MW00561465

BEN-GURION LOOKS AT THE BIBLE

BEN-GURION LOOKS AT THE BIBLE

By
DAVID BEN-GURION

Translated by
JONATHAN KOLATCH

JONATHAN DAVID PUBLISHERS
Middle Village, New York 11379

BEN-GURION LOOKS AT THE BIBLE
by
DAVID BEN-GURION

Originally published in Hebrew by Am Oved Publishers and the World Bible Society under the title, *Iyunim Batanach*. Copyright 1969.

English translation by Jonathan Kolatch

JONATHAN DAVID PUBLISHERS, INC.
Middle Village, New York 11379

Library of Congress Catalogue Card No. 70-167600
ISBN 0-8246-0127-0

Printed in the United States of America

Table of Contents

Translator's Note

This collection of addresses in essay form by the former Prime Minister of Israel was first published in Hebrew in 1969. They were presented before a select group of students of the Bible who met regularly, and were called the "Prime Minister's Bible Study Circle." Many prominent Bible scholars of Israel were members of the study group. Among them were: Professor Ezekiel Kaufman, author of *A History of the Israelite Faith;* Abraham Kariv, author of *The Seven Pillars of the Bible;* Professors P. Meltzer and B. Dinur; Dr. Haim Gevaryahu, Chairman of the World Jewish Bible Society; His Excellency Zalman Shazar, President of the State of Israel; and many others.

In accordance with the wishes of Mr. Ben-Gurion, this translation has adhered as closely as possible to the original Hebrew text.

JONATHAN KOLATCH

CHAPTER ONE

Uniqueness and Destiny

The army has the duty to carry out organizational, managerial, and supply roles. These duties are imposed upon particular soldiers or upon special branches at staff headquarters. But, there is one general function which is assigned to every army commander, from the lowest rank to the highest, and in every branch of the military, without exception—on land, on sea, and in the air—namely education. In part, it is technical education: training the soldier to use defensive and offensive weapons; and, in part, it is education in a personal, physical and spiritual sense: training the soldier in orderliness, cleanliness, punctuality, endurance, responsibility, economy, orientation, discipline, camaraderie, coordination, courage, fearlessness.

This responsibility for education is common to all armies in the world. But, the Israeli army has a special educational role which has no place, and is unnecessary, in other armies. The Israeli army cannot be satisfied with the calibre of education which is offered in any army—and I'm referring to superior modern education—but requires additional, special instruction because of the historical uniqueness of its people, and because of the destiny of the age in which we are living.

By historical uniqueness, I mean the intellectual-moral struggle which our people has engaged in with its neighbors since it became

---

From a lecture on the education of the army and the nation, delivered before the High Command of the Israeli army (19 Nissan, 5700—April 6, 1950).

a nation, and continues until this very day; and, also the messianic vision which was kept alive in the heart of the people throughout the generations.

By the "destiny" of the age, I mean the ingathering of exiles. This is the central event of our times and is unparalleled in world history—even in our own history—and has consequences for the future of our people, for our security, for our national and international posture and, perhaps, in no small measure, for the future of humanity.

In the history of nations, until this very day, there has always been a political struggle, and this struggle has degenerated from time to time into a physical confrontation between nations—that is, an armed struggle.

As has been the case with other nations, the Jewish people has also been engaged in political struggles with its neighbors and, more than once, has been engaged in battle. So it was in the days of the judges, so it was in the period of the monarchy in the days of the First Temple, so it was in the days of the Second Temple.

After scores of generations, we have returned to become an independent nation. And even before the State was established, war was declared on us, and the State of Israel was founded and built in the whirlwind of war. Even after the armed struggle ceased for a while, the political struggle remained, and no one knows how long it will continue, and whether it might not turn once again into a military conflict.

A pre-condition to our ability to prevail in the struggle, be it political or military, demands an assessment of ourselves and our situation; an assessment of the circumstances and conditions of our existence; an assessment of the basic and permanent factors which have long-range effect, as well as of factors which are in constant flux, and which determine our existence and the scope of our overall activity.

We will not see our situation as it really is, and many of the central visions of our history (not only of the past, but of the present and future as well) will not be understood, and we will not be prepared and equipped—and the decisive "equipment" is the spiritual equipment—either for a political struggle or a military struggle, if we do not grasp fully, and recognize the moral and intellectual struggle which transpires in human history. In such a case, we will not understand our place in this struggle.

In order to see into the ideological struggle, and to understand its place in the upheaval of history, there is no need to clarify and prove through philosophical debate whether an ideological struggle stems from economic, social or political problems, or whether it creates them; or if the economic and intellectual contradictions are bound up in each other, and one cannot differentiate between them. There is no practical value to such an abstract debate, just as there is no practical value in ascertaining if the chicken came before the egg or the egg before the chicken. It is obvious that one is impossible without the other: there is no way to raise chickens without hatching eggs, and there is no way to get eggs except by raising chickens.

We have seen ideologies in history which have altered regimes —politically and economically—and we have seen regimes which have introduced ideologies and implemented them. People fight for their views no less than for their government and their possessions; thus, from the day man learned to reason, intellectual struggle has not ceased. In the annals of our people this struggle occupies a more central position than, perhaps, in the annals of any other nation. There has hardly been a struggle in our history—political or military—which has not been bound up with an ideological struggle.

We are presently involved not only in a conflict with our Arab neighbors, but, to some extent, with most of mankind as it is organized in the United Nations—because of Jerusalem. Only a blind man does not see that the sources of this conflict are not political, economic or military alone, but also ideological.

When the Syrians, the Iraqis, and the Egyptians enthusiastically support the internationalization of Jerusalem, their motives are clear: It is better that the Mosque of Omar be under a Christian government than that a large part of Jerusalem be under a Jewish government. But, it is difficult to explain in mere political terms the stand of several nations in South America which generally have stood by our side in the United Nations in our political struggle, and which have turned against us on the question of Jerusalem. One cannot explain, in political terms, the position of France which had an important political and miiltary stake in helping us, and did help us quite a bit, not only in the General Assembly of the U.N., but in much more practical, productive matters. And such is the case with Czechoslovakia. Nevertheless, these nations came out against us on the question of Jerusalem.

We cannot ignore the fact that there is also an ideological struggle going on in the world.

On the question of Jerusalem we saw a very strange and mystifying combination. On one side there was arrayed, not the entire Christian world, but the largest bloc in the Christian world—the

Catholic bloc. On another side stood the Moslem bloc. On the third side, the Communist bloc.

There is no doubt that each one of these blocs had its own motives. And there is no doubt that even if not related, all three blocs had one thing in common. What unites all blocs is not just political interests, but also an ideology. There is an ideology in Islam, and there is an ideology in Catholicism. There is an ideology in Communism. And again, it doesn't matter, in order to understand our problem, if the ideology sets the policy, or if the policy sets the ideology; they both, jointly, stem from one source. To disregard ideology is to disregard one of the obviously central factors in human history.

The Jewish nation is not only a national and political entity. It incorporates within itself a moral will, and has borne an historic vision ever since it appeared on the stage of history; and the will and vision of the Hebrew nation have nothing in common with even one of the three great world-views which joined together in the General Assembly of the United Nations over the question of Jerusalem—not with the Christian-Catholic, not with the Moslem, not with the Communist, and not even with the other world-views that have contended for world domination in the chronicles of mankind from early times until today.

It is impossible to understand Jewish history, the struggle for survival of the Jewish people, the steadfastness of the people in all periods and in all lands—both as a people rooted in its own soil, more or less under its own control, and as a scattered, wandering people in exile—if we do not see the ideological uniqueness of the Jewish people and the stubborn struggle (not only the physical, economic, political and military struggle, but also the spiritual, moral and intellectual struggle) which the Jewish people faced and continues to face to the present. And it will face this struggle until the end of time; until the coming of the messianic age.

This struggle began in the earliest period of our history, as far back as authentic, recorded history will take us. One constant physical fact is permanent in our history, and from it flows many of the resulting phenomena of our history—both then and now: We have always been, and we remain, a quantitatively small nation. There is no doubt that it is our destiny to continue to be a small nation in the future as well—small in relation to our neighbors, and small in relation to the nations with whom we are involved. This physical-mathematical fact has many consequences for our destiny—both negatively and positively.

In days of old our neighbors were Egypt and Babylon. These

two nations were not only superior to Israel in number, in wealth, in military strength, and in the scope of their political power, but also in many spiritual attainments and scientific accomplishments.

The idea which we have about Egypt from the Book of Genesis and the Book of Exodus is one-sided. According to what we learned in school, Egypt was a slave-camp in which our forefathers did back-breaking work; and the exodus from Egypt is accepted to this very day in Israel as an exodus from slavery to freedom. But in fact, ancient Egypt was one of the few nations in the world which created an original, advanced culture.

More than 5,000 years ago, in the days of Pharaoh Sneferu, this land attained a lofty, cultural level and laid the foundation for several branches of science: arithmetic, engineering, chemistry and medicine; and, in the course of thousands of years, created a varied and rich literature in the fields of religion, history, morality, science, and works of poetry and prose, little of which has been preserved or discovered thus far. But the small remnant that is available testifies to great intellectual activity and cultural originality.

In one of the preserved stories about two brothers, we find the theme of Joseph and the wife of Potifar. And the love songs remind us of Solomon's Song of Songs. There are also hymns which resemble our Psalms, somewhat. The Egyptians were also great architects, as can be seen from the pyramids, and they also excelled in the art of sculpture and painting.

And the same was the case in Babylonia. Babylonia was superior to Egypt in its rich literature. The great Gilgamesh Epic (translated into Hebrew by S. Tchernichovsky), stories of creation, the Song of Ishtar, dirges, prayers, books on morality and wisdom, hymns and historical writings have all been preserved for us. Babylonia developed the science of measurement, medicine and engineering, and improved its system of jurisprudence long before other nations. The language of Babylonia was for a long time the international, diplomatic language in all the lands of the Bible which are today known collectively as the Near East.

The struggle of the Jewish people with these two mighty neighbors was not just political and military, but also cultural and spiritual. The work of the prophets of Israel was directed, principally, against the spiritual influence of neighboring nations on the religious and moral outlook of the Children of Israel as well as on its social fabric. The debate over orientations, which some think was originated in our day, is an old debate in our history. In the Book of Jeremiah we find clear expression given to this debate. The generals, and at their head, Jochanan son of Kareach, and Jezaniah son of Hoshaiah, were both oriented towards Egypt and not Babylonia. But Jeremiah was concerned with Israel and the God of Israel, and he said to the generals in prophetic anger: "If you are bent on going to Egypt . . . then the sword you fear will overtake you in Egypt, and the famine you dread will still be with you even in Egypt, and you will die there. . . . If you will stay in this land, then I will build you up and not destroy you, I will plant you, and not uproot you. . . . Do not be afraid of the king of Babylon whom you now fear. Do not be afraid of him, says the Lord; for I am with you, to save you and deliver you from his power" (Jeremiah 42).

This debate, without a doubt, did not originate in the days of Jeremiah, but had gone on for a long time, and the entire history of Israel in the days of the First Temple is filled with struggles between the different foreign influences emanating from Israel's neighbors, and the spiritual side of the nation that was personified in the prophets of Israel. It is not coincidental that political views and outlooks dealing with relations between neighboring nations were combined with social and moral utterances and messianic prophecies. The small nation surrounded by mighty neighbors and rulers of the world (the "world" that was known to our people at that time) was continuously under double pressure: political and military, on the one hand, and cultural-spiritual, on the other hand. These mighty neighbors not only cast fear, but also lured and attracted the people by their lofty culture. This attraction is the source of the internal struggle which went on in the life of the nation from its beginning until the Babylonian Exile, and from the Babylonian Exile until this day.

Faint overtones of this internal struggle reach us in the encounter between the false prophets and the true prophets. The words of the false prophets have not been preserved, and we do not know their content or intent, but everything which remains from the true prophets points to great spiritual efforts not only to stand up against foreign rule, but also to stand up against the foreign spiritual influence which these powerful neighbors imposed upon a nation that was small and weak, politically and militarily, but exceptionally gifted in terms of spiritual strength and moral independence.

The Israeli nation, of which we are the inheritors, was not the only people in the land of Israel and its environs which was faced with this double pressure. Several Semitic nations whose language was Hebrew (as can be seen clearly from Canaanite Phoenician writings and from the writing of Mesha, king of Moab) lived in Israel. But not a trace remains of all these people because they were unable to stand up to the cultural pressure of their mighty neighbors, and thus were absorbed by them without leaving footprints.

The Jewish people battled and was victorious, and it makes its appearance once again as a liberated nation, in a corner of the world where it first stepped on the stage of history four thousand years ago. The entire ethnic, political and cultural environment of the ancient, biblical world underwent a drastic change. The line of development of the ancient nations was completely severed: their language, their religion, their culture, their tradition, and their name—all vanished from off the face of the earth; and the Jewish people—though it was physically uprooted from its birthplace more than 2,000 years ago—is the only nation which continues its ancient tradition, its own language and culture, *as if* there had been no break in its historical continuity.

As if! But, it is obvious that the Jewish people of today is not like the Jewish people in the days of the First Temple or even of the Second Temple. The entire world has since changed, and it is only natural that the Jewish people has also changed. It is neither our intention nor our desire to return to that stage in which the existence of the kingdom of Judah was interrupted by Babylonia, or the government of Bar Kochba by the Romans. In the Babylonian captivity, and in everything that happened from then until now, our people absorbed new doctrines, principles and practices from the nations it met, and was influenced by, and also from, the surge of change which developed in the living conditions of society at large. The ancient Jewish outlook was intuitive and theocratic. In the Middle Ages, from the days of Saadya Gaon onward, attempts were made by Jewish scholars to combine Jewish theocratic thought with the Greek philosophical view which predominated among the educated at that time. And in the modern period, from the time of Spinoza onward—as was the case with all modern cultured peoples—the scientific, experimental approach became stronger and deeper within us.

Jews played a substantial and significant part in the advancement of science in the last 150 years—perhaps out of all proportion to their numbers—and have been full partners in the unraveling of the secrets of nature, and in the great intellectual revolution which has taken place in the world. Nevertheless, all of the changes which have taken place—both materially and spiritually—in our political and social condition, that occurred during the thousands of years of our existence, did not sap or weaken the vital inner strength which has preserved our people throughout all of the ravages of time. Nor did it negate its national uniqueness as happened to many of our historical counterparts in other countries. An amazing vitamin is stored up in this nation which preserves its existence and independence, and gives it the strength to face any foreign influence which threatens its national being and moral quality.

Quite obviously, not every Jew was favored with this miraculous quality. In the course of time many have defected: individuals, groups, tribes, and entire communities. In every generation and in every land—even in the birthplace of the nation—there have been Jews unable to stand up under foreign pressure—physical or spiritual—and were destroyed or converted. But, the backbone of the nation stood the test—it struggled and it prevailed. The history of our people is the history of this mighty struggle. And it has not yet abated, even after the establishment of the State of Israel.

We know very little about the history of our people during the period of Persian rule, from the return to Zion in the days of Zerubabel, Ezra and Nehemiah, up to the appearance of Alexander the Great. This was perhaps the only period in the life of the Jewish people in its own land when it was not under heavy external pressure, and did not have to struggle for its political or cultural existence. Generally speaking, Persian rule was based on tolerance and autonomy, and it permitted every nation to follow its own practices and beliefs, and to maintain a high degree of internal self-rule.

Although there were also instances of persecution and pressure, as can be gleaned from the Scroll of Esther and from a historical hint dropped by a Greek writer (Hecataeus of Abdera), it can be generally said that the Persian period—which lasted over 200 years—was a period of internal consolidation in Judaism, and the spiritual image of the Jewish people was molded and refined in this period perhaps more so than at any other time, although even then the Jews could not avoid the Persian influence which was subconsciously absorbed by Judaism.

With the conquest of the East (including the Persian kingdom) by Alexander the Great (331 B.C.), the Greek period begins in which we witness a desperate struggle between Judaism and a rich culture unparalleled in human history until then; a culture which influenced human society more than any other to this day, and which bequeathed to the world spiritual treasures in poetry, literature, philosophy, science, sculpture, painting and other branches of the arts which represent the ultimate in human creativity throughout the generations.

The struggle between the Hasmoneans and the Greek rulers was not just the political and military struggle of an oppressed people fighting against foreign rulers and oppressors. It was principally a cultural struggle—one of the most dramatic struggles in human history—between two outstanding nations who differed fundamentally in their material way of living, in their approach to political power, and in their concept of the world, but were like one another in their spiritual greatness, though each in its own way.

The Jewish nation was small, poor, confined within narrow borders of a portion of its ancient land, and enjoying only internal, self-rule; while the Greek nation looked out upon the entire world, on those parts of Europe, Asia and then known Africa; with its language and culture spread among all ancient nations, from the outer reaches of the western Mediterranean, to India in Asia and the banks of the Nile in Egypt. The Greeks conquered not only by their sword, but also through their rich and superior culture; and when the Greek government that succeeded Alexander became established in Egypt and Syria, and when Alexandria and Antioch became Greek cultural centers, it was impossible that small and weak Judah would not be influenced by this superior culture, even in its tainted form during the hellenistic period. (The Hellenists who arose in Israel were only "backscratchers" who flattered foreign rulers.) The appearance of Greece on the stage of world history was unlike that of Rome at a later date—which had only military and administrative power to its credit. Greece offered a powerful, cultural presence that opened a new spiritual era for mankind, and enriched the treasury of human culture more than any other nation.

Only the words of those who opposed the Hellenists and fought against them remain in our literature, and the picture received from them is not altogether objective and complete. Without doubt, this encounter enriched and elevated the Jewish spirit and left quite an impression on Hebrew literature which emerged after the appearance of Alexander the Great, and gave birth to a broad and rich Judeo-Hellenistic literature—historical, liturgical, exegetic and philosophical.

But, despite this awesome culture, the Greeks were unable to assimilate the Jewish people as it had absorbed many nations in the East. The Jewish people met the challenge and was victorious.

Not only did it preserve its uniqueness and independence, but it even strengthened and deepened them.

The entire Jewish nation was not victorious. We do not know how many Jews were lost in this struggle—both through physical annihilation and through assimilation. But the nation as a whole was victorious, and the Hasmonean period will always be one of the most marvelous political, military and spiritual trials in our history in which the few prevailed over the many, the poor over the rich; all this, only because of the mighty spiritual powers which propelled the elite of the nation and the masses—even if it did not touch the privileged and the ruling circles.

The most difficult and prolonged test in the struggle of the Hebrew nation came with the rise of Christianity. The cultures of Egypt and Babylonia, and later the culture of Greece (and Rome) were alien to Judaism. Not so Christianity. It was developed on the lap of Judaism and emerged from within it. The person on whom the new religion was dependent was a whole Jew, and his religious and moral outlook did not differ from the Jewish outlook of his day. Even the special emphasis of Jesus was not different in essence from the things which were commonplace among the different contending groups in Israel in the period before the destruction of the Temple. Like other contemporary Jews, Jesus refused "to take the children's bread and throw it to the dogs," and when he was asked to help a Canaanite woman, answered: "I was only sent to gather the sheep lost to the House of Israel."

The anti-Jewish direction was given to this new religion by Saul of Tarsus, the principal exponent and perhaps the main creator of "the new covenant," as contrasted to the ancient covenant, the Hebrew covenant. Saul of Tarsus, the son of an expatriated Roman citizen, was also raised on Judaism. He was a student of Rabbi Gamaliel and, like all the other students, was an ardent Pharisee. But he was a Jew from the diaspora, and he absorbed from it part of the Greek culture. Initially, he was among the ardent opponents of the Christian sect which was organized in Jerusalem. But after "he saw the light" on his way to Damascus, and turned into one of those who believed that Jesus was the son of God, he gave new direction to the new sect. In contrast to Jesus' disciples who lived in the land of Israel, and who considered themselves full Jews, Saul of Tarsus (called Paul) saw the thrust of his mission as directed toward the heathens, and he turned the new sect into a religion and a church, which was contrary to all the principles of Judaism as a people, as a religion and as an ideal.

While it was said in the name of Jesus: "Do not suppose that

I have come to abolish the Law and the Prophets; I did not come to abolish, but to complete. I tell you this: So long as heaven and earth endure, not a letter, not one iota will disappear from the Law until all that must happen has happened" (Matthew 5:17-18). Saul (Paul) worked hard at uprooting the Law and its precepts and at eliminating Judaism as a national entity oriented toward a messianic vision. Saul was perhaps the greatest of all the assimilationists who ever arose among the Jewish people. He negated all of the positive commandments which were, in essence, the entire foundation of Judaism, and set up, contrary to the Torah of Israel, an entire religion based on faith alone. He recognized the individual only, and not the people, and tried to uproot the faith of the Jewish people and its hope for national redemption. In place of the messianic vision of the prophets of Israel which looks to the future, and which links the redemption of the nation with the redemption of the world—to the rule of peace and justice in all nations—Saul of Tarsus predicated Christianity on faith in a heavenly redemption, by a messiah who had already arrived.

The growth of Christianity and its expansion took place during the period when Israel's independence was being undermined —during the fierce and hopeless wars which Jews fought against their Roman oppressors, from the days of Judah of Galilee and Zadok, until Simeon Bar Kochba and Rabbi Akiba—wars which ended in defeat for the Jewish people and in the loss of their independence. The nation experienced an intense and unprecedented spiritual, social and political upheaval. The zealous, daring warriors fell in battle or were taken captive. The nation's freedom was destroyed. The Temple was burned. The greater part of the homeland was devastated. Jerusalem was destroyed, and even its name was changed. It appeared as if Judah was utterly and finally destroyed and all the Jewish people would be completely obliterated.

Only the *faith* of the Jews remained; and even that was put to a bitter test—and not only through external decrees! Emperor Hadrian, who subdued Bar Kochba, prohibited circumcision, Sabbath observance, and the study of the Torah in the schools, and these decrees were carried out with great cruelty. The great leaders of Israel risked their lives to teach the Torah, and were put to death (the Ten Martyrs); among them was Rabbi Akiba who was the living spirit behind the war of Bar Kochba. However, the more dangerous encounter for Judaism came from within, from the doctrine of Christianity which initially grew out of Judaism, and pretended to rest on the words of the prophets; on beliefs, views and hopes which had become rooted in Judaism in the days of the

Second Temple. It rested, in particular, on a belief in the messiah and the resurrection of the dead.

Jesus' first disciples lived for a long time as full Jews and adhered to all the precepts of the Torah and the customs of Judaism, but they did not believe in the national revival of the Jewish people, and in its future redemption, for they believed that the messiah had already come. The attraction to it of Jews from the diaspora—whose knowledge of Judaism and whose links with the Jewish people were flimsy—and the acceptance of the new religion by Greeks and others from idol-worshipping nations (especially through the missionary work of Saul of Tarsus), accentuated the differences between Judaism and the new religion.

The Christian-Jews did not participate in the national struggle of the Jews against Rome. They even publicly acknowledged to the Roman authorities that they had no connection whatsoever with the Jews who were rebelling against the empire; and Saul of Tarsus ordered his disciples to submit to the authorities and accept its rule. It had already been said, also in the name of Jesus: "Then give to Caesar what is due to Caesar, and to God what is due to God" (Matthew 22:21). But Saul of Tarsus went further. "Every person," Saul taught in one of his Epistles, "must submit to the supreme authorities. There is no authority but by act of God, and the existing authorities are instituted by him; consequently, anyone who rebels against authority is resisting a divine institution . . ." (Romans 13:1-2).

The serious and dreadful losses which the Jews suffered in the wars of Vespasian and Titus, and later in the days of Hadrian, and the bitter disappointments which came in their wake, paved the way for these doctrines of Christianity. Thus, many of the Jews living in Israel, and even more among the Jews in the diaspora of the Roman empire, were captivated by the new religion. In the course of time, less than 200 years after the fall of Bar Kochba, the Christian religion became the dominant religion of the Roman Empire, and was forcibly imposed on the peoples of the Greco-Roman world of Europe, Inner Asia and North Africa. Only the Jewish people's rebellion persisted—though not without numerous and continued losses—and it preserved its uniqueness.

The nation which was first to bring tidings of the vision of universal redemption—a vision of peace, freedom and justice for all peoples of the universe—which based its teachings on one central precept: "Love thy neighbor as thyself"—was not led astray by the new religion which donned universal garb and preached that one should not strike back against another who intends to harm him.

And when the power to rule fell into its hands, it oppressed and persecuted anyone that didn't submit to it.

Dominant Christianity, which had under its control the entire world that was subject to Rome and its successors, would not forgive the Jewish people for its stubbornness, and in the name of the religion of love the Jews were viciously persecuted, and entire communities gave their lives for the sanctification of God's name. The Jewish people did not submit, and stood alone for hundreds of years in this historical struggle—and it prevailed. There are forces in Christianity which to this very day are unable to forgive us for our "rebelliousness."

About 500 years after the fall of Bar Kochba, the land of Israel was conquered by the Arabs. This invader, unlike most of the earlier conquerors, did not come with military might alone, but was armed with a new idea and a new doctrine: the doctrine of Mohammed. This doctrine was not created in Israel and did not grow out of Judaism, although it was substantially influenced by Judaism, since the prophet of Islam had contact with it through trade and also in a spiritual sense. The conquests of Mohammed and his disciples were quicker and more amazing than the conquests of Christianity. The spread of the doctrine of Mohammed among the Arabian tribes in the seventh century, and shortly thereafter throughout Asia and Africa, was unique in its awesome scope, its amazing speed and its profound cultural and linguistic influence. In a short while, most of the Mediterranean basin turned into an Arab-Moslem empire, and the language of Arabia became the spoken language among the nations of Syria, Assyria, all of North Africa, and the Iberian Peninsula. All the nations of the Middle East and North Africa accepted the new religion—some willingly and others unwillingly. The only ones to defy this mighty surge was the Jewish people.

Jews lived in the Arabian Peninsula from ancient times. Among Yemenite Jews there is a widespread tradition that their settlement in Yemen began in the days of King Solomon. But, there is no doubt that as far back as the days of the Second Temple Jewish merchants came to the edges of Arabia—to the south and to the north. King Herod sent a Jewish regiment of 500 men to South Arabia to aid the legions of Caesar Augustus in the conquest of South Arabia. Jews also came to Arabia from Babylonia and Persia. In the course of excavations at Beit Shearim, an ancient cemetery was uncovered containing the grave of a Jewish family from Himyar in Arabia dating back to the second or third century of this era. At the end of the fourth century, Abu Karib Assad, the king of

Yemen, converted to Judaism and propagated the faith of Israel in his country. The tragic fate of the Jewish king, Dhu Nawas, who ruled in Himyar at the end of the first quarter of the sixth century, and was overthrown by the Christian armies of Ethiopia, is well known. Many Jews who were persecuted by Christian Ethiopians fled to North Arabia and most of them settled in the City of Yathrib (Medina) and the surrounding areas.

In the days of Mohammed (570-632), many Jews lived in the Arabian Peninsula, and many of them worked the soil and raised sheep and cattle. The prophet of Islam would often meet with them during his business travels, and would hear them tell stories from the Bible about the patriarchs of the nation, the oneness of God, and the holiness of Jerusalem. During the first period of his prophetic mission, Mohammed instructed his believers that when at prayer they should face Jerusalem. He thereby hoped to win over the hearts of the Jews to his prophetic mission. Only after the Jews refused to accept his doctrine did he retract and give the order to face Mecca, his birthplace, at prayer-time. Thus did the new doctrine assume an Arab national character.

His hatred for the Jews grew, and he pursued them with his sword, and he demanded that they accept his doctrine. The Jews would not submit, though their resistance to this new force was costly. The Jews of Arabia—with the exception of their brothers in Yemen—were expelled or put to the sword. What remained of the Jewish settlement in Israel, especially the rural settlement, was likewise unable to stand up to the new conquerors. Some of them were assimilated among the conquerors, and some left the country. But the Jewish people in general survived, although the persecution was renewed from time to time. As far back as the twelfth century, more than 550 years after Mohammed, Maimonides had to send a letter to the Jews of Yemen to encourage them to stand up to the violent decrees, persecution, and rapacious actions of Islam.

A new ideological wave that opposed the existence of the Jewish people and its national uniqueness and moral independence emerged with the great revolutions of modern times: the French Revolution at the end of the eighteenth century and the Russian Revolution at the beginning of the twentieth century.

The French Revolution, that held aloft the vision of liberty, equality and fraternity was not limited to its own country, but had repercussions throughout Europe. It undermined the institutions of monarchical despotism and of feudal regimes, and also was the initial impetus in the drive for the emancipation and equality of

Jews in Western countries. But it was not mere accident that this revolution demanded of the Jews a denial of national identity. Many Western Jews accepted this demand willingly, and that is how an assimilation movement arose that threatened to engulf the entire Jewish people. "It appears as if this old man among the nations, which fought for its existence for thousands of years, and withstood the storms of history all over the world, cannot withstand the surge of the nineteenth century, but has succumbed and has denied its very being, and has reduced itself to the rank of a religious sect, an appendage of other peoples" (Dubnov); and quite a few were the victims of the assimilation, not only in the West but also in the East.

But, the determined historical will of the Jewish people also overcame this mighty surge, and emancipation led, not to assimilation, but to a new expression of its national uniqueness and its messianic yearnings. For the most part, Judaism shed its theocratic garb, and took on a secular form, but its attachment to its historical sources and its ancient birthplace increased. Its national language was reawakened, a secular Hebrew literature was created, and the "Lovers of Zion" and Zionist movements arose. The emancipation which came from without turned into auto-emancipation—a movement for independence from the shackles of foreign domination and influence, and the first foundations were laid for the renewal of national independence in the ancient homeland.

Just as with the French Revolution, the Russian Revolution was also not confined to the limits of the country, but had, and continues to have, repercussions throughout the world. Again, the Jewish people faced an ideological struggle and an historical trial —no less serious than any that had come before.

In 1917 the Balfour Declaration was issued. For the first time since the destruction of the Temple the Jews were recognized by a world power as a special people, and were promised the right to return to their land. The League of Nations, which was established at the end of World War I, gave international sanction to the Balfour Declaration and recognized the representation of the Jewish people as a body certified by international law.

In this same year, 1917, the Russian Revolution succeeded, and the new regime, which promised liberation to all, delivered a severe blow to the Jewish people. Russian Jewry, the largest and most fruitful Jewish community in the world, was forcibly cut off from the Jewish people and from its revived birthplace.

The Russian Revolution heralded national equality for all the peoples of Russia and her minority groups, and also kept its promise, in its own way: under the new regime, national autonomy was given all peoples, races and minority groups who resided within the empire of the Russian czars. The Soviet Union was planned as a federation of equal peoples—each in the autonomous national region in which it lives. As with all arrangements in the Soviet Union, this autonomy was subject to the absolute dictatorship of the Bolshevik party which is based in Moscow. And the central government determines the entire economic, civil, cultural and political order which prevails throughout the giant republic. But under the Bolshevik dictatorship, the rights of all nationalities—large and small—were made equal, and the culture, language and economy of every nationality and tribe, to the degree that they were independent, were free to develop.

Only one national entity in the Soviet Union—the Jewish people—was in effect sentenced to national and spiritual extinction; not because of any particular negative attitude toward the Jews on the part of the Bolshevik government, but because of the objective reality of a scattered people, without a homeland, which this government did not take into consideration. The other nationalities in the Soviet Union, which are concentrated in their own areas, received national territorial autonomy under the Bolshevik dictatorship, and their language, culture, education and economy, in large part, are under their own control; and they sponsor schools, a press, and a literature in their own language. Not only is the national tradition of every people not disturbed, on the contrary, it is encouraged and abetted as it never was in czarist Russia. But, the language of the Jewish people, its education, its literature, and its connection with its national past were paralyzed, smashed and strangled. In addition, contact by Jews of the Soviet Union with the Jewish people, and with the homeland of the Jewish people, was banned. The oldest of all the cultures in the Soviet Union was robbed of its historical inheritance. The Hebrew book was driven underground. All the Hebrew schools were closed. Silence, orphanhood, and national bereavement were decreed on a Jewish community numbering in the millions, which for generations had led the national creativity of its people.

The Jewish people had not received as severe a blow as this since the Bar Kochba-Hadrian war. The paralysis and isolation of Russian Jewry not only affected the millions of Jewish inhabitants of the Soviet Union, but was also a serious blow to the entire Jewish people in all parts of the world.

In order to have some idea of the terrible and colossal loss which the Jewish people has suffered since 1917, we have to ask ourselves what we would have lost had the thing which happened in Russia, in 1917, occurred in 1880. Had Russian Jewry been isolated and paralyzed at that time, we would have lost the Bilu immigration, the new Hebrew literature (Mendeli, Ahad Ha'am, Bialik and their group), the Zionist movement, the Jewish Workers' Movement, the Second Aliya, the founders of the kibbutz and "Hashomer," the builders of the workers' settlement and the founders of Tel Aviv—all the personalities who were at the head of the Zionist movement and the Yishuv for a period of 40 years, and all the assistance which Russian Jewry contributed toward the building of the land. We also would have lost the Jewish workers' movement in the United States, and all the creativity of Russian Jews in all countries.

The defeats and victories of the Bolsheviks during their first years of rule—defeats in the international sphere and victories and conquests in Russian territory—caused profound changes to be effected in the goals of the new regime. Starting as a government that seized power by force, it became a government that ruled by force; and dictatorial rule was converted from a temporary measure to a permanent policy.

The new doctrine of "one-country socialism," practically speaking, turned into a nationalistic striving, putting the interests of one particular country above international socialism. Instead of depending upon the working class of the world to be a liberating force in every nation and state, the only dependence was on the Soviet Union and its military power. It was not socialist attainment in their own individual countries, according to the particular needs and historical circumstances of each country—as Marx had taught—that was required of the workers' movement in every country outside of Russia, but absolute loyalty to the internal and international needs of the Soviet Union as they were interpreted from time to time by the heads of the ruling party.

Naturally, this same undivided discipline is demanded of all citizens of the Soviet Union—from the masses of the workers, farmers and intelligensia. And the duty of obedience is applied not only to social and political questions, but also to scientific and cultural questions; to questions of literature, fine arts, history, language, family life and personal conduct. From the time of the founding of the Catholic Church in Rome, and the establishment of the universal rule of the Popes, no power appeared on the world scene which claimed absolute international authority such as did the leaders of the Bolshevik party. And this claim, which in fact relies on the awesome military power of the Soviet Union, presumably professes the theory of revolutionary socialism, and declares its aspiration for perfecting the world and the redemption of humanity.

Without a doubt, the heads of the ruling party believe that whatever is good for their country is automatically good for the rest of the countries, and that their country is bringing redemption to the world. But, there is nothing at all new in this very faith—not in Russian history nor in world history.

The Jewish people, which never submitted to superior physical force, and which guarded its moral and intellectual independence even when it was not in a position to maintain its political and economic independence, has been confronted—more than any other nation in the world—with a severe and cruel test. There has been no people for which the vision of the redemption of the world has player a greater and more continuous role in its life, its history, and spiritual development than the Jewish people. No other people has yearned for peace among the nations, and for the oneness of humanity, more than the Jewish people which is scattered all over the world. The great personalities of the Jewish people in the last few generations have been those who have delved into the theories of the social revolution and given them a scientific foundation based on an analysis of the contradictions of the existing regime. The best of Jewish youth, throughout all the countries of the diaspora, stood in the vanguard of the wars of liberation. And more than anyone else, this is true of Jewish youth in czarist Russia. The hearts of almost all of Russian Jewry were with those who strove to crush the tyranny of the Russian Czars; and Jewish fighters stood in the front lines of the Russian Revolution.

The terror of the pogroms, which threatened the Jews in Russia for decades, disappeared only with the victory of the Bolsheviks. Millions of Russian Jews knew that under this government pogroms against the Jews could not happen. Lenin, the prophet, legislator and commander of the Bolshevik revolution, had several Jewish friends and disciples; and even after almost all of the Jewish members of Lenin's group were liquidated one by one, no one saw this as an anti-Semitic action. The memory of the troubles, persecutions and insults which the Jews suffered in the days of the Czars did not leave the Jews of Russia and Jews of the world for a long time. Even many of those who were unable to reconcile the socialist slogans of the Bolshevik party with the reality of its rule, did not want to deny the change which occurred in the legal status of the Jews after the destruction of the czarist regime.

The new regime abolished all traces of czarist discrimination against the Jews. The rights of the individual Jew were made completely equal to the rights of the non-Jew. But, the Jewish community was severely hurt by the Bolshevik regime and its totalitarian demands, because of the harm it did to Judaism itself. Not only was the Jewish community in the Soviet Union hurt, but the Jewish people throughout the world was hurt as well.

The agony of Russian Jewry for more than 30 years (since the establishment of the new regime) has proven that even the steel roller of the Bolshevik dictatorship could not completely crush the Jewish people. Yet, despite the fact that many prominent Russian Jews devoted themselves wholeheartedly to the new order, and accepted it completely—willingly or unwillingly—the spark of spiritual independence was not extinguished even among the masses of Russian Jews, and their deep spiritual connection with the Jewish people and its homeland was not severed.

Evidence of humiliation, degradation and spiritual servitude among the Jewish supporters of the Russian revolutionary movement was not lacking even long before the appearance of the Bolshevik party. It is known that even in the days of the Czars Jewish revolutionaries gave their blessing to the pogroms against the Jews, since they saw in the anti-Jewish pogroms the revolt of the Russian farmer against the land-owner, and to them Jewish blood was the lubricating oil for the wheels of the Russian revolution.

The initiators of the attacks on the Hebrew language and the Zionist movement were members of the Jewish department of the Bolshevik party (Yevskazya), whose hate for Zion and the Hebrew language was even greater than their communist orthodoxy. The personal intervention of Lenin was needed to permit the existence of the Hebrew theater, Habimah, in Moscow. And when the workers' alliance requested permission to participate in the World Agricultural Exposition which was held in Moscow in 1923, it was these members of Yevskazya who opposed their coming. But, the authorities did not accept the view of their Jewish advisors.

Nevertheless, it was this very same Russian Jewry, even after the Russian Bolshevik government took complete control, that gave the country some of its best pioneering youth; and the deeds of these young people in Israel testify to the ability latent within the Jews of Russia, and to the secret desires which they crave in their inner being. And all the oppression, physical and moral, cannot contain them or destroy them.

With the establishment of the State of Israel, the continuing struggle of the Jewish people seemed to be crowned with final victory. But this is no more than a misleading and dangerous illusion, not only because the task of building has not been completed and the job of ingathering the exiles is still in its initial stages. It is not only that the struggle of the Jewish people for its political and economic independence has not yet ended—but that the ideological struggle, the struggle for our moral independence, is more acute. The seriousness of this struggle is not in the ideological and moral wrangling between one or more of the world powers and the Jewish people. Power and numbers are never the decisive factors in an ideological struggle, and the Jewish people, "the smallest of all nations," has no reason to worry about the results of the encounter in the moral-ideological sphere, even if the powerful and mighty countries of the world oppose it. The Jewish people, faithful to itself, will not submit to the moral and ideological authority of a "world" power, and will not bow to it on questions concerning the organization of its society, science, spirit and culture as well as on values of freedom, equality, justice and peace—it will not bow before those who, by virtue of the power of their government and their military or economic power, have appointed themselves as the great judges of humanity.

The severity of the struggle for spiritual independence lies in the internal conflict. In a nation as small as ours, there are always groups which are attracted by the glamor and magic of mighty powers whose political, economic and military capacities are awesome, and whose world influence is tremendous. This attraction is due not only to self-interest—though we must not view this prosaic factor lightly. But, what is intriguing is the great capacity, the capability and the wealth of the world powers. In our modern history, they call this new trait of humbling oneself before the tyrant, "yes-manship," and "yes-man" Jews are found among these same groups of Jews who do not have self-respect and sufficient faith in their people. Among the rightist groups, they are called the American Council for Judaism, and are headed by Jewish financial tycoons in the United States. Among the leftist and revolutionary groups they are called *Yevskazya,* and at their head stand writers whose "masters' voices" always speak through their throats.

After the establishment of the State of Israel, these openly and conspicuously estranged and assimilated Jews are no longer particularly dangerous, because now there is a dependable and secure resting place for the masses of Jews wherever they are—the re-established State of Israel. But even within the State of Israel, there are many for whom the dichotomy between "man" and "Jew" still exists. The Jewish soul in exile has not been healed. The unfortunate and insulting teaching of the scholars of the Exile: "Be a Jew at home, and a man outside," also has supporters in new forms, in Israel. Freeing oneself from material exile is easy today—it is sufficient to immigrate to Israel. But, one cannot easily free himself from spiritual and moral exile. This is not possible through outer change, through travel from land to land, but comes from within, from a great spiritual, intellectual and moral effort for which not everyone is equipped.

In the State of Israel, "Be a Jew at home, and a man outside," is interpreted as: *We* determine such Jewish matters as immigration and settlement. But with regard to matters affecting mankind—problems of society and international politics—who are we, and what power do we have to deal with them alone, by ourselves? On these questions we must accept the judgment of the great and mighty, who know everything, who are qualified for everything, who determine everything. There is a big and mighty camp, somewhere, which is struggling for human redemption; and we have only to say "amen" to anything that the commander of this big and mighty camp tells us to do, to think, and to say. And if he tells us today the complete opposite of what he said yesterday, we are forbidden to suspect his motivation: he knows what he is doing; he alone knows what he is doing.

Those faithful to Jewish independence refuse to be bound by foreign judgment. They understand the limited areas of activity and capacity of the Jewish people, and know how to deal respectfully and critically with mighty superpowers who are responsible for the fate of hundreds of millions of people; and they realize that their great influence reaches out beyond the confines of their own country and extends over entire areas of the world. But, there is one realm in which the Jewish people sees itself as fully equal in every way—both in its ability and in its power to influence humanity in the coming generations—and that is in the realm of spirit and vision. In this area the size of one's army is not decisive. It was not through the strength of their numbers or their political and economic might that Jerusalem and Athens left their imprints on the culture of a large part of humanity.

The great powers, and the governments with far-reaching authority, do not necessarily have a monopoly over the way in which the world is to attain freedom, peace, justice and equality; redemption or perfection of this society, and the realization of man's most cherished hopes for today and future generations. The use of force by mighty countries, even when it accomplishes its intended goals, will by its very nature be transformed from a means to an end.

All of the great conquerors: the Persians, the Greeks, the Romans, the Arabs, the Mongols, the Spanish, the French, the British and the Russians have always pretended to share the blessings of their superior culture with the conquered peoples, and this was not always an empty gesture. Indeed, many of these conquerors bestowed on their protectorates improved rule and higher culture. But history does not know of one case where a "beneficent" conquest did not, in the end, turn into suppression and enslavement. Rule through lawlessness, rule which is not based on the free will of the ruled, has an inner logic of its own; and there is no escape from it. When all other methods are lost, the maintenance of control is impossible without the use of coercion and oppression; and also without the desire to maintain power.

On the other hand, the capacity for social and moral advancement and excellence is not necessarily dependent on the material strength and military might of nations. Not only mighty powers, but small nations as well are able to show humanity the way toward scientific, social and spiritual advancement, as history has proven in antiquity, in the Middle Ages and today. The long experience of the Jewish people gives it no cause to feel inferior to the strong and mighty of the world.

The Jewish people, which after thousands of years of wandering and hardships in all corners of the world, finally reestablished itself as a state in its homeland, will not renounce its historic vision and its great spiritual heritage in order to merge its national redemption with the general redemption of all nations of the world; it will not divest its national independence of its humane and universal principles; and will not become subservient to foreigners, to great and mighty powers, in the establishment of its future and its attitude toward the messianic vision.

In the State of Israel there is no dichotomy, whatsoever, between the Jew and the inner man. Nothing intellectual or moral contravenes the establishment of the State of Israel. Independence is not divisible. There is no such thing as *independence* only as pertains to Jewish matters, and *dependence* when it comes to world matters. The Jewish question includes the whole world, and nothing human is alien to it. The independence of Israel means, cognizance of our being, the roots, the source from which we come, and the direction of our lives in the present and in the future, in internal and external affairs, on questions dealing with the present and with the future—stemming from complete and full freedom according to our will, our needs, the conditions of our life, our wishes, and our hopes—without any dependence on any external, foreign authority, large or small.

Spiritual independence does not rule out concern for humanity as a whole, just as political independence does not negate international concern; and economic independence does not demand complete economic self-reliance. Mutual concern among nations, countries and peoples is an irrefutable fact and an historical necessity. Every nation takes from others, from the bequest of generations and from the conquests of the human spirit which lives on in all periods and in all countries. This mutual dependence is an eternal, cosmic law. There is nothing in the world, small or large, from the invisible electron to the largest bodies in the universe, which does not have an attraction both for those of its own kind and those not of its own kind. All of existence is an infinite series of mutual dependencies—in the spiritual world no less than in the material world. Thought, poetry, fine arts, the literature of the generations and of many nations, influence each other and draw sustenance one from another. And for a nation to dwell alone is less possible in our day than in all preceding generations.

With the establishment of our political independence, we became citizens of the world more than ever before. Though as a people, scattered throughout the world and wandering from country to country and from nation to nation, we always had a greater world-sense than many other peoples, our independence as a nation put our world-citizenship on a firm and normal basis. It is not for lack of a firm territorial and political grounding that we are concerned with the problems of humanity. We are aware of its needs and difficulties because we are equal partners with it. Modern methods of transportation on land, on sea and in the air, as well as radio communication, have erased distances and removed barriers.

The Jewish community in the diaspora also serves as a strong factor in our universal concern. Jews from 55 countries in five parts of the world have fought in the Israeli army. Knowingly and unknowingly, we cultivate pipelines to all countries where Jews are found. And just as we eat meat from Argentina and wheat from Russia, plow with American tractors, smelt Belgian steel, use Mexican gasoline, wear British cloth, and furnish our homes with Canadian wood, so we will read the literature of all nations and will seek wisdom wherever it is found. We will translate the spiritual, philosophical, scientific and political treasures of all nations and all generations into our language so that the spiritual bequest of all of mankind will be our national property. One cannot read our

Book of Books without listening to the early echoes of the great cultured nations which surrounded our people: Egypt, Assyria, Babylonia, Syria, Persia and Greece. Along with our great pride in the tremendous ability of our people to stand up to the mighty pressure of great and rich cultures like the Greek culture in the Hasmonean period, there are times when we regret the inability of the great past leaders of our people to differentiate between the dross and trash of the Hellenistic culture during the period of decline in the days of Alexander's successors, and the splendid spiritual riches of the Greek genius in its heyday—after the return from Babylonia in the days of the Great Assembly.

Perhaps many things would have been different in our history and in the history of the civilized world, had only those of our scholars who knew Greek translated the works of Sophocles, Thucydides, Plato and the other great scholars of Greece at the same time that our holy books were being translated into Greek; and had they learned the art of warfare and government from the Greeks and the Romans.

After our long adventure on the stage of world history for 4,000 years in all countries of the world, we returned to the point of our origin and founded the third government of Israel—and we will not divest ourselves of the vast and rich international experience which we have accumulated. We will not lock ourselves up in our shell. Rather, we will open windows to all civilized corners of the world, and we will bequeath unto ourselves all the conquests of spirit and knowledge of our day. We will learn from all who would teach us, but we will preserve our independence. We will not isolate ourselves; we will maintain our concern for the world-at-large. We will be concerned, but will not accept an external authority; not enslavement in any shape or form. Independence is enshrined in the heart, in the soul, in the will of the nation; and only through inner independence does one reach and maintain outer independence. The most dangerous form of enslavement is enslavement of spirit, of thought.

The test of spiritual and moral independence is freedom of judgment and conscience. We are only free and in control of ourselves if we ourselves judge and decide what is good and what is bad—what is good for *us* and what is bad for *us*. Anyone who at the outset accepts the jurisdiction of a foreign power forsakes his inner freedom and his personal independence.

The very essence of the spiritual struggle of the Jewish people ever since it became a nation, and to this very day, was its refusal to accept foreign rule which ran contrary to its conscience, even when confronted by superior physical force.

The Jewish people do not believe in physical superiority, in the superiority of physical power. But, the denial of the superiority of physical power does not imply a denial of its value. We would be rejecting Jewish history—from the days of Joshua son of Nun, up to, and including, the Israeli army of today—if we were to assign little value to the importance of physical power. A denial of physical power is a denial of this world, a denial of life. This type of denial has always been foreign to the spirit of the Jewish people. In this lies one of the basic differences between Judaism and Christianity.

The Jewish genius, from the days of the prophets until Einstein, has never recognized the dualism of matter and spirit, a dualism which several of the world's thinkers, from the Greeks and the Persians to Descartes and his disciples, have subscribed to. Jewish intuition, both religious and scientific, has always stressed the unity of the universe and existence, despite the multiplicity of these other manifestations and phenomena. Even though the Jewish people's most able sons: its prophets, scholars and teachers, have always seen Israel's higher destiny to be in the spiritual realm, they have never looked disparagingly at the physical body and the body's needs, because there is no soul without a body, and there is no universal human destiny without existence as a nation.

The victory of Jewish armaments over Arab armaments played an important and decisive role in the establishment of the Jewish state. The source of this victory lay in the moral and spiritual superiority of the Hebrew nation, and it was the Jewish spirit which bestowed victory upon the Jewish armaments. The belief in, and devotion to, the superiority of the spirit has accompanied the Jewish people on its long historical trek, from the revelation on Mount Sinai to Israel's war today. This faith was the bequest of all those same people who molded the Jewish people from its inception until today; who conceived and cultivated its Torah, its poetry, its prophecy, its literature, its jurisprudence, its messianic vision, and its messianic faith; who fought for its national and world uniqueness and destiny; who conducted the wars of its political and military independence; who sanctified God's name in the slaughter of the communities of Israel during the Crusades, in the flames of the Inquisition, in the pogroms of Chmielnitzki, and the Nazi massacre; and who conceived, built and cultivated the program of settlement which lead to the State of Israel.

The devotion of the Jewish people to the superiority of the

spirit has been linked to its faith in the value of man who, according to the faith of the Jew, was created in the image of God. No deeper, loftier, and more penetrating expression of the greatness and value and dignity of man is possible than this expression. The concept of God in Judaism symbolizes the epitome of good, beauty, justice and truth. The life of man has, in the eyes of the Jewish people, been dear and holy. Human beings who were created in the image of God all have equal rights, and are an end in themselves—not a means. The "image" demands it. It is no wonder that the scholars of this people based the Torah on one great principle: "Love thy neighbor as thyself." Love of one's neighbor is not to be for the Jewish citizen alone: "The alien that lives with you shall be treated as a native born among you, and you shall love him as a man, like yourself; because you were aliens in Egypt" (Leviticus 19:34).

At an early period in Judaism, a universal, all-embracing concept of humanity already predominated, and the echoes of this outlook reach us in the prayer of King Solomon at the dedication of the Temple. After the king prayed on behalf of his people, he added a universal prayer: "The foreigner too, who does not belong to thy people, Israel, but who has come from a distant land because of thy fame . . . when he comes and prays toward thy house, hear in heaven, Thy dwelling, and respond to the call which the foreigner makes to Thee . . ." (I Kings 8:41-43).

A complete book of the Bible, Jonah, is dedicated to the idea that the mercy of God is given in equal measure to all peoples, to the idol-worshipping peoples, as to the Jewish people. When the prophet complained to God for having pitied the city of Nineveh, God said to him: "You are sorry for the gourd, though you did not go through the trouble of growing it; a plant which came up in one night and withered in one night! Should I not be sorry for the great city of Nineveh, with its 120,000 people who cannot tell their right hand from their left, and cattle without number?" (Jonah 4:10-11).

The third thing which was tied up with the faith of the Jewish people as it relates to the superiority of the spirit was its messianic vision, out of which grew the messianic faith, and yearnings for national and universal redemption.

It was at an early stage that the Jewish people distinguished itself for its original historical outlook, not paralleled by any of the nations of the East or West; not by Egypt, Babylonia, India and China; and not by Greece or Rome or any of their successors in Europe, even until modern times. Our people did not look back, as did the other ancient nations, to the legendary Golden Age of the past which was gone and would not return, but directed its vision to the future, to the messianic age, to the time when "the world would be filled with knowledge as waters cover the sea," and "nations would beat their spears into pruning hooks; nation would not bear arms against nation, and would learn war no more."

Not useless yearnings for the splendor of a past that is no more, but hope for the realization of the vision of a more perfect future; a vision of the reign of justice and peace among all the nations of the world, for the good of peoples in all countries—this was the historical philosophy which the prophets of Israel bequeathed to their people. This expectation and faith in the future stood our people in good stead in the days of hardship and suffering in its long history, and it was this which brought it to this juncture, to the beginning of its national redemption, which also harbors the first sparks of overall human redemption.

This nation, which is faithful to itself, will not depend upon the direction that the strong and mighty may seek to impose upon it simply by virtue of their strength and power. It will choose for itself its own path towards an improved life and towards the reign of justice.

For a long time the Jewish people viewed itself as a chosen people, and it had sufficient basis for this view, so long as the sole criterion of the Jewish people was religio-moral consciousness. Modern Jews can no longer ignore the large role which other nations have played, in ancient times as well as modern times, in a civilization which is so interwoven and interrelated through thought, poetry, science, the arts, technology, geographic discoveries, and in social progress. We respect the great deeds and blessed creations of all nations, but we will not belittle ourselves; we will not be enslaved, and will not accept any form of spiritual servitude, intellectually or morally, just as we will not seek for ourselves dominion over others. In keeping with our conscience, we will follow our own special path.

In our own day, the Jewish people has had to do its own spadework: the cultivation of a desolate land and the ingathering of exiles; and this work will not be accomplished unless all of the resources of civilization, together with its positive values, are in full possession of the Jewish people. No development made by the civilized world will be foreign to it. There will be no need for the Jewish people to consider itself the best of all nations, but there is no reason for it to consider itself inferior. It is not inferior to any nation in its ability or in special talents. It must learn much from the advanced nations in the areas of economic performance, government organization, scientific research and technological capability. The difference between good and evil will be drawn from the moral genius which illumined the Jewish people since its inception, and did not diminish or fade. The true road to freedom, to justice and brotherhood will pave itself, through absolute intelectual and moral independence—without enslavement and without imitation.

Through mastery of the instruments of physical and social science and technology, and through the pioneering enthusiasm of those who are realizing a dream—national and universal—the Jewish people will create the image of a model people in its revived homeland, which will not disgrace the legacy of its prophets, its scholars and its leaders from ancient times to this day.

The maintenance of this moral and intellectual independence of the Jewish people requires no less a continuous spiritual effort than the maintenance of our political and economic independence, because our spiritual independence is threatened no less than our material independence. Moreover, the forces which face us in the ideological struggle are inestimably greater and more numerous than those confronting us on other fronts. But let us not panic. An intellectual struggle has never been decided by armies and by might, but by spirit. And the spirit of Israel will not forsake us. Our 4,000 years of history testifies to this.

The main subject of discussion in the education of the army, the young people, and the nation in general, is our national uniqueness—from a political and economic, as well as from a moral and intellectual point of view. National uniqueness is both an end and a means. An end, in that this uniqueness is a natural and historical right; and a means, in that it is necessary that we fulfill our destiny. It is the natural and historical right of every people to be the master of its own destiny, to go its own way and to mold its life and image in accordance with its own characteristics, needs, wishes and special conditions. And no nation has the authority to renounce this right, because a nation is subject to claims and has a responsibility which destiny has imposed upon it. Only through inner freedom and faithfulness to itself will it be within its power to fulfill its destiny and carry out the missions which history has imposed upon it.

The destiny of the Jewish people in our era, the destiny which characterizes this period in the history of the nation, is the repatriation of the Jewish people, the ingathering of exiles.

We have just experienced two marvelous revolutionary happenings in our history: the revival of the State of Israel and the victories of the Israeli army. But the revolutionary zeal of the modern period was not exhausted by these events; they served only as prologue and preparation for the crucial matter, and that is the repatriation of the Jewish people.

This is not the first time that Jews are returning to their land and renewing their independence as a State. Such a thing happened 2,500 years ago, in the days of Zerubabel, Ezra and Nehemiah when the exiles of Zion returned from Babylonia during the reign of the Persian kings, and laid the foundation of the Second Temple.

But the ingathering of exiles that is going on today is different. It is on a scale larger, and more difficult than the first return to Zion. In those days, only one exile existed: The Babylonian Exile; and that exile was in its infancy. Only about 70 years had passed from the day that the Jews were driven from their homeland; and the exile was closer to their homeland. Many of the exiled had family ties with those who remained. And the number of those in exile was not large, consisting only of about one-tenth of the number who immigrated to Israel in the last two years. Detailed, and apparently precise, statistics have been preserved for us in the book of Ezra, concerning those who returned from Babylonia together with all of their possessions: horses, mules, donkeys, and camels. And here is what was said there:

"The whole assembled people numbered forty-two thousand three hundred and sixty, apart from their slaves, male and female, of whom there were seven thousand three hundred and thirty-seven; and they had two hundred singers, men and women. Their horses numbered seven hundred and thirty-six, their mules two hundred and forty-five, their camels four hundred and thirty-five, and their asses six thousand seven hundred and twenty" (Ezra 2:64-67).

Not so the dispersion of our generation. The whole idea of a Jewish diaspora, in general, is ancient, and predated the destruction of the Second Temple and even the destruction of the First Temple. As far back as the seventh century B.C. we find Jews in Egypt. It is possible that they were exiled there after King Josiah was killed in his war against Pharaoh Necho. In any case, it is clear that the Jews who went down to Egypt in the days of Jeremiah already found Jewish settlements in the Egyptian cities of Tahpanhes, Noph, Migdol and Pathros. In Elephantine, at the gateway to the south of Egypt, there was a Jewish military colony in the sixth century B.C., which was joined by Jochanan, son of Kareach, and "all the captains of the armed bands and other Judeans" who didn't want to heed the voice of Jeremiah, and went down to Egypt.

With the destruction of the kingdom of Judah, a large center of Jewish life was established in Babylonia, of which only a part returned to Israel after the edict of Cyrus, king of Persia, who issued a proclamation throughout his kingdom, and also stated in writing: "Whosoever among his people, may God be with him, let him go up to Jerusalem, that is in Judah, and let him build the House of God, the Lord of Israel."

Only about 50,000 people answered this call and the Babylonian Exile was not liquidated, but rather continued to our times.

Egypt and Babylonia were not the only dispersions in ancient times. In the days of the Second Temple, the diaspora expanded and spread to many countries. In Syria and Asia Minor there were Jews even before the Hasmonean period and the Delphic inscriptions, in Greece, tell of the emancipation of Jewish slaves at the time of the Hasmonean rebellion (150-170). Even a little before that, the prophet, Joel, inveighs against Tyre, Sidon and the territories of Philistia for selling the people of Judah and Jerusalem "to the Greeks, and removed them far beyond their frontiers" (Joel 3:6).

In Isaiah, there is also a verse about Jews scattered across the sea: "On that day the Lord will make his powers more glorious by recovering the remnant of his people, those who are still left, from Assyria and Egypt, from Pathros, from Cush and Elam, from Shinar, Hamath and the islands of the sea" (Isaiah 11:11).

The Greek geographer, Strabo, who lived in the days of Herod the First, tells that "the Jewish people reached every city and province, and it is not easy to find a place in the settled world which has not absorbed people of this nation or was not influenced by them." And Philo of Alexandria, who was born 90 years before the destruction of the Second Temple, says in his book *Adversus Flaccum:* "One country cannot absorb all of the Jews, so great is their number. Consequently, they scout around for a livelihood in most of the prosperous cities of Europe, Asia, and in the islands of the sea, and on land. They consider their origin to be the Holy City on whose heights sits the Temple dedicated to Almighty God. They love the lands in which their fathers and grandfathers settled generations ago as their own birthplace, for they were born and raised in them."

The Jewish diaspora grew after the destruction of the Second

Temple in all parts of the Old World, and reached all the countries in Europe, Asia and Africa; and with the discovery of the New World—America and Australia—it spread there as well. And after the terrible massacre of the Jews of Europe by the Nazis in our own time, the population center of diaspora Jewry was shifted to the United States.

There is no people that is scattered among the nations of the world as the Jews. The terrible, bitter curse in the Torah was fulfilled: "The Lord will scatter you among all peoples from one end of the earth to the other. . . . Among those nations you will find no peace, no rest for the sole of your foot. Then the Lord will give you an unquiet mind, dim eyes and despondent spirit. Your life will hang continually in suspense, fear will beset you night and day, and you will find no security your whole life long . . ." (Deuteronomy 28:64-67).

All attempts to return to the homeland—and such attempts never ceased from the time that our people went into exile—were limited and, generally speaking, doomed to failure as long as foreigners ruled our country. And here, 1813 years after Israel last lost its independence, in the days of Bar Kochba and Rabbi Akiba, the State of Israel was established anew, and the gates of the homeland were opened wide to all our scattered people.

It is difficult, almost impossible, to pinpoint the beginning of events. Who can single out the first "wave" of immigrants responsible for the establishment of the state? The first foundations of our renewed agricultural settlement were laid with the establishment of Mikve Israel and Petach Tikvah; but Jewish immigration predated these attempts at settlement, and there are natives in the country going back five generations and more.

Before World War I, the Jewish community in Israel did not total even 100,000 people. During the war years it decreased in size substantially, and at the end of the war there were less than 60,000 Jews in the country. By the Second World War their number increased tenfold, and when the state was proclaimed in May, 1948, we reached approximately 650,000 Jews. But, in these last two years, more than 400,000 Jews immigrated to Israel. Not only did the numerical pace change, but a fundamental change took place in the nature and character of the immigration. Entire national blocs of people were uprooted, almost at one time, from the bulging exile and were transported to their liberated homeland: from Bulgaria and from Yemen, from Yugoslavia and from Morocco, from Germany and from Algeria, from Austria and from

Tunisia, from Turkey, from Egypt, and from several other countries.

The greatest ingathering of exiles took place in the Israeli army. During the War of Independence there were volunteers in the army who came from 21 European countries, from 14 countries in North and South America, from 10 countries of North, Central and Southern Africa, from five countries in Asia (Burma, India, China, Yemen and Turkey), and from two countries *down under:* from Australia and from New Zealand. I doubt if there was ever such a cosmopolitan army.

The number of foreign volunteers in the Israeli army was only the first sign of what was to come. With the end of the fighting, a massive immigration exploded, and the new "exodus from Egypt" began—not from one Egypt but from many Egypts. At present, more Jews immigrate in one month than immigrated in an entire year during the Mandate period. The quantity of this immigration calls for further explanation. On an American scale, this quantity would equal 40,000,000 people per year. On a Russian scale it is an immigration of 53 million people per year. It is doubtful if there ever was such a gigantic movement of people, if we take into account the dimensions of our small state.

.The return of the Exile is the central event and mission of our day. Without it, our independence cannot be assured, and our state will not be established. We reached the first million in our country this year and, from one point of view, this is the greatest event in our history since the victory of the Maccabees. But this is no more than a beginning. Without a fast, large-scale continuation of this process, we shall have no security, and this beginning will have served no purpose.

No one can predict whether or not all of the diasporas of Israel will be gathered in. The Jewish diasporas today can be divided into two: a diaspora which does not consider itself in exile, and is not about to emigrate to Israel, and a diaspora which neither can, nor wants to, remain where it is because of its miserable, wretched and insecure life. The latter is anxious to emigrate. Yet, the differences between these two diasporas is neither permanent nor unalterable.

A particular diaspora which at one point in time considers itself secure, content and integrated may quite suddenly find itself in an oppressive exile, as happened to the Jews of Germany. When that happens, it is no longer important to debate whether or not the complacency of large, present-day diasporas is justified or not. It is not the prognosis of the ideologist which determines immigration, but the feeling of the majority of the members of the Jewish community. This feeling is not even dependent on whether one is a Zionist, a non-Zionist, or an anti-Zionist. All of the segments of American Jewry feel that they do not need to immigrate. It is clear that even from countries such as these, immigration inspired by pioneering and by Zionist drive is possible. But this is personal immigration, immigration of individuals—although the number of individuals involved can run into the hundreds and thousands.

The greatest and most urgent mission which is imposed upon us at this time is the ingathering of those diasporas that have no no choice; that cannot, and do not wish to remain in exile. If only granted the right to leave, they would immigrate; and would continue to immigrate in great numbers. The Jewish diaspora in the Eastern European and Islamic countries wishes, and is compelled, to leave. Part of this Jewry is imprisoned, and the exit-gates are closed to them. But all those who are permitted to leave must come to Israel, even if the State is not yet ready to absorb them. The vast majority of these Jews have nothing; they have no possessions and no money. All this was taken from them. They were also deprived of education and culture, since it was never given to them. They are forced to come without means, without a trade, without an education, without any preparation, without language training, without a knowledge of Israel and its values. Because of a messianic urge they stream in by the thousands and ten-thousands to the State of Israel, and the efforts required for their absorption are even greater and more difficult than the war effort. The supreme mission of the ingathering of exiles depends upon two programs which require the supreme effort of the nation: a housing program and an education program.

There is no hope for the return of the people without preparing for a return to the land. Making desolation bloom, conquering the forces of nature on land, on sea and in the air, giant-scale housing projects, large scale irrigation works and power plants, the building of a diversified economy which maintains itself through agriculture and industry—these are the material conditions for the absorption of the immigration.

However, material and economic absorption alone will not suffice. The mission of this generation will not be carried out only through housing, settlement and employment for hundreds of thousands of immigrants. A people does not live by bread alone. The diasporas which are being liquidated, and which are reassembling in Israel, do not of themselves constitute a nation; just a conglomeration of people, of human dust, without a language, without education, without roots in the tradition and vision of the nation—not having been nurtured by it.

The Jewish people is one of the smallest in the world, and it has promoted general education for over 2,500 years. Even when it lost its independence and birthplace, it was careful to guard the education of its children, as the pupil of its eye, during its wanderings in foreign lands.

However, a large part of the immigrants come to us without the most elementary knowledge, without a trace of Jewish or general education. Two things brought this about: the time and the place. They are the products of a period of destruction and havoc in the world; a period of world wars and material and spiritual decline that is tied up with a shaking of the foundations of the world. They come from backward, remote, oppressed, deprived countries.

The spiritual absorption of this immigration—its blending, and molding, the conversion of this human dust into a cultured, creative, independent, vision-bearing nation—is not easy work, and its difficulties are no smaller than the difficulties of economic absorption. We will require a supreme moral and educational effort—an effort accompanied by deep and pure love—to unite these wandering people, to transmit to them the riches and values of the nation, to transplant these distant and deprived exiled communities into our society, our culture, our language and our creativity; not as benefactors, but as equal partners.

And so it is with the soldier that we created—the veterans of the Yishuv [the Jewish community in pre-1948 Israel]—the materialistic and spiritual soldier. We did not create him by ourselves. We were bequeathed a precious legacy from our forefathers, and we were able to stand on the shoulders of the generations that preceded us. This legacy is the legacy of the entire Jewish people, and it can endure only as the legacy of the entire nation. Within these education-starved immigrants is stored all of the same qualities and potential which made the builders of the Yishuv what they are now; there is nothing which we have done until now in the economic, political, military and spiritual realms which will, in the course of time, be out of the reach of these immigrants, if only they will receive from us the help which we received, in our day, from our parents and our communities.

This educational program, on which the fate of the State hangs, no less than the fate of the immigrants, will not be accomplished in schools alone. There is no doubt that the younger generation which will be born here, or will grow up among us from the new immigration, will strike roots and blend in, to no less an extent than the children of the veterans. But, we are neither permitted nor able to wait until a new generation grows up. It is imperative that this education and assimilative effort be applied to all immigrants regardless of their age. The deep and speedy change which can be effected in a child, naturally, cannot be effected at the same pace, and with the same ease, in an adult immigrant. But, aside from school, we have a powerful educational tool at our disposal —and that is the army.

A most vital mission of our generation has been imposed on the Israeli army: to safeguard the security of the State of Israel. This mission is important enough that the best of our youth give it all of their ability, energy and time. But this is not the only mission of our army. Our army was also charged with being a pioneering force, an educator, a nation-builder and the redeemer of desolate places. If we will not be a united nation and we will not settle the areas of desolation, our security will not be assured.

The problem of our security is different from the security problem of any other nation in the world; not only because we are few against many, but because we are still not a nation, and we still do not have a land. A land 90 per cent desolate, arid, and empty is not a land; and a population in which one person does not understand the language of his neighbor, a population which is not aware of the culture of the nation and has no knowledge of the land, and is not attached and committed to the nation's culture and outlook, is not a nation capable of facing its enemies and its problems in time of need.

It was not out of love of "superfluity" that we drafted a security-service law the likes of which is not found in other countries; a law which requires every 18-year-old boy and girl to undergo agricultural training. When the security-service law was submitted to the Knesset a year ago (20 Ab, 5709—August 1949) it was explained that it is imperative that our army be small, because we are small in number, and our manpower is needed for land development, for the absorption of immigrants and for economic and cultural creativity all of which are basic needs of our State. Consequently, the greatest problem of our army is how to attain excellence. All the technical and professional knowledge which any superior army in the world has, all the physical and spiritual needs of each soldier, all the organizational improvements which raise the collective capacity of the security forces—we need all of these no less than any other state. But, these alone will not be enough for us because, in view of our special geographic and historical situation, it is imperative that our army add its own important ingredient, namely: the pioneering touch. Only by raising our moral and intellectual advantage to the peak of its potential will our army fulfill its mission: to maintain the security of the state.

At the time that the security-service law was explained, it was stressed that we cannot view the pioneering aptitude as a monopoly of privileged groups among us. A pioneering spirit is not the legacy of the privileged and elite. It is stored within the soul of each one of us. Inside of every person there are latent spiritual powers, virtues and treasures, only few of which are ever revealed. The pressure of historical need, along with properly oriented educational programs which are able to uncover paths to the heart and to the inner reaches of his soul, can stimulate and energize secret resources which exist within man and raise him to the highest level of bravery and pioneering spirit. Every able army commander knows this secret, and has the power to turn his army, made up of ordinary flesh and blood, into an army of brave men.

The historical sense which has guided us in Israel has paved the road leading to these pioneering sources that were latent within Jewish youth in the towns of Lithuania, Poland, Galicia, Rumania and America. The immigration which will be arriving in the coming years will be, in large part, an immigration from the countries of the East, the Islamic countries, the countries of Asia and Africa. In recent generations, the Jewish communities in these countries have not had the means and the opportunities to draw on the human and Jewish cultural treasures, even to the extent that was possible for the Jews in Europe.

There is, however, no basis to the assumption that the Jews of North Africa or Turkey, Egypt, Persia or Aden are different in their make-up and nature from the Jews of Lithuania, Galicia and America. Rich resources of pioneering ability are hidden within them as well; resources of bravery and creativity. If we invest in them part of the efforts that we have invested in the Jewish youth of Europe, we will here also obtain blessed results.

The Israeli army is obliged to become the creative force of the nation's pioneers, and the cultural instrument for the assimilation of returnees; for their integration and their cultural advancement. The insipid prattle of the critics of the military—that by its very nature is an instrument which breeds stupidity, careerism, idleness, arrogance, etc.—let that not disturb us. The nature and character of the army, as of other institutions, depends on the content which we put into it; and we have to fill this institution with pioneering and cultural ingredients which contain what is needed to build a nation and create a homeland.

It is incumbent upon the army to implant within the youth under its influence—from the Youth Brigade and upward—the basic values of cleanliness—physical and moral, a knowledge of the language and the country, physical and mental dexterity, love of the homeland and fraternal loyalty, bravery and creative initiative, discipline and order, fitness for work and a pioneering drive —these in addition to the military and professional qualities which are needed for security in the most narrow sense.

The Israeli army is only two years old. However, this young army is but an offshoot of ancient military stock; one of the oldest armies in the world. Jewish military history is as old as the Jewish people—some 4,000 years. Abram, the first Hebrew, fought with Amraphel king of Shinar, Arioch king of Ellasar, Chedorlaomer king of Elam and Tidal king of Goyim, to rescue his relatives who fell captive in the War of the Nine Kings in the valley of Siddim (Genesis 14). The first war of the Jewish people came immediately after the exodus from Egypt—war with the traditional enemy of Israel, Amalek; and it was conducted by the first military commander in Israel, Joshua, son of Nun. The battle took place at Refidim, in the same area where the last battle of the Israeli army was conducted in our times—the battle to liberate the Negev from the Egyptians at the end of 1948.

After the battle of Refidim, the armies of Israel fought with the Canaanites and the Amorites, with Moab and Edom, with Philistia and Aram, with Egypt, with Assyria, with Babylonia and with Arabia, with Greece and with Rome. And its military history did not end with the destruction of the Temple, nor with the defeat of Bar Kochba.

As late as the seventh century, the Jewish army fought in alliance with Persia against the Byzantine army under the commander, Benjamin of Tiberius; and at the end of the eleventh century, in the year 1100, Jewish Haifa battled the Crusaders. Only after the Venecian fleet attacked Haifa from the sea, and the army of Tancred surrounded it by land, did Jewish Haifa fall after a desperate two-week battle.

The Jewish army, with a few exceptions, has always been a popular army. The Jewish fighters in the days of Joshua were those who settled the country and built it up. It was a fighting nation that conquered the land, and not mercenaries who were out for personal gain. The most serious transgression in the army of ancient Israel was for a soldier to take booty and keep it for himself. Such wartime robbery was considered a breach of the Covenant, and an outrage, and Achan, son of Carmi of the tribe of Judah, was punished for this transgression by Joshua, son of Nun, in accordance with the full severity of the law: the penalty of death and confiscation of his possessions. The place where this outrage took place was called, the Vale of Achor "to this day" (Joshua 7). The army of Joshua was basically a citizens' army. When Othniel ben Kenaz, brother of Caleb, conquered Dvir, which is in the Negev, Achsah the wife of Othniel (the daughter of Caleb), persuaded her husband to ask her father for springs of water "because you have given me the land of the Negev. . . . So Caleb gave her the upper pool and the lower pool" (Joshua 15:19). This was perhaps the first Nachal [Pioneering Brigade] in the army of Israel which attempted to irrigate the Negev.

It was not for naught that the Jews were warned to preserve the trees of the field in wartime, and even in time of siege. "When you are at war and lay siege to a city for a long time in order to take it, do not destroy its trees by putting the axe to them, for they provide you with food; you shall not cut them down" (Deuteronomy 20:19).

The laws of recruitment which Moses established also prove that the army of Israel was a citizens' army. "When you are about to join battle. . . . Then the officers shall address the army in these words: 'Any man who has built a new house and has not dedicated it shall return to his house, otherwise he may die in battle and another man will dedicate it. Any man who has planted a vineyard, and had not yet begun to use it, shall return home, otherwise he may die in battle and another man will use it. Any man who has pledged himself to take a woman in marriage, and has not taken her, shall return home, otherwise he may die in battle and another man take her' " (Deuteronomy 20:2-7). Because this was a citizens' army, and the entire nation were soldiers, they didn't want faint-hearted men to participate in war. This was also one of Moses' laws of recruitment: "The officers shall further address the army: 'Any man who is afraid and has lost heart shall return home, or his companions will be discouraged as he is' " (Deuteronomy 20:8).

Rabbi Jochanan, son of Zakai, one of the great scholars during the closing days of the Second Temple, said about the laws of recruitment: "Notice how deeply God is concerned with the dignity of man. When the fearful and weak-hearted return, people will say: 'Perhaps he built a house, perhaps he planted a vineyard, perhaps he was betrothed to a woman.' Hence, they were all required to bring witnesses, with the exception of the fearful and the weak-hearted—who bears witness to himself: 'He heard the sound of the closing of the shudders and he was frightened; to the sound of the neighing of horses, and he trembled; to the sound of the blowing of horns, and he became alarmed; he saw the unsheathing of swordsmen, and water started running between his knees. . . .'"

These exemptions from the army were not the result of a frivolous attitude towards the responsible role which is imposed on the army; on the contrary, they were instituted in order to strengthen its morale, and to free it from those who cannot devote themselves at all to military missions because of new family ties, unsettled economic affairs, or because of an organic, spiritual weakness which cannot be overcome. After the fighting nation was cleansed of these unwanted elements, strict discipline was maintained in the army, and stern measures were taken against deserters from the battlefield "because the beginning of defeat is flight." As a result, they used to station, in front of the troops and behind them, "sentries armed with iron sledgehammers, authorized to beat anyone wanting to turn back."

Exemptions from the people's army for economic or family reasons were permitted only during an offensive war, but during defensive wars, when the people of Israel were attacked, "everyone went, including the groom from his bridal-chamber and the bride from her wedding canopy," because the obligation of defending the nation from outside attack fell on every man and woman without exception.

Up to the period of the monarchy, there was no regular army in Israel. Saul was the first one to establish a regular army of 3,000 men: "And two thousand were with Saul in Michmash and the hill country of Bethel, and 1,000 with Jonathan at Givat Binyamin; and he sent the rest of the people home" (I Samuel 13:2). King Solomon also established an equestrian army of 12,000 men.

The army reached its peak of perfection in the days of the First Temple, during the reign of the greatest of the kings of Judah, Uziahu (Azariah) son of Amaziah, who ruled in the middle of the eighth century B.C. and was a contemporary of Jeroboam the Second, son of Joash. These two kings expanded the boundary of Israel to an extent not reached after the division of the kingdom following the death of Solomon. Jeroboam expanded the boundary of Israel in the north, and returned Damascus and Hamath to Israel, and Uziahu, king of Judah, expanded the boundary of his kingdom in the south. He battled the Philistines at Gath, Yavneh and Ashdod in the west of Israel, and the Arabs who lived at Gur Baal, and the Maonites in the eastern part of the country. He not only expanded the boundaries, but also developed the land, built new cities in the territories which he conquered, expanded the agricultural area, set up irrigation in the wasteland of the south, and promoted the raising of sheep and cattle as well as the planting of groves in the hills. "And he built towers in the wilderness and dug many cisterns, for he had large herds in the lowlands and in the plains. He also had farmers and vine-dressers in the hill-country and in the fertile lands, for he loved the soil" (II Chronicles 26:10).

One of his chief projects was the building up of Eilat. Solomon had already appreciated the great importance of the gulf of the Red Sea for both the economy and the status of his kingdom. He developed and exploited the copper mines in the Arava, and set up a factory for smelting the copper at Etzion Gever, adjacent to Eilat. (This factory was discovered several years ago in the course of the excavations of the American Jewish archeologist, Nelson Glueck.)

Solomon also appreciated the importance of the sea and navigation. "King Solomon built a fleet of ships at Etzion Gever, near Eloth on the shore of the Red Sea, in Edom" (I Kings 9:26). But there were no sailors in Israel then, and Solomon was compelled to make use of the Canaanite sailors of his ally, Hiram, king of Tyre. But Eilat did not remain for long in the hands of the Jews. In the days of Joram, son of Jehoshafat "Edom revolted against Judah and set up its own king" (II Kings 8:20), and Edom reverted to be an Edomite city. Only after King Amaziah, son of Joash, "defeated ten thousand Edomites in the Valley of Salt, and captured Selah . . ." (II Kings 14:7), was his son Uziahu able to reach the edge of the Arava in the south. He built Eilat and returned it to Judah.

Along with the settlement and development projects, and the expansion of the boundaries, this great king gave his attention to the fortification of the capital of his kingdom. "And Uziahu built towers in Jerusalem at the Corner Gate, at the Valley Gate, and at the slope, and he fortified them" (II Chronicles 26:9). But, the main activity of this king was the reinforcement of the army from the point of view of organization and armament. There was no king in Israel before him who did such wonders in strengthening the security forces and in increasing their battle capacity. In the days of Saul there was not one blacksmith in the entire land of Israel "for the Philistines were determined to prevent the Hebrews from making swords and spears. . . . And when war broke out, none of the followers of Saul and Jonathan had either sword or spear . . ." (I Samuel 13:19-22). King Uziahu saw to it that his army would have at its disposal every type of weapon that was then known to Egypt, Assyria, Aram and all the surrounding nations. He also perfected new types of weapons and set up the first artillery in the history of Israel: "In Jerusalem he had machines designed by engineers for use upon towers and bastions, made to discharge arrows and large stones. His fame spread far and wide, for he was so wonderfully gifted and he became very powerful" (II Chronicles 26:15).

The author of the Book of Chronicles gives the size of the army of Uziahu as "three hundred and seven thousand, five hundred, a powerful fighting force to aid the king against his enemies" (II Chronicles 26:13). It is possible that this number was exaggerated. The second number given in the same place seems more probable: "The total number of heads of families which supplied seasoned warriors was two thousand six hundred." But, from Uziahu's feats of strength and expansion in the land of the Philistines to the west, in the Arabian section to the east, and in Edom in the south, it is clear that he had a large army, and the strength of the army lay not only in its numbers, but also in its perfected equipment. "Uziahu prepared for the whole army shields, spears, helmets, coats of mail, bows and sling-stones" (II Chronicles 26:14). All these were the kinds of offensive and defensive weapons which existed at that time and for a long time afterward.

The special greatness of King Uziahu lies in the fact that he knew how to integrate settlement, development and irrigation projects with military and war activities. It is no wonder that he merited having his full biography ("The Other Events of Uziahu's Reign, from First to Last") written by Isaiah, son of Amoz, the prophet. However, this book, as with all of the books of the kings of Judah and Israel, did not come down to us.

The classic example in our history of the joining of work projects and defense occurred during the first return to Zion in the days of Ezra and Nehemiah. The first returnees from Babylonia found that "the wall of Jerusalem was broken down and its gates destroyed by fire" (Nehemiah 1:3), and they began to build the walls of the capital and its gates under the leadership of Nehemiah, son of Hacaliah. But, when "Sanballat and Tobiah, the Arabians and Ammonites and Ashdodites, heard that the new work on the walls of Jerusalem had made progress and that the filling of the breaches had begun, they were very angry; and they all banded together to come and fight in Jerusalem" (Nehemiah 4:7).

Then Nehemiah gave the command to continue with the building: "The builders had their swords attached to their belts as they built."

Thus does Nehemiah narrate in his memoirs: "From that day onward, half the men under me were engaged in the actual building, while the other half stood by holding their spears, shields and bows, and wearing coats of mail . . . some building the wall and some laden with burdens; with one hand engaged in work and the other grasping his weapon. . . . And they served as guards during the night and workers during the day. So neither I nor my kinsmen nor the men under me nor my bodyguard ever took off our clothes . . ." (Nehemiah 4).

Once again our generation has been charged with the double burden of the first returnees to Zion—on a scale several times as large. Not only the wall of Jerusalem, but the desolation of the country has been left to it to rebuild and cause to flourish. It is our duty to teach tens and hundreds of thousands of returnees from the Exile to fight and to work so that a nation may arise that will know how to rebuild the ruins of its country and to defend it from its foes.

The area of concern of the Israeli army cannot be limited to the military. It must also serve as a base for education and integration as well as for settlement and construction. Within the framework of the army, the young immigrants will acquire a knowledge of the language and the country, and within the framework of the army, the youth will be trained to rebuild the desolation, to erect border settlements, and to establish works to tame the Arava on the outskirts of Jerusalem, in the lowlands, and in the mountains. In the navy and in the air force they will learn to control the forces of nature on the sea and in the air.

Not all immigrants will be accommodated within the military, but the civilian community is also not exempt from the central mission of our generation: the material and spiritual absorption of immigrants. All of the modes of settlement, rural and urban: the kibbutz, the moshav, the moshava, cooperatives, business concerns, labor unions, artisans' guilds, farmers' and industrial associations, professional associations, local towns and councils and every man and woman in the country: workers, clerks, doctors, teachers, writers, contractors, store and factory owners, merchants and businessmen—all are called upon to extend a faithful, helping hand for the absorption of immigrants, for their guidance and education, and to help them get settled and to strike roots in the country. These efforts will not be demanded of us for only a year or two, but forever, and tirelessly, with increasing urgency. This is the noble destiny of our era.

The admixture of people which flows in from foreign exiles will be cleansed, refined and purified from harmful, foreign dross in the melting pot of Jewish brotherhood and through military discipline. The barriers between communities will be torn down, and true unity of a new nation reviving its youth will be forged which will draw from an ancient past saturated with struggle and experience, built and glorified through pioneering work and a struggle for freedom, aided by a spirit of bravery, heroism and strength, and bound to a messianic vision whose time has come.

CHAPTER TWO

The Bible Is Illumined by Its Own Light

To my friend Yitzchak Damiel-Schweiger: Greetings!

I read your article, "On Our Book of Life," in the Rosh Hashana edition of *Davar* with great pleasure. I especially enjoyed the fine story on the partnership between the town *maskil* [Jewish intellectual] and the *melamed* [teacher] Nahum Leib. Even though you ridicule the poor intellectual and his counterpart, I lovingly accept the derision despite the fact that I see nothing degrading about the title "intellectual." On the contrary, I would not be at all ashamed of this title, if I knew that I were worthy of it.

It appears to me that both traditional interpretation and modern inquiry have enriched our spirit, each in its own way, though it is possible to find defects and faults in both of them.

I do not accept the view expressed by Kariv at the gathering at the Maloh Club. It seems to me that this is also your view—that the Midrash [commentary on the Bible] is greater and more important than the Bible. Large segments of orthodox Judaism relate negatively to the Bible and see it as an almost heretical book. In any case, the Talmud, the Responsa and the Midrashim are closer to their hearts.

Even though this view is invalid in my eyes, and definitely in error, I attach importance to the Midrash and see a vast and precious spiritual legacy in it, even if it does not come close to attaining the standard of the Bible, neither content-wise nor style-wise, and it is not at all possible to place them on the same level. But I do not accept the contempt for the literature of the Haskalah [Enlightenment] and the intellectuals. It's easy to find defects in Haskalah literature, but it has been a great blessing in past generations. Without it, who knows if we would have achieved national revival in our day. Without the Haskalah, I am doubtful if Love of Zion (*Hibat Zion*) or Zionism would have arisen, and if we would have attained the renewal of the State of Israel.

But, it is not my purpose to defend the Haskalah or the maskilim, with or without quotation marks, but to correct a mistake you made about something that I said. I saw the letter *aleph* at the beginning of your essay, and from it I learned that you are still involved in the debate about what I said at the Maloh Club, and it is my duty, if possible, to rectify slander, because in your first words you distorted my position. I am sure that you did not do so maliciously. It is possible that my sketchy remarks at the Club brought this about, and I want to express my view to you as it is. I am not in agreement with you about everything, and you will have much room for disagreement, but I would prefer that you do not ascribe to me views that I do not hold and, as an old friend of yours, I would not want you to argue about things that never entered my mind.

First of all, I must tell you that I did not intend, in my remarks at the Club, to offer an evaluation of the Bible. I do not consider myself at all qualified for that. The Bible, you know, is not a book, but an entire literature which contains legend (others would say "mythology"), stories, history, laws and statutes, rebuke and elegy, poetry and meditation, words of wisdom and prophecy. In order to evaluate this literature, one must be not only well-versed in the Bible, but also a poet and a philosopher, a critic and a prophet, a historian and an archeologist, a linguist and an expert in the history of ancient religion, thought and literature. I do not possess even one of the mentioned qualifications, and I would not venture to appear at a gathering of writers, or at any gathering, and attempt to evaluate these immortal books.

I spoke at the Club as an average reader of the Bible. I admit that I read the Bible with great love and deep admiration. I appealed to the association of writers and artists that they might bring the Bible to our generation, using all of the artistic means and spiritual capability at their disposal: as writers, artists, sculptors, musicians, theatrical people, philosophers and educators. Our generation is not acquainted with the Bible, the greatest masterpiece of the Hebrew people to this very day. Without a knowledge of the Bible, a knowledge of ourselves, our origin, our spirit—our destiny and our future is impossible.

Up to this point, I imagine, there is no difference of opinion between us. But, in your essay, you put into my mouth an answer to a question that was asked in this manner: "Wherein is the special significance of the Bible that it has become so important to Israel and to humanity as a whole?" According to you, I answered the question as follows: "The strength and uniqueness of the Bible lies in its being the book of truth like no other—a book in which the truth is told about the nation and its people *as it is,* without any bias," etc. This is not completely correct, and contains a half-truth with which you justly take issue.

It is true that I stressed in my remarks, that truth—the bitter truth, completely unbiased—is one of the greatest and most precious characteristics of the Bible; and I recalled as an example the story about Uriah the Hittite and the words of Nathan the prophet to King David: "You are the man." Even after reading your essay, I hold to my view that the truth, the naked truth, is one of the most outstanding and marvelous characteristics of the Bible. You contend that such truth can also be found in other books; and, indeed, I also contend that there are other great books in the world, and they cannot remain alien to us. Truth is the seal of the Almighty, and there are not many books in the world which are impressed with this seal as is the Bible.

But, I did not say, as you indicate in your essay, that the special value of the Bible lies in its *only* being a book of truth. In the transcript of my remarks at the Club you will find that I said: "What is the greatness of the Bible, aside from its poetry, and aside from its other great treasures? First and foremost—the truth." And in my answer to Kariv I said that if the Bible were no more than the story of Samson—though it is important—or just the names of the generals of Edom, I do not know if the Bible would be an important book. "But when there is Hosea, Micah, Isaiah, Jeremiah and Psalms—all of these together comprise the greatness of the Bible." Hosea, Micah, Isaiah and Psalms do not involve themselves in stories about the life of the people and its notables, but express divine, moral ideas and deep and great thoughts.

At the end of my article in the *Government Annual* for 5714—1954—(called "Israel Eternal"), I devoted a few lines to the Bible. Even there I did not give an evaluation of this book, because I would not accept such a task, for reasons that I have already explained. But, if you read those lines, you will be convinced that the view of the Bible which you ascribe to me is completely alien to me.

Contrary to your essay, in my understanding of the Bible, I am both a partner of the maskil in the town and of the melamed Nahum Leib.

I learned in the Torah, along with the poor maskil, that Moses was born in Egypt, was educated in the house of Pharaoh, went out to see the travail of his brothers, smote the Egyptian because he hit one of his Hebrew brothers, fled to Midian, married a non-Jew and was Jethro's shepherd. These were all important episodes in the life of Moses, and in the Midrash there are several good interpretations about these episodes. And like your beloved melamed, Nahum Leib, I read the story of the burning bush that was not consumed, of Moses' mission to Pharaoh, of the exodus from Egypt, of the revelation at Mt. Sinai, etc. In one respect—and it is a very very important one—I differ from Nahum Leib, the melamed, and with you. In my humble opinion, the episode of the burning bush is a chapter in the biography of Moses, and not a chapter in the biography of the Almighty. The episode of the almond stick is also, in my opinion, a chapter in the life of Jeremiah the prophet, and not in the life of the Almighty. I believe in Jeremiah who tells us that the word of God came to him as follows: "Before I formed you in the womb, I knew you; before you were born, I consecrated you; I appointed you a prophet to the nations" (Jeremiah 1:5). Jeremiah, without a doubt, told the truth, and he heard the things that he described.

But from whose mouth did he hear these things? Perhaps you know. I do not. Perhaps it is because I accept the view of Maimonides (and others) that God has no mouth and utters no sound; he has no body, nor does he have any form resembling a body. This is not to say that Jeremiah invented these words. On the contrary, I am certain that he heard them in his heart.

From the Bible I am more or less familiar with the story of Abraham, Isaac and Jacob. These accounts not only describe the sheep and the herds which they had, but also the patterns of their lives, their spiritual world, and their conception of God. From the Bible I also know, more or less, the story of Moses and the Children of Israel, the words of the prophets and the songs of Psalms, the Proverbs of Solomon and the conversation of Job and his comrades. And, again, I am able to comprehend, more or less, the beliefs of our forefathers and their physical and spiritual struggles. But I do not believe that the Bible is a book about the history of God. Such is not possible.

In the Book of Genesis it says: This is the story of heaven and earth, this is the story of man, this is the story of Noah, and this is the story of the sons of Noah. But not once does it say: This is the story of God. And it is impossible for that to be said.

The patriarchs and the prophets heard the word of God; but I do not know where the sound came from, because I do not know, and it seems to me that no one knows, how God lets his utterances be heard; for every Jew says in his morning prayers: "The attributes of the human body cannot be attributed to him."

The Bible relates the history of the Jewish people and transmits to us the inner feelings, the thoughts, meditations, visions and beliefs of the nation's patriarchs, lawmakers and prophets—all of these are important and precious. We read in this book about great and deep experiences—physical and spiritual, moral and intellectual experiences—we read accounts of eye witnesses unparalleled in world history. But we read only of their experiences as they report them. Not one of us knows their source.

I do not believe—and I imagine that you do not believe either—that man originates only from dust. I do not even believe that the dust is just plain dust. The ideas of Einstein and Newton, the plays of Shakespeare and Sophocles, the dialogues of Plato and Buddha are not the products of a blind game of atoms and electrons running to and fro, but a living expression of something great and mysterious called "spirit," and this spirit is a part of the awesome and infinite being, no less than are the organs of man part of the human being. We stand before a great and awesome mystery which no one is able to solve. There are those who call it by the name "God." I do not believe that by merely giving something a name we clarify and explain what does not lend itself to clarification and explanation.

From the Bible I know what our forefathers thought about this great mystery. More than this I do not know. The mystery itself remains a mystery. And it is both the mystery of "spirit" and the mystery of "matter." Spirit and matter are the manifestations of a higher unity.

I am a great believer in the capacity of the human spirit; both in its intellectual capacity and its moral capacity. Many, many things which we do not know and understand today will be known and understood by the coming generations; a great deal of what has been spoiled until now, will be fixed in the future. "The spirit of man travels upward," despite the doubts of Ecclesiastes. But I do not know whether in the end of days man will attain an understanding of the infinite, and will fully know the "one and all."

And I do not know if we will ever attain ultimate perfection in the life of man.

The Bible, in my humble opinion, is the creation of the Jewish people, and did not come to it from outside. I also do not accept the explanation that Job was translated from another language. Without a doubt, the Bible was one of the chief factors in the molding of the image of our people; but this factor came from within, from within the people. The greatness of the Bible is the greatness of the spirit of the Jewish people; it is the fruit of its spirit, the fruit of the great men of our people.

Of course, you can ask: From where did this spirit come? Just as you can ask: What is the source of the spirit of Greece as revealed in the epics of Homer, the tragedies of Aeschylus, Sophocles and Euripides, the dialogues of Plato and the books of Aristotle, etc.? And, in general, where did man's spirit come from? And his body? From dust! All right. But from where did the dust come? It is part of the world! From where did the world come? Neither the Bible nor any other single book in the world has given—and I am afraid, will ever give—the answer to these eternal questions. The only answer which the Bible gave is what our forefathers thought and believed about this question—the answer that they gave to themselves. This answer left its mark on the history of the Jewish people, just as other answers—and they are not many, and not too different—left their marks on the history of other nations.

At the end of the great and moving poem attributed to Job, there is the answer of God out of the storm. Even in this reply only questions are posed, eternal questions with which the human spirit has struggled since the day it matured. But there is no answer to these questions.

In addition to its other great virtues, the Bible contains one more powerful feature. I do not find in the Bible what I find in Greek books and in the midrashic literature: two separate worlds—a separate material world and a separate spiritual world; in other words, a "now" and a "hereafter."

One of the first things that Moses heard from the mouth of his God, after the exodus from Egypt, was that the Jewish people would be "a people more treasured than any other, a kingdom of priests and a holy nation." And all of the blessings which Moses heard from the mouth of God—provided that the Israelites would obey the voice of God—were the blessing of the field and the city, the blessing of the womb and the earth, the offspring of cattle and sheep, the blessing of fruit baskets and kneading troughs, the blessing of strength and victory against all of the enemies that would rise up against them, the blessing of storehouses and toil—"And I will bless you with a land that the Lord your God will give to you."

Even when the later prophets spoke only of a God of righteousness and justice, of mercy and truth, and demanded of man, in the name of the Lord, "only to do justice, to love mercy, to walk humbly before your God" (Micah 6:8), they always stood on the firm ground of this world, but prophesied at the same time that "nation should not lift sword against nation" and "man will sit under his vine and under his fig tree and will not be disturbed."

This image of the Bible was later altered within the midrashic literature; and there are marvelous things in the Midrash not found in the Bible. Occasionally, there are descriptions in the Midrash which differ, on the very same matter, from those in the Bible. In the Torah, the revelation on Mt. Sinai is accompanied by thunder and lightning, a dense cloud, and a very strong blast of the shofar; and the entire people sees the thunder and lightning and shofar blast. Yet, the Midrash relates: "When God gave the Torah, a bird did not chirp, a fowl did not fly, an ox did not low, wheels did not spin, seraphim did not say 'holy,' and the sea did not move, living creatures did not speak; the world was completely silent. And the voice spoke out: 'I am the Lord your God.'" I admit that the description in the Aggada appeals to me more than the description in the Torah.

And there are also changes which were made purposely. In the Torah it says: "An eye for an eye." Our Rabbis later said: "An eye for an eye means monetary payment [for the value of the person's eye]." From a moral point of view, the sayings of our Rabbis are closer to us than the original verse of the Torah. But we cannot accept this statement of our Rabbis as an authentic interpretation of the verse in the Torah. When it says in the Torah "an eye for an eye," the intention is not money. If the Torah had wanted to say money, it would have said this in clear Hebrew: "Payment for an eye," or "money for an eye," and the like. Hence, if it said it as it did: An eye for an eye, a tooth for a tooth, a hand for a hand, a foot for a foot, a burn for a burn, a wound for a wound, a boil for a boil; we must understand these things as they are written, even if they are distasteful to us.

Truth comes before all. The books of the Bible and the books of the Midrash are certainly two different things. The latter are dependent on the former (though not completely, not always, and not in everything); but the former can only be explained through internal evidence.

Kariv, you and many others like you can hypothesize, if you wish, that the midrash on the Song of Songs, which is a song about nature and love attributed to King Solomon, is a conversation between the House of Israel and the Almighty, and that it is more important and more beautiful than the original Song of Songs. This is a matter of taste which cannot be debated. But the truth must surface. The composer of the Song of Songs sang about simple, natural, earthy love between a swarthy and comely maiden: a tender of vineyards, and her cousin—a garden watchman and a gatherer of lilies.

You might say: There are also such love songs in Greek and Latin and even among the Gypsies. There are! But the Bible would be impoverished if those who refused to include the Song of Songs in the canon had succeeded. We must remember that there are also conversations with the Almighty in Greek (in the writings of the Fathers of the Church), and in Latin, and Spanish, and other languages.

Kariv is certain that the midrash on the verse, "he will kiss me with the kisses of his mouth," which talks as if the Almighty kisses twice—once in this world and a second time in the world to come—is superior in its beauty and its spiritual content than the original verse, as we understand it literally. It is possible that this is an apt midrash. But kisses of the Almighty did not enter the mind of the composer of the Song of Songs at all—not in this world and not in the next world—and I'm doubtful if he would have believed at all that there is another world in addition to this one. In any case, in the Torah, in the Prophets, and in the Song of Songs there is no reference and no suggestions of the world to come.

The Bible, and the Midrash on the Bible, are two different things; not necessarily opposite or contradictory in all cases, but different. The Song of Songs is separate; the Midrash on the Song of Songs is separate.

The Midrash is beautiful in its own way, and the Bible is great and exalted in its own way; and in my humble opinion there is nothing like it. The Bible was great before the Midrash existed and is not dependent on the Midrash. It is not to be understood through the aid of the Midrash, but through its own inner content.

I am doubtful if the masters of the Midrash intended to comment on the Bible. They seized upon the verses of the Bible in order to express what was in their hearts, and very frequently they expressed wonderful and noble things, but these were their words, not the words of the Bible. The words of the Bible are to be found only in the Bible. "A Bible verse can never lose its literal sense." There is no poetic or moral importance at all to a list of the generals of Edom. And if an imaginative midrash is composed about it, then the midrash is more beautiful than what is being commented on. Money in place of "an eye for an eye" is morally preferable. But not every commentary and late Midrash is superior to the source. Most words in the Bible are peaks, and there is nothing higher than a peak.

I reject with all my moral and Jewish strength what Kariv said at that same gathering at the Maloh Club, that "every verse [in the Bible] started its universal and eternal life in a post-biblical period." Had I not known who Kariv is, I would have said that this is a desecration of the holy.

The eternity and greatness of the Bible is not dependent upon any book, commentary, or Midrash that came after it, although the books, commentaries and Midrashim that were written after the post-biblical period are a part of our spiritual legacy; and we must bequeath to our generation their revelations. But chapter 15 in Psalms, or chapter 19 or 24 or 37 or 42 or 72 or 89, or any chapter whatsoever in Psalms, did not require Midrashim and later commentaries in order to elevate them and to bestow upon them eternity.

Is it permissible to say, concerning the Book of Psalms as it is, without its Midrashim, that it is "a small book," and that "we must not delve into it too deeply?" The same applies to books of the Prophets, the Book of Job, and all the other books of the Bible, without exception!

I also do not understand the denigration of the natural history and the geography of the Bible. Kariv (and also you, according to your article in *Davar,* it seems to me) wants us to know about King David only what is written about him in Psalms, chapter 89: "I have discovered David my servant; I have anointed him with my holy oil." From this we see that "David was a discovery of God." But this isn't the the only verse written about David in the Bible. The end of First Samuel, all of Second Samuel, and the beginning of First Kings, deal with the life of David and his actions, and they say what they say, and no Midrash of yours or of Kariv will expunge these words. The authors of the Bible wanted us to know the entire truth, so let us be respectful of the truth.

There is a beautiful legend about the harp which David used to play. When midnight arrived, David would get up immediately, and study the Torah until the morning star appeared. David would appeal to the Lord "that all the kings of the East and West are sitting in groups, in all their glory, while my hands are soiled with blood, amnion, and afterbirth, so as to purify a woman for her husband." But this isn't the David of the Bible. The stories of the Bible stand as they are. Do you believe that First or Second Samuel should be concealed, or should not be taught in school; and only the words of the Midrash taught in their place?

This is what I meant when I spoke about the unmitigated truth of the Bible. The great writers of the Bible left us an image of King David based upon his mighty deeds and his ugly misdeeds, and let us study the Bible as it is, with its great and bitter truth. When our souls are faint, we read the marvelous verses of Psalms. The Bible is itself a ladder stationed on the ground whose top reaches into heaven.

If the Bible is, as you say, our identification card—and I agree with you on this point—let us recognize this document for what it is.

When we went into exile, our people was uprooted from the soil in which the Bible grew. We were removed from the political and spiritual setting in which it was woven. There are books in the Bible which have no temporal or spatial connection. Most of the chapters of Psalms, Proverbs and Job are like this. But, almost all of the books of the Pentateuch, and the Early and Later Prophets, are the result of, and an expression of, the political and intellectual struggle of the Jewish people in the territorial, political and cultural environment in which the nation lived in biblical times —from the days of the patriarch, Abraham, to the days of Ezra and Nehemiah—and even after. Without a familiarity with the environment, there can be no understanding of the Bible. During the exile, the image of our people was distorted, and the image of the Bible twisted. Christian Bible scholars, with Christian and anti-Semitic motives, turned the Bible towards Christianity. Even Jewish commentators who were uprooted from the environment of the Bible—from its spiritual and physical climate—have not yet been able to understand the Book of Books properly. Only now that we have again become a free nation on its own soil, and can again breathe in the air which surrounded the Bible at its creation, has the time come, it appears to me, to deal with the essence and truth of the Bible, historically and geographically, as well as religiously and culturally.

In the *shtetl* it was possible to make the artificial distinction between the earthly Bible of the despicable maskil, and the heavenly Bible of the exalted melamed, Nahum Leib. But the truth of the matter is that there is only one Bible. I do not believe at all in the artificial distinction between matter and spirit as it pertains to man, to a nation, or to the Bible. In it matter and spirit are mixed together without neat prearrangement. Both matter and spirit are eternal, and live forever. Anyone who does not believe in the "earthliness" of the Bible makes a fraud of the Book of Books no less than one who denies its "heavenly" spirit. The uniqueness and destiny of the Jewish people were revealed in the Bible. The books of the Bible tell of the glory of Israel. The glory of God—this the heavens declare. And the "heavens"—these are not the possession of our people alone; not even the possession of humanity. They are the possession of the Infinite One. And God is the God of the universe, the God of eternity and of all worlds. The Bible is our creation. You also call it, "Our identification card." The Almighty has no need for an identification card.

The greatness of the Bible is the greatness of the Jewish people, and if God's hand is in this greatness, then his hand is in everything.

"Our heavenly Father"—He is the Father of all. But there is such a thing as personal uniqueness, and national uniqueness, and the Bible is the ultimate expression of uniqueness.

The divine presence of our Creator did not completely abandon us during the 2,000 years of exile, but the luster of the Bible did fade during the exile, as did the luster of the Jewish people. Only with the renewal of the homeland and Hebrew sovereignty were we enabled to examine the Bible once again completely and truthfully.

The commentary of Rashi is very important, but it is no more than the *commentary* of Rashi. The Bible is illumined by its own light, and it is this light which we must explain to the younger generation. This task is imposed upon the educators, teachers, writers, scholars, poets and artists: to cause the light of the Book of Books to shine upon our people in Israel and in the diaspora, to the extent that our redeemed generation is privileged to see the light.

I am presently resting on Mt. Carmel, and I permitted myself to tire you with these words. Please forgive me.

Yours,

D. Ben-Gurion

September, 1953.

CHAPTER THREE

The Antiquity of Israel in Its Land

PART ONE

Gentlemen: I feel as though I have entered a lions' den. I'm afraid that one of the chairman's predictions will not be fulfilled. For the most part, I shall pose many questions. This, I consider, the central purpose of my remarks, because I myself have doubts regarding my own answers. What I will say, I will say with the greatest of respect.

Unlike the preceding lecturers in this group, I do not feel that I have any right to be numbered among those who study the Bible scientifically if, indeed, Bible study is a science. I am just one of the readers of the Bible which I view as a revelation of the original genius of our people; a book which molded the image of our people more than any other book did for any other people in the world.

In general, I consider myself a disciple of Professor Kaufman—as a student who is learning, not as a scholar; as a simple student when it comes to the antiquity of the monotheistic belief among the Jewish people. I consider Professor Kaufman one of the most profound and original thinkers in connection with the early faith of Israel and in arriving at an understanding of the Bible, though

---

Presented before the Bible Study Group, Jerusalem, April 4, 1959.

I do not accept his dogmatism. Nor do I regard monotheism as the one thing which distinguishes the Jewish people, as he does.

The Torah of the Jewish people, or the Torah of Moses, is based on a monotheistic concept—but it is, in addition to this, a national Torah; which is not in keeping with the view of Professor Kaufman that "the religion, for whose sake we separated ourselves from other nations, and which the people considered to be the basis of its uniqueness, was *really* the foundation of its uniqueness." I accept completely Professor Kaufman's refutation of the criticism of the Bible, by Wellhausen, his teachers and students, which to my mind, arbitrarily tortures the Torah and the Prophets by using unfounded, flimsy hypotheses.

There is a wholeness and a unity in the Books of the Bible, though here and there it is possible that a few, and perhaps many, verses were confused, deleted or added. But, the biblical evidence for the historical events of the time, not too distant from when it was written, is more faithful than the explanation of the Germans or other commentators of the nineteenth and twentieth centuries. It appears to me that the historical books of the Bible—such as some of the chapters of the Torah in Genesis, Exodus, Numbers, Deuteronomy, and in the books of Joshua, Judges, Samuel and Kings—were not written only for the sake of history, as was, for example, Thucydides' book on the Peloponnesian War which was written with surprising scientific objectivity based on an investigation of the events which occurred in his day, and many events which he witnessed and participated in. The books of the Bible were written with a clear and obvious religious purpose. Nevertheless, the events related in them, with the exception of the legends, should be accepted as historical fact. But, just as Thucydides did not write about the history of Greece, or even about events relating to his own day, so the Bible saw no need to write about everything, but only about those things which, according to its writers, offered instruction about God and his sovereignty over history; as well as about his sovereignty over nature. Had nothing more than the great book of Thucydides come down to us, we would not have the slightest notion about the marvels of the art, literature and philosophical inquiry of Greek thinkers, because the author of the history of the Peloponnesian War, even though he regards his book as of "eternal value," intended to reveal through it the personal and political factors which played a part in the war and in the relationship to many neighbors. He did not devote one word (perhaps with the exception of a few references in the speeches of Pericles) to the great cultural creativity of Greece, which is the essence of the greatness of Greece, and not the war between Athens and Sparta.

Even the books of the Bible which deal with history did not intend to include and exhaust all of the historical events of their day, or of earlier periods, but only treated those moments which contained moral lessons (which is mistakenly called "religious"—Hebrew *dati*—because *dat* in Hebrew is *law* and not *religion*), and have a connection with the covenant that the great leaders of Israel (Moses and Joshua) made between their people and the God of Abraham, Isaac and Jacob, Who is also the God of the universe, the God of nature, and the God of history. No wonder the Bible passes silently over many things to which present-day historians would devote much space.

The things which I would like to treat here are things which, in the main, are only hinted at in the Bible. Here and there perhaps the hint is deceptive (when I reach such hints, I will say that I do not see them as convincing evidence), and I must note at the outset that everything that I will say is no more than an hypothesis, perhaps even a strange theory, and I do not regard all the evidence which I will bring in its support as indisputable. I realize how easy it will be to question my hypothesis, but I have reached it after the establishment of the State and the War of Independence, which, at least for me, cast a new light on our distant past. Questions which previously did not occur to me as I read the Bible, were aroused within me with an intensity that allowed me no rest. And only this hypothesis can offer a plausible explanation.

I will start with the first question which arises in connection with the story of the crossing of the Jordan by the people under the leadership of Joshua. There it is written: "The Israelites camped in Gilgal . . . and they ate from the produce of the land . . . and the manna ceased on the morrow, after they had eaten of the produce of the land; and the Children of Israel no longer had manna, and they ate from the fruit of the land of Canaan in that year" (Joshua 5:10-12).

I ask: How did the nation sustain itself from the time it crossed the Jordan until the end of the conquest? The author of the Book of Joshua faced this question, and answered it twice: "And they ate from the produce of the land, they ate from the yield of the land of Canaan in that year." But the question is asked: Who supplied food to this vast people over a period of many years, when they were engaged in war with all the people surrounding them? Joshua was 110 when he died. It is not known how old he was when he crossed the Jordan, but there is no doubt that from then, until his old age and the end of the wars and the settlement of the land, many years had passed. Where did they get food for this vast people?

In Exodus (12:32) it tells that the Children of Israel were ordered by Pharaoh to leave, and to take with them their sheep and their cattle. Later, the tribe of Reuben, the tribe of Gad, and half of the tribe of Manasseh left "their women, children and herds" in Transjordan, and only the armed warriors—40,000 men —crossed the Jordan with the rest of the people. But the other tribes took their herds along. This aggravates the problem: Where was pasture and fodder to be found for this great herd? It is known that a pastoral people needs a greater land area than an agricultural nation. Where did the herds of the Israelites pasture during the entire period of the conquest?

It is possible to turn back to the past and to ask the same question about the subsistence of the nation in the desert for a period of 40 years: Where did the vast herds of the people pasture all this while? We are now well acquainted with the Negev, and also with the Sinai desert, and we know that there is no possibility there for the maintenance of vast herds belonging to 600,000 families. The people ate manna, but what did the herds of cattle, and the flocks of sheep eat? We know that it is written: "The sons of Reuben and the sons of Gad had very large herds" (Numbers 32:1). We also know that in Israel's war with the Midianites (as is told in Numbers 31), the Children of Israel plundered 675,000 sheep, 72,000 cattle and 61,000 asses. We must inevitably assume that these numbers are exaggerated. But, even if the numbers are smaller, food would have been needed for the people and fodder or pasture for the herds. How did the Children of Israel find this in the desert during the period of wars through the completion of the conquest and the settlement?

Another question also arises. In the days of Moses and Joshua, we see all the tribes of Israel functioning as one nation under one leader. Even the tribes of Reuben, Gad and half of the tribe of Manasseh, who had already settled in Transjordan in the days of Moses, worked together with the other tribes under one leader. And after they conquered the land and settled down, we find in the Book of Judges that in the course of almost 400 years, from Kushan Rishatayim until Ehud, which according to this book covered a span of time from the death of Joshua until Samuel the prophet, the tribes of Israel were scattered and divided. This is an unusual process which contravenes the processes known to us in the history of all nations—that unification comes after division and not vice versa. It turns out here that first the nation was united under the authority of one leader, and after him there was again one leader; but afterwards every tribe shifted for itself, or several tribes joined hands and all of the others were on their own.

And again we meet up with a strange phenomenon: In the days of Moses and Joshua, the Children of Israel believed in God, in Almighty God, and made a covenant with him; and immediately after the death of Joshua and the elders, we read in the Book of Judges, from time to time "the Israelites did what was evil in the eyes of the Lord and worshipped the Baalim. They forsook the Lord, their father's God, who had brought them out of Egypt, and went after other gods, gods of the peoples among whom they lived; they bowed down before them, and provoked the Lord to anger; they forsook the Lord, and worshipped the Baal and the Ashtaroth" (Judges 2:11-13). What is the reason for this change? Moses was the leader for at least 40 years; and Joshua was also a leader for several decades. All this time the nation believed in one God. Then, suddenly, after the death of Joshua, they began to worship idols and believed in other gods. One judge after another arose and returned the nation to the correct path, and again they do evil in the eyes of God. How do you explain this?

Above all, the question arises: Is it possible that the people of Israel, possessed of a national character so manifestly different from all the nations around it, could have been established as a people in a foreign land while in a state of enslavement? Is it possible that it preserved its own distinct language—if we accept as a fact that all the Israelites in the days of Jacob and Joseph consisted of just one family of 70 people, and all of them went down to Egypt, and that the Jewish people existed only in Egypt, and preserved its language amidst strangers?

I know the passage in the Talmud which says that they were redeemed from Egypt because they did not change their language. But how did a thing like this happen, and how is it possible that a single family, living in a strange land among foreigners for 430 years—as is written in the Book of Exodus (and even according to Rashi: 210 years)—was able to maintain its language and to refrain from speaking the language of the people in whose midst it was found?

I do not doubt the basic fact that the people of Israel, from then until today, throughout the generations, was a nation different in its nature, spirit and destiny from all other nations on the face of the earth; and that this difference also existed in the early history of the people, through the years of the First Temple, the Second Temple and in the 2,000 years of exile. And even now, there is nothing in world history to compare to the establishment of a renewed Israel. The difference was not only in a belief in one God, as Professor Kaufman maintains, but also in our people's character and its messianic vision. But even a nation different in its characteristics from all other nations in the world is subject to the laws of physics and biology; and also to the laws of sociology—if there are sociological laws. (I personally am not so sure that there are sociological laws.)

We have witnessed in our day how a Jewish community of 5,000,000 arose in the United States, and, behold, not even 50 years have passed, and they have not preserved the language which they brought with them from overseas, and have almost all switched to the use of the English language. And such is the case among the Jews in Latin America who adopted the Spanish language as their tongue. How, then, is it possible that one single family succeeded in preserving its language in a foreign country for hundreds of years?

I will ask another question which will appear strange, perhaps insolent: What motivated the people in Egypt to go to the land of Canaan? There is no doubt that the authors of the Bible believed in the promise which God made to Abraham, Isaac and Jacob, and later to Moses and Joshua. But, if we want to understand the matter naturally, we must ask ourselves: What in particular motivated those who left Egypt to go to the land of Canaan?

When we read the chapters of Joshua very carefully, we find an astonishing fact in which I see part of the answer. This is only a hypothetical answer. I am not absolutely certain about it, because there is no certainty about history that is thousands of years old, and of which only fragmentary documents remain. As I have already said, at that time no one engaged in the writing of a full and complete history that exhausted all of the geographic, demographic, economic, social, military, political, international and social facts available. We have only fragmentary documents pertaining to that period which were recorded, not for the sake of history, but to express faith in God. We must, therefore, draw indirect conclusions from bits of knowledge, incomplete traditions and random geographic notes about which there is no certainty as to their completeness, and for which it is clear we do not have all the information available.

The most difficult matter in the chapters of Joshua is the great disparity between the few cities with whom Joshua fought and captured, left in flames or unscathed, and the large number of cities in which the tribes settled. Joshua fought against Jericho and Ai; they surrendered to him without fighting and made peace with him in the pastures of the cities of Gibeon, Hakefirah, Beerot and Kiryat Yearim. Afterwards, Joshua fought with the kings of Jerusalem (and not in Jerusalem), Hebron, Yarmot, Lachish and Dvir, not in their own cities, but in Gibeon, Azekah and Makedah. Later, he seized Makedah and fought in Livnah, and after that he seized Lachish and later defeated Horam, king of Gezer. (It doesn't say that he captured Gezer.) From there he went over and fought with Eglon, Hebron and Dvir. Afterwards, he defeated, *en masse* "the entire region—the hill-country, the Negev, the Shephelah, the watersheds, and all their kings. Joshua continued the slaughter from Kadesh Barnea to Gaza, over the whole land of Goshen and as far as Gibeon. All of these kings he captured at the same time, and their country with them . . ." (Joshua 10: 40-42). All this went on in the south of the country. Suddenly, we read about a jump from the southern end of the country to its northern end, the Upper Galilee, to wage war at the waters of Merom with Javin, king of Hazor, and his allies, Jovav, king of Madon, the king of Shimron, and the king of Akshaph. "At this point Joshua turned his forces against Hazor, and conquered Hazor and killed its king with the sword, because Hazor was formerly the head of all those kingdoms. . . . And he burned Hazor with fire" (Joshua 11:10-11).

In Dr. Elitzur's first lecture to this group, the question was asked: How did Joshua get from the south—from Dvir which is on the boundary of the Negev—to Hazor in Upper Galilee, without the inhabitants of the central part of the country interfering or fighting against him? The answer that was given then, that this area was covered with forest and was uninhabited, does not agree with the description and list of cities in the Book of Joshua.

In chapter 12, the author lists 31 kings, "whom Joshua and the Israelites put to death on the other side of the Jordan, to the west, from Baal Gad in the Valley of Lebanon as far as the bare mountain that leads up to Seir" (Joshua 12:7). To this list were added sixteen kings and cities that were not mentioned in Joshua's earlier wars in the Book of Joshua, with the exception of the king of Arad who fought Israel in the days of Moses, immediately after the death of Aaron (Numbers 21:1-3); and Arad is again mentioned in the Book of Numbers (33:40). But in the chapters on the settlement, in the Book of Joshua (from chapter 12 until chapter 19), we find hundreds of cities which were not mentioned at all in the war of conquest. The tribe of Judah alone had 112 cities, of which Joshua only fought for a few. Benjamin had 26 cities, Zebulon 12, Issachar 16, Asher 22, Naphtali 19, Dan 16, Manasseh west of the Jordan, six; Simeon took possession of the cities of Judea. In all, the tribes of Israel west of the Jordan had over 230 cities, as against 31 cities mentioned in chapter 12. What is most amazing is that Shechem, the most important city in Jewish history from Abraham until after Joshua, and, practically speaking until the days of Rehoboam, son of Solomon (about which Professor Dinur said in our last discussion that it is the most significant episode in the story of the conquest; I differ about this), is not mentioned in the saga of the conquest, even though it is central to Joshua's life and spiritual activity. If we ignore completely the attitudes, readings and tradition of the Samaritans, and read the Bible according to our text and tradition, with open eyes, we see immediately the important and central position which Shechem held in the history of Israel from Abraham until Joshua, son of Nun (in my view, even after him, but for my purpose up to Joshua is sufficient).

When Abraham came from Haran, he passed through the country "to the sanctuary at Shechem, to the terebinth of Moreh" (Genesis 12:6), and there God appeared to him and said to him: " 'I give this land to your descendants.' So Abraham built an altar there to the Lord who had appeared to him" (Genesis 12:7). Here, in Shechem, the first divine revelation to Abraham occurs, and here he erected the first altar to his God. When Jacob returned from Paddan Aram with his family, it is written: "Jacob came safely to the city of Shechem . . . and encamped before the city . . . and he erected an altar there and called it *El Elohei Yisrael*—God, the God of Israel" (Genesis 33:18-20). And then comes the very strange story of Dinah and Shechem, son of Hamor, the Hivite, and about the circumcision of all the people of Shechem, and about the terebinth (oak) tree in Shechem. This oak is very important (and was still spoken of at the end of Joshua's life), because under it Jacob buried the idols and the earrings of the members of his family (Genesis 35:2-4).

We must pay attention to Jacob's conversation with Joseph before his death as is told in Genesis 48:21-22: "Then Israel said to Joseph: 'I am dying. God will be with you and will bring you back to the land of your fathers . . . which I took with my sword and my bow.' " The word *one* (in verse 22) after the word *shechem* lends itself to different explanations and makes interpretation difficult. The Septuagint says explicitly: "I will give you *shechem*—a better portion than your brothers—which I took from the Amorites with my sword and my bow." Rashi also comments: "Shechem refers to the actual city; and it will be your extra portion over that of your brothers." Ibn Ezra also says: "He alluded to the city of Shechem which also belonged to the children of Joseph." But Onkelos translated: "And I gave you one extra portion over your brothers."

We later hear from Moses about the importance and holiness of this spot: "When the Lord your God brings you into the land which you are to occupy, there on Mount Gerizim you shall pronounce the blessing, and on Mount Ebal the curse" (Deuteronomy 11:29). And again Moses commanded the nation: "When you have crossed the Jordan, you shall set up these stones [i.e., the stones on which were written the entire Torah] on Mount Ebal. . . . And you shall build an altar there. . . . And you shall inscribe on the stones all the words of this Torah, engraving them with care" (Deuteronomy 27:4-8). And in the same chapter, Moses continues his command: "Those who shall stand for the blessing of the people on Mount Gerizim when you have crossed the Jordan are the following: Simeon, Levi, Judah, Issachar, Joseph and Benjamin. Those who shall stand on Mount Ebal for the curse are the following: Reuben, Gad, Asher, Zebulun, Dan and Naphtali" (Deuteronomy 27:11-13).

Abraham, Jacob, Moses, Joshua—for all of these people this place was holy, and perhaps *the* holy place. For Abraham, the first divine revelation after he came to the land occurred here. Jacob invoked the name of the Lord, God of Israel, here after he returned from Paddan Aram. And Moses issued a command here to inscribe the entire Torah on stone on Mount Ebal which is outside of Shechem. In chapter 24 of Joshua we find that the sanctuary of God was in Shechem in the days of Joshua. We then come to the events in Joshua. Joshua brought down the walls of Jericho and afterwards seized Ai through a clever war strategem: "Joshua held out his spear and did not draw back his hand until he had put to death all who lived in Ai" (Joshua 8:26). Immediately, thereafter, after his first military victory, he rushes to Shechem.

Jericho was captured through a miracle—the trumpets brought down the wall; but in Ai they actually fought a battle. He reaches Shechem without any warfare or any conquest, and builds an altar on Mount Ebal. "There, in the presence of the Israelites, he engraved the Torah of Moses on the blocks of stone" (Joshua 8:32). This was still before the conquest of the land, just after the war in Jericho and in Ai. "And all Israel, elders, officers and judges, took their stand. . . . Half of them stood facing Mount Gerizim and half facing Mount Ebal, to fulfill the commandment of Moses the servant of the Lord that the blessing should be pronounced first" (Joshua 8:33). In chapter 17, during the settlement of half of the tribe of Manasseh on the western side of the Jordan, we read that this tribe included the sons of Aviezer, the sons of Helek, the sons of Asriel, the sons of Shechem, the sons of Hepher and the sons of Shemida. We can conjecture that these sons of Shechem are residents of Shechem, as is written in the same chapter: "The boundary of Manasseh stretched from Asher at Michmethath, which is before Shechem" (17:7). In chapter 20 we read that Shechem was one of the towns of refuge on the western bank of the Jordan: "They dedicated Kedesh in the Galilee, in the hill-country of Naphtali, Shechem in the hill-country of Ephraim, and Kiryat Arba, which is Hebron, in the hill-country of Judah" (20:7).

But the spiritual and political importance of Shechem in the period of Joshua is made clear to us in the chapter of the Book of Joshua which describes the climax of the great conquest, of the covenant which Joshua, son of Nun, made between the Israelites and their God. This is chapter 24 which we heard much about from Shazar at the last meeting. This chapter begins: "And Joshua assembled all of the tribes of Israel in Shechem." Here he told them of the historical journey, and gave them a choice: to fear God and to worship him wholeheartedly, and to remove the gods "which your forefathers worshipped beyond the river and in Egypt. . . . But, if it does not please you to worship the Lord, choose today whom you will worship: the gods which your forefathers worshipped beyond the river, or the gods of the Amorites in whose land you are living" (24:14-15).

After this comes the reply of the nation: "We dare not forsake the Lord to worship other gods." This is followed by a fresh warning from Joshua, and an additional, spirited reply from the nation: "The Lord our God we will worship and his voice will we obey" (24:24). Joshua rose and made a covenant for the people "and he drew up a statute and an ordinance for them in Shechem. And Joshua wrote these things in the Lord's Torah. And he took a large stone, and he erected it there under the oak near the sanctuary of the Lord." This was like a second revelation at Mount Sinai, repeated in the days of Joshua. This was the same oak, near Shechem, under which Jacob buried the idols and earrings (Genesis 35:14). The Septuagint translates verse 25 of chapter 24, not as we have it, but: "And Joshua made a covenant with the people on that day, and he drew them up a statute and ordinance in Shilo before the sanctuary of the God of Israel." It is difficult to accept the version of the Septuagint, and one should not negate our Hebrew version. In Joshua 18:1 it is written: "The entire community of Israelites met at Shilo and established the Tent of the Presence there; and the land was subdued before them." Yet, in Shilo, Joshua merely tended to the division of the property among the seven tribes, by lot. It is interesting that in the only place in the Torah which mentions Shilo—in Jacob's blessing to his sons, when he said about Judah, "The sceptre shall not pass from Judah, nor the ruler's staff from between his feet, as long as men come to Shilo, and unto him shall the obedience of the peoples be" (Genesis 49:10)—the Septuagint does not read *shilo* but *shelo* (his). Onkelos' translation doesn't read *shilo* either, but "His messiah is the king," and the same is true of the commentaries of Rashi and Ibn Ezra. That is to say, they do not read *shilo* there; hence, *shilo* is not mentioned in the Torah. But there is no doubt that our version (in chapter 24 of Joshua) is correct. It is possible that the translators of the Septuagint changed Shechem to Shilo intentionally because of the dispute with the Samaritans.

Shechem, which was already important in the days of Abraham, in the days of Jacob, and in the days of Moses; the place where Joshua made the covenant between Israel and its God, where Joshua wrote the Torah of the Lord, where even the sanctuary of the Lord was erected; this city which became the first royal city in the days of the judges, because Abimelech, son of Gideon-Jerubaal reigned there for three years—this city apparently maintained its importance for some time after the conquest of Jerusalem by David, and also after the building of the Temple there by Solomon, since we find in First Kings that after the death of Solomon all of Israel came to Shechem to crown his son, Rehoboam (I Kings 12:1). This is, indeed, something to wonder about: this Shechem wasn't conquered by Joshua, and Joshua didn't fight over it. How can we explain this puzzle?

Only recently, after I wrote my remarks, I received Professor Kaufman's new book on the Book of Joshua, and I noticed that even he deals with "the absence of any description of a war in the central portion of the territory of Joseph, and especially the absence of any description of the conquest of Shechem," and he notes that "this is considered the most striking contrast between narrative and form," and admits that "the absence of any narrative about Shechem is truly amazing at first glance, because Shechem was the main city in this region. Here, during the period of Tel Amarna, ruled Lavaya and his sons, who, at this time, played an important role in the feuds of Canaan. Shechem is mentioned in the stories of the patriarchs. In Joshua 24, it is a place of assembly for the tribes of Israel, and there is an Israelite sanctuary there." (Slightly mistaken: not an *Israelite* sanctuary, but a sanctuary of God. Dr. H. Gvaryahu: He means as opposed to a Canaanite sanctuary.) "In the days of Abimelech, an attempt was made to establish there a monarchy for Israel. How is it conceivable that this city is not mentioned in the story of the conquest of the land? The deficiency is especially significant if we accept the prevailing view that an Israelite settlement already existed in Shechem at that time, and that the ceremony was attached to the sanctuary of Shechem. If this is true, then we have here a clear hint of another account of our settlement in the country which is not to be found in the Book of Joshua and possibly has no connection with Joshua" (Kaufman, pp. 62-63).

However, Professor Kaufman comes to the baseless conclusion, in my view, "that the city was already sacked or that it contained some weak settlement which did not have enough strength to fight. Shechem no longer was what it had been in the days of Lavaya or the days of Hamor" (p. 63). In my humble opinion, these remarks have no basis, and contradict everything written in the Torah and the Book of Joshua about Shechem and its two mountains, as I noted in my previous remarks. To this, we must add the words of Jotham, son of Gideon, who said to the people of Shechem when they coronated Abimelech: "My father who fought for you and offered himself in battle and delivered you from the Midianites" (Judges 9:17). It is clear from this that its inhabitants were Israelites. Why would a Jewish judge "offer himself in battle," in order to rescue a Canaanite tribe from the hands of Midian? According to Professor Kaufman, one should not conclude from Joshua 8:30-35 "that Shechem had already been conquered in an earlier war or that there was an Israelite settlement there at the same time" (p. 63). As I noted earlier, these statements, in my view, are contrary to the words of Jacob to Joseph before his death (Genesis 48:22) that promised him Shechem "which I took with my sword and my bow"—despite the fact that there is no instance in the Torah where Jacob fought Shechem; only Simeon and Levi did.

And another puzzle: Even though the people was divided into 12 tribes in the days of Moses and Joshua, it was united and worked and fought as one national unit, and heeded one leader: first Moses and afterwards Joshua. Only after the death of Joshua do we find the nation split and divided into tribes, with every tribe fighting separately, or in a group, as in the days of the prophetess Deborah. But, it is still a long while before Saul was crowned, and after him David—before a united people was established. This is contrary to all of the historical processes known to us in the history of other nations: First they exist as separate tribes; then they unite. Here we have the opposite.

And one more puzzle (not the last): How can we explain the fact that in the days of Moses and Joshua, for more than 100 years, all of the Israelites believed in God, worshipped him and heeded his voice; and only after Joshua and the elders did they, from time to time, do evil in the eyes of God? What is the explanation of this?

And, finally, I must deal with a very significant chapter—Genesis 12)—in which it appears as if the history of our people starts; for in it God said to Abraham, a native of Ur of the Chaldees, "Leave your country, your birthplace, your father's house, and go to a country that I will show you. And I will make you into a great nation. . . . And Abraham set out as the Lord had asked him, and Lot went with him. . . . And they started on their journey to Canaan. . . . Abraham passed through the country until the place of Shechem, until the terebinth of Moreh" (Genesis 12:1-6). Incidentally, it does not say there that God showed Abraham the land of Canaan; rather that Abraham went there by himself.

Here I want to raise a question (which might not be a question at all) regarding two extremes. On the one hand, there are those who believe that every word in the Torah must be accepted literally, as if it were written by the hand of God himself before the creation of the world; and on the other hand, there are those who deny the existence of God, and believe that these are no more than mythological legends. On this question, I am in complete agreement with the view of Maimonides in the *Guide for the Perplexed* that "the Torah spoke in the language of man." This had already been said in the Talmud, but for Maimonides it was a central idea. He expains that we cannot believe literally that God speaks, because one cannot attribute speech or any other human action to the godhead, for this is vulgar personification and, in general, it is forbidden to ascribe any positive attributes to God, because all of these attributes smack of anthropomorphism and polytheism. It is possible that the authors of the Bible did not understand the meaning of God as profoundly as did Maimonides, and that they felt that God truly spoke, walked, descended, became angry, etc.

However, when we attempt to understand historical events as they really occurred, we are not bound by the manner of speech of the authors of the Bible, because we certainly cannot attribute speech to the godhead and conceive of God in the image of man. One cannot take these things literally, as if God came to Abraham and said to him as one man talks to another: "Leave your country . . ." but there are, as Maimonides explains, people who are superior by virtue of their intellectual, spiritual and moral traits (*Guide for the Perplexed,* Part II, Chapters 40-41), and they hear God's voice in their heart or in a dream, and they act in accordance with this inner voice. This is how I understand what is written in chapter 12 of Genesis, and this is how I interpret it to myself: Abraham, who attained a faith in one God by himself, and in opposition to the members of his people, knew of the existence of a Hebrew nation which believed in this one God—a people located in the land of Canaan; and an inner voice told him to go and join up with this nation which believed as he did in an Almighty God, Creator of heaven and earth. He left his land, his birthplace, and his father's home where they believed in many gods. He was unable to live with them because of his belief, and he went to the land of Canaan. Finally, he came to Shechem, to the oak of Moreh (this oak is the same tree that was found in the days of Jacob and the days of Joshua). There, the first thing he did was to build an altar to the Lord who appeared to him, because this city, Shechem, was the political or spiritual center of the Hebrew people, which believed in one God.

I am saying that the Hebrew people preceded Abraham. I know the difficulty with this theory, since almost everywhere—in the Torah and also in the Book of Joshua—this land is called the land of Canaan, because the various Canaanite peoples fought over it (Professor P. Meltzer: As is written there, "And the Canaanites were then in the land"); whose language was indeed very close to the Hebrew language, but whose faith was decidedly different from the faith of the Hebrews (Dr. Y. Elizur: They were the descendants of Shem). But, in the Torah and in the Prophets, we find early allusions to the "land of the Hebrews," and in the Bible they use the term "Hebrews" when they want to indicate their special faith and the difference between them and other peoples. The word Hebrew designates not only a certain identity, but a separation from others. And there is one very strange verse: Joseph says about himself in Egypt, "By force I was stolen from the land of the Hebrews" (Genesis 40:15). Where was the land of the Hebrews located? Even in the first divine revelation to Moses from the midst of the bush at Horeb, it was said to him, among other things: "And you and the elders of Israel must go to the king of Egypt and say to him: 'The Lord, God of the Hebrews, has met with us . . .' " (Exodus 3:18). Where did Hebrews suddenly come from? And again it is said to him: "Say to him, 'The Lord, God of the Hebrews sent me to you . . .' " (Exodus 7:15). The name Hebrew (in its masculine, feminine and plural forms) is found in the Bible wherever the intention is to specify a Jew, and to distinguish between him and a non-Jew. In Jeremiah, we find an identity between the name Hebrew and the name Jew. When Jeremiah commands, in the name of God, "that every man free his male and female Hebrew servants [to distinguish from non-Hebrew servants] so as not to keep their fellow Jews in servitude" (Jeremiah 34:9), Jew and Hebrew are identical. Abraham, who abandoned the faith of the gods of his people and left his father's house, and arrived at a belief in one God, left his country and went to the Hebrew people who professed this religion, and became a "prince of God" in their midst.

Here, it appears to me, is the key to the entire history of the Jewish people. Because the question is asked: Why did Abraham go from a rich and fertile land, with an advanced culture, to a poor and backward land in every respect? Two countries were the birthplace of human civilization: Egypt and Mesopotamia. Abraham was born in Mesopotamia, which was a rich land. Canaan was a poor country. What motivated Abraham to leave this rich and cultured land and go to a poor and backward land? Why did he go to Shechem and build an altar to God? And why did God's voice speak within him there saying that the land would be given to his offspring? Abraham went there because a people existed there which believed, as he did, in one God. He could not have stayed in a land which worshipped idols.

The answers which I will attempt to give to these questions, and to the earlier perplexities, as well, are not, as I said at the outset of my remarks, any more than a theory. There are refutations in the Bible to my theory. You can find contradictions to it as in the story about the spies who came to the land of Canaan and saw strong and mighty nations who were unconquerable. And there is not even a mention of the existence of a Hebrew people, of the existence of Hebrews. Even so, it is difficult to understand the evolution of our history from the days of Abraham until the judges unless we proceed along the general lines of this hypothesis which possibly, here and there, does not hit the target. But, it appears to me that, in general, it—and only it—coincides with the facts as they are related in Genesis, Deuteronomy, the Book of Joshua and the Book of Judges.

My first assumption is that the Jewish people or the Hebrew people was born in Israel and grew up in Israel, even before the days of Abraham, as one of the nations of Canaan, and, at that time, was scattered in the south, the central sector, and the north, with its spiritual and perhaps political center in Shechem.

I accept as an indisputable fact the exodus from Egypt, the appearance of Moses, and the revelation at Mount Sinai. These are the central and decisive events in the history of our people whose ramifications are recognizable to this very day. But in my opinion, only a few families—the most privileged, and perhaps even the most important—went down to Egypt: The Hebrew lived in the country among the peoples of Canaan even before Abraham; and their language was Hebrew, as was the language of the rest of the peoples of Canaan, Moab and Ammon. But they differed, at the outset, from all of their neighbors in one detail: they believed in one God—Almighty God, Creator of heaven and earth.

The land of Canaan was then a land weak materially and weak spiritually, but the existence of the people of Israel in its midst, with its unique belief—a belief in one God—is what set this land apart. There were other peoples in it whose language was also Hebrew, but their faith was different; they had other gods, many in number. The nations with advanced culture at that time were Egypt and Babylonia. One of the privileged inhabitants of Babylonia, Abraham, son of Terah, arrived by himself at a belief in one superior being and denied the predominant faith in his country. Because of this he was attracted to the land of Canaan where a large or small nation lived which professed this faith. The wealth and intelligence of this stranger-sojourner—so they called him in Genesis—and his enthusiasm for the faith which the Hebrew people professed, made him a prince among this nation, and Abraham joined up with them because of this common belief.

We find an allusion to this in the story in Genesis 14 about Abraham's war with the four kings. I will not take upon myself the task of solving the complex problem of the chronology of Abraham's period, or of discussing whether Amraphel was Hammurabi, or if the war of the four kings against the five kings is an historical fact. But the story of Abraham's war has all of the signs of a true historical event, with reliable documentation.

You recall that when Abraham heard that the *son* of his brother was taken captive "he assembled his charges, men born in his household, three hundred and eighteen of them, and pursued them as far as Dan" (Genesis 14:14). Abraham's brave and noble conduct—and his beautiful answer to the king of Sodom—befits the great image of this stranger-sojourner who, on the strength of his belief, left his country, birthplace, and father's home, and came to the land of Canaan, and identified himself with the nation which believed, as he did, in one God.

Abraham's army of 318 men was at that time a mighty force. The requests of several of the kings of Canaan to Pharaoh, in the Tel Amarna letters, to send ten warriors, or even four, to save them have already been recalled in earlier lectures. An army of 318 men was then a mighty force. There is no doubt that these warriors were of the same faith as Abraham, and there is no indication or reference to their having left the country. These 318 warriors had parents, wives, children, brothers and sisters; probably a group of several thousand—not an insignificant number for that ancient period. These people did not leave the country, and there is no doubt that they multiplied. If my hypothesis is not correct, the question would be: What happened to all these people? The Bible does not say anything about this, but we have to ask: What happened to these 318 "charges," to their children, their grandchildren and their great-grandchildren?

Joseph—he is also without a doubt a historical personality. Cast off in Egypt, he drew close to Pharaoh and became his chief aide (as occurred in Turkish history to Don Joseph, a prince in the sixteenth century). This high and influential Hebrew official brought several relatives to Egypt, and we can assume that they were also among the noble and privileged of their people. But only a few families went down to Egypt. The Hebrew people remained in its land together with the other peoples of Canaan.

Joseph's importance and his friendship with Pharaoh was cause for bestowing upon his relatives, who went down to Egypt, high status, and when a new king arose in Egypt, "who did not know of Joseph," his family's influence diminished, and they became slaves who worked "in mortar, bricks, and in all labor of the field." The Children of Israel, it appears, lived in Egypt for only two, three or, at the most, four generations. Among those who went down to Egypt were the grandchildren and great-grandchildren of Jacob, as is told in chapter 46 of Genesis. For example: Kohath, son of Levi; Hetzron, son of Peretz, son of Judah; Pallu, son of Reuben; Manasseh, son of Joseph and his son Machir were born in Egypt. And among those who left Egypt we find: Moses, son of Amram, son of Kohath; Dathan and Abiram, sons of Eliab, son of Pallu, son of Reuben; Zolophehad, son of Hepher, son of

Gilead, son of Machir; Nachshon, son of Aminadab, son of Ram, son of Hetzron, grandson of Judah who went down to Egypt. Even if we assume that the 70 people who went down to Egypt, listed in chapter 46 of Genesis, were couples, and we extend ourselves and say that on the average six children were born to each couple, and every generation trebled in this fashion, it comes out that in the second generation there were 420 of this people in Egypt; in the third generation 1,260; in the fourth generation 3,780, and in the fifth generation only 11,340 people. (Prof. B. Dinur: In the Midrash it says "six in the belly of one.") Even if you assume that every one had 10 children, the number will not increase by much.

In the Torah it is told that those who left Egypt, 20 years old and over, fit for military service, were counted in the second year of the exodus from Egypt; and the number of those 20 years and above, excepting the Levites, reached "six hundred and one thousand, seven hundred and thirty" (Numbers 26:51)—the Levites were not included in this number. This vast number, which (with women and children) reached two or three million, does not jibe with those who went down to Egypt in chapter 46 of Genesis, or with the data about those who left Egypt in chapter 26 of Numbers. Indeed, it was said to Abraham that his descendants would be aliens "in a land that is not theirs; and they will be slaves, and will be held in oppression for four hundred years" (Genesis 15:13); and in the Book of Exodus it says: "At the end of four hundred and thirty years . . . all the tribes of the Lord came out of the land of Egypt" (12:41). But, Rashi already dealt with this difficulty in his commentary on Genesis 15, and he counts the 400 years beginning with the birth of Isaac, and says: "From the time Isaac was born until Israel left Egypt 400 years elapsed. How? Isaac was 60 when Jacob was born, and when Jacob went down to Egypt he said: 'The years of my sojourn were 130' which adds up to 190, and they spent 210 years in Egypt, which brings us to a total of 400 years. If you say that they were in Egypt for 400 years, then Kohath would have to be one of those who went down to Egypt. Now, figure the years of Kohath and of Amram, and the eighty years of Moses when Israel left Egypt, and you only come to 350; and you must deduct from them all the years which Kohath lived after the birth of Amram, and that Amram lived after the birth of Moses." Ibn Ezra also had difficulty in counting the years in his commentary on Exodus 12:41 and said: "There are many numerical figures in the Bible about which we are not sure."

To me, one thing is clear: It was the privileged individuals of the Hebrew people that went down to Egypt, and from the beginning they assumed an important role in their new place of residence, thanks to Joseph's connections with Pharaoh. Only when a Pharaoh came to the throne who did not know Joseph did their situation deteriorate.

Among this privileged group of immigrants, which lost its influence, was born a child of genius, Moses, son of Amram, who along with his tradition of belief in one God absorbed all of the rich Egyptian culture, and was unable to accept the bondage which had been imposed on the members of his family and his people. He led them out of Egypt to the Sinai desert, and there he experienced a divine revelation; and his faith in a God of the universe, one God without form, was purified and refined, and He gave his people the Ten Commandments [literally: *ten words*]. (I do not understand why people say *aseret hadibrot*—the ten words, using the feminine form, when the Bible says *aseret hadevarim*—using the masculine form.) It is natural and understandable that to the writers of the Bible this is the central and principal event in the life of the Hebrew people in the biblical period.

Moses had a disciple gifted with military ability, Joshua, son of Nun, and Moses delegated some of his authority to him (Numbers 27:20). In his old age, he assigned to him the task of completing the work which he had begun: the emancipation of his people and their return to their birthplace and their people, because Moses died before he reached the Jordan. Joshua also inherited the Torah of God from Moses and completed the covenant between Israel and its God.

What happened after that is known to us from the Book of Joshua, if we read the book carefully and with a knowledge of the background of the return of the Children of Israel to their land. What it means is that those who went down to Egypt finally returned to their country and their people.

It is difficult—or shall we say, impossible—to know today, more than 3,000 years after the event, what was the numerical relationship of those who left Egypt and returned to their people and their country, in comparison with the veteran settlers of the Hebrew people. If I say a ratio of 31 to 230—which would include the number of cities which were supposedly conquered by Joshua and also those in which he fought, but did not conquer—as against the number of cities in which the various tribes settled, this would be no more than an arbitrary guess. Nevertheless, it is possible to understand the conquests of the Book of Joshua solely on the basis of this background which I described (the return of the elite of the Hebrew people to the land), though I admit that this is no more than conjecture, to which serious questions can be posed, and for which, in turn, there are not sufficient answers.

It is a fact that the writers of the Bible deal mainly with the exodus from Egypt and the wanderings of the Israelites in the desert, as well as the appearance of Moses, which was undoubtedly a central event in the molding of the image of the nation—even of those who remained in their country. It is also clear, according to the stories of the Bible which we have before us (and it is clear that much historical material and many documents were lost and destroyed in the course of time), that a faith in one God was known to the Israelites even earlier, and that Moses elevated, purified and refined this belief. Even the essence of the lofty saying in Psalms: "Righteousness and justice are the foundation of His throne" (Psalms 97:92), was also not foreign to the members of Abraham's generation. It is said of Abraham that he said to God: "Far be it from Thee! Shall the Judge of all the earth do what is not just?" (Genesis 18:25).

However, Moses, through the Ten Commandments, deepened the faith in one God, ordered the Israelites to have "true scales, true weights, a true *ephah,* and a true *hin*" (Leviticus 19:36), and not only taught the main principle in the Torah, "Love thy neighbor as thyself," but went further than anyone else of his time, as well as of later periods, and gave them teachings that continue to remain exalted and brilliant in their eternal splendor: "When an alien settles with you in your land, you should not oppress him. He shall be treated as a native born among you; and you shall love him as yourself, because you were aliens in Egypt. I am the Lord your God" (Leviticus 19:33-34). It is obvious that the word "alien" is not used here in its later talmudic sense: a non-Jew who was converted, but rather a non-Israelite who lived in their midst, because in the Bible they called converts by the name "Judaizers." (And so was it also at the time that the Scroll of Esther was written.)

The authors or editors of the Bible didn't always feel the need to write down all historical events, but only what was required for their own special historiography: to show and emphasize the sovereignty of Almighty God, not only in nature, but also in history; and to recount, in particular, the exploits of the main heroes of early history, Moses and Joshua.

The stories in Exodus, Numbers, Deuteronomy and Joshua are principally the stories of the exploits of these two leaders; what they did to strengthen the covenant between the nation and its

God, and what they did in the territorial and national realms, because they excelled in both these aspects. It is not the history of the Hebrew people, but the great deeds of the two leaders which is central to the stories of the Bible. Evidence of this type can also be found in Greek literature. The literature of Homer does not deal with Greek history, but is centered around the anger of Achilles. But Moses and Joshua are more important in the eyes of the Bible than is Achilles in the eyes of Homer.

There is no doubt that many documents and books were stored away and also lost in the course of time, and if by chance only the Book of Kings, and not Chronicles, had remained extant, for example, we would know almost nothing about one of the greatest kings of Judah, Uziahu (or Azariah) son of Amaziah. In Second Kings (chapter 15) it only says of this king that he was 16 years old when he came to the throne, and he reigned for 52 years; that the name of his mother was Jechaliah of Jerusalem; that he suffered from leprosy until the day of his death, and that Jotham, his son, ruled the nation after him. But, an ancient document was preserved in Second Chronicles which tells of wars that he conducted with the Philistines and the Arabs, that he expanded the boundary to the south, that he built Eloth or Eilat and returned her to Judah. It tells of the blessed task of settlement which was carried out in the desert and in the lowland, in the plains and in the hills; and of the army which he perfected and equipped with new weapons. "His fame spread far and wide, for he was so wonderfully gifted that he became very powerful" (II Chronicles 26:15). And this great king—the only one of all the kings of Judah and Israel—was worthy of having his story recorded by the greatest of the prophets, as it is written: "The other events of Uziahu's reign, from beginning to end, are recorded by the prophet Isaiah, son of Amoz" (II Chronicles 26:22). This is not said of any other king, not even of David. And we know all of this only from the Book of Chronicles. In the Book of Kings there isn't even a hint of this. If it were possible to find the book which Isaiah, son of Amoz, wrote about Uziahu, it would outweigh, in my opinion, all of the hidden scrolls from the end of Second Temple days, even though I recognize and appreciate the great importance of the Dead Sea Scrolls. (Dr. Y. Yadin: It could be among the Dead Sea Scrolls.)

In view of what I have described, it is possible to understand Joshua's unmolested journey to Shechem immediately after the collapse of Ai; and likewise, the two last journeys of Joshua in his old age. It is very possible—I raise this as a conjecture, for I am not convinced of it—that the first message in chapter 23 was spoken to the new immigrants who came with him from the desert; and the second message in chapter 24—the lengthier and more important message—to the people who did not go down to Egypt, namely, to the veteran residents of the land. If you pay attention to the difference between them, you will see that this is very plausible, thought it isn't certain.

Perhaps there is a hint to this effect in the words, "Joshua assembled all of the tribes of Israel in Shechem"—words that were not spoken in chapter 23. To them he also told the history of the exodus from Egypt which was not so well known to the veteran residents of the country. What is more, the phrase "all of the tribes of Israel in Shechem" should not be interpreted to mean that he gathered all of the nation in Shechem. Rather, what is alluded to are the elders among the veteran residents, the elders of the old settlement. In chapter 23 he doesn't mention the exodus from Egypt because there was no need to tell about it to those who came from Egypt. Perhaps this will explain why only in the second message did he give the people of Israel the choice "to worship the gods of their fathers or the gods of the Amorites." It is possible that it was not necessary to offer a choice to the veteran settlers who, for the most part, had heeded the faith of their fathers all the while. But, there were many among them who were influenced by their Canaanite environment and tended towards the faith of the people in whose midst they lived. To them it was necessary to say: Choose between a belief in God and a belief in the idols of other people. But there would be no logic in saying these things to those who left Egypt, who had been with Moses, and had accepted his Torah with the words, "we will do and we will hear," and who had been loyal to His teachings. They were the people who were trained by Moses, who received from him the Torah and the Ten Commandments, and who knew of all his brave exploits.

There is one important verse in Exodus which one can use to question everything that I have said. In chapter 23, verses 28-30, it says: "I will send the hornet before thee, which shall drive out the Hivite, the Canaanite, and the Hittite from before thee. I will not drive them out all in one year, lest the land become desolate and the beasts of the field multiply against thee. I will drive them out little by little until your numbers increase and you can inherit the land." If my conjecture is correct, there is a difficulty here. The chapter on the spies also raises a difficulty.

But, as against this, if we accept the foundation I laid down, then it also explains why, after the death of Joshua—the second great leader, who had become acceptable to the entire nation by virtue of the numerical strength of the "new immigrants," the disciples of Moses who had come up from Egypt and the desert—many of the veteran Israelites (who all the while had lived among other peoples") reverted "to do evil in the eyes of God." That is, they tended to assimilate among their neighbors. Among some of them (not all), the inclination toward assimilation was a religious one. From time to time a great man of the spirit arose, sometimes in one tribe, sometimes in another; sometimes a leader like Deborah the prophetess arose, who inspired many tribes and who, in addition to the struggle to bring the people back to the God of their fathers, fought the neighbors with whom the Jews tried to draw close. And so it continued until the time of Samuel and the establishment of the monarchy. Then, the people became one nation, and included among them were also the Hebrews who had been subjects of the Philistines.

I have finished my remarks. I advance a theory here which, it seems to me, can explain the events in the Torah, and the Books of Joshua and Judges. I know that there is no certainty to my hypothesis; that it is not beyond question; and that it even contains several problems. Nevertheless, it appears to me that it is plausible, and through it several puzzling matters are explained.

* * *

I will deal with one question which, although not the main question, is one whose seriousness has not been sufficiently understood.* This is the question: How did the division of the tribes after the death of Joshua, son of Nun, come about? We cannot accept the facts as stated by Professor Dinur or by David Zakai in the name of Ahad Haam. (Are we also bound by the words of Ahad Haam?) If we read the Bible as it stands, we see that tribes suddenly appeared after the death of Joshua, son of Nun. There was a man by the name of Jacob; and he had sons, and these sons also had sons, and they had wives. All told, counting those who went down to Egypt previously, and including one daughter, there were 70 people—as it appears 70 couples. They were together. Afterwards, they lived together in Egypt for 400 years, according to Professor Meltzer. They left Egypt together, 600,000 men of military age and, as can be deduced from this number, another 2,000,000 women and children. They were all subject to the leader-

* Continuation of the discussion of the Bible Study Group, 11 Nissan, 5719, April 18, 1959.

ship of one leader. They received the Torah on Mt. Sinai. They all died together in the desert. The others were all born in the desert.

What is told in the Torah about the tribes resembles the same division by which they divided the brigades before the establishment of the modern Israeli army: the Golani Brigade, the Alexandroni Brigade, etc. There was no common feeling. According to the Torah, at the outset there were no tribes; tribes were not formed with special leaders and with a special character which were later molded into a nation. There was, as has been said, one family which multiplied to two or three million people. They all left Egypt together; they all received one Torah; they had one leader; they fought together. Part of this nation conquered areas on the eastern side of the Jordan. The leader stipulated a condition to them: Even though you occupy territory here, you must cross the Jordan and help the rest of the nation in its war. There was no tribal character whatsoever. There was no separation. There was no difference at all between tribes. We know who was the father, and who his sons were, and also the sons of his sons, and the sons of the sons of his sons. We know how they all lived in bondage and servitude. They all went free. They all saw the miracles.

How did the tribes live? There was no special tribal character. They all conquered the land together under one leader. And here the leader died, and tribes arose. Some fought and some did not fight, as the words of the Song of Deborah testify. And so 400 years passed from the time of Joshua until Eli the priest. (President Y. Ben-Zvi: Until King David, 480 years.) From Kushan Rishatayim until Eli more than 400 years passed, according to the Bible. (Professor P. Meltzer: The question is whether every judge judged alone, or whether there were periods in which there were two or three judges together.)

Until the death of Joshua there was one people, one language, one faith, one leader. They all saw the miracles, they all came to the land. How is it that they suddenly fell apart after having been one people for such a long period? They lived in Egypt for 430 years, they wandered in the desert for 40 years—all told 470. It's difficult to ascertain how long the conquest went on. (President Y. Ben-Zvi: Twenty years.) For some 50 years they were one unified people, without any tribal differences, except that this one was called this, and that one, that (just as today in our army we have Brigade 7, Brigade 8, Brigade 15. Is there a difference between them? Tomorrow they can take a regiment from Brigade 7 and insert it into Brigade 15, and there will be no difference between them). If this is the case, how did this fragmentation occur after more than 500 years of life as one people, united by faith, experiences, suffering, redemption; united by all the signs and miracles which they saw; united by two great leaders with whom they travelled all the while? How did it happen that after the Children of Israel was unified and integrated as no other nation in history had ever been (there are things in Jewish history unparalleled in the entire world; there has not yet been a people in history that was born in such unity and remained united for hundreds of years)—how did it happen that suddenly it split into tribes?

We know about the division of countries. The country of Alexander the Great was divided after his death. The Swedes and Norwegians were together. The Norwegians said: We want a separate state. But our question is: How can a nation that was born together, that lived together, that suffered together, that was redeemed together, that received the Torah together, that saw signs and miracles together, that conquered together—how after all this was it divided into tribes? That was the question and no answer was given to it.

PART TWO

The Antiquity of Israel in Its Land

—By Way of Reply—

At the beginning of my remarks at our twelfth session (April 4, 1959), I emphasized that I do not consider the hypothesis which I am preparing to place before you as proven or final. Furthermore, I see several difficulties in having it conform to a number of stories in the Bible, such as the chapter about the spies in Numbers 13, Deuteronomy 1:23-25, the chapter on the hornet in Exodus 23; 28-30, Deuteronomy 7:20, Joshua 24:12, the story of the settlement as described in the Book of Joshua, and others. These difficulties remain unresolved. But I have noted several serious questions and problems which the accepted version concerning the birth of the Jewish people in Egypt and its entry into the land confront us with; and for which there is no reasonable explanation other than my theory. I have also found evidence, here and there, which lends some degree of validity to my hypothesis—evidence which may possibly be refuted. But more than hoping to convince you of the validity of my hypothesis (I am also not sufficiently convinced of it), I intended and hoped to receive an answer to these questions and problems from you. I regret that this reply has not come forth. On the contrary, in speaking with several of the disputants, I found evidence to strengthen my hypothesis (Professor Rabin, Mr. Luria, and others), but not convincing proof.

The legend which Dr. Meltzer related in the name of Rabbi Shimon Bar Yochai—whether we accept it as midrashic legend or as historical fact—offers no contradiction to the antiquity of Israel and to the exodus from Egypt as I see it. Rabbi Shimon Bar Yochai commented on the verse: "He stands still and shakes the earth" (Habakkuk 3:6), and mentioned events occurring centuries apart: the giving of the Torah on Mt. Sinai, which was in the third month of the exodus of the Israelites from Egypt (Exodus 19:1), and the building of the Temple by Solomon, 480 years after

---

Sde Boker, April 24, 1959.

the exodus of the Israelites from Egypt (I Kings 6:1). According to Exodus 12:40, the Israelites lived in Egypt 430 years, which offers no proof at all that before the exodus from Egypt there were no Hebrews in the country.

Regarding the question at hand, we have to distinguish between the forest and the trees, between the fundamental outlook —or what Professor Dinur calls the historical tradition—and individual and isolated events linked to it. I will begin with the "forest."

A discussion such as the one conducted here regarding the distant past took place 60 to 80 years ago relating to the near future. The discussion was not only between the free-thinkers and the religious, but also among the religious themselves.

According to an ancient tradition all Jews believed that redemption would come, and our freedom would be heralded by a mighty blast of the shofar; and a banner would be raised to gather in our exiles from the four corners of the earth. Our judges would return as of old, and our counselors as in early times. We would return to Jerusalem and rebuild it speedily, in our own lifetime, as an eternal city. For this, Jews prayed for hundreds of years, three times a day. They certainly believed that it would happen through the will of God, and not through natural means. The false messiahs who arose up until the time of Shabbetai Zevi (and including him) claimed that they would bring the redemption in a supernatural way.

In the nineteenth century, the Love of Zion (*Hibat Zion*) movement arose, followed by the Zionist movement, which professed to bring redemption in a natural way, through immigration to Israel, urban and rural settlement, the establishment of an armed Hebrew force, a political effort to organize the nation, and negotiation with world rulers.

Many of those who adhered to the old tradition—and this was a tradition of hundreds—perhaps 1,800 years, if not more—looked upon the new movement as heresy, and fought against the rabbis and their followers who supported this new approach.

In my youth, there were two followers of [the Rebbe of] Gur in my village who became Zionists: Simcha Isaac and Michaelson, the ritual slaughterer. They were persecuted by their friends—followers of Gur—until they were forced to leave town. Simcha Isaac immigrated to Israel, and Michaelson moved to America.

Among the younger generation in my town there were many participants in the Second Immigration. I was one of the few second generation Zionists. The majority were sons of chassidic Jews who rebelled against their anti-Zionist fathers and emigrated to Israel. The parents of one of them, by the name of Wolman (now living in Kfar Malal), observed the seven days of mourning, rent their garments, as if their son had died, and did not, afterward, ever ask whether or not he was alive, what he was doing, and how he was faring.

I remember from my youth the rabbinic literature which grew out of this debate and argument. The religious, who believed in redemption through natural means, won out. The Jews settled on the land, multiplied, proclaimed a Jewish state, and in the first decade we have achieved an ingathering of exiles unparalleled in the history of our people. In these ten years, 20 times more people immigrated to Israel than in the days of Ezra and Nehemiah.

The followers of Gur who were initially opposed to emigration —and from whom Agudat Yisrael [an ultra-orthodox group] was formed in Poland—later made their peace with the idea of settlement and immigration. They, themselves, also immigrated and joined the founders of the State, and even participated in the government of Israel.

But today there is still a remnant known as the Neturei Karta, who stubbornly stick to the ancient tradition which does not acknowledge the Jewish State, and sees its very existence as heresy and as a desecration of God's name.

Now, let us envisage how Dr. Meltzer would have written the history of the settlement in our day and of the establishment of the State. Perhaps, he would have added the words, "with God's help," but generally speaking, he would have written it as Professor Dinur or Zalman Shazar would have written it.

And if he were assigned the task of writing the history of the Holocaust, he would have written it like anyone else.

But, I am certain that if the authors of the books of the Early and Later Prophets had written the history of the Holocaust, they would have begun with these words: "The Israelites did evil in the eyes of God and he delivered them to Hitler. . . ."

And if they were to write the history of the new settlement, they would write: "God said to Joshua (Stampfer): 'Arise, leave Hungary, your country, and go to the land of your fathers, and you will settle there and build houses and plant vineyards. . . .' "

And when I look back and consider the history of our revival in the last three generations, from the establishment of Mikve Yisrael and Petach Tikvah to the Sinai Campaign; the laying of the oil pipeline from Eilat to Haifa and the immigration of a million Jews from 102 countries; the revival of the Hebrew language and the transformation of most of the immigrants into field and factory workers; the war of the few against the many, the expansion of the borders as compared to the boundaries of the U.N. General Assembly of November 29, 1947; the flight of the Arabs from the confines of the State which already had begun in December, 1947; and the setting up of Jerusalem as the capital of Israel contrary to the U.N. decision—I see a great and awesome miracle, even though I know that everything was done "naturally." I have known for over 50 years exactly how these things were done, through what means and by whom, and no supernatural miracle took place. But, I know that an occurrence such as this has not been equaled in all of human history, to the degree that we are familiar with it, and this is an event, or a chain of events, unique in the annals of the nations of the world. They call a thing of this type "a wonder."

And not only that. I know that all of Jewish history from its beginning—whether it begins with Abraham's trek from Haran to Shechem, or even prior to Abraham, as is very possible in my view (though it is not as clear to me as I would wish it to be) —I say *all* of Jewish history from then until today is unique, and the Jewish people is different from all other nations of the world. I know that the other nations also differ one from another, but our difference is unlike the differences of the rest of the nations. Here the difference is permanent, qualitative, fundamental—a crucial difference. The difference is both spiritual and material. It was not in vain that many Jews and non-Jews denied the very existence of a Jewish people after the loss of its independence, and after its dispersal among the nations of the world. If 100 or 80 years ago someone had written a fanciful story, and had merely described what actually transpired later in Israel—about Joel Moses Solomon's leaving the old city and joining Joshua Stamfer and his friends; the establishment of Petach Tikvah on the marshes of the Yarkon and the immigration of Jewish students from Russia in 1882 to work at Mikve Yisrael; the establishment of Rishon Le-Zion and Gedera by the Russian pioneers; also the establishment of Zichron Yaacov and Rosh Pina by pioneers from Rumania; the appearance of a person as mad as Ben-Yehuda who decided that Hebrew would be a spoken language; the immigration of the members of the Second Immigration who raised the banner of Jewish labor and self-protection; the establishment of a Jewish armed force in the days of Turkish rule; the issuance of the Balfour Declaration during the First World War and all that came afterward—if someone had written such a book, it would have been called an absurd imaginary utopia. It would have been said that Jews would not immigrate to a Turkish land which forbade the entry of Jews; that they would not live among Arabs who hate them, and that they would not be transformed from academicians—yeshiva boys and university students—to tillers of the soil; that Jews would not be able to build villages and cities and would not be able to stand up against the Arabs, forty times their number. But it did happen, and additional episodes are still in the making. And it happened, not in accordance with established tradition, but contrary to tradition, and in opposition to the orthodox elements within the tradition. It happened through free-thinkers and atheists, and through the orthodox who dared to veer from the tradition and see the future in a new light, in a rational light, without departing from a belief in Almighty God, Creator of heaven and earth.

From this I come to a question which perhaps is not historical. Call it philosophical, metaphysical or theological; the word isn't important.

Are there miracles in nature or history—as the accepted tradition understands the term? Or, are nature and history of themselves the greatest and most profound miracle that can be imagined?

"The heavens declare the glory of God and the firmament shows his handiwork" (Psalms 19:2). Man who stands in full amazement and reverence before the secret of life, searches his mind to understand insofar as his intellectual capacity permits, in order to unravel the secrets of the universe: the secret of the microcosm and macrocosm; man who makes an effort, a yeoman effort in this search, and penetrates the mysteries of the structure of the almost invisible atom, and through the use of a 200-inch telescope sees stars which are two billion light-years away from us, something which the human imagination cannot grasp; man who is able to divide the second, one thirty-six hundredth of an hour, into a billion parts faster than the blinking of an eye—yet he continues to stand in awe. As Einstein said, the more we try to understand nature, the more the mystery grows, because our knowledge is no more than a drop in the ocean of our ignorance. But from everything we have accomplished and learned and understand, we know that there is law, regimen and order in nature, which the Greeks called by the name *cosmos* (that is *order*), and though we are prevented from understanding everything, what we do understand is that things are arranged according to a certain order. And as with nature, so with history. There is no need for miracles which are supernatural, because nature itself is the ultimate miracle above which there is nothing greater. The same is true of history.

Our history is completely different from the history of other nations, but even it has developed naturally—namely through the great and ultimate miracle, but not in a supernatural manner—through the sorcery and superstition of primitive man.

We find traces of this discussion on historical tradition, and upon which Professor Dinur relied, in the writings of our sages. Among them there were also two contradictory views.

We read in Sanhedrin (99a) that he who says that the Torah does not come from heaven, or even if he says that the entire Torah does come from heaven, with the exception of this one verse, "Because he has despised the word of the Lord" (Numbers 15:31), and claims God did not say it, but Moses alone said it—he who speaks in this manner has no share in the world to come. Nevertheless, we find a debate between Rabbi Judah and Rabbi Shimon on this matter. It is written in Baba Batra 15a: "Joshua wrote the last eight verses of the Torah, beginning with: 'And Moses, the servant of God, died there.' Could Moses have written, 'And Moses . . . died there, after the event?' Therefore, we must say that Moses wrote until this point, and Joshua wrote from this point on. This is the opinion of Rabbi Judah. (Some say it is the opinion of Rabbi Nehemiah.) Rabbi Shimon said to him: 'Is it conceivable that a completed Torah scroll should be missing even one letter?' Yet, it is written: 'Take this scroll [as if it were complete] of the Torah.' We must, therefore, say that until this point God dictated and Moses repeated it, and wrote it down, but from this point on, God dictated (a future event) and Moses wrote it down with tears in his eyes.' " And Rabbi Joshua Bar Abba in the name of Rav Gidel, who reported it in the name of Rav, agreed with Rabbi Judah and not with Rabbi Shimon (that Joshua completed the last chapter).

This type of debate also took place with regard to the Book of Job. Rabbi Samuel, son of Nachmani, said: "Job never existed. The book is only a parable" (Baba Batra 15a). But Rabbi Levi, son of Lachma, believed that Job lived at the time of Moses; Rabbi Jochanan and Rabbi Elazar contended that Job was one of the returnees from the exile whose academy was in Tiberias; Rabbi Joshua, son of Karcha said: "Job lived at the time of Ahasueros" (15a).

Rav said something even more daring, in contravention of the established tradition. He made reference to the famous legend (Menachot 29b): "When Moses went up to heaven, he found God sitting and adding ornamental crowns (to the letters of the Torah)."

Moses said to Him: "Lord of the universe, who is interfering with Your work?" He answered: "There is one man who is destined to be alive several generations in the future. His name is Akiba, son of Joseph. He will interpret each and every letter, and will heap piles of law on them."

Moses said to Him: "Lord of the universe, show him to me."

He said to him: "Go back."

Moses went and sat eight rows back (in Rabbi Akiba's academy) and didn't know what they were saying. He became faint. When Rabbi Akiba came to the interpretation of one point, his pupils said to him: "Rabbi, how do you know that?" He answered them: "It is a law which Moses received at Sinai." Then Moses felt better.

The intention of Rav (or Rabbi Judah) is clear: Rabbi Akiba discovered interpretations for things which Moses would not have understood at all, and attributed those things for which he could not find textual support, or some other explanation, to "a law given to Moses at Sinai."

We find a textual change in Midrash Rabba (Exodus 63) for a verse explicit in the Torah which has a bearing on the matter before us. In Exodus 12:40 it says: "The Israelites had been settled in Egypt for 430 years." Rabbi Nathan, in Midrash Rabba, makes a correction and says: "The Israelites had been settled in Egypt and Goshen and *in Canaan* for 430 years."

The historical tradition on which Professor Dinur relies is not a tradition over which our sages did not differ. And since, in our times, the accepted tradition relating to the central question pertaining to the survival of Judaism—the accepted tradition concerning the redemption—has changed, and events have transpired contrary to what traditionally-minded people would have believed, we may allow ourselves (even the most orthodox among us—in my view), it is incumbent upon us—to take a new look at ancient history. And this, because the events of our day are shedding new light on ancient events, though I know that there are no valid comparisons in history, since every historical event is unique in itself. Nevertheless, it seems to me that the basic concepts of ancient history were not understood by most of our people after they were uprooted from their land and lost their independence. Because of this, tradition has become distorted.

Conquest, settlement, tribe, nation—I doubt if a scattered and dispersed people without a land and without independence is capable of knowing the true significance and full meaning of these words. They did not participate in conquests and did not know what is involved in conquest. And the same holds true for settlement. Only with the rebirth of Israel in our generation did these vague concepts take on flesh and we have become aware of their content and essence. Now that we are aware, we must delve anew into the stories of the Bible and try to understand what happened then in the natural course of events—this alone is historical knowledge and understanding—because even then, in ancient times, things were not done supernaturally, but naturally. Yet, what was then done naturally is the greatest miracle.

Let's start with Abraham.

Professor Dinur sees a vast difference between the things which Malkitzedek said to Abraham about "Almighty God, Creator of heaven and earth," and the things which Abraham said to the king of Sodom: "The Lord, Almighty God, Creator of heaven and earth." Professor Dinur sees in this addition of the word, "Lord" the new faith in which Abraham excelled. There are two rebuttals to this argument. Professor Dinur has already noted one of them himself.

In the days of Enosh (son of Seth) it was already said: "At that time men began to invoke the Lord by name" (Genesis 4:26); and that was 17 generations before Abraham. What is more, it is written of Cain: ". . . [he] brought a gift to the Lord from the produce of the soil" (4:4). And before Cain, Eve said upon giving birth to Cain: "With the help of the Lord, I have brought a man into being" (4:1).

Lamech, son of Methuselah, named his son Noah, "saying, 'This lad will bring us relief from our work, and from the hard labor that has come upon us because of the Lord's curse upon the ground' " (Genesis 5:29).

It is explicitly written of Abraham that he did not know the name of the Lord, but called him "Almighty God" (*El Shadai*). In Exodus (6:3), God says to Moses: "I appeared to Abraham, Isaac and Jacob as God Almighty, but I did not let myself be known to them by the name of 'God.' " Without a doubt, this verse has greater force than the addition of God's name when Abraham turned to the king of Sodom. However, there is no difference at all between the faith of Malkitzedek and the faith of Abraham. And Malkitzedek was not alone in his belief because he was a priest of Almighty God, as is written about him during his meeting with Abraham (Genesis 14:18). It appears that he stood at the head of a full community which believed, as he did, in Almighty God—the same faith through which Abraham was bound to them. And Malkitzedek and his people were natives of the land of Canaan.

Professor Dinur dealt with my question: Why did Abraham leave Ur of the Chaldees which was rich, developed and cultured, to go to Canaan, which was poor and of low calibre in all senses? He argued that not Abraham, but Terah went to Canaan, as is written: "Terah took his son Abram, his grandson Lot, son of Haran, and his daughter-in-law Sarai, wife of his son Abram, and they set out from Ur of the Chaldees for the land of Canaan. And they reached Harran and settled there" (Genesis 11:31).

From this we can deduce that Terah had intended to go to Canaan, but he changed his mind when he reached Harran; and he remained there. However, it is incorrect to say that Terah went to Canaan. We know from excavations made before the Second World War that Harran was also a rich and developed country. Therefore, Terah remained there, but not Abraham. Professor Cassuto has a useful explanation for this dual-faceted fact: the trip of Terah and his family was with the intention of going to Canaan, and to his remaining in Harran. His explanation goes hand in hand with my hypothesis.

Here is what Cassuto says in his interpretation of the above verse: Apparently the verse means that from the very beginning, when they were still living in Ur of the Chaldees, it occurred to Abraham, Sarai and Lot to go to the land of Canaan. They influenced Terah and the rest of the family that all should leave and proceed to settle wherever they wished. They traveled through the Fertile Crescent, and when they arrived at Harran, in the middle of their journey, they remained there and did not continue the journey. Only Abraham's group continued, after a while, to the previously intended destination. Under the influence of Abraham and his group, even Terah and the rest of the family felt an inner urge—though not sufficiently strong or clear—to head in the same spiritual direction to which Abraham had turned with all his heart and all his soul. But they did not succeed fully in overcoming the powerful attraction of idolatry, and they were unable to shed its influence. They did make some progress, but they remained midway. Concerning Abraham and his entourage it says (12:5): "They left on their journey to Canaan," in much the same way as it is written here (11:31). But, there, the narrative goes on to say: "And they came to the land of Canaan"—i.e. they accomplished what they had intended to—while here (regarding Terah) it says: "And they reached Harran and settled there" (*From Noah to Abraham,* pp. 158-159).

Notice that Professor Cassuto also felt that the journey from Ur of the Chaldees to Canaan was the result of an inner urge, not completely material—not like mere wanderers who move from place to place, but was "spiritually directed," something which Abraham planned with all his heart and all his soul, only that Terah, his father, was still not completely free from his attachment to idol-worship as was Abraham, and did not leave "the realm of idolatry." Apparently Cassuto also realized that Canaan had a spiritual attraction for Abraham and his group because here was an area not dominated by idolatry. He does not say so explicitly, but it can be surmised from what he says, and in my opinion he was correct. Abraham was attracted to Canaan because it contained a people or tribes who believed in one God, as he did, in the "Lord Almighty, Creator of heaven and earth."

Professor Mazar is of the opinion that Abraham's journey from Ur of the Chaldees and Harran to Canaan was very much like the normal migration of wanderers in that period. Such an opinion is not acceptable because Abraham's family was rich and privileged, while the land of Canaan was poor and small compared to Ur of the Chaldees and Harran. It is obvious that Abraham came to Canaan at the outset to settle there. It is only reasonable to assume that spiritual, and not economic, considerations impelled Abraham to uproot himself from his home. Abraham maintained relations with the members of his family in Harran, and sent his servant to take a wife from there for his son. At the same time he warned him: ". . . you must not take my son back there" (Genesis 24:8).

Dr. Meltzer quoted me accurately when he referred to my belief in the exodus from Egypt, the appearance of Moses, and the giving of the Torah—the central events in our early history, as well as my remarks on the truth of the testimony of the Bible regarding the historical events which came before it was written. Indeed, I believe in all of these things.

But the fact cannot be ignored that we find several internal contradictions in the books of the Bible which even earlier commentators, such as Rashi, Nachmanides, Rabbi David Kimchi and Ibn Ezra had difficulty with. I must deal here with the promise which was given to Abraham that the land would belong to his descendants, as Dr. Meltzer stressed in his remarks.

The first promise is not in the Covenant of Abraham (Genesis 15), which Dr. Meltzer sees as the center of gravity of the stories about Abraham (it appears to me that the covenant in chapter 17 is more decisive, because through it the Covenant of Circumcision was established). We read of the promise, "I will give this land to your descendants" (12:7) immediately after Abraham comes to Shechem; and again in chapter 13, verse 17, after Abraham's parting from Lot: "Now go through the length and breadth of the land, for I will give it to you." Again, later in chapter 15, verse 7 (in the Covenant of Abraham): "I am the Lord who brought you out of Ur of the Chaldees to give you this land that you might inherit it." And again in the same chapter: "To your descendants I give this land from the river of Egypt to the Great River, the Euphrates . . ." (15:18). All this before the birth of Ishmael and Isaac!

There is no doubt that Ishmael was of the seed of Abraham, and that he was not excepted from the promise. Even after the birth of Ishmael, when he was 13, Abraham again received a promise: "I will give you and your descendants after you, the land in which you now live, all the land of Canaan, for an everlasting possession" (17:8). Again, Ishmael was not excepted from the promise. Later, it says: "I will fulfill my covenant with Isaac, whom Sarah will bear to you at this season next year" (17:21). Only after Isaac was born, grew up and was weaned, and Sarah asked to have the maidservant and her son banished, was it said to Abraham: "Do everything which Sarah asks of you, because your seed will be established through Isaac" (21:12); again, Ishmael was not excepted from the promise. Evidently, we cannot always accept things literally.

In any case, there is no reason to assume from the Book of Genesis that, with the exception of Abraham, there were no believers in one God before and during his lifetime. The opposite is true. Malkitzedek was a priest of Almighty God (14:19), and immediately afterwards it is explained that Almighty God is "the Creator of heaven and earth"—a clear monotheistic view—and if he was a priest to Almighty God, then it is an indication that there were many who believed in God, because it is not possible that he was a priest for himself alone.

I do not understand why Dr. Meltzer denied and belittled the importance of Abraham's 318 charges while relying on the verse which came afterwards: "For me, nothing but what my servants have used up; as for the share of the men who went with me—Aner, Eshkol and Mamre—let them take their share" (14:24). Abraham agreed that the three parties to his covenant would receive their share and the lads would only receive, as their share, the food that they ate. But, the fact is that 318 charges were circumcised, and professed Abraham's faith in one God, and they did not go to Egypt. In any case, there is no mention of it in the

Book of Genesis. Where did they disappear? And what happened to their children and grandchildren? We know that from the days of Abraham to the Egyptian exodus, at least seven generations had passed, and in that time their number could easily have reached 40,000. That is a sizeable group for those days.

Dr. Meltzer belittles the significance which I feel should be attached to the words of Joseph: "I was kidnapped from the land of the Hebrews" (Genesis 40:15), since the Midrash says that Abraham was called a Hebrew because "the entire world was on one side and he was on the other side." But this interpretation does not fit all of the Hebrews mentioned in the Bible; and this adjective [Hebrew] is mentioned 26 times in the Bible.

Shazar already dealt with the Hebrews in the story of Saul. Indeed, the Septuagint translates it as *slaves* [Heb. *avadim*] and not *Hebrews* [Heb. *ivrim*]. But, then, there is no logic whatsoever to the verse: "Jonathan killed the Philistine governor in Geva, and the Philistines heard of this. Then Saul sounded the trumpet all through the land saying: 'Let the *slaves* hear' " (I Samuel 13:3). What is the meaning of the words: "Let the slaves hear?" It is clear that he was talking to the Hebrews. There is a special significance to verse 21, in chapter 14 of First Samuel: "The Hebrews who up till now had been under the Philistines, and had been with them in camp, changed sides and joined the Israelites under Saul and Jonathan." This is the first time that there is a clear distinction in the Bible between Hebrews and Israelites. Although the verse is distorted, its meaning is clear. That is how all of the commentators interpreted it: that the Hebrews who came with the Philistines to fight against the Israelites as in the past, were on the side of the Israelites after the confusion and fear that Jonathan planted through his clever ruse in the camp of the Philistines, with the result that each Philistine plunged his sword into his fellow Philistine.

This appears—I do not say this with absolute certainty—to be one of the few instances in which the ancient Hebrews were inferior in spirit, faith and bravery to those who left Egypt and their offspring, and who returned to the country with Joshua, son of Nun.

The question is asked: If Abraham found believers in one God in the land—and in my view, it is *because* of them that he came to the land—why did he send his servant to his birthplace to take a wife for his son?

We saw the answer right here a short while ago. The queen of Belgium was here. She is a native of Germany. Why didn't her husband, Albert, take a Belgian girl for a wife? The privileged were always accustomed to taking wives from privileged families, and there is no doubt that Abraham came from a privileged famliy in Ur of the Chaldees and Harran. In any case, it is *not* because the members of his family believed in one God, for they remained idolatrous, as Cassuto correctly states.

It seems to me that there is need here to explain that the word "Canaanite" has a double meaning in the Torah and in the Book of Joshua. It is both the name of one of the peoples of Canaan, like the Perizzites, Girgashites, Hivites, Jebusites, etc, and is also the general name for all of the peoples of Canaan, including Hebrews—if there were actually Hebrews in the country before the arrival of Joshua, son of Nun. Abraham did not necessarily search out a wife for his son from the believers in one God, because in the land of his birth such people did not exist. Rather, he sought a woman from his family, someone special, as was his son.

But, the main problem is the exodus from Egypt and the conquest of the land. If in order to rely on the words of the Bible we must rely on every verse, what do we do if some verses contradict others?

In Joshua chapter 1, verse 5, Joshua is promised that "no man will be able to stand up against you all the days of your life," and in chapter 11, verse 23, it says: "Joshua took the entire country, fulfilling all which the Lord had said to Moses; and Joshua gave it to Israel as an inheritance, dividing it according to tribes. And war ceased in the land." And immediately following, in chapter 13, verse 1 it says: "Now Joshua had become very old, and the Lord said to him: 'You are a very old man, and much of the country remains to be occupied.' " Here is a contradiction which cannot be resolved. Yet, both verses rely on God's word to Joshua. Five chapters in the Book of Joshua (6, 8, 10, 11 and 12) tell of wars in the south and the north, from Dvir until Hazor, and in chapter 24, verse 12, Joshua says to the people: "I set the hornet before you [B.G.: This is the hornet also threatened with in Exodus 23:28-30, and Deuteronomy 20:20-21] and it was this, not your sword or your bow that drove out the two kings of the Amorites." But, in the stories of the wars there is no mention of a hornet, and the Israelites did fight with their sword and bow. It is even written of Sihon, king of the Amorites, that "Israel defeated him by the edge of their swords" (Numbers 21:24). And the same thing is said of Og, king of Bashan (21:35).

In Joshua 21:24 it says: "Of all their enemies, not a man could withstand them; the Lord delivered all their enemies into their hands." But we know from the Book of Judges that Judah did not drive out "the inhabitants of the valley because they had chariots of iron" (Judges 1:19), and the tribe of Benjamin did not drive out the Jebusites who inhabited Jerusalem. Manasseh did not drive out the inhabitants of Beit Shean, Taanach, Dor, Yivleam and Megiddo. "The Canaanites were resolved to live in that land" (1:27), and Ephraim "did not drive out the Canaanites who lived in Gezer" (1:29). Zebulun did not drive out the residents of Kitron and Nahalol, and Asher did not drive out the residents of Acco, Sidon, Ahlav, Achziv, Helbah, Afik and Rehov. Naphtali did not drive out the residents of Beit Shemesh and Beit Anat. The Amorites forced the tribe of Dan toward the hills and did not allow them to go down to the valley, and "the Amorites were resolved to live on Mt. Heres in Ayalon and in Shaalvim" (1.35).

There are also contradictory verses on the duration of the Israelites' stay in Egypt. In the Covenant of Abraham, Abraham was told: ". . . your descendants will be strangers in a land that is not theirs, and they will be enslaved and oppressed there for 400 years" (Genesis 15:13), but in the Book of Exodus it says: "the length of time that the Israelites lived in Egypt was 430 years" (Exodus 12:40). And all of the commentators—Rashi, Ibn Ezra, Nachmanides—have difficulty with this calculation.

Abram was also told in the Covenant of Abraham: ". . . and the fourth generation shall return here because the Amorites will not be ripe for punishment till then" (Genesis 15:16), yet it was seven generations from Abraham to Moses: Abraham, Isaac, Jacob, Levi, Kohath, Amram and Moses.

And now a few more remarks about "the trees": The arguments that were heard regarding my doubts and questions, and the refutation of several details—even the details in themselves were very important, because without trees there is no forest.

His Honor the President, as well as several other members, replied to my question on how the Israelites were divided into tribes after having been initially united and unified, brought evidence from the division of the Arab empire which conquered the Arabian tribes, the division of the empire of Alexander the Great, etc. But there is an essential difference between the breaking up of an empire such as Austria-Hungary and the Ottoman empire of our day and of earlier ones, and the splitting of a nation into tribes *after* it had been unified and united. As I explained at the end of the last meeting, according to the stories of the Torah, the people of Israel was unified from the beginning—from the days of Jacob until Joshua—as was no other people in history. The children of Jacob lived in their father's house, and together tended his sheep in the area of Shechem. Together they went down to Egypt; together they performed backbreaking tasks in Egypt for 430 years; and together they left Egypt under one leader. Together they witnessed the parting of the Red Sea. Together they stood on Mt. Sinai to receive the Torah. Together they made the calf and ate manna and quail. Together they saw the earth swallow up Korach and his followers. They all died in the desert.

Again, under one leader, Joshua, son of Nun, they conquered the land and settled in it. Jacob was 130 years old when he went down to Egypt, and he lived in Egypt for 17 years. The entire people of Israel lived in Egypt for 430 years. By the time they reached Jericho another 40 years had passed; and the conquest also took several years. Until then, they did not live as tribes, each living on its own separate land, speaking a special dialect, with special habits and traditions. Rather, together they constituted a people unique in its unity.

Thus, it is difficult to understand the division into tribes and the distance between tribes, as well as the contention among tribes (viz. the narrative about the concubine at Givah), or the alienation between tribes (reflected in the Song of Deborah), for a period of close to 400 years which lasted from the conquest of Joshua until the kingdom of Saul. (It is written of Solomon that he built the Temple 480 years after the Israelites left Egypt, in the fourth year of his reign. If we deduct the 40 years of wandering in the desert, the two years of the reign of Saul, the 40-year reign of David, and the three years of Solomon's reign until he built the Temple, we get 395 years from the time of the entrance of Joshua, son of Nun into the land until the reign of Saul.) It is difficult to explain this phenomenon and it is surprising that after the receiving of the Torah from Moses, and the making of the covenant in the days of Joshua, and after all of the wonders and miracles that the people experienced when they left Egypt, while in the desert and during the conquest of the land, as well as the establishment of a historical tradition—which Professor Dinur relied on so much, and which without a doubt was stronger, fresher, and deeper at the time of the judges than in later generations—it is surprising that the Israelites should have forgotten the covenant, the miracles, and the Torah of God immediately after the death of Joshua and his generation, and that "the Israelites did what was wrong in the eyes of the Lord, and worshipped the Baalim. And they forsook the Lord, the God of their fathers, who brought them out of the land of Egypt, and went after other gods from among the gods of the peoples who surrounded them; and they knelt down to them, and they provoked the anger of God. And they forsook the Lord and worshipped the Baal and the Ashtaroth" (Judges 2:11-13).

From whence, then, did the judges come whom God supported? Surely there were two different strata of society: 1. The veteran community, from the days of the patriarch, Abraham, and earlier who always lived in the country—part of which maintained its faith in one God, known to it from an early period (from the days of Enosh); part of which was influenced by its neighbors; and part of which was assimilated among its neighbors such as the Hivites (I'll say a few words about the Hivites); 2. Those who left Egypt, and their descendants who were the elite of the people —people who had absorbed the tradition of Moses and Joshua, in whom the memory of the exodus from Egypt and the Torah in the desert lived in their hearts, and for whom attachment to the faith of the patriarchs and the Torah of Moses was strong and deep-rooted, and from whom arose, from time to time, judges who fought against the Baal and Ashtarot, as well as against the nations that overpowered and influenced various tribes, from time to time. The struggle of the people of Israel in that period—and not in that period alone—was both a spiritual and a political struggle, and the uniqueness of our people lies in its being both an ethno-political entity and a moral-spiritual entity. The faith in the teachings of the prophets is an organic part of its being, though many do not acknowledge these teachings, and are not familiar with them, because it is the faithful few who guard and preserve the uniqueness of the nation. And this vision continues to this day.

A few words about the Hivites who were associated with one of the central problems of those generations: the problem of Shechem. Shechem, son of Hamor, was a Hivite. The closeness of the Hivites to the sons of Isaac stems from the fact that Esau took a Hivite wife in addition to his Hittite wife. (There is a contradiction with regard to Esau's wives between Genesis 26:34 where it says: ". . . and he married Judith, daughter of Beeri the Hittite, and Basmat, daughter of Elon the Hittite," and Genesis 36:2 where it says: "Esau took his wives from the women of Canaan: Adah, daughter of Elon the Hittite and Ahalivamah, daughter of Anah, daughter of Tzivon the Hivite.") The Hivites were dispersed throughout the land. They lived both in the south (in the cities of Gibeon, Kefirah, Beerot and Kiryat Jearim), in the central sector (in Shechem), and in the north: "The Hivites [lived] below

Hermon in the land of Mitzpah" (Joshua 11:3), and they went to war with Jabin, king of Hazor, against Joshua at the waters of Merom. The Hivites are also described in Judges as "living on Mt. Lebanon, from Mt. Baal Hermon until the outskirts of Hamath" (Judges 3:3). From the story of Shechem in the days of Jacob, and of the Hivites of Gibeon, it is clear that the Hivites in the central sector of the country and in the south were close to a belief in one God. If there is not conclusive proof for this, there is a clear hint; more precisely, two hints.

In the days of Jacob all the men of Shechem were circumcised, and this place was holy to Abraham and Jacob. In the days of Joshua it housed a sanctuary to God. The Hivites from Gibeon, Kefirah, Beerot and Kiryat Jearim came to Joshua and said to him, among other things: ". . . your servants have come because of the renown of the Lord your God. We have heard of His fame, of all He did to Egypt, and to the two Amorite kings . . ." (Joshua 9:9-10). They also knew, according to the Book of Joshua, "that the Lord your God had commanded Moses his servant to give you the whole country and to exterminate all of its inhabitants; so because of you, we were in terror of our lives, and that is why we did this" (9:24). The children of Kiryat Jearim, Kefirah and Beerot (743 souls) were also among "the children of the province that rose out of the captivity of the exile which Nebuchadnezzar imposed . . . and that returned unto Jerusalem and Judah, each to his city" (Ezra 2:1), and they are not included among the Temple servants and servants of Solomon (see II Samuel 21:1). In the Book of Nehemiah the "children of Gibeon" (95) are also included among the "children of the province" (Nehemiah 7:25), and even they are not included among the subjects. Perhaps it is coincidental that the Hivites from Gibeon, Kefirah, Beerot and Kiryat Jearim heard about the Lord God of Israel, and that there was a spiritual bridge between them and the people of Shechem who worshipped God, and who were their tribesmen. (In the days of Solomon it was said: "All the survivors of the Amorites, Hittites, Perizzites, Hivites and Jebusites who did not belong to Israel—that is, their descendants who survived in the land, where ever the Israelites had been unable to annihilate them—were required by Solomon to pay a labor tax, until this day. But Solomon subjected none of the Israelites to forced labor, for they were his fighting men, his servants and his officers . . ." (I Kings 9:20-22).

The President asked why Jeroboam left Shechem and built Penuel (I Kings 12:25). It is possible that he did not feel secure in that city which had been holy for so long to the entire nation, but it is clear why he put the calves in Bethel in the south and in Dan in the north—because these were the boundaries of his kingdom. Why did he settle in Tirzah? (I Kings 14:17)—I do not know. But the departure of Rehoboam from Shechem after the period of the united monarchy does not detract from the spiritual importance of Shechem from the days of Abraham (and in my view even before him) until after Joshua, to which the stories in the Torah and the Book of Joshua testify. It is difficult to over-emphasize the value of the covenant which Joshua made at the end of his days in Shechem between the people and its God. This was much like a second revelation on Mt. Sinai. Even according to the interpretation of Dr. Meltzer, Joshua wrote there these words in the Torah of the Lord which was in the sanctuary of God; and this sanctuary was in Shechem.

In my lecture I already dealt with this, for in my view Joshua's first message in chapter 23 was delivered to those who had left Egypt, and for that reason Joshua does not present his audience the choice—whether they will worship the God of their fathers or the gods of the Amorites—because those who left Egypt, and came together with Joshua, received the Torah of Moses with the words, "we will do and we will listen." Whereas, the message in chapter 24 was delivered to all the tribes of Israel; that is, also to the representatives of the veteran Hebrew settlers who hadn't left the land at all. Since there were many among them who were influenced by their neighbors and worshipped the Amorite gods, it was to them that Joshua put the choice.

I must draw your attention to verse 23 in this chapter (23) in which Joshua says: "Banish the foreign gods which are in your midst at once." It does not stand to reason that these words would be spoken to those who left Egypt, because there were no "foreign gods" in their midst. Even before they crossed the Jordan, as well as afterwards, we saw that all the people who had come with Joshua were whole-heartedly with him, and with his Torah, and with the Torah of Moses. They were all circumcised, and they sacrificed the paschal lamb, and there was not a trace of idolatry in their midst. In verse 14 it says: "Banish the gods whom your fathers worshipped beyond the river and in Egypt, and worship the Lord." But those who had left Egypt were attached only once to the Baal of Peor because of the lewd behavior with the women of Midian (Numbers 25:3). Those who acted in this manner were killed (according to the story of Numbers, 24,000 were killed), and this catastrophe was not forgotten by those who left Egypt as can be surmised from the words of the Children of Israel which were spoken in the days of Joshua to the sons of Reuben, Gad and half the tribe of Manasseh (22:17).

All of chapter 22 also testifies to the fact that those who left Egypt were faithful to the God of Israel. The trepidation which was aroused in their hearts by the building of a large altar by the sons of Reuben, Gad and half of the tribe of Manasseh was cause for the entire nation to assemble. Through the emissaries whom they sent across the Jordan, they transmitted the stern warning: "Was our offense at Peor, for which a plague fell upon the community of God, so insignificant that to this day we have not been purified from it? If you defy the Lord today, and you rebel against the Lord, then tomorrow He will be angry with the entire community of Israel" (Joshua 22:17-18). We see here how much Joshua's followers who had left Egypt were in trepidation over loyalty to the Lord of Israel, while the existence of foreign gods was only possible among the old-time Hebrews whom Joshua found in the land, and to whom he spoke in chapter 24.

The President, it appears to me, erred when he said that after Baasha smote Jeroboam, he move the capital to Tirzah. Jeroboam already lived in Tirzah, and his son Abiyah died there (I Kings 14:17). The dispute with the Samaritans arose only after those exiled to Babylonia returned, and this does not pertain to the antiquity of Israel. I did not rely at all on the tradition of the Samaritans, but on the tradition of *our* Bible. According to our Bible, it is evident that until the conquest of Jerusalem, in the days of David, and the building of the Temple by Solomon, 480 years after the exodus from Egypt, there was no place as important as Shechem.

Dr. Elitzur raised the question: If Abraham came to join other Hebrews, why then should Ishmael have been declared unfit to live in the land? And such was the case with Esau who went to the land of Seir. The question is a real one, but it should not be addressed to me. It should be directed to the Torah. The land was promised to the descendants of Abraham. Ishmael was of the seed of Abraham. Why should he have been declared unfit? The Bible does not say that Ishmael worshipped Baal or other gods. Such a thing was also not said of Esau. He parted from Jacob and lived in Seir "because their possessions were too plentiful for them to live together, and the land where they lived could not support both of them because of their livestock" (Genesis 36:7). He left Jacob for economic reasons, not religious ones.

Dr. Elitzur put me in a select group, with Albright and other researchers, who speak of Hebrew tribes that lived on the other side of the Jordan. I willingly accept the status of this honored group, though my doubts as to the validity of my theory have not ended because of this. But, it is difficult to agree with Dr. Elitzur that separation after unification is a common process, well known in history. I differentiated earlier between the division or dissolution of an empire and the splitting up of a united and unified people, as—according to the Bible—were the Children of Israel from the days of Jacob until Joshua. They were divided into separate tribes. Such a process is not found in history.

Dr. Elitzur answers my second question: why the Israelites did evil in the eyes of the Lord after the death of Joshua. In his view such a thing has happened in our day as well. The settlement of the land in the course of the last three generations has turned the Jews from an ideo-theological factor into a politico-colonial factor. But such a thing did not happen in the days of the Judges.

I do not accept Dr. Elitzur's description of the change that took place in our day. But even if we agreed with his characterization of our era, it bears no comparison to what happened in the days of the judges. After their settlement, in the days of Joshua, the Jews did not become unbelievers. Rather than to worship one God, the God of the patriarchs, they worshipped the Baal and the Ashtoreth—that is, gods of other peoples. I question this turnabout, because it is difficult for me to imagine that those who left Egypt, who received the Torah, who witnessed all the miracles, and in whom the historical tradition lived, turned their backs on the God of their fathers and attached themselves to the Baalim. This can be compared to having Jews who have come to settle in the land today suddenly converting to Christianity or Islam.

And I do not concur that a change has taken place in our day. To the extent with which I am familiar with our settlement, through personal experience of the last 55 years, there has been no spiritual or religious change. Most of those who built up the country were free-thinkers from the outset, beginning with the members of Bilu, the Second and Third Immigrations, and stretching to the arrival of the Oriental communities after the establishment of the State. To the best of my knowledge, the percentage of orthodox is larger today than it was 20, 30 or 40 years ago.

Dr. Elitzur believes that Shechem [the city] was not Jewish, and he finds proof for his assertion in the words of Gaal, son of Eved. Gaal was banished from Shechem by Abimelech, and Gaal's followers were killed by Abimelech's army (Judges 9:40-41). There is no evidence at all to be found in the words of Gaal that Shechem was Canaanite. Its history was without doubt Hivite, because

Shechem, son of Hamor was still a Hivite, but it is known that they were circumcised. In any case, in the days of Joshua, Shechem was one of the three cities of refuge west of the Jordan, together with Kedesh Naphtali and Hebron in the hills of Judah, and it was given to the Levites. This proves that its inhabitants were Hebrews. (Joshua 20:7).

Dr. Elitzur was correct in saying that the land of the Hebrews from which Joseph was abducted might possibly have been small, because in the Book of Joshua (8:1) we also find the land of Ai. In any case, this proves that there were Hebrews already on their land, and they did not go down to Egypt. Dr. Elitzur is ready to admit that there was such a Hebrew community in the land all along, but he believes that the overriding majority had come out of Egypt. But, if we recall that from Abraham until Moses seven generations passed (Abraham, Isaac, Jacob, Levi, Kohath, Amram and Moses); from Abraham until the settlers of the land, eight generations; and only three generations lived in Egypt (Kohath, Amram and Moses); then it is clear that the 318 circumcised charges who remained in the land, and did not go down to Egypt with Jacob and his sons, multiplied in the course of eight generations several times more than the 70 souls who went down to Egypt with Jacob and who had lived in Egypt for only three generations.

I was happy to hear the remarks of Dr. Eliner because he also feels that we must assume that monotheistic groups whom Abraham joined existed in the land of Canaan. I will note here, parenthetically, that the addition of God's name in the words of Abraham—which are unlike the words of Malkitzedek—did not occur in Abraham's conversation with Malkitzedek, but only in Abraham's answer to the king of Sodom. This addition does not detract from the significance of the words of Malkitzedek about "Almighty God, Creator of heaven and earth."

Dr. Eliner feels that I did not answer the question as to how the Israelites maintained their language in Egypt. The theory relating to the existence of a monotheistic nation in the land of Canaan does not offer an answer to this question. My answer to this question is that the Israelites lived in Egypt for just two or three generations, as some of our distinguished commentators, including Rabbi David Kimchi, have already noted. And this small group of Jews who went down to Egypt was, in my view, part of the Hebrew intelligentsia. Many of them already knew the Egyptian language, as is clear from the conversations of Joseph, Moses and Aaron with Pharaoh.

I agree completely with Dr. Eliner that the uniqueness of the Jewish people is not purely religious, but religio-national. And so it remains to this day, because the Jewish people has always been unique, and there is nothing comparable to it among all nations. Its belief is national, saturated with national memories and yearnings. But beneath its nationalism there is a spiritual base which if abolished or destroyed, would undermine its nationalism. This is the secret of Jewish unity in the diaspora and the attachment of the Jews of the diaspora to Israel. But this is a subject, important by itself, which does not directly affect the question of the antiquity of Israel in its land.

At the opening of the last session, when our honored chairman, Judge Chashin, was summarizing, he erroneously attributed to me the statement that "the sole innovation which Abram brought to Canaan was a belief in God." On the contrary, according to my hypothesis—I stress this word because this is nothing but a hypothesis, and not a final and definite opinion—Abraham continued on to Canaan because there were Hebrew tribes there who believed in one God as he did.

The chairman asked why Abraham sent his servant to take a wife from Paddan Aram for his son, and why, if there were Hebrew tribes in Canaan, Isaac told Jacob to take a wife from among the daughters of Laban, the brother of his mother. Abraham and Isaac were from a rich and privileged family and wished to marry people similarly endowed, as I previously pointed out; and clearly, not because Laban believed in one God.

I have no doubt about the authenticity and importance of the exodus from Egypt, something which was etched so deeply in the memory of the nation and referred to by almost all of the prophets. Samuel refers to it when speaking to the Children of Israel (I Samuel 10:18, 12:6-8). When the Temple was built in the days of Solomon, it was noted that it was built 480 years after the exodus from Egypt (I Kings 6:1). The exodus is also mentioned in Solomon's prayer after he brought the ark to the holy of holies (I Kings 8:51, 53); in the words of Jeroboam when he made two golden calves (I King 12:28); in the words of Isaiah the prophet (11:16); Jeremiah (2:6; 11:4, 7; 16:14; 23:7; 31:31; 32:20-21; 34:13); Ezekiel (20:10); Hosea (2:17; 11:1); Amos (2:10); Micah (6:4); 7:15); Haggai (2:5); Psalms (81:11; 105:23, 38); 135:8-9; 136:10-11); Daniel (9:15); Nehemiah (9:18). And the community of the exodus from Egypt has not diminished to this day.

It is impossible that this ancient memory not be based on fact. There is also no room to doubt the unique historical significance of this event, because it is linked to Moses, the greatest personality ever to arise among the Jewish people and to the Torah which he gave his people on Mt. Sinai after the exodus from Egypt. But neither the true essence of the event nor its transcendental importance has any bearing on the number of people who went down to Egypt, the number that later left Egypt, or the length of time they spent in Egypt. About these things we have conflicting evidence, and because we know the names of all those who went down to Egypt, and the names of their descendants who were among those who later left, we must come to the conclusion that the totals in the census of those who left Egypt, given in Numbers (1:1-41; 26:5-51), are terribly exaggerated as are all totals in the early period. So large a group could not maintain itself in the desert for 40 years, and certainly could not provide food for itself and its herds in enemy territory after it crossed the Jordan, and the manna had ceased. Two or three generations after 70 people went down to Egypt, they could not possibly have numbered even 10,000.

Dr. Meltzer claims that the Children of Israel lived in Egypt for 400 years. According to the Book of Exodus (12:40), we find "the Israelites had been settled in Egypt for 430 years." But Rashi, Nachmanides and Ibn Ezra had a great deal of trouble with this reckoning because Kohath (one of those who went down to Egypt) and his grandson—Moses, son of Amram, son of Kohath—were among those who left Egypt. Thus, the reckoning of the demographer Peretz Carmeli is erroneous because he counted the years and not the generations. It is the number of generations which determines natural increase, and from Kohath until Moses there are only three generations. Thus far, no one has proven that the enumeration of generations in the Torah is erroneous. Carmeli also erred in the number of years. Our Rabbis also felt that 430 years did not apply to Israel's period of residence in Egypt. This is how the Midrash put it: "Rabbi Nathan said: 'It is an involved matter. The period which the Children of Israel spent in Egypt, and in Canaan, and in Goshen was 430 years' " (Genesis Rabba 63). The Septuagint also interprets: "The period during which the Children of Israel were in Egypt *and* Canaan was 430 years." In the tractate Megillah, chapter 9a, it says that the Lord put thoughts in the minds of each one of the men who translated the Torah into Greek so that all agreed to an identical interpretation. They wrote: "The period during which the Children of Israel lived in Egypt and in the rest of the countries was 400 years." (This is not correct. The correct Septuagint version is as I stated it earlier.)

Rashi comments that they changed the text of the Torah "so that it could not be said that a lie was told in the Torah."

Dr. Meltzer answered my question regarding the vast difference between the number of cities in which Joshua fought and the number of cities in which the Children of Israel settled. He claims—and it is very possible that he is correct—that the Book of Joshua did not tell of all the cities that were conquered. This leads us to the conclusion that the Book of Joshua did not relate all that took place in its day, and it is not impossible that for some reason or other it omitted several other facts. Although such omissions would be surprising, it is quite possible that it also occurred in connection with the existence of Hebrew tribes in Canaan with whom there was no need at all to fight.

Professor Rabin doesn't see any great difficulty in the fact that the Israelites preserved their language in Egypt, because there are many examples of this among nations who lived as a minority in foreign lands and did not alter their tongue. But, in this case, according to the view of Dan Meltzer, this was not a minority, but rather a people that emerged and developed entirely in Egypt—since only 70 people went down to Egypt and two to three million left; and they lived in Egypt for over 400 years, according to what is written in the Torah. Jacob was 130 years old when he went down to Egypt, and the language of Jacob's mother was the same as of Laban her brother—Aramaic; and the language of Jacob's wives was the same as that of their father and master Laban. Joseph spoke Egyptian, his wife was an Egyptian, and his children were born in Egypt. Is it possible that the 12 sons of Jacob, whose native tongue was not Hebrew, could bequeath the Hebrew language to two or three million of their descendants, who lived in Egypt for hundreds of years? I don't know of one such case in the history of mankind.

The question becomes even more involved since we know that the Jewish people itself did not preserve its language in the days of the Second Temple, and they spoke Aramaic, Greek, Arabic and other languages in accordance with the languages of the nations among whom they lived. Is it possible that in Egypt, before the receiving of the Torah, one family preserved its language for 430 years? It is explicitly stated in the Book of Exodus that the Jews lived among the Egyptians, and were, therefore, commanded to apply blood to the cross-bar and the two doorposts. "For when the Lord goes through to smite the Egyptians, he will see the blood on the cross-bar and the two doorposts . . . and will not allow the destroyer to enter and smite your houses" (Genesis 12:23). For this reason the holiday is called Passover, "because he passed over the houses of the Israelites in Egypt when he smote the Egyptians, but saved our houses" (12:23). The fact that they borrowed gold and silver objects from the Egyptians proves that they mingled with the Egyptians (12:35).

As Professor Mazar noted, in all my remarks I relied solely on the biblical narrative, mainly on the Torah and the books of Joshua, Judges and First Samuel. I do not belittle the value of external sources, and I should examine my hypothesis in their light (if I can free myself from the work imposed on me daily, maybe I'll do that), but when I find a contradiction between the words of the Bible and the external sources, I do not have to accept the version of the foreign source. Can they not err or distort the facts?

From a purely scientific point of view, I am permitted to accept the testimony of the Bible, even when an external source contradicts it, if there are no internal contradictions in this (internal) testimony, or if it is not absolutely certain that the testimony is in error. I arrived at my hypothesis solely from testimony in the books of the Bible, because of the contradictory texts found in it, and through the use of common sense which seeks to understand events naturally, just as I see the marvelous events of our day as a natural development.

But, I want to call Professor Mazar's attention to one point (and I'm not certain whether this point opposes what he said or not), because it is clear to me that Abraham's journey from Ur of the Chaldees and Harran to the land of Canaan was not just the wandering of a nomad looking for pasture for his herd, but rather was inspired by a spiritual urge, as the late Professor Cassuto noted in his commentary on Genesis 11:31 ("And Terah took his son Abraham . . . and they left Ur of the Chaldees with them on the way to Canaan and they arrived in Harran and settled there"), and on Genesis 12:5 ("And Abraham took Sarai his wife . . . and they set out for the land of Canaan and they arrived in the land of Canaan"). I have no doubt at all that there was a spiritual motivation at work here, in the same way as the spiritual drive has worked throughout Jewish history, to this day, and as it has not worked for any other nation—all this despite the fact that the Jewish people, like every other people, had to eat, drink, be fruitful and multiply naturally as all human beings; and was not exempt from obedience to all the laws of nature, as well as the laws of history, if there are historical laws.

Professor Dinur claims that one should not upset the historical tradition of a people, but he does except from it the tradition about the exodus of 600,000 people, and inserts into the tradition the departure of *all* of the Hebrews to Egypt, and not just one, or several, of the families. It appears to me that this distinction is arbitrary. If it is permissible to doubt that 600,000 left Egypt, then it is permissible to doubt whether or not those who went down to Egypt included all those in Canaan who believed in one God.

If my hypothesis is correct, then I agree completely with Shazar that it is difficult to understand the Bible's failure to refer to the existence of Hebrews in the country before Joshua's conquest. But I myself am not completely sure that my hypothesis contains historic certainty; on the contrary, the "probable exceeds the possible."

I have not heard one convincing answer from the discussants about the doubts and the questions which I raised at the beginning of my lecture. I admit that the answer that I gave to the question of Dr. Haran is not a decisive and final answer, and it is true that the answer itself raises new questions for which I, too, do not as yet have an answer. But I do not accept the reliance of my friend David Zakai on Ahad Haam. I think that this scholar denied completely the historical existence of Moses, and described the "legendary" image which was created about Moses among the Jewish people. He then established that this legendary image itself was an educative force. I believe in the historical existence of Moses, and in the great and decisive role he played in the molding of the spiritual image of our people, just as I believe is the fact of the exodus from Egypt. Consequently, I want to try to understand them in a natural way.

When I delve into biblical sources, I find serious contradictions and problems which have not yet been resolved. The old commentators have alluded to several of the problems: Rashi, Ibn Ezra, Rabbi David Kimchi and others. They missed several problems, because as members of an exiled people, dispersed among foreigners, they did not properly grasp the meaning of the concepts of the conquest and settlement of the land, and were not aware of the nature of the country or the desert. But our generation, which has been able to strike roots in its land again, and renew its national independence through continuous settlement, political struggle and wars with our neighbors (which are not identical to those of our forefathers, but greatly resemble them)—our generation is able to see things in their proper light, though it is not easy to penetrate the mysteries of a past that is 3,000-4,000 years old. I am not certain if the answer which I offered to my question is correct, but if it is not correct we face serious doubts and problems. To conclude my remarks, I will reformulate in chronological order the problems and the doubts, which now total 30:

1. Why did Terah and his family leave Ur of the Chaldees—a developed and rich land—in order to go to the land of Canaan?

2. Why did Terah remain in Harran, and why did Abraham and the members of his family leave Harran, which was also a remarkably rich and developed land, and go to Canaan, a poor and culturally deprived land?

3. Why did Abraham come to Shechem where God appeared to him and where he built an altar to the Lord?

4. Why was it said to Abraham: "Your offspring shall be strangers in a land not theirs . . . for four hundred years" (Genesis 15:13), while in Exodus (12:40) it is written: "The length of time that the Israelites lived in Egypt was 430 years?"

5. Why was it said to Abraham: "The fourth generation shall return here" (Genesis 15:16), when in fact the eighth generation returned? Abraham, Isaac, Jacob, Levi, Kohath, Amram and Moses add up to seven generations, and Moses' generation did not enter the land (with the exception of Joshua, son of Nun, and Caleb), but the generation that followed him did.

6. What was the fate of Abraham's 318 charges who were circumcised together with him—they and their families—in the course of eight generations, until the Israelites returned from Egypt to the land of Canaan? It is known that they, the charges of Abraham, did not go down to Egypt!

7. Why did only Jacob's family go down to Egypt because of famine, and not the other inhabitants of Canaan?

8. What was the fate of the Hivites in Shechem who were circumcized in the days of Jacob? And why did Jacob say to his son Joseph before his death that he [Jacob] had taken Shechem from the Amorites with his sword and bow (Genesis 48:22)?

9. Exactly what is the land of the Hebrews which Joseph said that he was kidnapped from (Genesis 40:15)?

10. How is it possible to square the number 70 who went down to Egypt with Jacob, with the huge number that later left Egypt—approximately two to three million—when Kohath, son of Levi, was among those who left Egypt? (We also find Pallu, son of Reuben among those who went down to Egypt and Dathan and Abiram, the grandchildren of Pallu, among those who left Egypt.) Is it possible that in a span of two or three generations 70 people grew into millions of people?

11. How did the Israelites preserve their language in Egypt for 430 years, before the giving of the Torah, though the wives and children of Jacob were born in a land where Aramaic was spoken (Aram Naharaim)?

12. How did such a large group, with such great herds, maintain itself for 40 years in a desert which had neither pasture nor water?

13. Why did the Israelites—a people of millions—leave Egypt, a rich and fertile land, to go to the land of Canaan—a land for the most part poor and arid? Why didn't they try to conquer Egypt itself, to destroy its people and take over its land?

14. Why were the 12 leaders of the tribes sent to the land of Canaan as spies (Numbers 13)? Is it possible that 12 spies traveled from the wilderness of Zin in the south, to Rehov on the outskirts of Hamath in the north, and traveled in a foreign land for 40 days without it being known to the nations of Canaan, and without even one of the kings of Canaan being aware of them? Yet, when two anonymous spies were sent by Joshua to Jericho, and hid in the house of a harlot by the name of Rehab, it was immediately known to the king of Jericho (Joshua 2:2).

15. By what means did this large nation support itself, after they crossed the Jordan, when the manna had ceased; and where did they find pasture for their sheep and cattle in enemy territory, until the completion of the conquest?

16. Why did Joshua go to the Hivite city of Shechem to build an altar there to the Lord God of Israel on Mt. Ebal immediately after conquering Ai? And why did not the Hivites of Shechem, who constituted one of the nations of Canaan still to be engaged in battle, not hinder them?

17. Why was it the Hivites from Gibeon, Kefirah, Beerot and Kiryat Jearim—the only ones among the nations of Canaan—who surrendered and made peace with Joshua?

18. Where did the Gibeonites, and the rest of the Hivites from Kefirah, Beerot and Kiryat Jearim, hear of the Lord God of Israel, as is recorded in Joshua (9:9), and who revealed to them that God commanded his servant Moses to destroy all the inhabitants of the land (9:4)?

19. Why is there no mention at all of the conquest of Shechem in the days of Joshua, since it did become a city of refuge in the days of Joshua, together with Kedesh in the hills of Naphtali, and Hebron in the Judean hills (Joshua 20:7), and was also transferred to the Levite children of Kohath (21:21)?

20. How did Joshua and all his warriors get from Dvir on the

southern end, to the waters of Merom on the northern end, in order to do battle with Jabin, king of Hazor and his allies without the interference of the nations of Canaan situated between the two boundaries.

21. How can we resolve the contradiction between Joshua 11:23 ("Thus Joshua took the whole country, fulfilling all of the commandments that the Lord had laid on Moses; he assigned it as Israel's inheritance, allotting to each tribe its share; and the land was at peace"); and Joshua 13:1 which says: "Joshua had become very old, and God said to him: 'You are now a very old man and much of the country remains to be occupied.' "

22. Why is there no mention at all of a hornet in all the wars of the Israelites on the two sides of the Jordan? We find recorded in the Book of Exodus (23:28): "I will send a hornet before you which will drive out the Hivites, the Canaanites and the Hittites from before you"; and in Deuteronomy (7:20): "The Lord your God will also send the hornet among them until all who are left or have gone into hiding will perish before you." Even Joshua himself said to the people at the end of his days (24:12): "I will send the hornet before you, and it was this, not your sword or your bow that drove out the two kings of the Amorites," though it explicitly says of Sichon, king of the Amorites (Numbers 21:24): "Israel put him to the sword and occupied his land"; and of Og, king of Bashan it also says (21:35): "They smote him and his sons and all of his people, until there was no survivor left, and they occupied his land."

23. Why did Joshua in his last speech say to the people (Joshua 24:23): "And now banish the foreign gods that are in your midst" —despite the fact that those who had left Egypt had not worshipped foreign gods, in any case, not between the time that they had attached themselves to Baal Peor, and the day they had crossed the Jordan.

24. By whom, and at what time, was a sanctuary to God erected in Shechem concerning which Joshua wrote in the book of the Law of God (Joshua 24:26)?

25. What is the historical significance of the covenant between Israel and its God at the end of the days of Joshua (chapter 24), and what is the meaning of the two speeches which he delivered one after the other—one in chapter 23 and the other in chapter 24—and why only in the second speech did he give the people a choice between the God of their fathers and the gods of the Amorites? Wasn't Joshua present when the Torah was given; didn't he hear the nation's response: "We will do and we will listen,"

and wasn't the nation faithful to the covenant with God all the while?

26. Why did the Book of Joshua conceal the conquest of 230 cities which the Israelites settled west of the Jordan in the days the Jordan.

27. Why did the nation split into separate tribes after they had been united as one nation and one family while in Jacob's home in Canaan, on their way down to Egypt, through 430 years of residence in Egypt, during the trek through the desert for 40 years, and as a people which had conquered the land together under one leader—first under Moses and later under Joshua—a unity which continued for over 500 years?

28. And why did the Children of Israel begin to do evil in the eyes of the Lord and to worship the Baalim after the death of Joshua and the elders, though the historical tradition of the exodus from Egypt, the opening of the Red Sea, the giving of the Torah, and the wonders and miracles in the desert, and the conquest of the land, as well as the greatness of Moses, and Joshua were all, without a doubt, still alive amid the descendants of those who had left Egypt and those who had conquered the land to a much greater extent than in the days of Ezra and Nehemiah?

29. Who were the Hebrews who, together with the Philistines, came to fight with the Israelites in the days of Saul (I Samuel 14:21), and in the end joined Israel when Jonathan and his servant caused confusion and trepidation to befall the Philistine camp?

30. And above all, the central question remains: How were the grandchildren of 70 couples, who went down to Egypt, able to occupy the land of Sihon, king of the Amorites and Og, king of Bashan on the eastern side of the Jordan, and most of the nations of Canaan on the western side? Such an action is questionable and appears to me impossible, both from a military and a demographic point of view.

My hypothesis on the antiquity of Israel contains the answer to most of these questions, and especially to the last question, which is the most difficult of all. But I admit that there are questions to be raised concerning my theory, and if it proves unacceptable, then another answer must be found. If my words will give any impetus at all to the search for an answer which will satisfy us, this will be sufficient reward for me.

CHAPTER FOUR

Messianic Vision

On behalf of the government of Israel, I have the great honor to welcome the third World Congress for the Study of Judaism, which is again meeting in Jerusalem, and to say to the many distinguished guests from different countries: Blessed are you who come!

We rejoice that the Torah has been returned to its rightful place. Jerusalem, which we have been privileged to establish as the capital of the renewed and independent Israel, is increasingly becoming the world center for the study of every facet of the history of Judaism, its literature, and its creativity. With the increase in the number of Jewish scholars in Israel and in the diaspora, the number of non-Jewish investigators is not decreasing.

I welcome with special gratification the delegate from Iran, Professor Pureh Daud, of the University of Teheran, who will lecture on Cyrus and the messianic concept in the Zoroastrian faith. I hope that many other scholars from the other countries of Asia and, in the course of time, from Africa, will follow in his footsteps; and that the scholars of Arabia, too, will in the future not be absent.

The Jewish people is an eternal people. And though its cradle was located in the land of Israel, its great forefathers and teachers came from other places. The first Hebrew, the patriarch Abraham,

---

Presented to the third World Congress for the Study of Judaism. Jerusalem, 12 Ab, 5721—July 25, 1961.

was a native of Mesopotamia, and the greatest of the prophets and leaders of Israel, Moses our teacher, was a native of North Africa, in the Nile Valley. The great Jewish scientists and philosophers of the last few generations—Spinoza, Einstein, Freud, Robert Oppenheimer and others—were natives of Europe and America.

As one of the dabblers in Jewish scholarship, I am full of appreciation and respect for those involved in it, whether they are from my people or another. And I am gratified at the proliferation of sessions on Jewish scholarship which will be dealt with at this Congress, beginning with the Bible, and including modern Hebrew literature, folklore and popular art forms.

If it is permissible for a layman to make a request before his teachers and masters, I would hope that at the next Congress a special session be devoted to the investigation of a central topic which is perhaps the soul of Judaism and the source of its strength, something from which our nation has drawn the will and capacity to renew the kingdom of Israel in our day. And that is the messianic vision of the prophets of Israel concerning the redemption of their people and all the peoples of the world; that is, the vision of Jewish and universal redemption.

The Jewish vision of redemption has two aspects: the ingathering of exiles and the continuation of the Jewish people in its land as a chosen people, and as a light to the nations. And the universal vision of redemption also has two aspects: peace among nations, and the reign of justice and brotherhood between men and between nations.

This double messianic vision is really one, because the redemption of one nation is inconceivable without the redemption of all of humanity, and all of humanity will not be redeemed if every one of its members is not redeemed. The belief in this messianic vision was the principal strength which kept our people alive through all the years of its wandering and suffering, reaching a peak with the horrible Nazi Holocaust that killed six million European Jews—men, women, old people and children. This faith provided us with the strength and will to rebuild the ruins of our land and to lay the first foundations for the renewal of the kingdom of Israel 13 years ago.

I know that many scholars from Israel and from the nations of the world have dealt with this subject in Hebrew, Italian, English, French and German, but as yet no exhaustive study has been made of the messianic vision in all of its manifestations as found in the Bible, the Apocrypha, the Talmud, the and later more modern literature. What is primarily lacking is a full and comprehensive description of the revelations of this vision and its function throughout all of the generations: the full range of the messianic movements in ancient times, in the Middle Ages, and in modern times which led to the revival of the State of Israel in our day, and to the first indication that the messianic prophecy concerning the ingathering of exiles and our being a chosen people would be realized. And also lacking are insights into the world-wide phenomena of the rising up of enslaved peoples in Asia and Africa, and the increased yearning all over the world to insure the perpetuation of the declaration of Isaiah, son of Amoz, that "nation shall not lift up sword against nation, neither shall they learn war anymore."

In the international realm as well, there is hope for human redemption. For the first time, despite the fact that mankind is still divided and embroiled in conflict, the human race is coming closer and closer together. Mutual dependence of nations, large and small, is increasing, and the desire in the world to insure international peace and the reign of human brotherhood is becoming stronger—that is to say, social government built on the Jewish precept: "Love thy neighbor as thyself."

Jewish scholarship cannot be complete and truthful if it is not based on a messianic belief; on the Jewish and universal vision of redemption.

My wish to the Congress is that it increase and deepen this research and that it may help convert the messianic vision into a Jewish and international reality.

CHAPTER FIVE

The Exodus from Egypt

I am certain that you, yourselves, understand that I am not speaking in the name of any group or organization, but as a journalist, and that you may disagree with me. This time I will speak about the exodus from Egypt.

There are modern scholars who do not believe in the exodus from Egypt because there is no mention of it in Egyptian literature. But a person need not be a blind believer, or bound by the written tradition, to understand that the exodus from Egypt is an undeniable historical fact. An event which has been etched so deeply into the consciousness of the nation and whose reverberations are heard in almost all of the books of the Prophets, and in several of the books of the Writings, is without doubt an historical event; indeed, a central event in our history. In addition to the books of the Torah, the exodus from Egypt is mentioned in the Early Prophets and the Later Prophets, as well as the Holy Writings: I Samuel 10:18; 12:6-8; I Kings 6:1; 8:51, 53; 12:28; Isaiah 11:16; Jeremiah 2:6; 7:22, 27; 11:4, 7; 16:14; 22:7; 31:31; 32:21; 34:13; Amos 2:10; Micah 6:4; 7:15; Haggai 2:5; Psalms 81:11; 105:23-38; 135:8-9; 136:10, 15; Daniel 9:15; Nehemiah 9:9.

This does not mean that we must accept all of the traditional assertions linked to this event as given. Through a thorough study of the books of the Bible and the Prophets one must arrive at conclusions different from those commonly accepted. I will try to

---

Lecture before the Press Guild, May 12, 1960.

prove this mainly on the basis of the stories in the Torah, but also based on the stories in the rest of the books of the Bible. Our sages of old sensed several contradictions between the two, and corrected statements in the Torah proper. But, it appears to me that they did not draw compelling conclusions from their studies. It is this that I have in mind to do now.

This elucidation is part of my view on the early history of Israel in its land as I lectured on it before the Bible Study Group. It meets in my home every other week, and the greatest Bible scholars in Israel participate in it, including those who hold traditional views as well as those with freer and more critical views. These remarks were published in a book entitled, *Studies On the Book of Joshua*. I doubt if most of those assembled here saw this book or read it. It is not my purpose to repeat here what I have said there, but I will present several questions which I outlined before the group, stemming from a renewed investigation—after the establishment of the State—of the stories of the patriarchs, the exodus from Egypt, the conquest and the settlement of the land.

The rebirth of Israel and the War of Independence placed the Bible before me in a new light. After I delved into it, considering the facts of the War of Independence and the settlement of Israel in our day, questions were raised within me to which Bible commentators in Israel throughout the generations had not paid sufficient attention, because to them the concepts nation, tribes, conquest, war, geography, Israel, settlement, and mother-tongue were abstract concepts. I will note here the questions which I posed to the group, and to which I did not receive a satisfactory answer, as well as several questions to which I received no answer at all. All of these questions were spelled out in detail in this essay.*

These questions led me to different conclusions regarding the early history of Israel in its land, the essence of which is that the Hebrew people always lived in the land, and only one of its families went down to Egypt. The third generation of those who went down to Egypt left Egypt and returned to its land after wandering in the desert, during which time Moses, through the lofty revelation of a Torah, refined the ancient faith of the Hebrews in one God. But the tribes of Israel remained in the land throughout the years.

The event of the exodus from Egypt only attained its historical importance in our annals, thanks to Moses—father of the prophets and the greatest of them—and the role which he played in shaping

* The essay on the antiquity of the people.

the image of those who had left Egypt, and also the image of the entire Hebrew people. As is known, Moses was reared in Pharaoh's house (Exodus 2:5-10). In this house he absorbed all the rich Egyptian culture of that day and because of the belief in one God which he imbibed from his parents, he was able to rise above all of his brethren, not accept their slavery, and to take them out of the land of Egypt. It was not in vain that the Rabbis said that "Moses was equal to 600,000 Israelites."

At this gathering, I will only attempt to clarify one chapter of this early episode and to deal with it as exhaustively as possible through the study of the books of the Torah, and the rest of the books of the Bible. We will try to ascertain how many generations of Israelites were born in Egypt, and how many people left Egypt. First, I will note the primary texts among the Bible stories dealing with the journey to Egypt as well as the exodus from Egypt, and will try to prove through the very traditional texts that the prevalent viewpoint is in error.

We possess detailed data about those who went down to Egypt in the Book of Genesis:

"These are the names of the Israelites, Jacob and his descendants, who came to Egypt.

"Jacob's first-born Reuben; Reuben's sons: Hanoch, Pallu, Hezron and Carmi. Simeon's sons: Yemuel, Yamin, Ohad, Yachin, Zohar, and Saul, the son of a Canaanite woman. Levi's sons: Gershon, Kohath, and Merari. Judah's sons: Er, Onan, Shelah, Perez and Zerah—but Er and Onan had died in the land of Canaan; and Perez's sons were Hezron and Hamul. Issachar's sons: Tolah, Puvah, Yov and Shimron. Zebulun's sons: Sered, Elon, and Yachleel. Those were the sons whom Leah bore to Jacob in Mesopotamia, in addition to his daughter Dinah. Persons in all, male and female—33.

"Gad's sons: Ziphion, Haggi, Shumi, Ezbon, Eri, Arodi and Areli. Asher's sons: Yimnah, Yishvah, Yishvi, and Beriah, and their sister Sera. Beriah's sons: Chever and Malkiel. These were the descendants of Zilpah whom Laban had given to his daughter Leah. These she bore to Jacob—16 persons.

"The sons of Jacob's wife Rachel were Joseph and Benjamin. To Joseph were born in the land of Egypt, Manasseh and Ephraim, whom Asenath, daughter of Potiphera, priest of On, bore to him. Benjamin's sons: Bela, Becher, Ashbel, Gera, Naaman, Echi, Rosh, Muppim, Huppin and Ard. These were the descendants of Rachel who were born to Jacob—14 persons in all.

"Dan's son: Hushim. Naphtali's sons: Yachzeel, Guni, Yezer and

Shillem. These were the descendants of Bilhah whom Laban had given to his daughter Rachel. These she bore to Jacob—seven persons in all.

"All the persons belonging to Jacob who came to Egypt—his own issue, excluding the wives of Jacob's sons—all these persons numbered 66. And Joseph's sons, who were born to him in Egypt, were two in number. Thus, the total of Jacob's household who came to Egypt was 70 persons" (Genesis 46:8-27).

I want to direct your attention to two things in this section.

First observation: The number of the sons of Benjamin and their names. According to the Book of Genesis (46:21), Benjamin had 10 sons and their names were: "Bela, Becher, Ashbel, Gera, Naaman, Echi, Rosh, Muppin, Huppim and Ard." But in First Chronicles 8:1-2 it says that Benjamin had only five sons: "And Benjamin begot Bela his first born [as in Genesis], Ashbel the second [in Genesis he is third], Achrach the third [no such name exists in Genesis], Nachah the fourth [this also is not found in Genesis] and Rapha the fifth" [again a name which does not appear in Genesis, but is found in Numbers 13:9 as Palti's father, though there the spelling of the name is slightly different—not Rapha, but Raphu whose son was the leader of the tribe of Benjamin].

Also in the Book of Numbers (26:38), only five sons of Benjamin are mentioned: "The descendants of Benjamin by their clans: of Bela, the clan of the Belaites: of Ashbel, the clan of the Ashbelites [two names common to the listings in Exodus and Chronicles]; of Achiram, the clan of the Achiramites [this name isn't found in Genesis, and it is possible that the name Achrach in First Chronicles is a corruption of Achiram]; of Shephupham, the clan of the Shuphamites [in Genesis it says: Muppim]; of Hupham, the clan of the Huphamites [as in Genesis]." The number of sons equals the number in Chronicles, but four out of five of the names are similar to those in Genesis, and it seems to me that three of the names in Genesis: Echi, Rosh and Muppim were scrambled, and in place of these three names, Achiram and Shephupham should be read. The "r" of Rosh and the "m" of Muppim, belong to Echi [i.e. Echiram], and the "sh" of Rosh belongs to Shupham or Shephupham.

However, I am ready to accept the number of the sons of Benjamin as 10, according to the Book of Genesis, though according to the Book of Numbers (26:40), Ard and Naaman were the sons of Bela—that is, Benjamin's grandsons, as it is written: "The sons of Bela are Ard and Naaman." According to First Chronicles (8:3-5), Bela, son of Benjamin, had sons whose names were Adar (a corruption of Ard) and Naaman.

Second observation: In Genesis 46 it is written that three generations went down to Egypt: Jacob, his children, and his grandchildren. But together with the two grandchildren went their two children (the great-grandchildren of Jacob); Perez, son of Judah, went down with two children: Hezron and Hamul; and Beriah, son of Asher, also went down with two sons: Chever and Malkiel.

The number of those who went down to Egypt, however, was —exclusive of the wives of Jacob's sons (as is recorded in this same chapter, Genesis 46:26)—66: Jacob, 11 sons (because Joseph already was living in Egypt), the four sons of Reuben, six of Simeon, three of Levi, four of Issachar, three of Zebulun, seven of Gad, five of Asher, 10 of Benjamin (if we do not accept the enumeration of Numbers and First Chronicles), one of Dan, four of Naphtali, and four more great-grandchildren—two sons of Perez and two sons of Beriah—66 in all. If we add Joseph and his two sons, we get 69 (in the Book of Genesis it says "70 persons"). It is possible that Machir, Manasseh's son who was born in Egypt (Genesis 50:23), is included in this figure.

How many years did the Israelites live in Egypt?

In the Bible there are two slightly different answers to this question. In Abraham's Covenant, Abraham is told (Genesis 15: 13-16): "Know well that your offspring shall be strangers in a land not theirs, and they shall be enslaved and oppressed four hundred years. . . . And they shall return here in the fourth generation." But in Exodus (12:40-41) it says: "The length of time that the Israelites lived in Egypt was four hundred and thirty years; at the end of the four hundred and thirtieth year, to the very day, all the ranks of the Lord departed from the land of Egypt." The ancients have already dealt with the contradiction between the number of years in Abraham's Covenant and what is stated in the Book of Exodus, as well as the contradiction that exists between the time span (400 or 430), and the time that elapsed between the descent to Egypt and the exodus from Egypt. In the *Mekhilta of Rabbi Ishmael* they ask: "It says [in the Torah], 'the length of time the Israelites lived in Egypt . . .'—one text says, 'four hundred and thirty years,' and another text says, 'they shall be enslaved and oppressed for four hundred years.' How can these be reconciled?"

Nachmanides says simply (in his commentary on Genesis 15:13): "This is a confused phrase. It intends to say: 'your offspring shall be strangers in a land not theirs for four hundred years; and they will be enslaved and oppressed.' It does not refer to the number of years that they will be oppressed and enslaved."

This is how Rashi explains the same verse in Genesis 15: "From the day that Isaac was born until the day that the Israelites left Egypt, 400 years passed. How? Isaac was 60 when Jacob was born, and when Jacob went down to Egypt he said: 'The years of my sojourn have been 130,' for a total of 190 years. And they spent 210 years in Egypt . . . for a total of 400 years. But, if you were to say that they were in Egypt for 400 years, then Kohath is one of those who went down to Egypt. Add up the years of Kohath and Amram, and the eighty years of Moses at the time that Israel left Egypt, and you come up with only 350 years. Yet, you must deduct from them all the years that Kohath lived after the birth of Amram, and the years that Amram lived after the birth of Moses."

On Exodus 12:40, Rashi again comments: "In all, from the birth of Isaac until the present, 400 years passed. . . . It is impossible to say that [they dwelled] only in Egypt, for Kohath was among those who came with Jacob. If you add up all of his years and all the years of Amram his son, and the eighty of Moses, you will not find the appropriate total. Many years must have passed before Kohath went down to Egypt. Many of Amram's years are mixed in with the years of Kohath, and many of the eighty years of Moses are mixed in with the years of Amram. You will not arrive at a total of 400 years from their coming to Egypt. You are forced to say that the other 'dwellings' [in the land] are called 'sojournings,' including that of Hebron, as it is stated: 'Where Abraham and Isaac sojourned.' And it further states: 'The land of their sojournings where they sojourned.' Thus, one must conclude that 'for your offspring will be a stranger,' was said after he had a child. If you count 400 years from the birth of Isaac, you will find that from their coming to Egypt until their leaving, 210 years passed. That is one of the things which they changed for King Ptolemy."

Rashi is referring here to the Septuagint, the translation of the Torah into Greek, which was carried out before the Hasmonean period. In this translation it says: "The period which the Israelites sojourned in the land of Egypt and in the land of Canaan comes to 430."

The Rabbis confirmed this translation, which differs from the version in the Torah. In the tractate of Megillah (9a) we find "Rabbi Judah said: 'Even when our Rabbis permitted the use of Greek, they only permitted it for the Torah, and because of the actions of King Ptolemy, who assembled 72 elders and didn't reveal to them for what purpose he had assembled them. He met with each one of them individually and said to them: "Write for me the Torah of Moses." The Lord gave each one of the elders wisdom, and they agreed on one approach and wrote for him: "The period of time during which the Israelites sojourned in Israel and in the rest of the lands was 430 years." ' " The Talmud was not particularly precise. In the Septuagint it doesn't say "in the rest of the lands" but "in the land of Egypt, and in the land of Canaan." But this does not change the gist of the matter. The Mekhilta corrects the Torah version in a simple way, and says: "The period of time during which the Israelites sojourned in the land of Egypt, and in the land of Goshen was 430 years. This is one of the things which they wrote for King Ptolemy" (the reference is to the Septuagint).

The same thing is said in *Seder Olam* 83, in *Pirkei D'Rabbi Eliezer,* in *Pesikta D'Rav Kahana,* in *Midrash Rabba,* etc. In *Genesis Rabba* it says: "Rabbi Nathan said, 'It is a very profound matter: 'The period of time during which the Israelites sojourned in the land of Egypt, and in the land of Canaan, and in the land of Goshen was 430 years.' "

It is obvious that neither the details in Abraham's Covenant nor the number of years in Exodus can be accepted as the true measure of the time that the Israelites lived in Egypt.

But the decisive problem as far as our discussion is concerned—and it involves how many people really left Egypt—is not the number of years that the Israelites lived in Egypt, but how many generations were born in Egypt after Jacob, his children, his grandchildren, and several of his great-grandchildren came to Egypt in the days of Joseph. For, the number of generations is what decides the number of those who left Egypt, since we know from the Book of Genesis almost precisely how many went down to Egypt.

It appears that we have a clear answer to this question in the Book of Exodus, and an even clearer and more detailed answer in the Book of Numbers. In Exodus it says: "The Israelites journeyed from Raamses to Succoth, about six hundred thousand men on foot, aside from children. Moreover, a mixed multitude went up with them, and much livestock, both flocks and herds" (12:37-38).

More detailed figures are given in the Book of Numbers (1:20-47). According to what is related there, the Israelites were counted in the Sinai desert on the first day of the second month of the second year of their exodus from Egypt. Only the Israelite males, 20 years and older, and fit for military service, were counted. There are detailed figures from each tribe excepting the Levites, as is written there: "The Levites were not recorded among them by their ancestral tribe. . . . All the Israelites, aged 20 years and over, enrolled by ancestral houses, all those in Israel who were able to bear arms—all who were enrolled, came to 603,550." According to this, the number of Israelites who left Egypt together with their wives and children, as well as the Levites, amounted to close to 3,000,000 people (there the "mixed multitude" is not mentioned).

But when the books of the Torah are carefully studied, completely different conclusions must be reached. Just as the figure "430 years" did not stand up even to the critical analysis of the ancients, because it conflicted with other data in the Torah, so the precise data concerning the generations which were born in Egypt lead us to completely different conclusions if we accept as a basis—and there is no reason not to accept it—the number of those who went down to Egypt given in Genesis 46 that I noted at the beginning of my remarks.

In order to remove, to some extent, all doubt about the conclusions which emerge from the investigations made, and so that everyone can view it without prejudice, the meaning of one word in the Bible must be explained: the word *elef* (lit. "a thousand"). Its accepted interpretation is ten hundreds, and generally this is the correct interpretation, though not the only one.

The word *elef* is also used in the Bible to express the concept of a family, as can be seen from Gideon's words to the angel of God: "Behold *alphi* [my *elef,* my family] is the poorest in Manasseh, and I am the least in my father's house" (Judges 6:15). The *Targum of Jonathan* says: "Behold I am the smallest of the descendants of the tribe of Manasseh, and I am the weakest of my mother's family."

Rabbi David Kimchi interprets the word *alphi* (translated above as my family) as *aluf,* meaning officer or sir. The word *elef* in the sense of family is found several times in the Bible: In Numbers (1:16) it says: "The chieftains of their ancestral tribes: they are the heads of the contingents [i.e. families] of Israel." "And if only one is blown, the chieftains, heads of Israel's contingents [i.e. families], shall assemble before you" (Numbers 10:4). "Phineas the priest and the leaders of the community and the heads of the families of Israel, who were with him . . ." (Joshua 22:30). "Now take up your positions before the Lord tribe by tribe and clan by clan" (I Samuel 10:19). "I will search him out among all the clans of Judah" (I Samuel 23:23). And it also says in the Torah: "When the ark was carried out. . . . And when it rested, he would say: 'Return, O Lord, unto the myriads of *alphai* Israel.' " (Numbers 10:36). It is clear that the reference is to the tens of thousands of families and not to tens of thousands of thousands (i.e. tens of millions).

There is no doubt that this double meaning of the word *elef* caused many corruptions and exaggerations in biblical literature in the course of time.

The Torah doesn't contain the names of all those who left Egypt. We have the names of all those who went down to Egypt, and the names of a small number of those who left Egypt—the parents who were born in Egypt and the children who left Egypt —and from these we derive the true number of those who left Egypt. Our rabbis (*Pesikta D'Rav Kahana, Midrash Rabba* and others) have already set us straight regarding the crucial fact that only two generations were born in Egypt to the grandchildren of Jacob who went down to Egypt. Rashi goes further, and in his commentary adds to what is written in Abraham's Covenant: "And they shall return here in the fourth generation." He seems to assert that only one generation was born in Egypt and left and then returned to the land. This is what Rashi says (Genesis 15:16): "After they will be exiled in Egypt, they will be there three generations and in the fourth they will return to this land. For in the land of Canaan He was speaking with him (God with Abraham) and made this covenant, as it is written: 'To give you this land as an inheritance.' Thus, Jacob went down to Egypt. Add up his generations: Judah, Perez and Hezron [these three were among those who went down to Egypt, as is mentioned in Genesis 46] and Caleb, son of Hezron [not to be confused with Caleb, son of Yefuneh] was one of those who entered the land." This is as far as Rashi goes (excepting what is enclosed in parentheses).

Caleb, son of Hezron, is also called Chuvai, son of Hezron (I Chronicles 2:9) and he had two brothers: Yerachmiel and Ram. The three generations which Rashi enumerates—Judah, Perez and Hezron—all went down to Egypt as is related in Genesis 46. Hezron, as I noted above, was one of the four great-grandchildren of Jacob who went down to Egypt; all the other grandchildren were born in Egypt. Consequently, Rashi's projection was not successful, for according to it, only one generation was born in Egypt—Caleb, son of Hezron. In this case, it is true—though regarding most of Jacob's grandchildren it is not true—that only ten children of Jacob: Reuben, Simeon, Levi, Judah, Issachar, Zebulun, Gad, Benjamin, Dan and Naphtali went down to Egypt with their children; and their grandchildren were born in Egypt. Only Perez, son of

Judah, and Beriah, son of Asher, went down to Egypt with two children. Joseph's sons—Manasseh and Ephraim—were born in Egypt.

Among those who left Egypt, we find these grandchildren of people who went down to Egypt: Datan and Aviram who were born in Egypt to their father Eliav who was also born in Egypt; the son of Pallu who was the son of Reuben; Moses, Aaron, and Miriam, the children of Amram, all four of whom were born in Egypt (Exodus 6:18), and Amram was the son of Kohath, son of Levi who was among those who went down to Egypt; Korach and his son Yitzhar who were born in Egypt to the family of Kohath who was among those who had gone down to Egypt (Numbers 16:1); Carmi, son of Zavdi, both of whom were born in Egypt and stemmed from Zerah, son of Judah (Joshua 7:1); Zelophehad, son of Hepher who were born in Egypt and descended from Gilead, son of Machir, son of Manasseh who were also born in Egypt because Manasseh was the son of Joseph (in the case of Joseph, who went down to Egypt before his family, we find three generations which were born in Egypt).

According to First Chronicles 8:1, Rapha, son of Benjamin, was among those who went down to Egypt. Palti, son of Rafu, who was the leader of the tribe of Benjamin according to the Book of Numbers (13:9), was among those who left Egypt. There is hardly a doubt that Rapha and Rafu are one and the same person.

It is consequently clear that the Israelites did not live in Egypt for more than two generations (and only one generation as pertains to the great-grandchildren of Jacob). This is also proven by the two Pharaohs who came after the death of Joseph: the first started to oppress the Israelites and the second expelled them from Egypt. As it is written: "Joseph died, as well as all his brothers, and all that generation. . . . And a new king arose over Egypt, who did not know of Joseph" (Exodus 1:6-8). Moses grew up in the home of this Pharaoh, who oppressed the Israelites, after Pharaoh's daughter drew him out of the Nile. As it is written: "When the child grew up, she brought him to Pharaoh's daughter, who made him her son. She named him Moses, explaining 'I drew him out of the water' " (Exodus 2:10).

Moses grew up and killed an Egyptian who had beaten a Hebrew (2:11). He fled to Midian and married Tziporah, daughter of Reuel or Jethro (2:22). Then the king of Egypt died (2:23). A third Pharaoh arose to whom Moses was sent after a revelation at the bush. During the lifetime of this Pharaoh, the Israelites left

Egypt. From this we can again conclude that the Israelites left Egypt two generations after the death of Joseph and his brothers.

Now the question is asked: How many grandchildren who left Egypt were born to the grandchildren of Jacob, who themselves were among those who had gone down to Egypt? The Bible does not supply, through the names of those who left, a detailed answer to this problem which is crucial to our understanding of our entire early history, both before the exodus from Egypt, and after the exodus until the establishment of the monarchy in Israel. But there is enough fragmented information to form a general picture.

We have full information about the descendants of the sons of Levi who left Egypt: Gershon, Kohath and Merari. Although precise conclusions concerning the number of those who left Egypt cannot be drawn from the numbers of those who left Egypt, as are mentioned in the Bible, we can arrive at a general estimate of the number who left. The grounds for this conclusion are twofold:

1) The fact that only two generations were born in Egypt, and that it is possible to estimate how many children could have been born in two generations to the seventy couples who went down to Egypt.

2) The given number of those of the family of Levi who left Egypt—according to their ages, the names of their parents, and the names of their grandparents.

As is well known, Levi had three sons who went down to Egypt: Gershon, Kohath, and Merari. Gershon had two sons: Livni and Shimei (Numbers 3:19; I Chronicles 6:2).

Elsewhere, in First Chronicles (23:7), the sons of Gershon are listed as: Ladan and Shimei, and in the same place, the three sons of Ladan are listed as: Yechiel, Zetan and Joel (23:8).

Shimei had four sons: Yachat, Zina (or Ziza), Yeush and Beriah (23:10). All these grandchildren of Gershon were among those who left Egypt and to their number—seven—I add seven wives for a total of 14.

Kohath had four sons: Amram, Yizhar, Hebron and Uzziel (Numbers 3:19; Exodus 6:18; I Chronicles 6:3).

Amram, son of Kohath had two sons and a daughter: Aaron, Moses and Miriam. Yizhar, son of Kohath had three sons: Korah, Nepheg and Zichri (Exodus 6:21). Uzziel, son of Kohath, had three sons: Mishael, Elzaphan and Sitri (Exodus 6:22). Hebron, son of Kohath had four sons: Yeriah, Amariah, Yachaziel and Yekamam

(I Chronicles 23:19). Kohath had 13 grandchildren to which 13 wives must be added for a total of 26.

Merari, son of Levi, had two sons: Machli and Mushi (Exodus 6:19; I Chronicles 6:4). Machli, son of Merari, had two sons: Eleazar and Kish (I Chronicles 23:21); and Mushi, son of Merari, three: Machli, Eder and Yeremot (23:23). Merari had five grandchildren, and if we add five wives to them, we arrive at ten.

Altogether the grandchildren of the sons of Levi numbered 25, and if we add to this their wives, we arrive at 50 people as the number of grandchildren of Levi who left Egypt. If we accept the birthrate of the sons of Levi as average, and ascribe the same average number of grandchildren to all the sons of Jacob, we arrive at 600 people (12 multiplied by 50) including their wives who, with the exception of isolated instances, were not mentioned in the Bible. If it is true that only two generations were born in Egypt —and the stories of the Bible leave almost no doubt that no more than two generations were born in Egypt (and according to Rashi only one generation, as I explained above)—we arrive at the conclusion that approximately 600 people left Egypt.

If my hypothesis is correct—that with the exception of Joseph's family, the Hebrew people lived in the land continuously from the days of Abraham—then there is no doubt that the number of Hebrews believing in one God, who remained in the land, was several times larger than the number of those who left Egypt and returned to the land. This hypothesis is based on the Bible stories about Abraham's 318 charges with whose aid he was able to fight with the four kings (Genesis 14:8-16). The charges were born in Abraham's house, and all of them were circumcised, and without doubt adhered to Abraham's belief in one God. These 318 soldiers of Abraham had wives, brothers, and sisters who did not go down to Egypt. Consider, also that from Abraham's generation to that of Joshua eight generations passed (Abraham, Isaac, Jacob, Levi, Kohath, Amram, Moses and Joshua). It is natural that their number, in the course of eight generations, was several times larger than the number of grandchildren of Jacob's sons from whose lifetime until the entrance into the land a period of only three generations elapsed (Amram, Moses and Joshua).

If Jacob's 50 grandchildren (100, including their wives) amounted to 600 in two generations (this means that they increased sixfold), then Abraham's 318 charges must have reached approximately 400,000 in eight generations, though this figure seems exaggerated to me in view of the sparse population in those days. It is possible that this was close to the number of Hebrews who had been in the land when those who left Egypt returned. This explains several of the questions which I posed at the outset of my remarks, and this fits in with what was said to Abraham during Abraham's Covenant: "In the fourth generation they shall return here." But, whereas Rashi begins to count from the generation of the children of Jacob—and comes to the conclusion that only one generation was born in Egypt—I am of the opinion that the count should begin with the grandchildren of Jacob who went down to Egypt such as Kohath, his son Amram, his son Aaron, and his son Eleazar who entered the land. For, as I have shown, two generations were born to the grandchildren of Jacob in Egypt, and only in two exceptional cases (Hezron, son of Perez, son of Judah, and Chever, son of Beriah, son of Asher) was one generation born in Egypt.

If the number of those who left Egypt was only 600, or even several hundred more—and in this early period this was not a small figure—then we can explain their wanderings in the desert, their entrance into the land, and their eating from the produce of the land immediately after arriving there. They had returned to their countrymen who had always lived in the land along with several of the Canaanite nations. For even before Joseph went down to Egypt, a "land of the Hebrews" existed, as Joseph said to the chief cupbearer: "I was kidnapped from the land of the Hebrews" (Genesis 40:15). There is additional evidence testifying to the existence of Hebrews in the land of Canaan, such as the existence of Malkitzedek, king of Shalem (the Rabbis said that he was Shem, son of Noah—Nedarim 32), who was a priest to Almighty God and believed (as did Abraham) in Almighty God, Creator of heaven and earth (Genesis 14:19). Further, there was a sanctuary to the Lord in Shechem, which was a holy place to the Hebrews in the days of Abraham, Jacob, Joseph and Joshua, and where Joshua wrote the book of the Torah of the Lord (Joshua 24:26), and made a covenant with the people of Israel ("He set them up a statute and an ordinance in Shechem"—Joshua 24:26). All of the tribes of Israel came to Shechem to crown Rehoboam, son of Solomon, though Jerusalem was already the capital of Israel, and a Temple had already been built there (I Kings 12:1).

The descent to Egypt and the exodus from it was limited to one large privileged family with many children, and the importance of the exodus from Egypt centers about the story of Moses and the giving of the Torah to the nation. Moses was the greatest figure who had arisen in Israel through the generations, and yet he was born outside of the country and was not privileged to enter the land.

CHAPTER SIX

Father of the Hebrew Nation

The constant expansion of Bible study groups in Israel is one of the most outstanding and invigorating manifestations of our "return" to ourselves, which stems from, and is tied up with, our return to Zion and the independence which we have won in our homeland. It is natural that in an independent Israel, a young Jew should feel closer, from a Jewish point of view, to the biblical period than in a village in the diaspora.

This does not reflect any alienation or aloofness toward diaspora Jewry, just as the fact of our national independence does not reflect conflict with the Jews of the diaspora. But it is natural that the stories of the patriarchs, the events surrounding the settlement in the land, and the entire way of life which sprouted from the soil of the homeland in early times—both in the days of the First Temple and in the days of the Second Temple—are much closer to the younger generation in Israel than are events which took place in the diaspora over the last 200 years, and even in earlier centuries.

There is no basis for the false assertion that Israeli youth have no connection with diaspora Jewry. But it is natural and understandable that the experiences of the patriarchs in the Negev, Joshua's wars during the conquest of the land, the adventures of David in the south when he fled from Saul, or the letters of Bar Kochba written 1,800 or more years ago, speak more to the heart of our youth than do accounts of the rootless lives of the Jews in Poland or Galicia.

There is no justification to the claim that of all the literary creations of our people over a span of more than 3,000 years, the Bible was closest to the youth. I remember that in the town in which I was born, there was a group of Hasidim that opposed the study of the Bible, just as they opposed Zionism and immigration to Israel. These Hasidim viewed the study of the Bible as an act of heresy. There is nothing more natural, healthy and fruitful than the devotion to the Bible which is increasing among the masses of Israel, and especially among the youth. Through the return to Zion and to the Bible, the process of the revival and renewal of the Jewish people reached its highest point, and the more this process increases, the closer we will come to complete political and spiritual redemption.

There is no basis to the fear that our attachment to the Bible will cut us off from the diaspora, for the diaspora is not a post-biblical phenomenon either. As early as the Book of Genesis, we read of the first instance of exile. In the Book of Exodus it tells of the Jewish people while in exile, and in the Book of Deuteronomy it says: "The Lord will disperse you among the peoples, and you will be left few in number among the nations . . ." (4:27). In the same book there is also the promise: "The Lord your God will restore your fortunes. . . . He will gather you from all the peoples where the Lord your God has dispersed you" (Deuteronomy 30:3). The same thing is to be found in the Early Prophets and in the books of the Literary Prophets: Isaiah, Jeremiah, Ezekiel, and others. The diaspora did not begin with the destruction of the Second Temple. According to tradition, it predated the birth of the nation and its settlement in the land of Canaan. Even the story of Abraham, the first of the Fathers of the Hebrew people, began not in Israel, but in foreign lands—in Ur of the Chaldees and in Harran—or, in contemporary geographic terms, in Iraq and in Turkey.

In the last 150 years, Bible research has principally been the domain of non-Jews: Germans, French, British, Scandinavians and Americans. We are not ungrateful, nor do we deprecate the contribution of these scholars for revealing hidden meanings, and for useful, instructive interpretations, though, in my humble opinion, one should not consider Bible study a science capable of revealing to us unequivocal historical truths. Nor is it my intention to belittle the importance of archeology and its useful discoveries which have contributed towards a better understanding of the past. But for a long time, it was impossible to free oneself from the sad and depressing feeling that even in this realm our legacy had been taken over by foreigners. It was the return to Zion in our day which brought us back to a deep attachment to the Bible. It produced for us original and profound Bible scholars who were no longer influenced by Christian scholars.

Christian scholars—with the exception of a few distinguished ones, such as Travers Herford, Albright and the like—could not free themselves from their attachment to the Christian view which saw the teachings of Jesus as the epitome of spiritual greatness for the Jewish people, as well as the demise of our people. Working from this point of view, they believed that everything which came before the appearance of Jesus was only an introduction—preparation for the final revelation of the highest religious and moral truth. Some of these scholars could also not free themselves from their hatred of Israel, which intentionally and unintentionally distorted the results of their research and its direction. This hatred prompted them to search for the origin of all the exalted and luminous moral and religious truths that are recorded in the books of the Bible—including the belief in one God, the Creator of heaven and earth—in the early literature of the peoples of Egypt and Mesopotamia. Even those who were not afflicted by a hatred of Israel were driven to search out all sorts of doubtful reasons and theories to prove that the most exalted chapters in the Torah, the Prophets and the Holy Writings were the product of a later period, post-dating the destruction of the First Temple, and were thus nothing more than a preparation for the appearance of the sublime teachings of Jesus and Paul. Even Jewish scholars such as Bernfeld, Chajes, and even Klausner were more or less carried away by these false views.

History owes a great debt to the dean of Bible scholars of our times—and not just in our times, but of all times—Professor Ezekiel Kaufman, who brought about a Copernican revolution in Bible scholarship. He approached his research without preconceived notions, without apologies to non-Jewish scholars; and also without being bound by tradition. Through his marvelous erudition in all the books of the Bible, as well as their commentators in and out of Israel, and through deep and original delving into the internal structure and historical significance of these books, their content, and style, he shook to its very roots the system of biblical criticism of Wellhausen's school that dismembered the Bible and erased, altered and transposed complete verses and chapters from place to place, arbitrarily and needlessly. They post-dated complete, early, historical books, and distorted the entire image of the Bible and of Jewish history covering the period of the First Temple.

In his monumental work, *A History of the Israelite Faith,* Professor Kaufman constructed an original, magnificent, lustrous and complete structure for the study of the Bible, the Hebrew faith and prophecy. And he proved its antiquity and originality. It was not his intention to restore the tradition to its pristine splendor, as he himself states in the Introduction to the above book; nor was it to criticize "biblical criticism" out of preconceived notions motivated by apologetics. Rather, he made a daring, revolutionary and successful attempt—(in my humble opinion, not completely convincing)—to prove that in the books of the Bible historical truth was achieved to a much greater extent than Wellhausen's school imagined. The most important thing which Professor Kaufman stressed, with skill backed by irrefutable evidence, is that the belief in one God, God of the world and God of history, is an early discovery of the Jewish people; that it is an original contribution, and is not drawn from other national sources that existed before Israel came into being, or in whose midst Israel dwelled—but that it was the product of an independent national Jewish culture which emerged from the depths of the spirit of Israel, from the earliest days of the Jewish people. He also proved that all attempts to move the date of writing of most of the books of the Bible to the days of the Second Temple, have no firm and abiding basis.

No useful and fruitful investigation into the books of the Bible is possible in our day and age without reliance on the great work of Professor Kaufman.

The greatness of Professor Kaufman's book lies in the fact that it is not bound to tradition, and does not completely negate the conclusions of biblical criticism. Rather, he posits truthfulness as the essence of the Bible, and proves the antiquity of the Jewish belief in one God, as well as in the originality of this belief.

In the tenth anniversary year of the national Bible assemblies, held under the auspices of the Israel Society for Biblical Research, we are again returning to the Book of Genesis after completing the study of the entire Bible in recent years.

This book does not begin with the life of Abraham, but rather with God's creation of the world and with everything in it, as well as with the oneness of all human beings, *all* of whom were created in the image of God, and who only after the passage of time did separate into tribes, nations and races. We have before us two of the basic universal themes of Judaism which made our people different from all nations (who preceded it, or who existed before the period ending with the Second Temple): 1. a belief in one God, creator and guide of the world, and 2. the oneness of the human race.

According to the biblical view, the difference between the Creator and man is not absolute, the factor common to the two is the divine spirit. Already in the second verse of Genesis we read of the divine spirit which hovers over the water. The word *spirit* doesn't refer to the motion of the air or to a physical breeze, but to one of the revelations of God which, from time to time, are reserved for, and serve as a kind of adhesive, so to speak, between the Creator of the world and of man. This is the essence of the image of God in whose likeness man was created. Man's body—in the Bible it is called flesh [Heb. *basar*]—came from dust and returns to dust. The special characteristic which elevates man above *mere* flesh is the spirit or soul which God breathed into him.

When God instructed Moses to engage Bezalel, son of Uri, to erect the sanctuary, he said to him: "I have endowed him with a divine spirit of wisdom, understanding and knowledge in every kind of craft" (Exodus 31:3 and also 35:31). Of Othniel, son of Kenaz it says: "The spirit of the Lord came upon him, and he became judge over Israel" (Judges 3:10); and also of Samson: ". . . the spirit of the Lord began to drive him" (13:25). The Bible uses the words "the spirit seized," or "the divine spirit possessed," or "the divine spirit rested upon." For example: "The spirit of the Lord took possession of Gideon" (Judges 6:34); "The spirit of God took possession of Zechariah" (II Chronicles 24:20). Of Samson it says: "The spirit of the Lord seized him" (Judges 14:6, 19); of Saul it says: "The spirit of the Lord will take possession of you" (I Samuel 10:6); and later, again: ". . . the spirit of God took possession of him so that he too was filled with prophetic rapture" (10:10). And again: "The spirit of God seized Saul" (11:6). Also of David: "The spirit of the Lord came upon David" (16:13).

Moses' ideal was that God would bestow His spirit upon all of the people; and when Eldad and Medad were acting as prophets in the camp, and Joshua, son of Nun, ran to Moses and said to him: "My Lord, Moses, stop them!" Moses answered him: "Are you jealous on my account? Were it only so that all of God's people are prophets, and that the Lord would confer His spirit upon all of them" (Numbers 11:29). All of Hebrew prophecy is a product of the divine spirit fermenting within the prophet, and which is bestowed upon him from above, as Isaiah states: "Until a spirit from on high is bestowed upon us" (Isaiah 32:15).

In reading the stories of the Bible, we want, or must, first of all, try to understand what the Bible, or the editor of the Bible, wanted to tell us: how the masters of the Bible saw and understood the events which are related. I will limit myself this time to the first task; I will deal only with what the Bible tells us about Abraham.

I doubt very much that history is a science like the natural sciences, and whether we have sufficient tools to examine the truth or exactness of the events which occurred thousands of years ago. Despite the fact that the Jewish people was the first of all nations to write books of history, the main thrust of the writers of history in the Bible was, if we may use the jargon, not historiography *per se* but "historiosophy"—that is, the religious lesson derived from the narrative of events. In my outline of the life of Abraham, I will note only how it is reflected in the Torah narrative. In Abraham, more than in the other patriarchs (Isaac and Jacob), we see not only the father of the Hebrew nation, but also a profile of the Hebrew nation from its inception to our times.

Abraham believed in one God even before he came to Canaan, because it was by command of God that he left Harran. In the Book of Genesis it is written: "The Lord said to Abraham: 'Go forth from your country, from your native land, and from your father's house to the land that I will show you. And I will make you into a great nation . . ." (12:1-3), but the country to which Abraham was commanded to go was not specified. Abraham went to the land of Canaan, and his first stop was Shechem. And in Shechem he built an altar to God who appeared to him (12:7). It is clear from the Torah that even before Abraham's arrival, there were believers there in an Almighty God, as we learn from chapter 14 where it says that Malkitzedek, king of Shalem, was a priest to Almighty God. And he blessed Abram, saying: "Blessed be Abram by God Almighty, Creator of heaven and earth" (14:18-19). Abram also used the expression "God Almighty" when he later spoke to the king of Sodom (14:22). Abram used the term "Lord" before he used "Almighty God," but in the Book of Exodus it explicitly says: "God spoke to Moses and said: 'I am the Lord. I appeared to Abraham, Isaac and Jacob as *El Shaddai* [Almighty God], but I did not make myself known to them as *Jehovah*' " (6:2-3). From the words of Malkitzedek, who was a priest of Almighty God in whom Abraham also believed, we must conclude that even before the arrival of Abram there was already a group of believers in "Almighty God" in the land, because it is impossible that Malkitzedek was a priest to himself alone. It is even possible that this fact—the existence of believers in an Almighty God—is what attracted Abraham from the land of Harran to the land of Canaan which was, without doubt, much poorer than Harran as we know from the excavations carried on by a French archeologist in Harran in the 1930's. It is also not mere chance that Abraham's first stop in the country was in Shechem. In this city, as we know from the Book of Joshua, "God's sanctuary" existed from antiquity (Joshua 24:26). Jacob, upon returning from Harran with his wives and children after his meeting with Esau, his brother, came to Shechem, as it is written: "Jacob came safely to the city of Shechem . . . on his journey from Paddan Aram. . . . He bought the parcel of land where he pitched his tent. . . . And he set up an altar there and called it *El-Elohei-Yisrael*—the Lord God of Israel" (Genesis 33:18-20).

The great event that carries decisive significance in Jewish history is the promise of the land of Canaan to the descendants of Abraham and Sarah—and this event also took place in Shechem as we read in Genesis 12:6: "Abram passed through the land as far as the site of Shechem. . . . The Lord appeared to Abram and said: 'I will give this land to your offspring.' " And then Abraham built an altar to God who appeared to him and later moved from there to the hill country: "Then Abram journeyed by stages toward the Negev" (12:9).

Why did Abraham settle in the Negev? It is clear that then, as today, the Negev was the most barren and lightly populated area in the entire country. In the northern part of the land of Canaan —in Hebron and Shechem—Abraham and Jacob had to acquire a plot of land for full payment: Abraham, the field of Efron in the Machpelah for 400 *shekels* (Genesis 23:16) and Jacob, the plot of land where he pitched his tent, from the sons of Hamor, the father of Shechem, for 100 *kesitah*. But the Negev was an open expanse without owners—as it is now, so was it then—and it contained pasture-land for Abraham's great herds. But, as in our day, there were drought years in the Negev, and from time to time Abraham was forced to wander northward to Bethel, as is related in the Torah. Here we find the first division of the country between Abraham and Lot: '. . . the land could not support both of them, for their possessions were so great. . . . And there was quarreling between the herdsmen of Abram's cattle and those of Lot's cattle. . . . Abram said to Lot: "Let there be no strife between you and me, between my herdsmen and yours. . . Is not the whole land before you? Let us separate. . . . 'So Lot chose for himself the whole plain of the Jordan. . . . Thus, they parted from each other . . ." (Genesis 13:6-11).

Now comes one of the great events which reveals Abraham's valor and compassion: the assembling of all of Abraham's charges —318 in number, which in those days was considered a mighty force—to save his nephew, Lot, who had been taken captive by Chedorlaomer and his three allies during their war with the five kings of Sodom and Gomorrah and their allies. "When Abram heard that his kinsman had been taken captive, he mustered his followers . . . and went in pursuit as far as Dan. At night, he and his servants deployed against them and defeated them. He brought back all the possessions; he also brought back his kinsman, Lot, and his possessions, and the women, and the rest of the people" (Genesis 14:14-16).

Abraham was an excellent strategist and chose the most suitable time to attack: at night, when the enemy was weary and lay down to rest. The Israeli army in our day has also preferred night operations: in the War of Independence, in the Sinai Campaign, and in the many operations which we have carried out between the two big campaigns, and of late on the eastern side of the Sea of Galilee.

When the king of Sodom said to Abraham: "Give me the persons, and take the possessions for yourself," Abraham said to him: "I swear to the Lord, Almighty God, Creator of heaven and earth, I will not take so much as a thread or a sandal-strap of what is yours . . ." (Genesis 14:21-23). Abraham went to war to save captives and not to plunder.

After this comes the first indication of exile, spelled out in the Covenant of Abraham. God said to Abraham: "Know well that your offspring shall be strangers in a land not theirs, and they shall return here in the fourth generation" (15:13-16). Our early commentators already had difficulty with these verses, among them: Rashi, Nachmanides, Ibn Ezra, and so on. Nachmanides simply says: "This is a distorted text." In the Book of Exodus it says that the Children of Israel lived in Egypt for 430 years and here it says 400 years. All of the early commentators, as well as our Rabbis, investigated this and found that the Israelites did not spend such a long period of time in Egypt. They also had difficulty in enumerating the four generations, because from Abraham until the exodus from Egypt not four generations, but eight generations elapsed: Abraham, Isaac, Jacob, Levi, Kohath, Amram, Moses and those who left Egypt, but died in the desert and did not reach Israel—only the eighth generation returned to the land. Rashi comments: "After they are exiled to Egypt, they will remain there three generations, and in the fourth they will return to this land. For in the land of Canaan was He speaking with him [B.G.: God with Abraham]. . . . So Jacob went down to Egypt. Count his generations: Judah, Peretz and Hetzron, and Caleb, son of Hetzron were among those who entered the land" (Rashi, Genesis 15:16). This is as far as Rashi goes.

According to Rashi, it appears that only one generation was born in Egypt: Caleb, son of Hetzron. For Hetzron, together with his father, Peretz, and his grandfather, Judah, son of Jacob, was among those who went down to Egypt (Genesis 46:12). But, in my opinion, Rashi erred in this matter: Not one generation was born in Egypt, but two or three generations. Levi and his son Kohath were among those who went down to Egypt; and Amram, son of Kohath, and his son, Moses, were born in Egypt. Gershom, son of Moses, was not born in Egypt, but in Midian while the Israelites were still in Egypt (Exodus 2:22). Reuben, and his son, Pallu, were among those who went down to Egypt, and Eliab, son of Pallu and the two sons of Eliab, Dathan and Abiram, were among those who left Egypt. Zerah, son of Judah, was among those who went down to Egypt, while his son, Zavdi, and his grandson, Marmi, were among those who left Egypt.

This clarification has no connection with the story of Abraham, and I will not dwell on the conclusions to be derived from these considerations. Here, it is important to note that according to biblical tradition, the land was already promised to the Hebrew people in the days of Abraham, and the promise applied to the descendants of Abraham and Sarah, and not to the descendants of Abraham by other wives.

The event which transpired in the wake of the promise is the Covenant of Circumcision which was made between God, Abraham, and all his descendants, and it exists among the Jewish people to this day, both in Israel and in all the countries of the diaspora. This covenant also applied to the descendants who were not from Sarah. It appears to me that nothing has been so doggedly maintained, through all the generations and throughout all the countries of the diaspora, to this day.

The essence of the covenant between God and the Israelites is one of the basic aspects of the biblical concept concerning the relationship between God and his people. God not only imposes his laws and decrees upon Israel, as Master of the universe, but makes a covenant with her, as if the two sides are equal, and God is an elected king.

The first covenant was made with Noah and his sons after the flood (Genesis 9:9), and the rainbow became the symbol of the covenant (9:13). This covenant applied to all of humanity: "I will maintain my covenant with you, and never again shall all flesh be cut off by the waters of a flood, and never again shall there be a flood to destroy the earth" (9:11).

The covenant with Abraham (Genesis 15:18) was, for practical purposes, also the beginning of the covenant between God and the Israelites, and was based on the Covenant of Circumcision; while the later covenant, with the Israelites themselves, is based on the Sabbath: "The Israelites shall keep the Sabbath, observing the Sabbath throughout the ages as a covenant for all time" (Genesis 31:16). In Exodus 34:10, God says to Moses: "I hereby make a covenant before all of your people." And again in Exodus 34:27 God says: "Write down these commandments, for in accordance with these commandments I make a covenant with you and with Israel." This covenant was renewed after the conquest of the land by Joshua. After he put the choice to the nation: "Choose here and now whom you will worship: the gods whom your forefathers worshipped on the other side of the river, or the gods of the Amorites in whose land you are living." And the people answered: "No, we will worship the Lord" (Joshua 24:15-21). "And He made a covenant with the people, and he drew up a statute and an ordinance for them in Shechem. And Joshua wrote these things down in the Torah of God" (24:25-26).

In Genesis 18, the type of hospitality which both Abraham and Sarah, his wife, excelled in is described: hospitality accompanied by great humility. Abraham sees three men—it later becomes clear that these were angels of God—standing near him, and he entreats them to be his guests. He says to them modestly: "Let me fetch a morsel of bread that you may refresh yourselves; and then go on" (18:5). But, in fact, he prepares a lavish feast for them, and says to Sarah: "Quick, get three measures of choice flour! Knead and make cakes!" And he himself ran and "took a calf, tender and choice, and gave it to a servant boy, who hastened to prepare it. He took curds and milk and the calf that had been prepared, and set these before them" (18:6-8)—apparently mixing milk with meat was still not forbidden.

And here came the tidings about the birth of Isaac, despite the advanced age of Abraham and Sarah. In a beautiful interpretation, the Rabbis said that the Almighty distorted the truth for the sake of peace. After Sarah laughed at this surprising prophecy with the cry: "My husband is old!" God said to Abraham: "Why did Sarah laugh, saying 'Shall I, in truth, bear a child being old as I am?' " Sarah argued that Abraham was old, but God told Abraham that

Sarah had said about herself that *she* was old. The prophet Zechariah said: "Love truth and peace" (8:19), but it appears as if God prefers peace over truth when there is good reason for so choosing. So important is the love of peace in the Torah of Israel and in the Prophets!

Now comes one of the most exalted events in the life of Abraham, and one of the most marvelous stories in world literature: when God reveals to Abraham, "The outrage of Sodom and Gomorrah is so great, and their sin so grave!" and when he tells him that he intends to destroy them, Abraham turns to God with the argument: "Will you sweep away the innocent along with the guilty? . . . Will you not forgive the place for the sake of the innocent fifty who are in it?" And he concludes with daring forceful words: "Far be it from you! Shall not the Judge of the earth deal justly?" (Genesis 18:20-25). This sensitivity toward justice as expressed by Abraham, and the courage that he possesses to argue his case fearlessly before his Creator, is one of the most sublime moments in the Bible. This is the sole example, it seems to me, of man forcefully demanding justice from his God. Abraham was not afraid of being a nuisance, and he repeated his request five times in different ways. First, he argued on behalf of 50 just people who might be found in Sodom; then on behalf of 45; on behalf of 40; on behalf of 30; on behalf of 20; and finally on behalf of 10—and each time God assented.

The greatness of Abraham's staunch, stubborn and daring stance before God in asking for justice and mercy lies in the fact that he not only asked to save 50 or 10 honest people, but that he argued to pardon all of Sodom for the sake of the few righteous people living there. This greatness stands out even more in light of the great episode which follows the defense plea for Sodom: the story of the sacrifice of Isaac, which tells of Abraham's unequivocal surrender to God and his willingness to sacrifice his only son, Isaac, born to him by Sarah in his old age. This is one of the grandest and most amazing chapters in the Torah. *Grand,* because it demonstrates the deep faith of Abraham and his limitless and boundless trust in God—Abraham did not hesitate for a moment to carry out the order of his God and to offer his son as a sacrifice; and, *amazing* because it bears resemblance to the idolatrous and cruel practice of sacrificing one's son to the *Moloch* (a pagan deity), such as we also find in the Book of Judges, in the story of Jephtha's daughter (chapter 11). True, the sacrifice of Isaac was only a test, and God who told Abraham to sacrifice his only son on one of the mountains, later told him—through an angel—(after

Abraham had already taken the knife to slaughter his son): "Do not raise your hand against the boy, nor do anything to him; for now I know that you fear God, since you have not withheld your son, your favored one, from Me" (Genesis 22:12). In any case, this episode teaches that such actions were common in those days, as well as afterwards.

If we study all of these events in the life of Abraham—and I only dealt here with the main ones—we find, indicated in them, a sort of veiled summary of all of Jewish history through all the thousands of years that have since passed. The belief in a Creator of the universe; in only one God who rules His universe with justice and mercy; the settling of the Hebrew nation in the promised land; the exile of the nation and its suffering in foreign lands; and the sacrifice of thousands, tens of thousands, and millions of Jews throughout the entire period of exile. If you prefer, you may include the dividing of the land as was arranged between Abraham and Lot; the readiness to redeem captives to save Lot; the military and strategic ability to save the captives; the Covenant of Circumcision which has been adhered to in Israel for some 4,000 years, from the days of Abraham to this day; devotion to the rule of justice and mercy, and the demand that it be adhered to even by the Almighty. For this reason did our rabbis say: "The deeds of fathers are guidelines to sons." In none of the other patriarchs is the history of Israel so symbolized as in the life of Abraham.

In conclusion, I should note that the Prophets and Holy Writings also mention the name of Abraham as "a friend of God." In Isaiah (41:8) it says: "But you, Israel my servant, you, Jacob whom I have chosen, descendants of Abraham my friend," and in Second Chronicles (20:7), King Jehoshaphat says: "Did you not, our Lord, dispossess the inhabitants of this land in favor of your people Israel, and give it to the descendants of Abraham, your friend, forever?" The patriarch, Abraham, is the only personality in the Bible who was given the esteemed title, "Friend of God."

CHAPTER SEVEN

The Early History of the Hebrews in Canaan

Professor E. Kaufman: Let's get to the matter at hand.

Chairman H. Gevaryahu: We have gathered for a friendly chat and to discuss Torah in honor of the publication of Professor Kaufman's commentary on the Book of Judges. Our distinguished member, the Prime Minister, prepared a speech in reply to Professor Kaufman's lecture delivered at the gathering of the Bible Society in April of this year, dealing with the Hebrews at the beginning of the history of Israel—the beginning of monotheism. The members gathered here have received the Prime Minister's speech, and it is now on the table. Now Professor Kaufman will reply to some of the Prime Minister's criticisms. The reply will be divided into four areas. The first matter that we will deal with is the question of the genealogy of the descendants of Ever. This is one of the points about which there is disagreement.

Professor Kaufman: We will not be able to deal with all of the matters that Mr. Ben-Gurion touched on. I will attempt to exhaust several of these as much as possible. The first question: Does the Book of Genesis contain the genealogy of the descendants of Ever? The second question: Should the Hebrews and Israel be considered as one people; should they be considered identical? The third

---

A conversation with the late Prof. Ezekiel Kaufman, Jerusalem, 17 *Sivan,* 5722, June 18, 1962.

question: The matter of Shechem: Was Shechem a Hebrew city during the patriarchal period? The fourth question: What is the purpose of chapter 24 in the Book of Joshua?

I will begin with the first question. I opposed Mr. Ben-Gurion's view that there were peoples at that time called "Hebrews." In my opinion, there were no Hebrews—certainly not as one people. Indeed there are many peoples which belong to the group that are the descendants of Ever, and a list is given in the Book of Genesis. Not one of them is called a Hebrew people; not one lived in Canaan in that period; not one was monotheistic, as we understand the term monotheistic. They were polytheistic as were the rest of the nations outside of Israel. Mr. Ben-Gurion replied that he didn't find a genealogy of the descendants of Ever; in his opinion there is no such list. In my humble opinion there is.

I want to try to show here where there is a list of the descendants of Ever. When the narrative in the Book of Genesis moves to the list of the sons of Shem, it begins with the story of Shem, but it immediately stops and says: "ancestor of all of the descendants of Ever" (Genesis 10:21). What does this mean? It means that here begins the genealogy of the descendants of Ever. It is clear that the narrator knows the group of peoples which emanated from (or was related to) the descendants of Ever, and he contends that Shem was not just a part of these peoples, but the progenitor of them all, for it says: "Sons were also born to Shem, ancestor of all of the descendants of Ever." It fixes Ever's position as one of the fathers from which several nations descended.

In this chapter, one of the branches of Ever is listed: "Two sons were born to Ever: the name of the first was Peleg [i.e. division] for in his days the earth was divided . . ." (10:25). This means that an important personality, after whom the period is named, is the symbol of the period. And afterwards the narrative adds: ". . . and the name of his brother was Yoktan" and gives a list of the nations which emerged from Yoktan: "Yoktan begot Almodad and Sheleph . . . all of these were the descendants of Yoktan" (10:26-29). It does not say at the end: "these are the descendants of Ever," but rather that Yoktan, their father, is among the descendants of Ever; that they are a part of this branch. The narrative doesn't always have to summarize. For example, the chapter begins: "These are the descendants of the sons of Noah: Shem, Ham, and Japheth," and later it continues: "the sons of Japheth" and enumerates his sons, and also "the sons of Ham." But, here as well, the narrative does not conclude: "these are the sons of Ham, these are the sons of Japhet." It is inherent in the text.

Where does the story of the sons of Ever continue? When the narrative says of Abraham: "I make you the father of a multitude of nations" (Genesis 17:5)—the father of families of nations—it means that Ever is a part of the genealogy. They belong to the same group. The narrative could not have said: "these are the descendants of Ever." It doesn't cite a special list, because the lives of the descendants of Ever are the essence of the Book of Genesis, from this point until the end. The first of Ever's sons is named after the period—a period of division; and from him came Israel—a young nation. The narrative has to tell about the sons of Peleg; it can't say: "these are the sons of Ever." This it doesn't say anywhere, because it doesn't cite one single genealogy as it does in other places. It tells not only of the genealogy of the descendants of Ever, but tells about the lives of the descendants of Ever. It doesn't tell of the lives of the descendants of Ham; it doesn't touch on that at all; except to reveal as much as necessary about what transpired in Canaan. In essence, all that it tells is the story of the descendants of Ever.

I want to show that in chapter 11 the narrative once more returns to the descendants of Ever (beginning with Genesis 11:14). It mentions Peleg, and later lists Reu, Serug and Nahor, who "begot Terah." None of these is important, but when it reaches Terah it again comes back to the development of the nations. Between Terah and Ever there are several generations. This is the ethnographic reality of new nations. The longer the genealogy of any particular nation, the younger it is. The longest genealogy is of Israel, as I recall. And when the narrative reaches Terah, it tells us of his three sons: "When Terah had lived 70 years, he begot Abram, Nahor and Haran" (11:26). Afterwards, it does not tell us the stories of the descendants of all the generations, but rather it tells us how Ammon and Moab came into being.

Later, we see that there are other genealogies. There are several genealogies here. In chapter 22, beginning with verse 20, the genealogy of Nahor is mentioned: "Milkah, too, has borne children to Nahor." Later the narrative cites the genealogy of Ishmael: "And these are the descendants of Ishmael, son of Abraham" (25:12)—perhaps the most recent of nations. Before the genealogy of Ishmael, in the same chapter, there is the genealogy of the descendants of Keturah: Zimran, Yokshan, Medan, Midian, etc. (25:2). They belong to the nations of Ever; and later, as already mentioned, to the descendants of Ishmael. Without a doubt, they belong to the nations of Ever.

Afterwards comes not the genealogy, but the life history of the descendants of Abraham, Isaac and Jacob. From here on, we do not have a genealogy but a history. This is the history of the descendants of Ever. All of these nations are the descendants of Ever. There is a list here of the descendants of Ever beginning with chapter 11. The list is given in sections. Afterward, we are given the history, a complete history. The narrative tells us about the life of these peoples. There are also genealogies among them, but the main emphasis is on history.

If someone should come and say that these are not the descendants of Ever, my question, in essence, still stands. For I ask: How is it possible that the Book of Genesis is careful to give the history of all of these peoples, mentioning small nations whose place in history we do not know, and who did not play a substantial role in history—while it does not mention one Hebrew people, which, as we are arguing here, was monotheistic before Abraham and Moses. This should be a part of the story about the descendants of Ever. How could a people that was so important that Abraham came to live in its midst, and which would later certainly combine with Israel—how could it be forgotten?

B.G.: I must correct you: I was not speaking about Hebrew peoples. I am saying that there was one Hebrew people.

Kaufman: That is even stranger. Why doesn't the narrative mention this Hebrew people? Why doesn't it record anywhere that there was a Hebrew people?

B.G.: In my opinion it does mention it many times. It is possible to say that Ever is the father of Israel, though this isn't vital, because the name Ever is found several times in the Bible without any connection with peoplehood. We find in Nehemiah 12:20: "Of Sallai, Kallai; of Amok, Ever." In Chronicles, among the descendants of Gad were "Yakan, Ziah, and Ever" (I Chronicles 5:13); and among the descendants of Benjamin: "The sons of Elpaal: Ever, Misham, and Shamed" (8:12). All these are "Ever" and they have no connection whatever with the nation.

Kaufman: What about "all the descendants of Ever," and "Shem, father of Ever?"

B.G.: I'll get to it in a moment. First of all we have the words "Ever" and "Ivri" [Hebrew] many times in the Bible. *Ivri* and not *Ever,* begins to appear only with Abraham the Hebrew. It is not used before Abraham the Hebrew, and then only in a place where the matter concerns the Jewish people that believed in one God.

Abraham was called a Hebrew, and when Moses was ordered to go before Pharaoh it was said to him: "You shall say to him: 'The Lord, God of the Hebrews, manifested himself to us'" (Exodus 3:18). There was such a people which was called "Hebrew" (*Kaufman:* the people of Israel). He didn't say to him: "God of Israel," but, rather "God of the Hebrews."

Kaufman: O.K., granted. Why then wasn't the nation mentioned before Abraham, if it existed?

B.G.: I still haven't gotten to what came before Abraham.

Kaufman: Why does it [the narrative] begin to call them Hebrews beginning with Abraham? If Abraham goes to settle among a Hebrew nation, why doesn't the narrative mention it?

B.G.: I'll get to that, too.

Kaufman: Why is there no mention of it before Abraham?

B.G.: I will explain why no mention is made before Abraham. The history of the people has some kind of beginning. I want only to note that we have "Hebrew" [Heb. *Ivri*] to distinguish from "Ever." It is possible that Ever is connected to Ivri, and it is possible that there is no connection. I rely on the fact that "Hebrew" and "Hebrew people" are mentioned 26 times: six times in the Book of Genesis, twelve times in the Book of Exodus, and eight times in the Book of Samuel.

Kaufman: Where is it mentioned before Abraham?

B.G.: It is not mentioned before Abraham.

Kaufman: That is the question: The name Hebrew is not mentioned before the existence of the people of Israel.

B.G.: The people of Israel existed only after Jacob; before Jacob there were Hebrews. Only Jacob was called Israel, and his descendants, the Children of Israel. If we accept the genealogy as it is—though Professor Kaufman says that you cannot rely on genealogies—then it is clear that Abraham is not an Israelite, and cannot be an Israelite. Only his grandson was called by the name Israel, and only after him can there be Israelites.

Kaufman: "Israel" as in the "patriarchs of Israel."

B.G.: Abraham cannot be called an Israelite. Even after Israel there are other Hebrews.

Kaufman: Why not? The father of Israel—father of the nation?

B.G.: Abraham is not the father of Israel. Abraham is not once called by the name of Israel, his grandson.

Kaufman: There were no Hebrews. That is what I claim. There was a people of Israel which was not called the Hebrew people.

B.G.: There were Hebrews before Israelites and Hebrews after Israel. There were no Israelites in the days of Abraham.

Kaufman: Nor a Hebrew people.

B.G.: It is not mentioned in the Bible before Abraham. I will use the term "Jewish." That is the last name found in the Bible.

Kaufman: That is dangerous. I ask one question: The term Hebrew appears for the first time in conjunction with Abraham. Why doesn't the term Hebrew appear before Abraham, if Abraham went to such a people? Indeed, is there even a hint that there was a Hebrew people?

B.G.: This term does not appear before Abraham. The term Hebrews also does not appear in the Book of Joshua or the Book of Judges. But it does appear in the Book of Samuel. Were Hebrews suddenly born in the days of Samuel? You can claim that before Abraham the term Hebrews does not appear, but that does not necessarily prove that there were no Hebrews.

Kaufman: I did not want to show any more than that.

B.G.: I am saying, that according to the Bible, our history begins with the times of Abraham; and he was a Hebrew. And I say that there were Hebrews in the land of Israel—not just idol-worshipping Canaanites, but also Hebrews—and that they believed in one God, in Abraham's faith, and that it was this belief which attracted Abraham to the land of the Hebrews. That is to say, the land of Canaan to which he came was also the land of the Hebrews.

Kaufman: We have only one testimony to this fact: that of Mr. Ben-Gurion.

B.G.: When Abraham was circumcised it said: ". . . and all his household, his homeborn slaves and those that had been bought from outsiders, were circumcised with him" (Genesis 17:27).

Kaufman: These were slaves, members of his household.

B.G.: The term slave in the Bible is not meant in the same way as slave is today, such as in South America.

A. Ginsburg: "Bought . . ." [implies slavery].

B.G.: Not only "bought." He mustered his charges, born into his household, numbering 318" (14:14). It doesn't say that they were bought.

Kaufman: It doesn't say that they were Hebrews either. And now to the second question. . . .

B.G.: I am saying that our people had three names in three periods. In the early period, Hebrews; later, Israelites; and, finally, Jews. This is one people which in different periods was called by different names.

B. Dinur: And it became narrowed down.

P. Meltzer: "Son of the Israelite woman" (Leviticus 24:11).

B.G.: Right, son of the Israelite woman; this is one people. There are reasons why it was first called Hebrew and later Israel, and that at the same time it was called Israelite. There were Hebrews—this is one people. Later the name changed to Jew, because the kingdom of Israel was destroyed. After the destruction of the kingdom of Israel, they were called Jews.

B. Dinur: Hebrew son of Abraham.

B.G.: That isn't written in the Bible. In the Bible it says: Abraham the Hebrew.

Kaufman: They were called all of these names. I want to deal with the question: Is the Hebrew people identical with the Israelites? Can we view it as one nation in all periods which only changed its name? I recall my sins. I didn't deal with it in my critique, but several scholars have already asked this question: there were Hebrews and there were Israelites. The assumption is that this is basic. There was a Hebrew people. There were Canaanites, and at the same time there were also Hebrews similar in culture and language; and they helped conquer the land. But, how can it be said that the Hebrew people and the Israelite people is one people and that it just changed its name? I would never have thought of such a thing. I thought that this was a mere metaphor, and I didn't give an answer to this question as to whether or not it is possible to view them as one people.

I thought that Mr. Ben-Gurion's assumption was that there were two peoples there. Abraham went to the Hebrews, to their academies, because they were monotheistic. I simply don't understand this identity. What does it mean that only the name was changed? I want to ask several questions about this. It had been fixed in the consciousness of the Hebrew people that Israel is the descendant of Abraham, Isaac and Jacob. Before Abraham there was not an Israelite people. It also did not exist in the days of Isaac, and not even in the days of Jacob, except after they went down to Egypt. Now, we hear that Abraham went to the Hebrew people which lived in the land of Canaan, and which was a monotheistic people. How is it possible to say that it merely changed its name, when Israel did not yet exist and Jacob had not yet been conceived in the womb of his mother; his father had yet to be born? How is it possible that this people existed, when this people had not yet been born? Abraham came to join them before Isaac was born. This is another people; he was born afterward. We have no information about a Hebrew people, not one word. About the people of Israel . . . we do. How is it possible to say that this people existed hundreds of years before the second son was born, and that when Jacob was born, only the name changed—a new nation was born? This is the first question. There are others of the same type.

B.G.: I'll add a second question. For some reason Professor Kaufman did not take notice that in another period they call our people Jews. They do not call us Israelites or Hebrews.

Kaufman: They are the descendants of Abraham, Isaac and Jacob.

B.G.: But earlier Professor Kaufman argued for the Israelites. Before Jacob there were neither Israelites nor Children of Israel. But in the days of Jeremiah they are called Jews.

Kaufman: They consider themselves the children of Abraham, Isaac and Jacob. That doesn't apply here. There was no Hebrew people here before Abraham, nor after Abraham. Only several generations afterward did a very young people emerge, the Children of Israel called, the Hebrew people. How can there be an identity, how is it possible to say that they united, or that it is the same people, with only a change of name?

B.G.: There were also other people, descendants of Abraham, and other people, descendants of Isaac. But the Jewish people had three names. We know that present-day Jews call themselves by different names in different countries. They feared that this name or that would arouse anti-Semitism. There are countries where they call themselves "Jews," in Russia they call themselves Yevrei, meaning Hebrew. In our day there are different names, and in the Bible we also find different names. In the days of Jeremiah they were called Jews; in the days of Samuel and Saul we hear of both Israelites and Hebrews.

Kaufman: There are those who say that the Hebrews are a different element.

B.G.: Is Abraham also another element, because of his Hebrew name? Also Joseph? I believe that this is one people—Hebrews, Israelites, Jews.

Kaufman: They can't be one people if one of them already existed hundreds of years beforehand.

B.G.: In the days of Saul it says: "The Hebrews were under the Philistines as beforehand" (I Samuel 14:21).

Kaufman: But before Abraham?

B.G.: The narrative of our history begins only with Abraham. This is no proof that there were no Hebrews before Abraham. What went on before Abraham I do not know. It isn't related in the Bible.

Kaufman: In any case, there were no Hebrews.

B.G.: How does Professor Kaufman know this? He can only say, that before Abraham the Bible does not speak of Hebrews. Since we do not know exactly who lived then, there are several questions which arise in the human mind.

Kaufman: I have many questions and I won't ask all of them. But there are several questions which I must ask. That it is possible to say, as Albright does, that the Hebrews in the land of Israel were one people—I understand. But what Mr. Ben-Gurion says, that the Hebrews, Israelites and Jews are one people that merely changed its name—that I can't grasp. The Israelites are divided into 12 tribes; we know their names. If this was one people, was the ancient Hebrew people also divided into 12 tribes?

B.G.: This is a question for which I have no answer. But, Joseph, when he comes to Egypt, speaks of a land of the Hebrews from which he was brought. Would you say that Joseph did not belong to the Israelites? According to a plausible theory, there were many Hebrews in the land of Canaan. They were there in the days of Abraham, and of course, after Abraham. They didn't all go down to Egypt. If we were to assume that the Hebrew people—which later was called the Jewish people—this was its latest name—if we were to contend that the Hebrew people, or the Israelite people, was born in Egypt, then it would be difficult to understand how after being there for several generations they spoke Hebrew. What is more, how is it possible that such a vast people consisting of several millions survived in the desert, as we are told, for 40 years?

Kaufman: I know all the arguments. There are answers for them. There is a question to which I want an answer. If it is the same people, then it should be divided into 12 tribes. If this is not so, then how is it possible to speak of identity?

B.G.: In Egypt the Israelites were not divided into tribes, but were one people. My answer is that a large segment did not go down to Egypt.

Kaufman: That doesn't answer my question. Were there 12 tribes in the Hebrew people?

B.G.: Not in Egypt. In my opinion, if we accept the fact that the Hebrew people were only the descendants of Jacob that went down to Egypt, then it is impossible to understand how the tribes were formed. In Egypt there was one people, not separate tribes. They left Egypt under one leadership, entered the land under one leader, and conquered it. There were only tribes in the land of Israel.

Kaufman: I have a clear idea about this matter, but I don't want to respond. Now I want answers from you. I want to know how it is possible to speak of a people which is not divided into 12 tribes, and was not comprised of the descendants of Abraham, Isaac and Jacob to be identified with the Israelites? How can this have occurred *before* the matriarchs and their maidservants were born? All of this happened after Abraham. And if what came before Abraham was divided into tribes, then how was it divided? And if it wasn't divided into tribes, how then can we speak of identity? (*P. Meltzer:* Actually, there were 13 tribes.) If there is no record of this, then how is it possible to speak of identity?

Another question: The Hebrew people, according to you, was a native people which did not have to fight to conquer its land. At a certain point it assumed the name Israel. Let us suppose that Israel was a part of this people and was also part of the native population. Why did they lose their privilege with the appearance of the patriarch Abraham? Why were they now strangers? Was this the same people that was called Hebrew, and later did it lose its privilege when it was called Israel? This people has troubles. It has to go down to Egypt. How is it possible to speak of identity? They are strangers. Abraham was promised that the entire land would be given to his descendants. That is to say that it would not be settled by Hebrews or by Israelites; and this at a time when the Hebrew people already lived in the land.

How is it possible to speak here of the history of one people, which only changed its name? When they changed their name and called themselves Jews, it didn't say that there were two completely distinct peoples in the land of Israel. Did they cease to be dwellers of the land by changing their name? Why did they go down to Egypt? Because there was a famine. Well, didn't the Hebrews who remained in the land require food? Why didn't the rest of the Hebrews go down to Egypt?

B.G.: Did all who lived in Canaan go down to Egypt? Apparently, not all went down to Egypt; not all of the nations of Canaan went down. Only the children of Jacob went down, and not even all of them.

Kaufman: Jacob didn't go down, and the rest of his family didn't go down either.

B.G.: Why couldn't the nations of Canaan have remained?

Kaufman: It is not mentioned that they left together with Israel. They needed food. Everything is confined to a generation which was hungry in the land. The Children of Israel are mentioned, but not the Hebrews. It's convenient to identify the Israelites with. . . .

B.G.: It is not true that our people are always called the Children of Israel, neither before Jacob, who became Israel, nor after Jacob. Joseph says: "I was kidnapped from the land of the Hebrews" (Genesis 40:15).

Kaufman: There is an explanation as to how they conquered the land; there are other explanations. Scholars generally say that the Israelites were a small people, and were not able to fight. They entered the land, not through war, but were peacefully assimilated with the Canaanites and became one people. From this it is possible to draw a conclusion. But absolutely nothing at all is said about Hebrews; and at least something is said about the Canaanites.

B.G.: Joseph mentions the land of the Hebrews. What is the significance of this?

Kaufman: I already explained that.

B.G.: I interpret it differently.

Kaufman: It is impossible to base the history of an entire people on that.

B.G.: It is also impossible to build a complete history on the name *Israel.* It says of Moses: "He saw an Egyptian beating a Hebrew, one of his kinsmen" (Exodus 2:11). And it also says: "When he went out the next day, he found two Hebrews fighting" (2:13). It doesn't say that he saw Egyptians fighting. He didn't see Egyptians; he saw Hebrews. Moses was a Hebrew, a Jew, an Israelite. A Jew related the story in Moses' name. They were Hebrews.

Kaufman: The Israelites were called Hebrews.

B.G.: Abraham wasn't an Israelite. Joseph was familiar with the land of the Hebrews; there was a land of Hebrews.

Kaufman: There is a simple explanation. It is impossible to build a complete theory on this; that there was a Hebrew people; to make an identity with the Israelites; to say that there is a land of Hebrews. The word has. . . .

B.G.: It says in the Bible: "the father of all of the descendants of Ever"—but there is nothing there about the Hebrews (Heb. *Ivrim*). You say that it says: "the father of all of the descendants of Ever," and you draw many conclusions from that. It is possible that these conclusions can be drawn. It says: "a Hebrew," "a Hebrew boy," "from the land of the Hebrews," "the Lord God of the Hebrews"—this is how God reveals his name to Moses. It is impossible that everything is a mistake or a chance occurrence. There were Hebrews.

Kaufman: They are all the descendants of Abraham, Isaac and Jacob. At no time are others spoken of.

B.G.: Joseph didn't say that he was the son of Jacob or an Israelite.

Kaufman: Hebrew families lived in the land. But, these were the families of Abraham and all those related to them.

B.G.: Joseph didn't say that he was from the family of Abraham.

Kaufman: He was certainly interested in them not knowing of his Amorite antecedents. He wanted to put up a front when he arrived in a foreign land. His manner of speech is not precise. In my view it is possible to interpret the verse that the descendants of Abraham lived in this place, and he lived in the land of the Hebrews. There is no indication that there was a Hebrew nation before Abraham. There isn't a half or a third of a verse on that.

B.G.: Before Abraham, there is no mention of Hebrews in the Bible.

Kaufman: I have another question: We hear, according to one theory, that the Hebrew people—unlike Israel—was native to the land, native to the land of Canaan, before Israel lived there. . . .

B.G.: Before they went down to Egypt.

Kaufman: When the narrative lists the nations living in the land of Canaan, it does not list the Hebrews!

B.G.: It only lists the Canaanites. I rest on the words of Joseph. Joseph's words came from his heart. He speaks about the land of the Hebrews. There was a land of the Hebrews.

Kaufman: He came from the land of the Hebrews.

B. Dinur: The region where his family lived. That isn't a country. It is a stretch of land where the household of Jacob lived. That is the land of the Hebrews.

B.G.: Joseph did not speak of a country, but of a land. How do you know that there were only the twelve sons? Abraham had 318 charges who accompanied him in battle. It is possible that these were Hebrews. (*B. Dinur:* These were slaves.) All of these concepts which we have today didn't exist then. When he returns from the war with the four kings, Malkitzedek, king of Shalem, goes out to meet him (Genesis 14:18). Shalem isn't Jerusalem; Jerusalem isn't mentioned in the Torah even once. "And he was a priest to Almighty God" (14:18); he believed in the same faith as our patriarch, Abraham. Was he a priest to himself?

Kaufman: Why wasn't he called a Hebrew? He should have been called by the name Hebrew. The Hebrews were monotheists. No one is spoken of as a Hebrew. Who knows if these weren't Syrians or Canaanites, who went with him.

B.G.: That is possible, but it doesn't say that in the Torah. I don't think that we can tell in our generation with any certainty (knowing something of the Khazars) that the Jewish people was formed from just one family. Could there not have been different tribes which joined up with the Israelites and intermingled with them? There is no genealogy. Can a people be formed from one person?

Kaufman: There were slaves who were circumcised. . . .

B.G.: I am only interested in the Bible. The changes that took place later don't interest me. I want to understand the Bible and I have been striving for that from my earliest days.

Kaufman: There is one decisive fact: that the first person called a Hebrew is Abraham, and his descendants were called Hebrews. Nowhere is there a person called a Hebrew who is not a descendant of Abraham. The existence of such a nation cannot be proven. Such a people is not mentioned anywhere, except the one beginning in the days of Abraham.

B.G.: What about the Book of Samuel?

Kaufman: That is in a different period.

B.G.: There were Hebrews then.

Kaufman: I'm discussing whether or not there were Hebrews before Abraham.

B.G.: Before Abraham . . . nothing is known. The Bible doesn't tell about the origin of the Israelites. It begins with Abraham and Abraham is called a Hebrew.

Kaufman: Maybe we should skip over to the third question: Was Shechem a Hebrew city? I don't think that there is any case so clear as the case of Shechem. Not one of the patriarchs is mentioned as having been in Shechem. There was an altar adjacent to Shechem, but they were not in cultural or religious contact with it. According to one version they belong to the Hivites; according to another, to the Amorites. But there is no mention that they belonged to the Hebrews. The only city which the patriarchs fought in and destroyed is Shechem, the residents of whom were all Hivites. But they didn't destroy all of them. If any of the residents of Shechem survived, then they were Hivites. It is not mentioned at any time that there were Hebrews there. They were hostile to Jacob's children who had fled from Shechem. And Mr. Ben-Gurion considers it a Hebrew city. Why they should choose Hebron [sic.], isn't known. They make friends with the local people and see themselves as their allies. Why they had an altercation with the people of Shechem is not told. In the days of Jacob, the Israelites attack all of the people of Shechem. This isn't one people; this isn't an identical people. How can we explain how the Israelites—before the birth of the nation—attacked a part of the Hebrew people and annihilated it? There is no basis for these things. How can we say that there were Hebrews there? Jacob goes to Bethel, Abraham goes to Shechem, Jacob goes to Shechem, and in the days of the conquest, Joshua goes to Shechem. Adjacent to Shechem they are building sanctuaries, but they have no contact with Shechem. Much is said about relations with Shechem, but much more is said about Bethel: A ladder stationed on the ground, the house of God, the gate of the heavens. It is impossible to compare the importance of Shechem with the importance of Bethel. Why don't we say that there were Hebrews in Bethel? The Israelites destroyed the people of Shechem. Why was it suddenly necessary to make the city a Hebrew and monotheistic center?

B.G.: Because it says so in the Bible.

Kaufman: Not in my Bible.

B.G.: In my Bible it says that God appeared to Abraham in Shechem, and the sanctuary of God was located in Shechem—not the sanctuary of *El,* but the sanctuary of *Adonay.* What is written about Bethel and what is written about Shechem—this I will commit to writing.

Kaufman: Doesn't it say that they were uncircumcised?

B.G.: Initially they were uncircumcised, but later they circumcised themselves. The Israelites also entered the land uncircumcised: "Joshua circumcised them; they were uncircumcised because they had not been circumcised on the way" (Joshua 5:7). The people of Shechem were uncircumcised and later they were circumcised.

Kaufman: They were circumcised for a practical purpose.

B.G.: They were circumcised.

Kaufman: There are many circumcised nations. The Egyptians were also circumcised.

B.G.: It doesn't say in the Bible that the Egyptians were circumcised. Shechem is mentioned in the Bible many times, and things are written about Shechem not written about any other place. It is imperative that we find an explanation for this. Lofty statements are made about Shechem, but not about Bethel. God appeared to Abraham only in Shechem—(*Kaufman:* Not in Hebron?) and in Shechem God said to Abraham: "I will give this land to your offspring" (Genesis 12:7). The first revelation in the Bible was in Shechem.

Kaufman: The first, but not the only revelation.

B.G.: The first revelation—which is not a small thing. It took place in Shechem, and it is there that Abraham was promised the land. Subsequently, Jacob came to Shechem. In the Torah, the Israelites were commanded to go to the land of Israel, and when they arrived there, they were commanded to accept the blessing and the curse on the two mountains adjacent to Shechem.

Kaufman: Shechem benefitted, and not the other way around.

B.G.: There are many facts for which an explanation must be found.

Kaufman: There is an explanation.

B.G.: Only this place housed the sanctuary of the Lord. It says in the Torah: "I did not make myself known to them by my name *Adonay*" (Exodus 6:3), though this contradicts what was said several times in the Book of Genesis. Abraham uses the same words that Malkitzedek uses: "Creator of heaven and earth" (Genesis 14:19), and it is said explicitly to Moses: "I was not known to them by this name." Later on, in the Book of Joshua, it says that the Lord's sanctuary was located in Shechem. This is the most important thing about Shechem. At this point, I have to discuss chapter 24 in the Book of Joshua. If this chapter in Joshua is read carefully, one sees in it a dialogue the likes of which is found nowhere else in the Bible—a complete and clear statement of the covenant which the Children of Israel enters with their God. There is a dialogue there between Joshua and the people. It is possible that later things were added, but there are things in this chapter which ring with truth, and which it is difficult to doubt: "Joshua mustered all of the tribes of Israel in Shechem" (Joshua 24:1). In contrast, it says in chapter 23: "Joshua summoned all of Israel, their elders, the heads of their families, their judges and their officers" (23:2). Here he summoned the heads of the people. And in the course of the story: "Joshua told the people: 'You cannot worship the Lord, because he is a holy God, a jealous God, and he will not tolerate your iniquities and sins. . . .' The people said to Joshua: 'No, we will worship the Lord' " (24:19-21). Again Joshua says: "And now banish the foreign gods that are among you, and turn your hearts to the Lord, God of Israel" (24:23). In Egypt, the Jews didn't worship foreign gods; in the desert the Jews didn't worship foreign gods; and in the stories in Joshua up to chapter 24 the Jews didn't worship foreign gods. Why does Joshua suddenly say: "Now banish the foreign gods that are among you?"

Chapter 23 was spoken to those who had left Egypt, and chapter 24 to the tribes who had been living in the land. Joshua assembled all of the tribes, including those who left Egypt, but he was mainly speaking to the Jews (or Hebrews) who had lived in the land all the while. We see a difference between the two chapters, and if we emphasize the words: "the father of the descendants of Ever," this also has some significance.

Kaufman: What significance? He's talking about the Hebrews in Shechem.

B.G.: There is a difference.

Kaufman: In chapter 24 it specifically talks about the people who left Egypt.

B.G.: The opposite can be proved. Joshua told the Hebrews who had not gone down to Egypt about the exodus from Egypt.

Kaufman: The opposite? Are Hebrews mentioned here?

B.G.: In chapter 23, he doesn't tell what happened in Egypt, as if he is speaking to people who had left Egypt.

Kaufman: He also speaks to those who had left Egypt in chapter 24: "I brought your fathers out of Egypt" (Joshua 24:6).

B.G.: I want to express my view. He had no need to tell all that happened in Egypt and in the desert in chapter 23; he told that only to the Hebrews who had been living in the land, whom he assembled in Shechem. The chapter opens: "Joshua assembled all of the tribes of Israel in Shechem." I contend that there were no tribes in the desert. There was one people. There was no basis for division into tribes. One family went down to Egypt, and they lived as one family.

Kaufman: These were Hebrews?

B.G.: In chapter 24 these were Hebrews, and the author used these proofs.

Kaufman: It says of them: "Terah, father of Abraham . . . I took your father Abraham." Were the Hebrews the descendants of Terah?

B.G.: Abraham was the son of Terah.

B. Z. Lurie: It could be that he also assembled the descendants of Terah.

B.G.: Since the history begins with Abraham, Terah was not of interest to him.

P. Meltzer: And what about verse 6?

B.G.: I know, I read it, those who had lived in the land.

Kaufman: It says: "I brought you out" (Joshua 24:5).

B.G.: The Jews which he took out of Egypt were also Jews, or Israelites, or Hebrews.

Kaufman: "I brought you out of Egypt"—how can that be? After that they are crossing the desert, and later he says: "I brought you into the land of the Amorites" (24:8). It is clear that he is speaking to those who had left Egypt.

B.G.: From where did they get foreign gods?

Kaufman: From where did Jacob get them?

B.G.: Joshua didn't speak with Jacob.

Kaufman: They bought them in Sodom (?!).

H. Ginsburg: Jacob stole the household idols.

B.G.: The first time that Joshua spoke, he didn't ask for the removal of the foreign gods. In Egypt they didn't have foreign gods. All of a sudden, at the end of his days, Joshua demands of them to remove the foreign gods. From where did they come?

Kaufman: This isn't a problem.

B.G.: Nevertheless. . . .

P. Meltzer: Balaam, son of Beor, cursed them.

B.G.: Balaam didn't curse Israel. On the contrary, he blessed them not once, but three times. Why does Joshua tell the entire story? He is talking to those who weren't in Egypt, to those who had remained in Canaan. They were one people that had one belief. But those that remained in the land were more influenced by the neighbors than the small segment that had been in Egypt, who were with Moses and with Joshua. This was the elite of the Hebrew people. In chapter 23 he spoke with those who returned from Egypt. He did not have to tell them all this. Afterward, he wanted to speak with the entire nation. Naturally, he didn't assemble all of the people who lived in the land; only the representatives of the nation. He told them what had happened in Egypt and also what had happened on the way through the desert. They did not have this experience. The most important thing is mentioned only here—unless you want to say that this isn't truth—this is the only place where it says that the Children of Israel chose God.

H. Ginsburg: We even have that in the Torah.

Kaufman: "I brought you out"—how can you speak in clearer language?

D. Dinur: What is the significance of "Let us do and listen?" This is a choice. The people is choosing God.

B.G.: It doesn't say that there. Perhaps that was thought of as an heretical idea, that the Jews chose God. It doesn't say that anywhere in the Bible—not in the Torah, not in the Prophets, not in the Writings.

P. Meltzer: In Joshua 24:13 it says: "I gave you land on which you had not labored, cities which you had never built; you have lived in those cities and you eat the produce of vineyards and olive-groves which you did not plant." Is this how he spoke to those who were veterans of the land, or those who had come to the land recently?

Kaufman: Are these the Hebrews who came from the other side of the river?

B.G.: I didn't say that the Hebrews came from the other side of the river. They had been living in the land all the while, even before Abraham had come. The Book of Samuel speaks of Hebrews. Is the Book of Samuel invalid?

Kaufman: We are speaking of Hebrews before Abraham.

B.G.: I feel that even in the days of Abraham there were Hebrews in the land, and that Abraham was attracted to them.

Kaufman: That is the question.

B.G.: The question is about the development of the Jewish people before they were in the land. It is not possible that they were all born in Egypt. They were only the descendants of Jacob. Only 70 people went down to Egypt. They were there for 210 or 430 years. They spoke only Hebrew, though the Jews who were exiled in Babylonia were there for only 50 or 75 years, and barely knew Hebrew when they returned.

H. Ginsburg: The Germans who were in Russia for generations preserved their language, and even the Germans in Transylvania.

B.G.: They were born there? They came as a group rooted in the culture and the language, and they preserved their culture and their language. In our case, a people was formed in Egypt—in your view, the entire people.

B. Dinur: The Israelites went down to Egypt as a united family.

B.G.: We know that 70 people went down to Egypt. This isn't the Jewish people.

President Y. Ben-Zvi: Not counting the women.

B.G.: I think that the figures are exaggerated. If we have to accept everything that was written, then close to 3,000,000 people left Egypt.

H. Ginsburg: No one accepts the figure 3,000,000.

B.G.: You can't say that no one accepts it. I'll show you people who do accept it, who don't doubt one word. If they were 20 years and older, excepting the Levites, 600,000. . . .

H. Ginsburg: Even Segal admitted that the figures are exaggerated.

B.G.: Why? Because it is against his sense of logic. He can't believe that. It contradicts simple logic. Was the people born there? A grand total of only 70 people went down there.

H. Ginsburg: Do you accept that?

B.G.: That, yes.

H. Ginsburg: It is clear that Jacob, his sons, and the sons of his sons numbered 70 people. We find a family of 70 people in an Aramean inscription; the family of Jerubaal amounted to 70 people (Judges 9:5).

B.G.: The Torah records all of the children of Jacob, all of the names.

P. Meltzer: Not the women.

H. Gevaryahu: Do you accept that as history?

B.G.: If you mean that you do not accept things because they go against logic, then it is illogical to assume that all the people of Israel were born in Egypt. Let us assume that 70 people did not go down to Egypt: let us assume that 150 went down, and let us include the women as well.

H. Ginsburg: It is even possible that there were thousands.

B.G.: If thousands went down, then that changes the entire matter. You build yourself a history like that, and I build myself a history on what is written in the Bible. According to the Bible, only a few score went down to Egypt.

Kaufman: Is it possible that there were secrets in the Torah? There were things that we don't know. Everything that is written is about 70 people or more than 70 people. All of chapter 24 in Joshua is directed only to those who left Egypt.

B.G.: Since Professor Ginsburg raised the point that if something goes against logic, he doesn't accept everything word for word, I say the same thing: It is not possible that a people was formed in a foreign land over the course of several generations, and that it preserved its language there. Secondly, it is not possible that suddenly the Hebrews appeared in the days of Samuel. Samuel was also close to those times. There are Hebrews and there are Israelites.

Kaufman: We are not saying that it is another name for Israel. How many times is it necessary to say that? Do you believe that even then it was one people?

B.G.: It was one people. Only a privileged family went down to Egypt.

Kaufman: That is another question. That wasn't known to them. In the days of Samuel that was already forgotten.

B.G.: It wasn't forgotten. The name "Hebrew" existed. In Jeremiah there is an identity between Hebrew and Jew.

H. Ginsburg: He is quoting from the Torah.

B.G.: We are dealing with the matter of Shechem. There are so many things told about Shechem which are not told about Bethel. There was no sanctuary for God here. This is a new "Mt. Sinai-type" revelation, and it didn't take place at Bethel. Chapter 24 describes the revelation, and it is more plausible. The Talmud describes the revelation at Mt. Sinai. We learn this from several expressions: "Choose today yourselves whom you will worship. . . ." And Joshua says to the people: "You are witnesses against yourselves that you have chosen the Lord and will worship him." And they answered: "We are witnesses." This is also a dialogue. The brevity of the dialogue points out something. It stands out for its conciseness, as does the short answer of the people: "We are witnesses."

Kaufman: He is speaking to the entire people and they all left Egypt. That is obvious.

B.G.: That is not obvious. He conducted two assemblies and this time he was speaking with those who had left Egypt.

Kaufman: How do we interpret: "I brought you out?"

B.G.: He says that to those who went down to Egypt, not to those who remained in Canaan.

Kaufman: He is speaking to the entire people. The entire people was assembled, and he says to them: "I brought you out." For what reason did he say: "To Isaac I gave Jacob and Esau. I put Esau in possession of the hill-country of Seir, and Jacob and his sons went down to Egypt?" (Joshua 24:4). He doesn't make a distinction. Afterwards, he says to them: "I brought you out." Science can surmise what it wishes, but you can't depend on that. Who can decide?

B.G.: There is a responsible Jew who explains that differently, who heard God's voice in his heart. I read a book by an important scholar who also explains it this way: God didn't come to Jeremiah, but spoke from within him. He made several prophecies which were not kept. (*H. Gevaryahu:* Do you mean Maimonides?) Maimonides also said that, but I was referring to Professor Ezekiel Kaufman. What I am getting at is: Did God come to Abraham? He experienced a revelation; he experienced a revelation in Shechem. This is the first revelation. It came from the north, from Turkey. . . .

Kaufman: And what does it say later about Hebron?

B.G.: The first revelation took place in Shechem. There God said to him: "I will give this land to your offspring" (Genesis 12:7).

B. Dinur: "The Lord said to Abraham: Go forth from your land . . ." (12:1).

B.G.: That was before he came to the land.

B. Dinur: That is in the center of the country.

B.G.: Even if you extend the boundaries of the land to the maximum, Harran is very distant. Abraham came from Harran—no small distance—reached Shechem, and in Shechem he experienced a revelation. Why necessarily in Shechem? How is it that this revelation came to Abraham in Shechem? It is possible to say that these were just stories? I don't accept that. If there was only one such happening. . . . You say that it is in the center of the country; that is man's view today. You know that it wasn't one country. In every city there was a king. There were many kings in Canaan. There was no center to the country. According to Joshua, God's sanctuary was located there. Whoever wrote the Book of Deuteronomy told the Israelites to come to the two mountains—Gerizim and Eval—adjacent to Shechem.

Kaufman: That doesn't prove anything. Why didn't he invite the inhabitants of Shechem?

B.G.: The Bible doesn't tell everything that transpired.

Kaufman: That isn't true.

B.G.: The Bible isn't an encyclopedia.

Kaufman: The sons of Jacob killed all who lived in the city.

B.G.: Professor Ginsburg has already said that there are things which are not plausible—that two people should kill an entire city. The people suffered pain after they were circumcised. Jacob says: "I give you one portion more than to your brothers. . . ."

Kaufman: ". . . which I wrested from the Amorites with my sword and my bow" (Genesis 48:22). He didn't conquer any place with his sword and bow. He only fought in Shechem. How can this city have been the center of the Hebrews if Jacob conquered it with his sword?

B.G.: But before his death Jacob said to Joseph: "I give you one portion which I wrested from the Amorites with my sword and bow." How do you interpret these things in the days of Abimelech?

Kaufman: How does that apply here?

B.G.: In the days of Abraham, Hebrews lived there. Jacob went down to Egypt after children and grandchildren were born to him, and they lived in Egypt for 210 years. They wandered in the desert for 40 years. Joshua also fought for many years. How is it that there were still traces of the Hivites in Shechem? Another great commentator said that this was a Hebrew city. I accept the fact that this was a Jewish city. Jotham, son of Gideon says: ". . . my father who fought for you, and risked his life . . ." (Judges 9:17). Did he risk his life to save a Canaanite city? This was a Jewish city. Hebrew, Israelite.

Kaufman: An earlier period is being spoken of. At the end of the days of Joshua, Israel conquered the place and built a sanctuary.

B.G.: There is no mention in Joshua of the Jews building a sanctuary to God in Shechem. Rather Joshua wrote these things in the Torah of God and instituted laws and statutes in Shechem and put all of this in the sanctuary of the Lord.

Kaufman: At the end of Joshua's life there was a sanctuary there, but how does that pertain to this case? They built sanctuaries all over the land.

B.G.: They didn't build a sanctuary to God. There is no mention of that in Joshua.

Kaufman: They brought the ark of God to Shilo. Why didn't they bring the ark to Shechem? They brought it to Shilo when Israel had nothing. In Shechem there was a trace of the Hivites, not of the Hebrews.

B.G.: The Hivites possessed a sanctuary of the Lord? If up until Abimelech there were Hivites there, and they were uncircumcised, where did the Jews come from?

Kaufman: In the days of Joshua, Jews settled there.

B.G.: That isn't recorded.

Kaufman: It isn't necessary to tell everything.

B.G.: If it isn't necessary to tell everything, then why was it necessary to tell about the Hebrews before Abraham came to the land? Let's take what is written and let's look at it logically: How is it possible that a nation, born in its entirety on foreign soil, was Hebrew? How is it possible that, suddenly, when the narrative is describing Saul's war with the Philistines, it speaks about Hebrews? Why does it say: "Now, the Hebrews that were with the Philistines as beforetime . . . even they also turned to be with the Israelites . . ." (I Samuel 14:21), when it speaks of both the Israelites and the Hebrews who were with the Philistines?

Kaufman: What does that show, that there were Hebrews before Abraham?

H. Ginsburg: If they say: "Now the Hebrews that were with the Philistines as beforetime," then who are the Hebrews who are not Israelites, or the Hebrews who are Israelites?

B.G.: That is what I have been arguing, that they are one people. Not all the Jews live in Israel today, but they are one people. There are Jews from Asia and Africa whose mother tongue is Arabic; there are Jews from Russia whose native tongue is Yiddish. I read the newspaper of the Agudah [ultra-orthodox group] or the Neturei Karta in New York. They have a weekly in Yiddish, and it begins with a saying: "Why did the Israelites merit leaving Egypt? Because they didn't change their language." I am gratified, and am waiting for them to say that Hebrew must be spoken. But this paper uses this talmudic saying to prove that we must speak Yiddish, because there are Jews who have been speaking Yiddish for a thousand years. But, it forgets that there are Jews who have never spoken Yiddish. Nevertheless, we are one people. That is the nature of the nation in its land. In the days of Abraham there were

Hebrews in the land of Canaan, because Joseph says that he came from the land of the Hebrews. They would not have put something in Joseph's mouth that was untrue. Certain stories that were not repeated in the days of Abraham continued to survive. In the days of Moses there were Hebrews. Moses said: "God, the God of the Hebrews, sent me." Moses saw an Egyptian hitting a Hebrew, and the next day he saw two Hebrews fighting. Moses wasn't an Egyptian. He didn't go to the Egyptians in the name of the God of Israel, but in the name of the God of the Hebrews. Among the laws it is also written: "When you acquire a Hebrew slave . . ." (Exodus 21:2). Here a Jew is speaking to a Jew. Many years later, Jeremiah speaks about Hebrew slaves. He always says Jew. He considers "Jew" and "Hebrew" as identical. There is something to this.

It is impossible to claim that there were no Hebrews. We have Israel, and afterwards, they stopped saying Israel. Later on they stopped saying Hebrew and said only Jew. I have an explanation, a plausible explanation: There were Hebrews who all the while had been living in the land. One, two, or three families lived in Egypt for a short while. We have a genealogy. It is true that Professor Kaufman says that we should not rely too much on genealogies, but they can be relied on to some extent. The story of Egypt speaks of three Pharaohs; Joseph's Pharaoh, the Pharaoh after Joseph, and the Pharaoh of the exodus from Egypt. I imagine that there was one more who was not written about.

Moses is a Hebrew. All the books of the Torah are centered about this personality, and from this I learned that he is a historical personality. We know who his father is, and who the father of his father is: Moses is the son of Amram, Amram is the son of Kohath, and Kohath came to Egypt. Amram and Moses were born in Egypt. It is possible that they lived in Egypt for two or three generations. That is plausible. In two or three generations, how many could have been born? Let us say that 150 people went down to Egypt (*H. Ginsburg:* According to one Qumran text—75). I have made it a rule to understand the Bible from the Bible, but if it doesn't contradict the Bible then I am ready to accept it. Abdihaifa, one of the kings of the Tel Amarna period, writes that Lavaya (I would pronounce his name somewhat differently) gave Shechem to the Habiru. I know the discussion about the Habiru. I cannot accept this as proof that the Habiru are the Hebrews when I have additional evidence from the Bible, from Abraham, from Jacob, from Moses, from Joshua, that Shechem assumed a unique position—unlike Bethel. There, there was a sanctuary.

Kaufman: It is written that they were Hivites, Amorites.

B.G.: The Hivites came before the Amorites.

Kaufman: Why don't you accept the view of Bible scholars?

B.G.: I don't accept a view which is not based on the Bible. They say that this is a natural process. Why do the four Hivite cities make a covenant with Joshua? I wouldn't rely on that alone. They were Hivites and they became Jews. There, there was a holy place. Precisely four Hivite cities—these suddenly believed in the greatness of God and in the victory of the Israelites?

Kaufman: They turned them into slaves.

B.G.: We are using contemporary concepts; we must examine the concepts in force at that time. It wasn't a unified, tight-knit people such as we are today (even now we aren't so tight-knit, now there is a separate, assimilating group). But then, why would other tribes—Kenites, Midianites—join with Israel?

Kaufman: The Hivites were close by; they begged for mercy. The people wanted to kill them and Saul pursued them to Charmah. There was no friendship between them.

B.G.: What did David do to Saul for this?

Kaufman: There are different aspects to the matter; this matter isn't so simple. Perhaps Joshua is written from a different perspective. The Gibeonites were ancestors of the Temple servants.

B.G.: In the Bible the term servant [Heb. *eved,* also slave] doesn't have the same significance as it does in South America. Joshua was called the servant of Moses.

Kaufman: That has no connection with this matter.

H. Gevaryahu: If our honored teacher isn't too weary from the war of the Torah, can we sum up?

Kaufman: The summation is simple: There was no Hebrew people according to the Bible.

B.G.: I don't know anything about what came before Abraham. There's no argument about that.

Kaufman: Genesis tells the story before Abraham. This isn't recorded. There is no basis for this hypothesis. There isn't even a word which substantiates it. There are problems and stories about the exodus from Egypt and the formation of the Hebrew people. Why weren't the Hebrews mentioned earlier?

And as far as Shechem is concerned—it was a heathen city. The descendants of Jacob fought over it. You want to infer that in the days of Joshua there were Hivite and Gibeonite cities in which the Israelites settled. The Israelites settled in Shechem and built a sanctuary in the days of Joshua. There is textual evidence that this was an old sanctuary. This doesn't prove that there was a Hebrew people which existed before the Israelites.

B.G.: You are not arguing with me. I do not contend that there was a Hebrew people before Abraham. I only want to understand why Abraham came to the land of Canaan.

Kaufman: You claim that Abraham came to be associated with monotheism.

B.G.: I am saying that Abraham came to the land because there were monotheists in this land. Malkitzedek was a monotheist.

Kaufman: Job was a monotheist and his friends were monotheists.

B.G.: Job never existed. So it says in the Talmud.

President Y. Ben-Zvi: I just want to say something about Shechem. I have no doubt that Shechem was also a holy place; it seems to me one of the 70 holy places mentioned in the Bible. Abraham was in Shechem first and later in other places. I have this question: If it was such a holy place that according to Ben-Gurion —as he learned from the Book of Joshua—a second revelation took place there, then when this place fell into the hands of Rehoboam's great adversary—into the hands of Jeroboam—he should have kept it and made a capital city of it. But he went to Dan and to another place; he went to Penuel and to Tirzah. Tirzah is mentioned several times ("you are as beautiful as Tirzah") and Shechem isn't mentioned at all. It is mentioned twice only in connection with the sanctuary of God; and in the Septuagint it is only mentioned once.

H. Gevaryahu: According to the Septuagint the sanctuary of God was in Shilo.

President Y. Ben-Zvi: But I have the impression that the verse was completely out of place. There are the Samaritans for whom Shechem was certainly the focal point, the center. They say that the sanctuary was high up on Mt. Gerizim, on the site where they now perform the paschal sacrifice. It was not Shechem which was the focal point for them, but Mt. Gerizim, which to them is the holy mountain.

B.G.: I am not a Samaritan, I am a Hebrew. And from the time that King David conquered Jerusalem, this city is dearest to the Hebrew people. To the Samaritans, Shechem is holier, and I understand and honor this; but I do not identify with the Samaritans.

President Y. Ben-Zvi: To them Mt. Gerizim is the holy place. They do not speak of Shechem at all, which is proof that Shechem is no more than one of *the* holy places.

B.G.: Your remarks strengthen my hypothesis, because it was the Samaritans who wanted to do that. For them Mt. Gerizim is *the* holy mountain. But those who wrote the Bible were not Samaritans and, nevertheless, did not expunge what was written about Mt. Gerizim and Mt. Eval. This shows that it is possible that a great deal more was written about Shechem, but that not all has come down to us. In the days of Solomon there was already another center. He built a temple in Jerusalem in order to bind the entire nation to Jerusalem, but after his death they came to Shechem to crown Rehoboam, son of Solomon, in Shechem.

P. Meltzer: Shechem is the center of the country.

B.G.: Right. It can be explained that way. But, when the country extends to Eilat, Shechem is not its center.

President Y. Ben-Zvi: In any case, the Bible talks about all the cities. The Bible was not written to compete with the Samaritans. Competition with the Samaritans began several hundred years after that. There was no competition in the days of Nehemiah, but much later—100 or 200 years. They accepted the Torah as it is; they only changed a few passages.

B.G.: Another fact: In the days of Joshua, Shechem was designated as one of the three cities of refuge on this side of the Jordan. A city in ruins cannot be a refuge city because the whole purpose was that someone who killed unwittingly should flee there (*Kaufman:* They lived there in the time of Joshua). This is proof that it was an inhabited city, not that it was conquered. There was no war over the conquest of Shechem, because it was a Hebrew city.

Professor Kaufman's strong opposition is not directed towards me. He is in disagreement with others who argue that monotheism did not exist until the end of the days of the Second Temple; and that other nations were not monotheistic either. What happened before Abraham, I won't know until new scrolls are discovered.

Kaufman: Quod erat demonstrandum that there was no Hebrew nation before Abraham.

B.G.: If one were to gather all that is written in the Bible about all of the cities, what is written on Shechem would stand out. What went on before Abraham, I don't know. I am discussing what is written in the Bible about Shechem and about the rest of the holy cities.

President Y. Ben-Zvi: Shechem was under Israelite rule for close to 300 years, nevertheless, the city has no special significance. Jeroboam went to Tirzah.

B.G.: The main event in the life of the Hebrew people took place in Shechem. Abraham was told that the land would be given to his offspring and he came to Shechem. And so it was with Jacob. Moses issued a command to go to these two mountains. After the death of Solomon, the nation went to Shechem, and not to Jerusalem, to crown his son.

CHAPTER EIGHT

Eilat

I do not know if there is another place in Israel like Eilat which combines both the grandeur of our past with the many hopes which we have for the future. I am very sorry that I will not be able to be at the gathering tomorrow to listen to the lectures on Eilat, Ophir and Tarshish—places which interest everyone who studied the Bible in his youth. While I admit that the future of Eilat concerns me much more than its past—even though I am one of those who is very interested in the past of the Jewish people, and particularly of the Jewish nation—one can learn quite a bit about the future of Eilat from its past, and I would like to devote a few words to one basic point.

In the days of the monarchy, we had three periods during which Eilat was the only port of the Jewish people in its own land. These were the days of Solomon, Jehoshaphat and Uziah. But, it is very interesting that each one of these kings was able to make Eilat a Hebrew port—and at that time it was the only Hebrew port in Isarel—because their fathers had conquered the Negev during their respective reigns. (At that time the area wasn't called "Negev" but "Edom.") So it was in the days of King Solomon, who was the first to make this port a Hebrew port after David, his father, or more precisely his two generals, Avishai and Joab, had conquered the area. (One incident is recalled in I Chronicles 18:12; the second in Psalms 60:2.)

Presented before a meeting of The Study of Israel and Its Antiquities, Eilat, Succot 5723; October 14, 1962.

The second king to make Eilat a port was Jehoshaphat. During this period, when Edom was under the domination of Israel, it was possible to send boats from Etzion Gever, but they fell apart.

The third king to make Eilat a port—and perhaps the greatest of the kings of Judah—was Uziah. He was able (thanks to his father Amaziahu who had conquered the Negev) to establish here a large port which existed for three generations until Rezin, king of Aram, came and returned Eilat to Edom. "And he expelled the Jews from Eilat, and Edomites entered Eilat and lived there until this day." The Israeli army erased the words "until this day" from reality—not from the Bible, but from reality—13½ years ago. At the end of March, 1949, about a year after the proclamation of the State, when the War of Independence was over, Eilat became a part of Israel.

I happened upon this place several years ago, in 1934. I say: "this place," and not "Eilat," because Eilat did not exist then. The place was then called Umm Rashrash. One could not spend a night there. I found a few policemen—one or two of them Jews—at a Palestine police station. It was obvious to me that this had never been Eilat. I came here via a route which is difficult for a Jew to pass through today; I came via Transjordan—through Salt, Maan, and from there to Aqaba. Aqaba was at that time the only town on the gulf of the Red Sea. We stayed in Aqaba a few days, and from there we came here. Here we found three shacks with the address: Palestine Police.

A long time ago Eilat was on the eastern side and I am doubtful if we will get there in our day. I said then to myself: "This place which is called Umm Rashrash soon will be Eilat." I walked around and saw that the land was empty, and that this place had a future. Now, after 13 years of Eilat's existence—when there is free navigation as a result of the Sinai Campaign—it is difficult to describe its great economic future.

From there we came to Kusima, via Ras-a-Naqab, and from there to Kadesh Barnea. We saw the rock which Moses hit and from which water came forth. And from there we returned to Beersheba. Beersheba was a small Bedouin town of 3,000-4,000 people, and not one Jew lived in it.

I travelled all that great distance and saw what a fine future awaited this place, if we could first succeed in establishing ourselves along the entire gulf of the Red Sea.

That year I was appointed to the Zionist Executive for the first time. It was in the summer of 1933, and I came here during Passover, 1934. I made up my mind to meet with one man whom I knew and respected, and who I knew would understand the importance of the situation, Louis Brandeis—a member of the Supreme Court of the United States. I went to him and presented him with a memorandum on the importance of the Negev and the future of Eilat. Among other things, I wrote in this memorandum:

> In the near future, Eilat will fill a political and economic role greater than the one which it played during the biblical period. The Suez Canal, which served as a main artery of the British Empire, may easily lose its importance. England, sooner or later, will leave Egypt. The Suez Canal is too narrow for large boats, and in wartime can easily be blockaded. It is enough to sink just one boat in order to tie up the whole canal. There is no other way to India, unless one uses the Red Sea, going from Haifa via Eilat. Because of this, these two places take on additional importance. Through the Gulf of Eilat and the Red Sea we have an open water-route to the Indian Ocean, and to the largest continent in the world which contains more than half of the human race. It is important that we stake a claim on this place; that we establish a pioneering Jewish settlement here. It will not bring a profit, and it might cost $100,000.

Brandeis had no sooner finished reading the memorandum when he said: "Here's $100,000."

I said, "Mr. Justice, I didn't come to ask you for money, I came to get moral support for this matter."

"I want the privilege of being the first to help stake a claim on this important spot," replied Brandeis.

I couldn't refuse him and I took the money and passed it on to the two people who handled the acquisition of lands: Joshua Henkin and Dr. Joshua Thon, so that they might buy land here.

This was in the summer of 1935. They promised me to do whatever necessary to acquire that land, but apparently they did not attach great importance to it; no real urgency. Years passed in the negotiations with the Arab governor of Beersheba, Ahraf al-Ahraf, until the issuance of the 1939 White Paper of Nevil Chamberlain and Malcolm McDonald which shut us off from the Negev. And nothing came at that time of all my dreams.

In the meantime, the disturbances of 1947 came. The General Assembly of the United Nations decided on November 29, 1947, to partition Palestine, and to set up a Jewish state in one part, and an Arab state in the other. Almost the entire Negev area was included in the Arab portion together with Umm Rashrash, where I had said we would establish Eilat anew.

Disturbances began even before the proclamation of the State, and I proposed to the Jewish Agency Executive to send 5,000 men to the Negev desert to capture this place. There was a big debate in the Executive Council about this. They opposed it and gave two reasons.

First, it was a death trap; there wasn't one Jewish settlement there; the Negev was surrounded by three Arab nations—Egypt, Jordan and Saudi Arabia—and it would be a death trap for the men who would be sent there. Second, it would endanger the position of the Jewish community in Palestine (the Yishuv) if we were to deploy 5,000 men of the Hagana. "There are 1,200,000 Arabs in Palestine and, therefore, we cannot weaken our forces and send such a large number of men to the desert," they argued.

Nevertheless, the majority accepted my view. It was decided not to send the 5,000 that we had asked for, but only 3,000. I then approached the Security Committee of the Yishuv, and there, too, the same debate arose, namely, that here we are sending people into a death trap and weakening the defense of the Yishuv. Nevertheless, the view that men should be sent there was accepted, and men were sent.

One day an officer came to me who had greater military knowledge than all the other people in the Hagana. (He had served in the Austrian, German and English armies.) He said to me: "There are eleven points south of the Gaza-Beersheba line which we must evacuate immediately because there is no chance of holding them." I called him then by his German name, Fritz. I said to him: "Fritz, get the evacuation of these spots out of your head. Instead, prepare for me a plan showing how to defend them."

He was a disciplined soldier and said to me, "Yes sir."

After a few hours he brought me a plan for the fortification of the spots. I immediately convened the Central Committee of the Agricultural Alliance, and in short order we implemented the plan which we got from Fritz. All eleven of these settlements exist to this day.

There is no need to tell you what happened after the proclamation of the State—how we stood our ground. All of you know this, more or less. On January 7, 1949, the last battle ended, and the head of operations, later Major General Yigael Yadin—and now Professor Yigael Yadin—was sent to Rhodes to conduct negotiations with Egypt about the armistice.

After the armistice was signed, we knew that from one side of the Negev—from the western side, from Rafah to Umm Rashrash—we were secure; that Egypt had ceased hostile acts and had committed herself not to renew them. But, on the second side, the eastern side of the Transjordan—we were not secure.

I gave an order to the head of operations to send soldiers to the gulf of the Red Sea. At that time, Jordanian soldiers were still located on that side. When the Arab Legion heard that our army was approaching the Gulf of Eilat, they retreated. I do not know if this was British politics (Glubb was the commander), or if they were afraid of the Israeli army. But, as soon as they heard that the Israeli army was approaching, they retreated to Transjordan without even one shot being fired. At the end of March, I got a telegram: "Israeli flag planted on the Red Sea." This was 13 years ago.

Eilat was established. But I must add: the Eilat that was destined to be, had not yet been established. Eilat will become a great international port. I already mentioned that the Eilat of the days of Solomon, Jehoshaphat and Uziah seems most probably to have been on the other side—on the eastern side—in a place called Aqaba, opposite Etzion Gever. In Aqaba, one meter [three feet] down, water can be found, while here there is complete desolation. But, even so, I was sure when I came here for the first time, 28 years ago, that Eilat would be built here.

This is still not the Eilat which will eventually be established in this place, because without populating and settling the Negev, it is inconceivable that the Eilat of which we are in need will be established—the Eilat that the historical imperative dictates we do establish.

From time to time I travel through the Negev and proceed along the highway which leads from Beersheba to Eilat. I see the tourists who are streaming to Eilat, but although this is gratifying, I know that this is nothing to rely upon. I see the heavy vehicles of 20 to 25 tons going down to Eilat laden, and returning empty, but I know that this is not enough. Unless we succeed in settling and populating the Negev; unless we succeed in establishing ourselves in the Negev (I would prefer to say, "in the land of Edom," rather than Negev. Esau was the brother of Jacob. This name is closer to us. This name says much more to us than Negev. But, this word Negev has already taken root, and I accept this decree); unless we establish agricultural settlements here in the Negev in sufficient numbers, that will be able to supply the needed food for the biggest port city in Israel which must emerge on the gulf of the Red Sea, and that will become a city of hundreds of thousands of inhabitants, and that will receive milk, fruit and vegetables from Yotvata, Ein Gedi and other places near to Eilat; and unless we set up factories which will create finished products from raw materials which will be brought in from the countries of Asia, and unless we sell them in the markets of the biggest continent, namely Asia—unless all this is achieved, the establishment of this port city for which we yearn and which we are sure must be established in spite of everything, will not be possible.

We are the only country, with the exception of Egypt, which has direct access to the two parts of the world: to Europe and West Africa and America via the Mediterranean, and also to Asia and East Africa via the Red Sea.

We have a perfect right, in accordance with international law, and in accordance with the decision of the Security Council, to have access to the Suez Canal. Yet, Egypt has violated international law and has blocked Israeli passage of the Suez. Nevertheless, we were blessed with an "overland" Suez Canal which extends from Haifa to Eilat, and even if the Suez Canal is destroyed or closed, it will not matter to us, because we do not need it. In 1956, we received from the army one of the greatest gifts which it could have given us: free passage in the Straits of Eilat and free access via the Red Sea to East Africa and to the large Asian continent, to India, Japan and Australia.

The little things which happened here in the meantime have proven that this is not a mere dream. We have designated this year as the "Year of the First," in honor of those who founded the first Hebrew collective settlements approximately 80 years ago: Petach Tikvah Rishon Le-Zion, Zichron Yaacov, Rosh Pina, Gedera, Yesod Hamaaleh and others. Whoever has not read something of the birth pains of these collective settlements—about their difficulties even after they were founded, and of the means by which we overcame them—will not be able to understand how an agricultural settlement of Jews, Jews who for hundreds of years were thought of as people unsuited to agriculture, and who could not succeed in working the land, grew up in such a short time. Nor will they understand how we succeeded in this short time to develop the most advanced agricultural procedures on the entire Asian continent, with the exception of Japan; and how we succeeded in the fourteen years of the State to set up hundreds of new agricultural settlements—more than we set up in the 70 years before the establishment of the State.

We can certainly be confident of the realization of this dream in view of what we did accomplish in the country as a whole, as well as in the Negev—in Beersheba (which a mere fourteen years ago was a Bedouin town of 4,000 inhabitants and today has 50,000). A few "crazy" people established Kfar Yerucham, which became the town of Yerucham. Thirty families which came from Morocco seven years ago set up one of the most flourishing towns in the Negev, Dimona. Other crazy people—so they called them—set up what they did in Mitzpe Ramon.

In Sde Boker there is one crazy man (it's not me, though I consider such a title one of honor) who said that Mitzpe Ramon didn't have to serve as a source of livelihood for a mere three or four people from Sde Boker, but that a large settlement could be set up there. And he went out to look for simple Jews who had not read Herzl, Hess, Pinsker, Brenner, Berdichevsky and Karl Marx. He went to Lod and Ramla and Jerusalem and brought back immigrant families to Mitzpe Ramon—and one of the most flourishing settlements in the Negev grew up there.

Not long ago there were several crazy ones, and among them one from here, from Eilat (they call him Moshe-and-a-Half, because he was taller than all of his friends) and they established Neot Hakikar.

Anyone who is familiar with this place knows; and anyone who is not—let him go and see that this is one of those marvelous places in Israel. It has saline soil, salty water and a successful economy.

I have no doubt that this year a new city will be established here, a city which Jews came upon during the second war after the exodus from Egypt. The first war was at Refidim against the Amalakites; the second in Arad. In Arad a new city is being set up, and already hundreds of people have signed up to settle in it. In that place, which is thought of as desolate, empty and poor, deposits of phosphates and natural gas were discovered. Within the environs of Eilat, in Timna, copper mines were discovered. And all the hidden deposits have not yet been uncovered! I am not referring to the undiscovered archeological finds. I am more interested in the future than in the past. We still have not discovered all the treasures of the Negev.

I am sure that the dream of a big international port city of hundreds of thousands, and afterwards perhaps of 1,000,000 inhabitants on the Gulf of Eilat, will be achieved. It will carry the produce of the hundreds of thousands of inhabitants of the Negev —agricultural, industrial and mineral products—to the four corners of Asia. This dream, this legend, was not recorded in the Bible, but it is materializing today.

And you, the residents of Eilat, have the honor of being the first. The coming generations will be amazed at how people dared come to this desolate and forsaken place, hundreds of kilometers from Jewish settlements in the northern part of Israel, and to live in this very hot area.

This legend, like the legend of the State of Israel, will become reality, and coming generations will see the degree of latent strength inherent in this amazing people which dared to do the things that appeared to practical people, to wise men, to experts, to be impossible. This dream of a populated, settled, flourishing Negev, of a big international port city of hundreds of thousands of inhabitants will, in the not too distant future, become a living and blessed reality. And all those who were privileged to be the first, who dared to lay the first stone, to stake the first claim, will be among those who turned Israel into one of the most productive places in Asia, and perhaps even in the entire world. They will be remembered with admiration. May you be blessed.

CHAPTER NINE

Southward

Son of man: set thy face and preach toward the south, and prophesy against the forest of the field in the south.

EZEKIEL 21:2

In the south and in the Negev lay the cradle of our nation. They form both the most vulnerable points of the State, and its greatest source of hope.

When the patriarch, Abraham, was commanded to leave his land, his birthplace, and his father's house in Ur of the Chaldees, and to travel to the Promised Land, he went southward. After spending time in Egypt because of the famine, he returned to the Negev.

For a while, Abraham lived in a tent amidst the oaks of Mamre which is in Hebron, because the arid land of the south could not sustain both Lot and himself, for both of them had large flocks of sheep and herds of cattle. But after the destruction of Sodom, "Abraham returned to the land of the south, and dwelt between Kadesh and Shur; and he lived in Gerar" (Genesis 20:1).

Abraham's neighbors were Philistines who settled in the south-west. The father of our nation made a covenant with these neigh-

Delivered at Sde Boker, Elul, 5716—August, 1956.

bors after having quarreled over the well which he had dug in this land of little rain. And Abraham called the place Beersheba, "because there the two swore" (Genesis 21:31). Our Book of Books, which excels in its dramatic conciseness even when it is talking about some colossal event, notes within one ten-word verse two deeds of Abraham which, when combined, arouse considerable amazement over the marvelous grasp of our ancestors. In one breath, a prosaic and everyday occurrence is related: the planting of a tree; and then the flashing of the great idea that was basic to the original Jewish world-view: the concept of a supreme being.

These are the words: "And he planted a tamarisk in Beersheba and there he invoked the name of God, the Eternal God" (Genesis 21:33). Only the ancient Jewish genius was sufficiently wise and daring to include in such pithy simplicity two such different and multi-faceted events as these.

Isaac, the son of Abraham, also lived in the land of the Negev and here he met Rebekah on her way from Aram Naharaim (Mesopotamia); and he also became embroiled with his Philistine neighbors over the digging of wells which they had sealed. "And Isaac's servants dug in the valley and they found there a well of living water. And the shepherds of Gerar argued with the shepherds of Isaac saying: 'The water is ours.' And he named the well 'Contention,' because they contended with him. And they dug another well and quarreled over it too, and they called it 'Enmity.' And he left that place and dug still another well, and they did not quarrel over it. And he called it 'Spaciousness.' And he said: 'For now the Lord has granted us ample space, and we shall be fruitful in the land.' And he went from there to Beersheba" (Genesis 26:19-22). And again Isaac continued here in the Hebrew tradition of his father: "And he invoked the name of the Lord, and he pitched his tent there, and the servants of Isaac dug a well there" (Genesis 25:25).

The pitching of a tent, the digging of a well, and the invocation of the name of the Supreme Being—all in one breath!

It is clear why the first patriarchs of the nation went southward: This was the least settled and least populated part of the country—as in our days. The first immigrant from this land, which is known today as Iraq, and in those days was called Aram Naharaim, found in the Negev a free and deserted expanse, to a degree not found in any other part of the Promised Land. It also devolved upon him to be a pioneer in his new place of residence: to search for water and to plant trees. And there, in that desolate expanse, he reaffirmed the supreme unity of God.

Even the spies whom Moses sent to search out the land first turned to the Negev, and from there went to Hebron. The first Canaanite ruler whom the Children of Israel encountered during their trek from the south to the north was the king of Arad, who lived in the Negev.

In the Bible the distorted expression "to go down to the Negev" isn't used. In the Bible they "went up" to the Negev.

As then, the Negev today is the largest and most desolate expanse in Israel. From the time that the feet of the patriarchs trod here, many changes have come over the Negev, and the destroyed cities of the Negev are testimony to the efforts of the generations—from the days of the patriarchs until the seventh century, until the end of the Byzantine period—to settle and make this desolate land bloom. The archeological excavations which have been conducted in recent years have also revealed a large number of ancient settlements throughout the Negev. The Arab conquest in the seventh century negated the efforts of the Hebrew settlers and the Nabateans, and today there is hardly a trace left of the cities of Judah and Simeon—the two tribes which settled in the south and the Negev.

The Book of Joshua (15:21-32) lists the cities in the territory of the tribe of Judah: ". . . toward the border of Edom in the south were Kabzeel, and Eder and Jagur; and Kinah, and Dimona and Adadah; and Kades, and Hazor, and Ithnan; Ziph, and Telem, and Bealoth; and Hazor, and Hadattah, and Kerioth, and Hezron which is Hazor; Amam and Shema, and Moladah; and Hazar Gaddah, and Heshmon, and Beth Pelet, and Hazar Shual, and Beersheba, and Biziothia; Baalah, and Iim, and Ezem; and Eltolad, and Chesie, and Hormah, and Ziklag, and Madmanah, and Sansannah; and Bebaoth, and Shilhim, and Ain, and Rimmon."

The tribe of Simeon that settled within the territory of Judah also resided in several of the towns mentioned above (Beersheba, Eltolad, Moladah, Hazar Shual, Ezem, Hormah, Ziklag, Ain and Rimmon). But Simeon also retained cities in the Negev, in which the tribe of Judah did not live: Bethul, Ballah, Sheva, Beth Hamarkavoth, Hazar Sussah, Shoruhen, Ether and Ashan (the last two cities are also mentioned among the towns of Judah in the lowland—in the Shefelah—Joshua 15:42).

The Bible distinguishes between six sectors of the Negev: Negev-Arad—this is the Judean Desert east of Beersheba to the Dead Sea; the Judean Negev—the central Negev; the Yerachmieli and the Kenite Negev—both of them apparently in the southern part of the Negev; Cherethite-Negev—apparently the western Negev on the Philistine side; the Negev of Caleb—possibly a part of the Judean Negev.

The prophets were never willing to think of a Negev in neglect. The prophet Isaiah, son of Amoz, prophesied: "The wilderness and the parched land shall be glad; and the desert shall rejoice and blossom as the rose. . . . Then shall the lame man leap as a hart; and the tongue of the mute shall sing; for in the wilderness shall waters break forth, and streams in the desert. And the parched land shall become a pool, and the thirsty ground springs of water. . . . And a highway shall be there, and a way, and it shall be called 'The Way of Holiness. . . .' But the redeemed shall walk there . . ." (Isaiah 35:1-9). Here was spelled out all the basic work required for the development of the Negev; and it still holds true until this day. Jeremiah prophesied: "For so said the Lord, 'Just as I have brought all this great evil upon this nation, so will I bring all of the good that I have promised them.' And fields will be bought in this land of which you say: 'It is desolate without man or beast. . . .' Men shall buy fields for money, and register their deeds, and seal them, and call witnesses in the land of Benjamin, and in the suburbs of Jerusalem, and in the cities of Judah, and in the cities of the hill country and in the cities of the lowland, and in the cities of the Negev; for I will cause their captivity to return, said the Lord" (Jeremiah 32:42-44).

In ancient times the first mines were located in the Negev, and these resulted in the increase of trade during the reign of the first kings of Judah. In the Torah, the country was already praised as one "whose stones are iron and out of whose hills you can dig copper" (Deuteronomy 8:9). And one of the later prophets speaks of "hills of copper" (Zechariah 6:1). On the hills of Timna, located in the southern Negev, King Solomon operated copper mines. The copper was melted down in refineries which this king built in Etzion Gever, as has been revealed through the excavations of the American Jewish archeologist, Nelson Glueck.

The copper concentration in the days of Solomon was so great that it was said of it: "And Solomon left all the vessels unweighed, because they were exceedingly many" I Kings 7:10). It is also said in the chronicles of David: "And no measure was taken of the copper and the iron, so great were they" (I Chronicles 22:14). Indeed, copper deposits have been found in the Negev in our day, even though there is no doubt that several of the mines had been depleted in earlier generations.

Asphalt, which is found in the vicinity of the Dead Sea, was also well known to the ancients ("And the valley of Siddim was full of asphalt pits"—Genesis 14:10), as were methods of making use of it.

Extreme importance was attributed to the Negev of antiquity because of the gulf of the Red Sea located south of it. This was the primary access route of the Jewish people to the sea in the days of the kings of Judah. Three kings (Solomon, Jehoshaphat and Uziah) of the dynasty of David made an effort to reach the southern limit of the Negev, and to make Eilat into a Jewish port on the "tongue of the Red Sea."

The road to Eilat—through the Arava, and the city which is on the shore of the Red Sea, were at first within the domain of Edom, as is written in the Torah: "So we passed by from our brothers the children of Esau, which dwell in Seir from the way of the Arava, from Eilat and from Etzion Gever" (Deuteronomy 2:8). In the days of David, Edom was conquered: "And all of Edom were slaves to David" (II Samuel 8:14). The successor of David, King Solomon, directed all of his efforts toward increasing the wealth of his land through peaceful means and, as a result, increased the economic importance of Eilat: "And King Solomon built a navy of ships in Etzion Gever, which is beside Eloth, on the shore of the Red Sea, in the land of Edom (I Kings 9:26).

The division of the monarchy in the days of Rehoboam led to the loss of Eilat. But the fourth king after Rehoboam, Jehoshaphat, son of Asa, was wise enough to make a covenant with Ahab, king of Israel, and as a result was able to reconquer Eilat; and he again attempted to cultivate the Hebrew navigation which King Solomon had started there.

After the death of Ahab—one of the great kings of Israel—the relationship between Jehoshaphat, king of Judah, and Ahaziah, the son of Ahab, worsened. Ahaziah also wanted to participate in navigation in the Red Sea, but Jehoshaphat rejected his proposal of partnership. "Then Ahaziah, the son of Ahab, said to Jehoshaphat: 'Let my servants go with your servants in ships'—and Jehoshaphat did not consent" (I Kings 22:50). Because of this quarrel, Judah grew weak and Eilat once again was lost to the Hebrews. Again, four generations passed until Amaziah, the son of Joash, king of Judah, defeated Edom at Gai Hamelach and conquered Selah (capital of Edom), and his son Uziahu (Azariah) built up Eilat and restored it to Judah (II Kings 14:22).

Uziahu, one of the great politicians to appear in Judah, maintained friendly relations with the king of Israel, Jeroboam II. He, too, was one of the great kings of Israel. And the two expanded the boundaries of their land: Uziahu, the son of Amaziah, in the south, and Jeroboam, the son of Joash, in the north.

King Uziahu was a great commander, a successful conqueror. He transformed desolation into blooming areas. In his time, the Jewish army gained in strength; settlement and irrigation were improved; the port of Eilat was built; and side by side with political and economic prosperity, moral and spiritual culture grew amazingly.

In the days of Uziahu, the first great author-prophets arose: Amos, Hosea, Isaiah, who bequeathed to the Jewish people and to the whole of mankind laws of justice, compassion, brotherhood and equality, along with the prophecy of Jewish redemption in the end of days. It was not an accident that this king merited the chronicling of his life by the great prophet Isaiah, the son of Amoz —something which no other king in Judah or Israel achieved.

Thanks to the conquests and the development works of Uziahu in the Negev, Eilat remained in the hands of Jews for three generations: in the days of Uziahu, Jotham and Ahaz, kings of Judah.

Jotham, son of Uziahu, continued with the development works of his father, and expanded the boundaries of his land in the east: "And he built cities in the hills of Judah, and in the forests he built castles and towers. And he fought with the king of the Ammonites and he prevailed over them" (II Chronicles 27:4-5).

With the destruction of the kingdom of Israel in the days of King Hoshea, son of Elah, the kingdom of Judah also declined, and, Rezin, king of Aram returned Eilat to Edom: "And he expelled the Jews from Eloth, and Edomites came to Eilat and they lived there until this day" (II Kings 16:6).

In our times, in March 1949, the Israeli army entered Eilat and returned it to Israel, and in place of the traditional boundary, from Dan to Beersheba, the boundary of Israel stretched some 250 kilometers [185 miles] south from Beersheba; thus, for the first time in our history a Jewish state borders on two seas: the Red Sea in the south and the Mediterranean Sea in the west. From the point of view of world transport, the Negev is similar to the Suez Canal: it serves as a passageway between the two areas of world navigation—to the Atlantic Ocean via the Mediterranean, and to the Indian and Pacific Oceans via the Red Sea.

The Negev has been blessed with one additional "sea" which does not have a great deal of value transportation-wise, because it is a closed, internal sea—and this is the Dead Sea. But this sea is unique in the world. It is sunk in the deepest depression on the earth—some 400 meters [1,350 feet] below sea level, and it is richer in bromides and minerals than any other sea in the world. It has some two billion tons of potash, over 20 billion tons of magnesium chloride, over 10 billion tons of sodium chloride, some six billion tons of calcium chloride, close to a billion tons of magnesium bromide, and more. And it is abundant in health spas which have, as yet, not been properly investigated. There is little doubt that great potential for health and recuperation are stored within them.

Since the time when the expanses of the Negev were redeemed by the Israeli army, the Negev has been reinvestigated and re-surveyed—though not sufficiently; and that which is obscure and concealed is still far greater than the revealed and the known. It turned out that copper and iron are not the only ores in the Negev. Many sources of phosphate were discovered which are, in part, extractable, and have yielded the precious material for atomic research: uranium sources of gypsum, marble and granite; deposits of sand for high quality glass, bituminous rock, kaolin, and more were found. But, still, one cannot say that all the treasures stored in the bosom of the great desert, and in the bowels of its earth, have been discovered. The animal and plant life in the Negev still demand detailed investigation, as does the climate, the quantity of dew, the quality of the soil, and the geological structure.

The marvelous advances of natural science in the last 300 years have, until now, been concentrated, in the main, in the northern countries—mostly Europe and America. In these countries there is no shortage of water and sources of energy such as carbon, oil, gas, waterfalls. The rains in these countries fall in abundance almost all months of the year. Carbon and iron resources paved the way for their great Industrial Revolution which took place in the nineteenth century.

As one of the few cultured peoples which has returned to its ancient homeland in the subtropical and, for the most part, arid land, it is incumbent upon us to concentrate on such surveys as had never been vital to the nations of the North. It is in the south that the ability of Jewish science and research will be tested. But, research alone will not be enough.

The triangular Negev is wedged between two threatening nations: Egypt and Ammon (Jordan). Across the southwest border of the Negev stretches the Sinai desert; and across the eastern border, the Arabian desert. The Arabs have succeeded in turning quite a few flourishing and populated lands into deserts. Desolation in Arab lands doesn't interfere with their existence or independence. But, the little State of Israel will not be able to tolerate a desert in its midst for long—a desert which occupies more than one half its area. If the State doesn't "liquidate" the desert, the desert is liable to liquidate the State. The narrow strip between Jaffa and Haifa, 15-20 kilometers [9-15 miles] wide, which contains most of the Jewish population, will not flourish for long without strong settlements throughout the expanses of the south and the Negev.

The indomitable spirit of the nation's pioneers in the course of the last three generations, and their creative initiative and hard work, have changed the face of the land while it was still under foreign rule. Those who paved the way for the establishment of the State made sand and rock bloom; they dried swamps, dug wells and planted vineyards and citrus groves; they afforested mountains, built villages and cities; and developed industry and craftsmanship. But their work was limited to the northern half of the western part of the country—and primarily to the coastal plains and the two valleys: the Jordan valley, whose land is generally fertile and whose rains fall in sufficient amounts, and to the Jezreel valley. The southern half of the country remained desolate for hundreds of years, since the Arab conquest. Both the Turks and the British did not try to make this desolation bloom—they had no need to. And the curse of Jeremiah hovered over the Negev: "The cities of the Negev were closed—and there is no opening them" (Jeremiah 13:19). From 1939, beginning with the publication of the White Paper of Chamberlain's government, the Jews were prohibited from setting foot in the Negev and in most of the south.

Foreign rule and alien ownership of the land limited our area of settlement. There were far-sighted people among the settlers of the Negev and the redeemers of the land before the establishment of the State, and there was a great deal of planning behind their attempts to acquire land under difficult conditions established by Ottoman and Mandate rule.

The noted Jewish philanthropist—that marvelous Jew who emerged from assimilated Jewry in France to favor the soil of our homeland, and to dedicate his entire life and a large part of his fortune to agricultural settlement, stands out notably in this regard. But, the foreign regime, for the most part hostile, and the restrictive laws stood as barriers to the nation's plans. And the dream of settlement in Transjordan which Rothschild hoped to realize, vanished with the new political reality—and the entire southern part of the country fell outside the area of renewed Jewish settlement. Thus, the entire Jewish settlement was limited to the narrow strip between Jaffa and Haifa, with a few offshoots to the south and the north.

The War of Independence put the entire territory of the State at our disposal—from Metulla in the north to Eilat in the south. The areas which the United Nations General Assembly proscribed on November 29, 1947 were enlarged first by the Israeli army, and was aided by the flight of the Arab residents which began in December of 1947—apparently in keeping with a plan which the mufti of Jerusalem had devised several years earlier. With the cessation of the fighting in the beginning of January, 1949, the boundaries were again enlarged without resorting to war; first, through the entry of Isareli army units into the southern part of the Negev and Eilat, after the armistice was signed with Egypt; and afterwards, in political negotiation with the rulers of Transjordan, when it was agreed to transfer to Israel the entire strip through which the train route from Lod to Jerusalem passes, as well as Nahal Eron (the road from Hadera to Afula) and land to the east of this road.

All the land of the south, from the west of the armistice line in the Hebron area, and all the Negev from Beersheba to Eilat, was redeemed as the property of the young State. The legal and political obstacles to the settlement of most of the State's land were removed and, at present, most of the territory of new Israel is in the south and in the Negev. The only obstacle which still remains to our expansion and to populating the south derives from the hostile environment: the desolation; and the paucity of rainfall. The pioneering ability, the indomitable spirit, the creative, conquering initiative of Jewish youth, and the scientific and technological ability of the scientific and research community in Israel will have to overcome the problems of this environment, and to open the south and the Negev to a mass migration based on farming, agriculture, handicrafts, mining, industry, fishing, navigation —and based on exploitation of the new opportunities made possible by the discoveries of science and the perfection of technology in our day. The law of survival—economic and from a security point of view—demands that the State direct its attention to the south: that it direct the country's water and rainfall southward; that it orient pioneering youth and new immigrant settlers southward; that it direct development budgets southward; that it move southward several of the scientific and research institutes which deal with the geography of Israel, its soil structure, vegetation, climate, and the mysteries of its soil; that it direct the thinking of Israeli scientists and researchers towards an examination of the open and hidden forces with whose help we will be able to cause the land of the south and the Negev to bloom and flourish.

Without populating the south and the Negev, the security of

the State is not viable, and we will not achieve economic independence. Such a feat will not be possible without effecting a change in the laws of nature, and this change is not beyond the potential of science in our day, nor beyond the reach of the pioneering initiative of our youth. With the aid of science and the pioneering spirit, we will be able to achieve this miracle.

Our entire enterprise here in Israel is one of the wonders of history. Not a supernatural wonder; for in miracles of this type, if they exist, there is nothing miraculous. If it is possible to create the planet Earth, and to send it rotating endlessly around the sun, then it is possible to command it, or the sun, to stand still. Man's genius has not yet reached—and it is doubtful if it will ever reach—an understanding of the secret of creation and an unraveling of the mystery of existence that constantly renews itself. The more our intelligence and experience tell us about the world around us, the more does the mystery deepen; and the unraveling of the secret of the universe moves farther away from us. However, man's experience is constantly being enriched, his ability increases, his control over his environment and himself grows; and the instruments which he creates to increase his ability to understand nature and to dominate it, to some extent, are constantly being perfected; and they widen man's horizons without surcease. The amazing instrument, the one with the most ability and power to help man subdue nature, is man himself. The ability latent in this marvelous being does not have a parallel among all the most complicated and marvelous instruments and machinery which man has created. Only because of the intuitive understanding of the latent ability of man and his capacity and will to make use of this ability (the capacity which we call "pioneering spirit") has our undertaking in Israel, which apparently went completely contrary to all the accepted laws and concepts at the time of the initiation of the undertaking, been able to succeed. Who would have believed, decades ago, that Jews, urbanized for hundreds of years, weaned from work and land for centuries, would become a nation of builders? Who ever thought that a nation scattered and separated for more than 2,000 years would reassemble in its ancient homeland, once conquered by foreigners, and would reestablish its national sovereignty? Who would have thought that a dead language, embalmed in prayerbooks and poems, would again be the everyday language of a people of many languages? Or, who would have dreamed that a people oppressed, humiliated and helpless for generations would suddenly reveal a spirit of bravery, and would destroy an army 40 times its own size?

The indomitable and naive faith of the early pioneers of 80 years ago, and the strength of their creative initiative when they founded new Hebrew villages in the ancient, captive homeland; the pioneering momentum which grew from generation to generation, over the last three generations, until it resulted in the revival of the Hebrew State and in the glorious victories of the War of Independence; the daring deeds in settling tens of thousands of immigrants from backward countries in the desolate expanses of the south, people who for thousands of years did not know the fragrance of the field; the cultural, social and economic transformations which took place in the lives of hundreds of thousands of immigrants within two or three generations—changes which have no equal either in the experience of our people since our very inception, or in the experience of any other people in our time—all these are the result of the great human miracle which happened in our recent history, and which we call "pioneering spirit." This is no more than man's deep faith in his power and capability, and in his burning spiritual need to alter the course of nature and the course of his own life for the sake of a vision of redemption.

Through the power of the pioneering miracle, we were able to confront the lifestyles we developed during the exile and to uproot them; we faced political difficulties and were able to overcome them; we faced the enmity of our neighbors and their hatred and we were able to overcome them; we faced the impoverishment of the country and its spoliation—and we rebuilt its desolation.

This time, precisely during the period of our sovereignty and our independent control over all areas of the State and its treasures, we were confronted by the greatest of all difficulties: the curse of nature which decreed sterility and desolation for most of the land of the State since the six days of creation. The State, the people, the youth and scientists were confronted this time by the supreme test of our history, since achieving national independence and regeneration. Only through the united effort of a working state; of a willing and brave people; of a strong-spirited youth girded with creative courage; of scientists free from all routine and capable of delving into the special problems of this land—only through an all-out attack by all the creative powers in Israel will we be fit for the great and decisive mission of developing the south and the Negev.

Water and power are the two things whose shortage is most felt in our country—even in the north; and in the south they are almost completely absent. The developed countries of Europe were endowed with the blessing of the heavens above: with water which falls throughout the year. The vast majority of them have also been endowed "with the blessing of the deep that couches below," with power resources hidden in the bosom of the earth.

However, it is due only to a deep-rooted, ingrained feeling that stems from our past that makes us imagine that the Negev expanse must remain desolate forever. Actually, it contains sources of power and water in abundance that were not used until now because we did not know the secret of their use. However, if we did not know it until yesterday, this does not imply that we will not know it tomorrow.

The subterranean waters, wells, rivers and streams in our country are very limited. And even these, we are not exploiting fully. The waters of the Jordan flow down to the Dead Sea, and the waters of the Yarkon spill into the Mediterranean. Much of the waters of the Sea of Galilee is evaporating; and the greater part of the abundant rainfall in the north, and the sparse rainfall in the south, spills uselessly into the Mediterranean or the Dead Sea without dispensing their full blessing to the parched soil. We are even wasting quite a bit of the water already at our disposal—especially in the northern part of the country that is blessed with rain or with the waters of the Jordan or the Sea of Galilee.

We have still not learned to collect all of the rain so that it does not flow uselessly into the sea, and to exploit the water at our disposal to maximum advantage and with maximum economy.

But, the solution to supplying water to the greater south and the Negev is in the distillation of sea water from salt water. The big mission which Hebrew science must accomplish is to discover a cheap and practical process for desalinating sea water so that it will be possible to irrigate the arid land of the Negev.

In the United States of America, rich in mighty rivers and huge lakes, research and experimentation has been going on for years to desalinate sea water so as to be able to irrigate the deserts in the western part of America. We are much more in need of a new, reliable source of irrigation-water than the United States, and it will not be beyond the reach of our scientists and technologists if they will dedicate their finest research to this end, and receive for it all possible aid from the government so that they may find a cheap process of desalinating sea water.

Irrigation of the desolate areas with desalinated sea water may appear to many today as a dream, but more than any other country Israel must be wary of considering as visionary those "dreams" which are likely, through the power of vision, science and pioneering ability, to alter the order of creation. Everything which exists in Israel is the result of dreams which materialized through vision, science and pioneering ability.

A cheap process of desalinating sea water is not just a vital Israeli need, but also a world need. Hundreds of millions of inhabitants of the big continent on which we live suffer from a shortage of food, but to date only a small part of the available land has been cultivated. In Asia, Africa, and also in America, there are vast wildernesses which, if water is found for their irrigation, are liable to double and triple the earth's produce, and will be able to supply food in abundance to tens of millions of people. If Israel succeeds in desalinating sea water, she will bring a great blessing to all humanity; and the matter is not beyond the reach of Israeli science.

Science stems from two sources: the creative ability of the human mind, and the essential needs of society. The human mind applies itself fully only under the pressure of the needs of society. Without this pressure man diverts his energy to other matters. The two factors which can cause hydrology to advance are found in Israel to no less a degree than in any other country. The Jewish mind is not inferior to that of any other nation. The need for additional sources of water is not just essential, but critical for Israel. And we must not be frightened by the novelty and difficulty implied in the idea of making use of sea water for irrigation.

Now to the problem of power—its importance is greater than that of water. Making use of water, in all of its forms, requires power. As the culture of man is enriched and his needs increase, the need for power and energy increases. Primitive man needed up to 3,000 calories, which he received through foods prepared for him by nature. After man learned to use fire and to domesticate certain animals, he needed 10,000 calories per day in order to produce food for his animals as well. The perfection of technology and the invention of machines increased the daily consumption of energy. If we take into account the machines, the airplanes, the trains, and the lighting devices, and we divide them per capita, we find that in the United States, on an average, each man needs 160,000 calories of energy per day.

If we want to maintain a high cultural level in Israel—and we must strive for a cultural level in Israel that will not be lower than that of any other country—then we must see to it that sources of power are created which will supply us with all the energy needed for man, animals and organic matter; for modes of transportation by land, sea and air; for lighting and communication devices and for machinery for all branches of the economy; and for all educational and cultural needs.

Our scientists are asked not only to continue the study and research in which they were engaged in the diaspora, but also to invest their scientific and research energy into those very problems which the "nature" of our country and the demands of our existence have placed before us—especially since the reestablishment of Israel.

We are on the eve of one of the greatest revolutions in the history of man, and of his control over nature; we are on the threshold of the era of atomic energy. Even though the principal sources of power in the most developed nations are still coal, oil and electricity there is no doubt that in a few, short years man will harness the marvelous and mighty power stored up in the still invisible atom, for the needs of industry, agriculture and communications just as he is already exhibiting it for war use. Although our country is, in the main, poor in natural resources, and not everything stored in the bosom of our earth is yet known to us sufficiently, the use of atomic energy is dependent, first and foremost, on the ability of that biological-psychological instrument known as the human brain. And this instrument, which we have at our disposal, is in no way inferior in its capabilities to that which is at the disposal of the richest and most developed nations.

A short time after the end of the War of Independence a scientific council was set up in Israel, and a board of atomic energy was established which has dealt with this matter with considerable ability and success. This board came to an agreement with the French and British governments on the production of heavy water, which is one of the materials needed for the development of atomic energy. The chief producers of heavy water at present are Norway and the United States, both of whom have inexpensive electricity. Our young scientists have already discovered by themselves the secret of the production of heavy water, although we are still far from producing it in substantial quantities.

The main substances needed to produce atomic energy are uranium and thorium. Although uranium is not found in Israel in as large quantities (as far as we know today) as it is in the Belgian Congo or several other countries which are rich in uranium, this substance is not completely absent in Israel; and we are able to build atomic reactors, because we have the two requirements: uranium and heavy water. Their extraction and production will require great effort, and we will not reach our goal quickly. However it is incumbent upon us to recruit manpower—to educate physicists and technologists of the required quality, and in adequate numbers, to make use of the available raw materials—so that within the next decade we shall accomplish the production of atomic energy. This will open new horizons for our economic development, in general, and the blossoming of the Negev, in particular.

With Albert Einstein's revolutionary discovery of the identity of matter and energy, and with a grasp of the complex structure of the atom, inestimable resources of power have been put into the hands of man. This marvelous conquest will not remain the possession of the superpowers alone, and the growth in cooperation between scientists of the world of atomic research is a good sign for our times. What Einstein, Oppenheimer and Teller—all three Jews—did for the United States is not beyond the reach of the scientists of Israel to accomplish for their people.

Atomic energy is not the only source of power which will immeasurably increase the ability of man. The mightiest source of power in our world, the source which feeds all animal and plant life, and of which only a small amount has been exploited by man until now, is the sun. It showers upon us daily astronomical quantities of energy which go to waste. Experts have computed and found that the solar energy which reaches the earth during a three-day period, is equal to the quantity of energy which can be produced through the combustion of all the coal, oil, natural gas, peat resources and all the forests on the face of the earth.

It is the Negev, in particular, which is the area of the country most blessed with this energy, because the cloudy and rainy days are so few here, and on almost all days of the year the sun shines on us with its full potency. What has been exploited from this abundance of energy until now is just a drop in the ocean. It has been utilized by the plants which we grow, and whose secret of growth is nothing more than the absorption of solar energy according to a process known as photosynthesis. The Negev today profits least from the absorption of the rays of the sun by its plant-life. But, it is possible to turn this energy into effective dynamic electrical energy; for even after all the sources of uranium and thorium on the face of the earth are exhausted, solar energy will continue to flow to us almost without end. It is incumbent upon scientists and technologists to discover efficient instruments which will absorb—if only in the tiniest amount—this mighty energy, and to channel it into the great needs of our multi-faceted economy. It is not impossible that through solar energy we shall be able to desalinate sea water and prepare it for the irrigation of the vast aridity of the south and the Negev.

Use of atomic power and solar energy, production of electrical power from the winds and the waves, exploitation of the many natural resources in the Dead Sea (one of the richest sources of minerals on the face of the earth which intercepts the flow that would proceed wastefully into the seas, and dams them up for drinking and irrigation needs), and all the rest of the development projects so vital to us (or expected of us): discovery of metal ore mines, granite, marble and the like—all these are matters of concern for physicists, geologists, chemists and engineers.

However, the energy which is stored in nature, in the bosom of the earth, in waterfalls, in the atom and in the sun will not be supplied to us if we are unable to make use of the most precious energy: the moral-spiritual energy which is stored in man, in the recesses of his divine being, whose mystery and meaning are unknown, but whose existence, strength, might, actions and influence are recognized by all. This marvelous energy has been revealed to us, both in its moral and intellectual potential, as it has not been revealed, perhaps, to any other human group. It is only through the power of this energy that the miracle of our existence in exile for 2,000 years was made possible and the miracle of our revival in our time has taken place. Accomplishments, unparalleled in human history, have been achieved in this small country by our forefathers in antiquity and by our youth in our time.

Not nature—which has not changed for millions of years—but the human spirit which is boundless, changed the face of the earth. Through the power of his thought and his spiritual strength, man overcomes nature, reveals its secrets, and employs it for his material and spiritual needs. There is no mightier example in human history of the power of the spirit to stand up to difficulties, obstacles, suffering and danger than that which has been demonstrated through the Jewish people from its beginning, in the days of the patriarchs, to our times.

Eight years ago, a new chapter was opened in the history of this marvelous people. Reestablished Jewish sovereignty set the Jewish people face to face with its own fate, without obstruction. Immediately, upon the declaration of its independence, the young state was forced to stand up to the attack of five neighbors, and it overcame them. Israel cannot exist without armed might as long as mankind is divided into opposing camps and man bears arms against his neighbor. But, the profound truth about the superiority of the spiritual dimension—whose outstanding proof is the long and tried experience of the Jewish people—is still valid; and upon this truth is based the faith of the Jewish people in its future. The supreme test of Israel in our generation is not in the struggle with hostile forces from without, but in overcoming the desolation of its country along the vast stretches of the south and the Negev through the power of science and the pioneering spirit.

CHAPTER TEN

Chapters 23-24 from the Book of Joshua

PART ONE

Those who study the Book of Joshua come across several contradictions. Especially puzzling are the last two chapters of the book: 23 and 24. In both of them Joshua assembles the heads of the nation and calls upon them to worship God. Yet, the content, structure and importance of the two chapters are essentially different.

In chapter 23, the place of the meeting is not given; just its time: when Joshua was "old, getting on in years." In chapter 24, the time is not fixed, but rather the place: Shechem. As will become clear later, great importance is implicit in this fact. In chapter 23, Joshua calls on the elders of the people—on its leaders, on its judges, and on its officers; and there is no mention of tribes. In chapter 24, he assembles all of the tribes of Israel. Only Joshua speaks in chapter 23. In chapter 24, there is a dialogue; Joshua speaks and the people respond; Joshua argues and the nation listens. And then Joshua assembles the tribes of Israel and calls to the elders, the leaders, the judges and the officers "stand before God." Nothing of this kind occurs anywhere else in Joshua. It can be felt, immediately, that this is a unique festive scene.

Delivered at the President's House, February 24, 1963.

In chapter 23, Joshua says to the people: "You have seen all that the Lord your God has done to these people for your sake," and he doesn't tell them anything. Rather, he asks them "to observe and perform all that is written in the Torah of Moses." Joshua starts his remarks in chapter 24 with a lecture on the ancient history of the nation. He starts with the days of Abraham, Isaac and Jacob and tells about the mission of Moses and Aaron; about the exodus from Egypt; about the parting of the Red Sea; about the trek of the Israelites through the desert; about their entry into the land of the Amorites on the other side of the Jordan; about the war of Balak, son of Zippor (unlike what is written in the Torah: "Moab was alarmed because the people were so numerous" —Numbers 22:3); about the battles with Jericho (unlike what is written in Joshua 6 that the walls fell down with the blasts of the shofars, as if Jericho was conquered without any battles); about the sending of the hornet (which isn't mentioned once in the Book of Joshua in connection with any of the wars described in it), as though it were that which was the cause of the expulsion of the two Amorite kings. And he [Joshua] said: "not with your sword, and not with your bow" (contrary to what the Torah says in Numbers 21:24 and 21:35 where it states, explicitly, that the Israelites "defeated them by the sword").

When we compare the words of Joshua in the two chapters, from the point of view of their religious demands, they leave us with the impression that in chapter 23 he is speaking to those loyal to God and to those who are observing his covenant; and in chapter 24, to those turning toward other gods and who were not the least bit aware of God's covenant. In chapter 23 Joshua is speaking to an audience which has clung to God all the while ("You must hold fast to the Lord your God as you have done down to this day"—23:8), and which knows what is written in Moses' Torah. He even mentions the Torah of Moses and asks the people not to deviate from it to the left or the right (23:6); not to go the way of other peoples, and not to transgress God's covenant under the influence of their neighbors—an indication that they already knew of the covenant existing between God and Israel.

But in chapter 24, Joshua speaks to the nation as if it had not yet professed a belief in God and had never made a covenant with him, as if it were a people among whom foreign gods were still to be found. Joshua places before them a choice: If it is wrong in their eyes to worship the Lord, then let them choose for themselves the gods which their ancestors worshipped on the other side of the river; or let them choose the gods of the Amorites in whose land they were now living.

The most puzzling thing about the history which Joshua tells the assembled tribes in chapter 24, is that no mention or hint is made of the revelation at Mt. Sinai or the Torah of Moses, though in the earlier chapters of the Book of Joshua, the Torah of Moses or "the Torah which Moses commanded" is mentioned more than once.

In Joshua 1, God says to Joshua: "Only be strong and resolute; observe diligently all of the Torah which My servant Moses has given you. You must not turn from it to the right or to the left if you are to prosper wherever you go. This book of the Torah must ever be on your lips; you must keep it in mind day and night so that you may diligently observe all that is written in it" (Joshua 1:7-8).

After the victory at Ai, Joshua went to Mt. Eval and built an altar there "following the commands given to the Israelites by Moses, the servant of the Lord, as is described in the Torah of Moses: an altar of blocks of undressed stone on which no tool of iron had been used" (8:30-31); "he engraved on the blocks of stone a copy of the law of Moses in the presence of the Israelites" (8:32). Later, it is told that the Israelites stood "half of them facing Mt. Gerizim, half facing Mt. Eval in fulfillment of the command of Moses, the servant of the Lord, to bless the people of Israel first" (8:33), after which he recited the whole of the Blessing and the Curse as they are written in the Torah. "There was not a single word of all that Moses had commanded which he did not read aloud before the whole congregation of Israel" (8:35).

In chapter 22:2 it says that Joshua called to the tribes of Reuben and Gad and half of Manasseh, and said to them: "You have observed all the commands of Moses the servant of the Lord, and you have obeyed me in all the commands that I have laid upon you." And he warns them: "But take good care to keep the commands and the Torah which Moses the servant of God gave you: to love the Lord your God, to conform to his ways . . ." (22:5). And in chapter 23, as well, Joshua tells all of Israel: "Be resolute, therefore, and perform everything written in the Torah of Moses, without deviating from it right or left" (23:6).

We note the recurrent emphasis, warranted and unwarranted, of the phrases "the Torah of Moses servant of the Lord," and "the command of Moses, servant of the Lord."

Joshua also recalls the mission of Moses and Aaron to Pharaoh in chapter 23, but the Torah of Moses is not mentioned once in chapter 24.

Since he seems to be speaking in these two chapters to two peoples who did not share a common religion, Joshua warns those assembled in chapter 23 "that they should not transgress the covenant which the Lord their God prescribed for them." From here it can be inferred that the covenant had long been in effect, and was familiar to the listeners. However, in chapter 24, he does not mention "the covenant which the Lord prescribed for them," but says: "On that day he made a covenant with the people and drew up a statute and an ordinance for them in Shechem," as if until that time there had not been a covenant with this people. And there is a dialogue here between Joshua and the people, which I will deal with a bit later.

Micah Joseph, son of Garion (Berdichevsky), concludes from this—I quote from his book, *Sinai and Gerizim,* which has just appeared in Hebrew—"that Joshua's covenant, which is thought of as the last of the covenants of Moses [the first at Sinai or Horeb, the second in the wilderness of Moab, and the third in Shechem] is in truth the very beginning, and no other covenant came before it." To this end, he removes chapter 27 from the Book of Deuteronomy (in which it says, in verses 12-14: "After you have crossed the Jordan, the following shall stand on Mt. Gerizim when the blessing for the people is spoken. . . . And for the curse, the following shall stand on Mt. Eval. . . . The Levites shall then proclaim in a loud voice to all the men of Israel . . ."), and transfers it to the Book of Joshua before verse 8:30—where it tells that they came to Mt. Gerizim. And he adds: "Only at a later date, when they thought that it was not to the credit of Moses that the decisive act in the establishment of the faith of Israel be performed by Joshua alone, did they remove the chapter from the Book of Joshua, and transfer it back to the Book of Deuteronomy, changing the past tense to the present tense, giving the impression that the covenant came at Moses' initiative." Thus Berdichevsky.

These statements of this renowned author do not make sense to me. The image of Moses, and the giving of the Torah by him in the Sinai desert (in Horeb) were so deeply engraved in the memory and soul of the people that it is inconceivable that this event never occurred, and that chapters 19-20 in Exodus, as well as the Ten Commandments, are mere legend.

Almost all of the books of the Bible—including those not in the Torah: the Early Prophets, Isaiah, Jeremiah, Micah, Psalms, First and Second Chronicles, Ezra, Nehemiah, Malachi and Daniel

—mention the name of Moses as well as his deeds. Without doubt, in the course of time many legends were woven around the figure of Moses, just as many legends were woven around the exodus from Egypt. (Without a doubt there are several among us who are not helped very much by the legends surrounding the exodus from Egypt. I beg their pardon.) But, the authenticity of the exodus from Egypt should not be doubted, and doubt should not be cast on the giving of the Torah by Moses in the desert.

Ahad Haam's essay on Moses is well known. Ahad Haam negates completely the value of the historical truth (in his words "the archeological truth") regarding the existence and accomplishments of Moses. According to Ahad Haam it does not matter at all if Moses actually existed or if he were no more than "a figment of the imagination," who was later converted into an educative force among the people. In his article on Moses, Ahad Haam establishes (*At the Crossroads—Al Parashat Derachim*—Vol. 3, pp. 209-211) that: "The matter is clear that the true historical heroes—those who were moving forces in the lives of humanity for generations—are in no case tangible beings who existed in reality at any time. For there is no case of an historical hero whose spiritual image was not created in the imagination of the people in a manner completely different from what it was in reality; and this fanciful creation, which the people created according to its needs and the inclination of its spirit, is the true hero whose influence sometimes extends over thousands of years, and not the true person who lived in real life for only a short time, and whom the people did not see at all as he was. . . . Even if you were to succeed in showing clearly that Moses the man never existed, or that he was not as described, this would not detract one bit from the historical reality of Moses as an ideal, who not only led us in the Sinai desert for 40 years, but for thousands of years in all the deserts through which we walked from Egypt to here." These are the words of Ahad Haam.

Ahad Haam's error, in my humble opinion, is in saying that "a figment of the imagination" can be turned into an educative force for the nation. Only a living person who is very active, blessed with excellence, magnanimous, and of great influence and inspiration is deeply etched into the soul of a people. Moses isn't a fictitious creation, and the revelation at Mt. Sinai—though not necessarily true in all its detail—is a fact (although our Rabbis described the revelation at Mt. Sinai in a different manner than it is described in the Book of Exodus, chapters 19-20).

In the story of Jethro (Exodus 19-20) there is a description of the revelation at Mt. Sinai and the giving of the Ten Commandments: "Now, Mt. Sinai was all in smoke, for the Lord had come down upon it in fire; the smoke rose like the smoke of a kiln, and the whole mountain trembled violently. The blast of the horn grew louder and louder [19:18-19]. . . . All the people witnessed the thunder and lightning, the blast of the horn . . ." [20:15]; yet, Rabbi Abihu says in the name of Rabbi Jochanan: "When the Almighty gave the Torah, not a bird chirped, not a fowl flew, not an ox lowed, cherubs did not fly, seraphim did not say 'Holy!' the sea did not rock, living creatures did not speak. The world was silent, and a voice came forth: 'I am the Lord your God.'" There is no doubt that Rabbi Jochanan's description is much more enchanting than the description in the Book of Exodus. But the details of ornamentation placed about a great event are of no consequence.

Had Joshua and not Moses performed the decisive action in the establishment of the faith of Israel—that is to say, had he made a covenant—it is inconceivable that coming generations would distort this central and decisive fact in the history of the nation and would ascribe the making of a covenant not to the man who did it, but to "a figment of the imagination."

To study chapter 24 of Joshua thoroughly and to compare it to chapter 23 which came before it in no way requires the far reaching hypothesis of M. Y. Berdichevsky.

Professor Kaufman, in his commentary on the Book of Joshua, established without any substantive proof that chapter 24 in Joshua is a later addition. He says (and I quote): "The Book of Joshua acts as a special prophetic and historic coagulant; it begins with chapter 1 and concludes with chapter 23 (chapter 24 is an addendum)." Without a doubt, there are verses in chapter 24 that are later additions, just as there are such verses in chapter 23 and in the other chapters of Joshua. It is clear, for example, that verses 17-18 in chapter 24 were inserted later, with the exception of the words: "The people answered . . ." at the beginning of verse 16, and the words: "We too will worship the Lord; he is our God" at the end of verse 18. According to my conception, these are historical truths. Because, logically, it is safe to assume that if after Joshua's words in verses 14-15 in the earlier version it says: "The people answered: "We, too, will worship the Lord; He is our God"; and if afterward comes Joshua's warning, in verses 19-20, and again the nation replies (and the people's answers were always brief): "No! We will worship the Lord" (24:22)—then it can be assumed that verses 11-13 are a later addition. Indeed, this raises problems, and I will deal with them later on. I will not read all the verses here.

In the earlier chapters of Joshua we find contradictions in its central theme—the matter of the conquest of the land. In the Book of Joshua we read several times that the entire land was conquered "just as the Lord had said to Moses"; and it says in chapter 10: "So Joshua defeated the population of the whole region—the hill-country, the Negev, the Shephelah, the watershed—and all their kings. He left no survivor, destroying everything that drew breath, as the Lord God of Israel had commanded. Joshua defeated them from Kadesh Barnea to Gaza, over the whole land of Goshen and as far as Gibeon. All these kings he conquered at the same time, and their countries with them, for the Lord God of Israel fought on the side of Israel" (10:40-42). Later, it says in chapter 11: "And so Joshua took the whole country, the hill-country, all of the Negev, all of the land of Goshen, the Shephelah, the Arava, and the Israelite hill-country with the adjoining lowlands [11:16]. . . . Thus Joshua took the whole country, fulfilling all the commands that the Lord had laid on Moses; he assigned it as Israel's patrimony, allotting to each tribe its share; and the land was at peace" (11:21). And again in chapter 21: "Thus the Lord gave Israel all the land which he had sworn to give to their forefathers; they occupied it and settled in it. The Lord gave them security on every side as he had sworn to their forefathers. Of all their enemies, not a man could withstand them; the Lord delivered all of their enemies into their hands. Not a word of the Lord's promises to the house of Israel went unfulfilled; all came true" (21:43-45). And also in chapter 23: "And now I am going the way of all mankind. You know in your hearts that none of the good things that the Lord your God has promised you has failed to come true. Everything has come true; not a word has failed to come true" (23:14).

But in chapter 13 we read: "By this time Joshua had become very old, and the Lord said to him: 'You are now a very old man, and much of the country remains to be occupied. The country which remains is this: all the districts of the Philistines and all the Geshurite country, from the Shichor to the east of Egypt as far north as Ekron. All this is reckoned as Canaanite territory, and it belongs to the five lords of the Philistines, those of Gaza, Ashdod, Ashkelon, Gath and Ekron. Also the Avvim to the south; all the land of the Canaanite and Mearah which belongs to the Sidonians as far as Aphek, as far as the Amorite border. And the land of the Gebalites and all of the Lebanon to the east from Baal Gad at the foot of Mt. Hermon to the outskirts of Hamath. I will drive out, in favor of the Israelites, all the inhabitants of the hill country from the Lebanon until Misrephot Mayim, and all the Sidonians. You are to allot all this to the Israelites for their patrimony, as I have commanded you' " (13:1-6).

It also says in chapter 12 that Joshua defeated the king of Jerusalem, the king of Gezer, the king of Megiddo and "Joshua gave their land to the Israelite tribes to be their possession according to their allotted shares" (12:7, 10, 12, 21). Yet, in chapter 15:63 it says: "At Jerusalem, the men of Judah were unable to drive out the Jebusites who lived there, and to this day Jebusites and men of Judah live together in Jerusalem." And in 16:10 it says: "They did not drive out the Canaanites who dwelled in Gezer . . ." and in Joshua 17:12: "The children of Manasseh were unable to occupy these cities [referring to Taanach and Megiddo], and the Canaanites were resolved to live in that land."

As is known, in the Book of Judges further particulars are given about the areas and cities which the various tribes were unable to occupy: "The Lord was with Judah and they occupied the hill-country, but they could not drive out the inhabitants of the valley because they had chariots of iron" (Judges 1:19). "But, the children of Benjamin did not drive the Jebusites out of Jerusalem, and the Jebusites have lived on in Jerusalem with the children of Benjamin till this day" (1:21). "Manasseh did not drive out the inhabitants of Beit Shean and its suburbs, nor of Taanach and its suburbs, nor the inhabitants of Dor and its suburbs, nor the inhabitants of Ibleam and its suburbs, nor the inhabitants of Megiddo and its suburbs. The Canaanites were resolved to dwell in that land. Later, when Israel became strong, they put the Canaanites to forced labor; but they did not drive them out" (1:27-28): "And Ephraim did not drive out the Canaanites who lived in Gezer; and the Canaanites dwelled in Gezer among them" (1:29). "Zebulun did not drive out the inhabitants of Kitron and the inhabitants of Nahalol, but the Canaanites lived among them and were put to forced labor" (1:30).

It is difficult, however, to say that the Book of Joshua from chapter 1 through chapter 23 is "one prophetic historical unit," when in the main plot of the Book of Joshua—the conquest of the land—there are such striking contrasts. But a thorough study of chapter 24 must lead one to the conclusion that the gist of this chapter was neither written later, nor added, but includes the main contents of the Book of Joshua and, in any case, is its earliest and most reliable portion (though several verses were added later);

because in it we find one basic fact—the fact that Joshua put a free choice to the nation to worship the Lord, God of Israel or to worship the gods of the other nations. And the people chose God.

This fact—the choice of God by the people—which was established in Joshua 24, stands contrary to several other sources in the Bible and to the accepted tradition of our people according to which God chose Israel, as it says in the Book of Deuteronomy (and also Exodus) : "For you are a people consecrated to the Lord your God; of all the peoples on earth the Lord your God chose you to be His treasured people" (Deuteronomy 7:6) . And it says again: "For you are a people consecrated to the Lord your God: the Lord your God chose you from among all other peoples on earth to be His treasured people" (14:2) . And only once in the Book of Deuteronomy does it say: "You have affirmed this day that the Lord is your God. . . . And the Lord has affirmed this day that you are His treasured people . . . and that he will set you, in fame and renown and glory, high above all the peoples that he has made; and that you shall be as he promised, a holy people to the Lord your God" (26:17-19) . This might be interpreted as if there were a mutual election here: the people chose God, and therefore, God chose the people.

The theme of God's choosing Israel also recurs in the other books of the Bible (Amos 2:2; Isaiah 14:1, 41:9, 48:10, 49:17; Psalms 135:4; Haggai 2:23; Nehemiah 9:7) .

But the matter of the Almighty's choosing Israel from among all the nations puzzled the Rabbis, and they taught: When the Lord revealed himself to give the Torah to Israel, He not only revealed himself to Israel, but to all the nations. There was not one nation to which He did not come and talk and knock at its door, to see if they wanted to accept the Torah. They said to Him that they could not accept the Torah. And afterwards He came to Israel. They said to him: "We will do and we will listen." The Torah was, thus, first offered to the rest of the nations, but only Israel chose it. I see in the fact that the Rabbis allowed themselves to interpret the giving of the Torah in this fashion, historical evidence that reinforces the assertion that the people chose God.

And truly, in chapter 24 on the Book of Joshua we hear that Israel chose God, and not the other way around. It is inconceivable that this chapter was inserted later, because no one would dare to contradict the accepted tradition that God chose the Israelites, and to fabricate a story that the people chose God. But it is understood that if the people did choose God—i.e., was captivated by a faith in one God—it became a chosen people by virtue of having been the one and only nation which for many hundreds of years believed in one God. All the other nations throughout the span of the Bible, and also for a long while after the conclusion of the Bible, worshipped many gods. However, the nation could be justly proud throughout the generations that "You chose us among all the nations." There is no doubt that we have in chapter 24 an authentic early document which in no way contradicts the revelation at Mt. Sinai and the giving of the Torah by Moses in the desert. And the imagined contradiction which M. Y. Berdichevsky saw disappears if we notice the difference between the last two chapters of the Book of Joshua—between chapter 23 and chapter 24.

In chapter 23 Joshua speaks to those who left Egypt. There is no need to tell them of the early history and of the exodus from Egypt, because they participated in these experiences no less than Joshua himself. They were no longer divided into tribes, because those who went down to Egypt and those who left Egypt were united all the while by one faith, one hope; and were led by one leader and teacher—by Moses, son of Amram. And Joshua, in his words to them before his death—in chapter 23—contented himself with the request that they cling, in the future, to the Lord their God as they had done "until that day" (23:8). And he warned them that they should not cling to "the rest of these nations," because when they came to the land such a danger truly existed, since there were still peoples in the land who worshipped other gods. There was no need to make a covenant with those who had left Egypt because they had made a covenant on Mt. Horeb, and later in the wilderness of Moab, as is related in Deuteronomy (28:6-9), under the great leader Moses, son of Amram. Thus, there was no need for Joshua to draw up a "statute and ordinance" for them, since they had received these from Moses. Therefore, Joshua does not make a covenant in chapter 23. But in chapter 24, Joshua talks with the tribes of Israel who were the veteran dwellers of the land; who never left their land, and who never went down to Egypt or returned from Egypt before Moses' generation—that is, before the exodus from Egypt, according to tradition. Apparently, the descendants of Ephraim mentioned in First Chronicles 7 (verses 20-21) belonged to this group, and it was after them that the land was called the "land of the Hebrews" in the days of Joseph (Genesis 40:15), and the God of Israel was called "the Lord, God of the Hebrews," in the days of Moses (Exodus 7:16). There is not one mention of "Hebrews" in the

Books of Joshua and Judges. Hebrews are only mentioned in three books of the Torah: Genesis, Exodus and Deuteronomy; and in First Samuel (4:6, 9; 13:3, 7; 14:11, 21; 29:3), Jonah (1:9), and Jeremiah (34:9, 14). In Samuel, the Hebrews appear as part of the nation enslaved under the Philistines (14:21), and in Jeremiah the name Hebrew is identical with the name Jew (34:9).

It is the veteran residents of the land that were divided into tribes according to their place of settlement. Consequently, chapter 34 begins with the words: "Joshua assembled all of the tribes of Israel in Shechem." Here they "stood before God," because Joshua assembled them in the Lord's sanctuary which was in Shechem, and from the outset he called upon them to make a covenant with God (which had not yet been made with them), because Moses only made this covenant with those who had left Egypt. The history of the Hebrew people was not known to the veterans in the land, and as a result Joshua began his words with the story of the early history up until the exodus from Egypt. Though a belief in one God was their historical legacy, they also had "foreign gods" in their midst, since they had lived for several generations among idol-worshippers, and the patriarchs' belief in "God, Creator of, heaven and earth" was not maintained in its purity and fullness among them. They had not been present at Mt. Sinai when Moses made a covenant with those who left Egypt, and gave them the tablets with the Ten Commandments. Therefore, Joshua put a choice before them and said: "Hold the Lord in awe then, and worship him in loyalty and truth. . . . But, if it does not please you to worship the Lord, choose here and now whom you will worship: the gods whom your forefathers worshipped on the other side of the river, or the gods of the Amorites in whose land you are living. But I and my family, we will worship the Lord" (Joshua 24:14-15).

Now, imagine that like the rest, these also had left Egypt, and had been together with the others at the revelation at Mt. Sinai where they said: "We will do and we will listen," and there they made a covenant. How is it possible that Joshua would come to these Jews and would say to them: "Choose yourselves other gods?" Something like this is inconceivable. But the leaders of the people answered: "We too will worship the Lord; He is our God" (Joshua 24:18). And Joshua reiterated: "You cannot worship the Lord. He is a holy God, a jealous God. . . ." But the people answered: "No, we will worship the Lord" (24:21). How could he have said this to people who had been in Egypt with Moses? After this answer, Joshua said the following very clear and significant words to them: "You yourselves are witnesses that you have chosen the Lord and will worship Him." And they answered: "We are witnesses" (24:22). Here Joshua established the historical fact that the Hebrew people which lived in its land in a historic moment chose the Lord to be its God. And then, after they had acknowledged the Lord, Joshua said to them: "Then here and now banish the foreign gods that are among you, and turn your hearts to the Lord God of Israel" (24:23). Nowhere in the Book of Joshua is there a mention that the Jews worshipped other gods. Why then would he have said to them: "Choose!" It is clear that there were no foreign gods among those who had left Egypt; only among the native Jews who had lived in the land all along.

This is the hypothesis that I am proposing: that there were Hebrews who had always lived in the land. Of course, this is only an hypothesis. It is possible that they didn't live there continuously, but returned to "the land of the Hebrews" or the land of Canaan before the exodus from Egypt in the days of Moses, and that they were influenced by their neighbors; and the ancient original faith was still strong. This nation then promised Joshua that: "We will listen to the Lord our God, and heed His call." And then comes the important story which is a cornerstone in the history of the faith of Israel, and which bears the stamp of historical truth; because it is inconceivable that this is a later insertion intended to blur and diminish the image of Moses, son of Amram, or to increase the stature of Joshua, son of Nun. We find no attempt in the later books of the Bible to enhance the image of Joshua, son of Nun, and to detract from the importance of Moses. In fact, there are those who feel the very opposite is the case. However, there is no reason to doubt the historical veracity and importance of the four verses which come immediately after the people's promise to Joshua that they will worship the Lord their God and will heed his voice. These are the verses: "So Joshua made a covenant that day with the people; and he drew up a statute and an ordinance for them in Shechem. And Joshua wrote these things in the Torah of God [Heb. *Elohim;* throughout the entire Book of Joshua up to chapter 23 *Jehovah* is used]. He took a great stone and erected it there under the oak by the sanctuary of the Lord" (24:25-26).

This oak is also mentioned in the days of Abraham (Genesis 12:6—where they call the tree *aylon Moreh:* the oak of Moreh) as well as in the days of Jacob (35:4—where they call the tree, *ha-elah*). Joshua made of the stone a sign—which he put under the oak, as was the custom in those days. Joshua said to all the people: "This stone shall be a witness against us, for it has heard all the words which the Lord has spoken to us. If you renounce your God, it shall be a witness against you." And, then, when he had completed all this, "Joshua dismissed the people, each man to his patrimony" (24:27-28).

This was a great and decisive historical revelation in the history of the veteran Hebrews who were not with Moses during the exodus from Egypt and at the revelation on Mt. Sinai. There is no clearcut reason, foundation or proof for considering this basic and important chapter in the history of the Israelite faith as a later addition, and to falsify it, anymore than there is any convincing reason in this chapter for denying the veracity of the revelation at Mt. Sinai in the days of Moses and those who left Egypt. This was, without a doubt, Joshua's greatest prophetic act, and one of the most decisive acts in the history of the Israelitish faith. Nothing testifies, as does this document, to the greatness of the Jewish people and its inclination to believe in one God—creator of heaven and earth; the God whom Abraham, the Hebrew, believed in, as did the other Hebrews who did not leave the land and did not go down to Egypt even in the time of the famine. They lived to see the return to their land of those among the Israelites who had gone down to Egypt. And Joshua, who was one of those who had left Egypt, and was Moses' disciple as well, made a covenant with them, like the one which Moses had made in the Sinai desert with those who had left Egypt.

PART TWO

Chapters 23-24 from the Book of Joshua

— By Way of Reply to Professor Kaufman —

I will make just one or two comments to Professor Kaufman. In my humble opinion, in the last 80 years no Hebrew book as important, original and as useful has appeared as Professor Ezekiel Kaufman's, *A History of the Israelite Faith.* I only regret that it has not yet been completed. I learned more from this book than I learned from all the Hebrew books which have appeared in the last 80 years on the history of religion. But this does not mean that we have to accept all that he says without question. If I cannot accept everything that is contradictory in the Bible, then it is obvious that I cannot accept everything that puzzles me in Professor Kaufman's work. He proves that monotheism is Moses' creation, but I find in the Bible that this belief predated Moses. There is nothing unnatural or contradictory in this. Why should I not accept the fact that there was an early belief in one God? Indeed, it says explicitly in Exodus: "I did not make my name *Adonai* known to them." But they said: "Almighty God, creator of heaven and earth."

Professor Kaufman takes exception to one thing which I will not deal with, and that is: the remainder of the conquest. The matter of the conquest is a very puzzling thing. It presents many difficulties. I only noted a few contradictions which exist in the Book of Joshua, and by chance they are in those chapters which Professor Kaufman speaks of as "a special prophetic historical unit." This is not one historical unit. Even a traditional Jew, such as Professor Segal, speaks of three authors to the Book of Joshua.

I want to remove one question. People ask me: "Why are you obsessed with the idea that there were ancient Hebrews?" I answered that this is my hypothesis. And the question as to why there are no "Hebrews" mentioned in Joshua or Judges is no question at all. No one answered the question: "Why are there Hebrews in the Torah, in Samuel, and after Samuel—and why in the years from Joshua to Samuel they disappeared? What happened? Nobody explains where the Hebrews disappeared to. There are those who say that only non-Jews used the word Hebrew. But non-Jews didn't write the Torah. Moses saw two Hebrews fighting. The word Hebrews is found several times in the Torah. Moses says to Pharaoh; "The Lord God of the Hebrews sent me to you." The word Hebrew or Hebrews appears six times in the Book of Genesis, and twelve times in the Book of Exodus. In the Book of Samuel it appears eighteen times. Why they are not mentioned in the Book of Joshua and in the Book of Judges, I do not know. But this is no proof that they did not exist before Joshua and before the judges.

When I come to the Book of Samuel which is, without a shadow of a doubt—for the most part, though not entirely—a historical book, and not a book of stories, I find Hebrews in it. If this is the case, then what happened in the interim? Did the Hebrews all die after the Torah period—in the days of Joshua and the judges—and suddenly rise again in the days of Samuel?

There are many puzzling points. Dr. Malamet was correct when he said that the Bible contains the earliest history of humanity. But the Jews didn't write history as did Thucydides, though he, too, didn't write about *all* of history. He only told about the Peloponnesian War; he didn't describe what went on at that time. There isn't a word there about the cultural, philosophic, literary, tragic and dramatic creativity of Greece. This is history, but not systematic comprehensive history.

The entire Bible is historiosophy. If they found a need for something, they included it; if not, they didn't include it. Why didn't they include the Hebrews in Joshua and Judges? I don't know. But, I haven't found anyone who could explain this puzzle. Professor Kaufman insists on saying that there are only Israelites. What can I do if despite what he says there are Hebrews and Jews in the Bible? We are the same people. They called the Hebrew language "Jewish" [Heb. *yehudit*] in the days of Hezekiah. And Jeremiah sees Hebrew as identical with Jew. There are both Hebrews and Jews there, and not just Israelites. Professor Kaufman calls his book *A History of the Israelite Faith.* I would have called it *A History of the Jewish Faith.* Again, why were Hebrews absent from these two books—Joshua and Judges? I don't know.

I don't know whether Joshua intended to tell about the rest of the conquest or not. You don't get a good picture of the conquest from the Book of Joshua. When I read it—and I read it carefully, especially in these last 15 years; years in which we have seen similar events in our own day, it is easier to deal with the difficulties. I find great contradictions. I cannot accept both sides of a contradiction. I have dealt mainly with the matter of the people's choice.

If I understood the words of Professor Dinur correctly, this is what he said: Chapter 23 is a story and chapter 24 is a story; one story is like this and another like that. It isn't vital that there be compatibility between a story by Hazaz and a story by S. Yizhar, because both are fictitious. But, I do not accept Ahad Haam's thesis that central figures in Jewish history are imaginary creations. If there is a contradiction, I want to understand it. There is a contradiction between these two chapters; and there is also a difference. If there is a piece where I can remove the contradiction through a plausible hypothesis, then I choose to do so, rather than leave the contradiction. But I will not say that this is a fabricated story and that the other is a fabricated story. I believe that it is history. It interests me whether the thing happened or not. Did the Jewish people decide, after Joshua's speech, to choose God and not gods, or not?

I will say just one thing, and not with the idea of persuading anyone. I am not at all sure that when it says in the Bible "an eye for an eye, a tooth for a tooth, a hand for a hand, a foot for a foot, a burn for a burn, a wound for a wound, a bruise for a bruise," it means, payment of money. The author of the Torah really meant an eye for an eye, a tooth for a tooth, etc. It was only later that a change in outlook occurred among the rabbis of the Mishnah. The rabbis had difficulty explaining this cruel punishment, and so they said: "money." But I don't accept the idea that they were alluding to money in the Torah. The matter recurs in the Book of Leviticus: "If anyone maims his fellow—as he has done, so shall it be done to him: a fracture for a fracture, an eye for an eye, a tooth for a tooth. The injury he inflicted on another shall be inflicted on him" (24:19-20). And again, in the Book of Deuteronomy: "Nor must you show pity: a life for a life, an eye for an eye, a tooth for a tooth, a hand for a hand, a foot for a foot" (19:21). Can we doubt the intentions of the narrators? The Rabbis changed the laws of the Torah, and did so justly.

I respect the view of anyone who thinks that what the Rabbis said reflects the original meaning of the words of the Torah, but I am not obligated to think likewise. If you say that what is written in the Book of Exodus about the voices and the sound of the shofar that grew louder and louder is not correct, and that only what the Rabbis said—that the world was still—is correct, or that both of these are correct; this is not plausible. It isn't reasonable to believe that there was was shouting and loud noise, at the same time that not a bird chirped.

Prof. P. Meltzer: My argument wasn't based on faith.

B.G.: What Prof. Meltzer said is correct. Joshua was also a political leader and not just a conqueror. I don't go as far as Micah Joseph Berdichevsky, who negates all that was said earlier. I don't accept this.

To Dr. Malamet: I don't feel that the history of the Jewish people was necessarily exactly like that of the Hivites—a vassal nation, and the like. Such a thing is possible but it isn't mandatory. Why do I feel that it didn't have to be like this? I am familiar with Jewish history. Jewish history is like the history of no other nation. I have been living for only 60 or 65 years (I don't count the first 10 years), but I have seen that in our day as well, things have happened to us quite unlike that which has happened to any other people.

Prof. P. Meltzer: Things happen to us which are contrary to logic.

B.G.: It isn't contrary to logic. A U.N. meeting on aid to developing nations just took place. One of the things which everyone noted, admiringly, was Jewish agriculture. They saw it as a marvelous thing. But I remember, when I came to the country no one believed that Jewish agriculture was possible. When I came to the Moshava-type of cooperative settlement, which was to be Petach Tikvah—while still in the diaspora, I had envisioned it as redemption itself, as the Garden of Eden. When in Rishon Le-Zion, I saw daily that a Jewish laborer could almost not get work, while hundreds of Arabs were working steadily; and when Jews wanted to drink a glass of milk or eat some eggs, they had to buy them from Arabs who lived in the area, just as they once had to buy from the local Polish farmers in Plonsk. When we saw this we said: Is this Petach Tikvah? Is this Rishon Le-Zion?

There were those who drew a conclusion from this, and said: Jewish labor was impossible. The most profound Jewish thinker of our generation, and not an anti-Zionist—Aham Haam, didn't believe in Hebrew agriculture and labor; and he felt that the masses of laborers should be Arabs.

I know what happened in the fifth century in Greece, in Athens. Something occurred which was unparalleled in all of human history. The Jews didn't have dramatists like theirs or artists like theirs. But, Jewish history is unique. I am sure that England can justly feel—certainly up until the nineteenth century—that her history is unique. But Jewish history is truly unique. Professor Kaufman insisted upon this. He showed that there is no truth in what German Bible scholars said: that Jews accepted a belief in one God only after the Babylonian captivity. They took this position because of anti-Semitic leanings on the one hand, and Christian leanings on the other; out of a desire to bring everything closer to the Christians. And they purported to prove it by quoting the sources and all sorts of proofs. Professor Kaufman came and said: No! This faith is rooted in the Jewish people from its antiquity.

I do not accept his dogmatism. Every time there is something in the Bible contrary to his view, he says: This is not right. But, that the Israelites were the first people in the world to present the great idea of one God—of this there is no doubt. I differ with Professor Kaufman's view that this was the only thing which made the Jewish people unique. Even the entire matter of the return to Zion did not occur only because the Jewish people is a monotheistic people.

Professor Meltzer, I will even show you contradictions regarding the belief in one God and the covenant with God. In Joshua 23:12, it says: ". . . for if you do turn away and attach yourselves to the peoples that still remain among you, and intermarry with them, and associate with them and they with you . . ." and Joshua warns them to continue to observe the covenant. That means that he is speaking with people with whom he made a covenant. It may be that all of chapter 23, as Dinur says, is just "a story." There is one type of story and there is another type of story, and there are other stories which were lost. But, I find contradictions between chapters 23 and 24 as *historical* chapters, and not as stories. In Chapter 23, Joshua speaks to the nation which already has made a covenant with God; they are not idol worshippers. He only asks that this covenant be preserved and conserved, and that they not turn to the nations among whom they live. In chapter 24 he speaks to an assembly which is not yet included in the covenant.

Prof. P. Meltzer: In chapter 24 it says: "The people answered: 'God forbid that we should forsake the Lord to worship other gods. . . .' "

B.G.: That means that they did heed Joshua. All of chapter 24 proves this. Why do I say that this chapter is special? Not because it does not fit my theory, but because it does not fit the context. Joshua says to them (24:15) : "But if it does not please you to worship the Lord, choose here and now whom you will worship: the gods which your forefathers worshipped on the other side of the river, or the gods of the Amorites in whose land you are living. But I and my family, we will worship the Lord." By the way, it says here "in their land," not in Egypt.

Dr. H. Gevaryahu: It says this earlier.

B.G.: If it says "Egypt," where in the Torah, in the entire story about Egypt, does it say that the Jews worshipped idols in Egypt?

Prof. B. Dinur: In Ezekiel.

B.G.: The calf wasn't a god. I don't imagine that Aaron worshipped a god that was a calf. He thought that the calf was God.

Joshua says to them: "Choose here and now whom you will worship. . . . The people answered: 'God forbid that we should forsake the Lord to worship other gods. . . .'" That is plausible. Afterward, they say: ". . . for it was the Lord our God who brought us and our fathers up from Egypt, from slavery. . . . The Lord drove out before us the Amorites and all the peoples who lived in that country. We too will worship the Lord; He is our God." How does "We, too, will worship the Lord," fit in with "The Lord drove out. . . ?" It didn't fit in.

Prof. P. Meltzer: That depends upon the interpretation of the word "too" [Heb. *gam*].

B.G.: The word "too" has a simple interpretation. Even the Rabbis don't disagree on this interpretation. It is possible that after Joshua said: "I and my family, we will worship the Lord," they answered: "We too will worship the Lord."

Prof. P. Meltzer: This isn't the interpretation of the word "too" in Jeremiah: "Yes, and there is blood on the corners of your robe—the life-blood of the innocent poor" (2:34). [*Gam* ("too") is translated here as *yes.*] And it is like this in other places as well.

B.G.: I am dealing with the Jews to whom Joshua spoke, not Jeremiah; and they said what they said. Professor Meltzer charged me with an excess of logic, but he can't charge me with a lack of logic. Joshua 24:18 makes no sense as it is. There are verses here which it is obvious Joshua could not have spoken. It says in verse 12: "I sent the hornet before you, and it was this, not your sword or your bow that drove out the two kings of the Amorites." Did Joshua say something against the Torah? In all of the wars in the north and the south there is no mention of a hornet. It is written explicitly in the Torah that they defeated them by the sword.

Prof. P. Meltzer: By the sword, which the Lord put in motion.

B.G.: But, there is a difference between a sword and a hornet. In any case, it is not conceivable that Joshua spoke this verse. It is obvious that there are later insertions here. These verses were inserted by someone who wanted to match things up. He found a hornet in the Bible, and inserted a hornet here. But it is not possible that Joshua himself who was present when the Israelites fought with Sihon and Og, and saw that they defeated them by the sword, would say that they didn't defeat them by the sword. Therefore, this is a later addition, if I am to believe what is written there—and I have no reason not to believe it.

There are also later verses in chapter 24. But the central episode, in my view, is the matter of the covenant with God. Berdichevsky concludes from this that this is the only covenant and, consequently, all that is written in the Torah is incorrect. I do not accept that. There is no contraction whatsoever between this covenant and the covenant which Moses made.

Let's try to understand this rationally. God created man and gave him intelligence so that he would understand things, and it is obvious that there are verses here which are implausible, because they are incorrect. It says in the Torah that Balak did not make war. It says that Balak was afraid to make war. Consequently, this too is a later addition. There are other verses which, logically, Joshua could not have said.

Prof. B. Dinur: What is the meaning of the verse: "Moab dreaded the Israelites" (Numbers 22:3)?

B.G.: He could not endure them, but did not fight with them, because the fear of this nation enveloped him.

I know that occasionally contradictory verses are found. And if there is an obvious contradiction, I have to accept either this or that. But I don't have to contradict the fact that the Israelites defeated Sihon and Og. Abraham's army numbered 318 men and he defeated the four kings with his sword. Jacob said that he conquered Shechem from the Amorites with his sword and his bow, and gave it to Joseph. This doesn't particularly fit the story about Dinah. According to what is written there, Jacob didn't conquer it with his sword. It is obvious that there is one version here and another there. This isn't exactly history, and we have to make an effort to understand it. It is possible to say that the one is just a story and the other is history. And if it is possible for me to salvage a historical portion, I make every effort to do so.

In chapter 24 there are later additions. But, there is one essential bit of common sense in this chapter that is basic to the Israelite faith.

Professor Meltzer says that there is no difference at all between God choosing Israel, and Israel choosing God. I don't accept this.

I am saying that it is inconceivable—if I believe in God—that God chose this nation or any other nation. Here we have a basic chapter in the history of the Jewish religion.

The Book of Exodus does not say that God exerted strong pressure upon them, and that he said to them: "If you accept the Torah, fine; and if not, you will meet your doom there." I know that there is such an interpretation. There have been such interpretations. I beg Professor Meltzer's pardon. But, I contend that 1,600-2,000 years ago people were human beings, not angels. There was a rabbi in one of the academies who held this interpretation: "You will meet your doom there." But there is no hint in the Bible that God exerted strong pressure on them. It is written only that "Mt. Sinai smoked, and its smoke rose as smoke from a furnace; and the entire mountain shook; and the sound of the shofar intensified." I'm not quite certain that this is important to the Israelite faith.

But there is one principle here. I accept the belief in God—not a crude belief; not in a God who ascends and descends and with whom one talks. Consequently, I say that chapter 24 of Joshua is one of the most important chapters in the history of the faith, and there is no basis for saying that this chapter was a later addition. It is inconceivable that after the tradition was accepted that God chose Israel, someone would come along and say, *no!* But Joshua says this. Therefore, I am compelled to say that chapter 24 is history. There are things which arouse doubt within me. In one place it says that Joshua conquered all of the land, while in other places it is written that many parts remained unconquered. The whole narrative about the war also does not seem so plausible to me after having had a little experience in military matters. The most important thing in chapter 24 is the choice of God by the Jewish people. It is of this that we are proud. The Jewish people stood out more than any other people because it arrived at a belief in one God; that one superior force created everything and rules over everything.

Prof. P. Meltzer: Before the Jewish people, there was the patriarch, Abraham.

B.G.: Neither of us was alive then. I respect your belief. If you are telling me that there exists an interpretation of Rabbi Shimon bar Yochai which runs counter to the Torah, and you accept his words, I respect that. Rabbi Shimon bar Yochai was a good and loyal Jew. There are various types of interpretations.

Here the greatness of the Jewish people is established; and it is properly and truthfully explained how the Jewish people arrived at this belief. Not Joshua, nor Moses was the only person to bring this about. It is told that after Moses lived with Jethro, and returned to the desert, he saw a bush burning, and at that time God was revealed to him, and he brought the tidings to the Jewish people. You can't change the outlook of a people in one minute. Since the Jewish people existed before Joshua and before Moses, I arrive at my conclusions based upon what is written in the Bible (and I do not find any contradiction there to logic or intelligence) that they believed in one God at an earlier date as well—even if this belief was not as lofty as it was in the days of Maimonides. Maimonides' definition of divinity appears to many as heresy. But Maimonides was not a heretic. He had a more developed concept of divinity than those who spoke of Him as one who "ascended and descended, shouted and was angered."

Since we were the first people to arrive at a belief in one God, there is an important matter to be pointed out here, in chapter 24, which reveals the importance of the Jewish people. To me, it is not of the essence that there were veteran Jews in the land, in addition to those who went down to Egypt. I must accept this in order to understand these two chapters in Joshua. There is here an original, important, basic revelation about the history of the Israelite faith, and it must be taken literally. Professor Dinur said that this whole chapter proves the importance of Shechem; that is 1) the greatness of Joshua, 2) the greatness of the Jewish people, and 3) the importance of Shechem.

Prof. B. Dinur: The holiness of Shechem.

B.G.: It doesn't stand to reason that in order to build up Shechem's importance they invented a tale about a sanctuary of the Lord, and about such a speech of Joshua's, and about such a dialogue with the Jewish people, and about the choosing of God by the Jewish people. Was all this in order to build up the holiness of Shechem? Shechem was already a truly important center. We know this from the story, or from the history of this place in the days of Abraham and in the days of Jacob.

I know what Professor Gutman said. I read the Septuagint. There are places in the Septuagint that makes sense to us. We dealt with this when we read the marvelous chapter in Samuel on "David's last days." Things are blurred there and cannot be understood, while in the Septuagint they are clearer. But it is not reasonable that in Joshua 24 it should have said Shilo instead of Shechem. Apparently, this was translated at a time when there was a serious dispute between the Jews and the Samaritans, and the Jews did not want to glorify the name of Shechem.

But this chapter was not written in praise of Shechem. It was written in praise of the faith of the Jewish people and the great thing they did in choosing the Lord. This is not new. This theme is constantly repeated in the Torah. There were those who had left Egypt, and there was an old settlement, or even another group which had also left Egypt, but earlier. If the rabbis could have allowed themselves such "heresy," so can we. In the tractate *Sanhedrin* it says explicitly that they were not all killed, but that they erred in their count and left Egypt before the appointed time. This was a large group, perhaps not only the children of Ephraim. But it doesn't matter if it was this way or that way; Joshua spoke with the Jews or the Israelites and put a choice before them: God or gods. There were idolaters among them, and Joshua said to them: "Remove the foreign gods which are in your midst."

Professor Kaufman has a theory that gods are a fetish. Let's assume that he is correct. Joshua wanted them to worship the Lord and not a fetish. When did he say this to them? After they had publicly acknowledged: " 'We, too, will worship the Lord. . . .' He said to them: 'You are witnesses against yourselves that you have chosen the Lord and will worship Him.' And they answered: 'We are witnesses.' " After this he says to them: "Remove the foreign gods in your midst." ". . . And he drew up a statute and an ordinance for them in Shechem."

Professor Meltzer asks: Why did the narrative have to say here "the Torah of Moses?" This is puzzling. The emphasis on "the Torah of Moses" is repeated in other chapters of Joshua, though there is no such need; while here, in this chapter, this emphasis is absent! Joshua, who saw all that Moses had done and had not sinned by worshipping the calf—this Joshua doesn't mention the Torah of Moses?

In my view this chapter is one of the earliest documents of the Jewish people, though I am not saying that there was nothing earlier. It is highly certain that it predates all the other chapters in Joshua, and certainly chapter 23, though not all of the book, because there are verses which we cannot reasonably assume were spoken by Joshua.

But there are things which, quite clearly, Joshua did say. The people didn't deliver speeches; Joshua delivered speeches. They said: "We too, shall worship the Lord," and they answered: "We are witnesses." According to this context, it appears that the answer was not to the long story but to that part which said: "But if it does not please you to worship the Lord. . . . But I and my family, we will worship the Lord." In answer, they said: "We too will worship the Lord." Once again he asked them, and once again they answered: "We are witnesses." Then he said: "Remove the foreign gods in your midst" and he drew up "a statute and a covenant for them in Shechem." This was a great revelation; though not the revelation on Mt. Sinai. This was the revelation at Shechem; the revelation at the sanctuary of Shechem. Thus, we understand the importance of "and they stood before God." Nowhere else in Joshua do they stand before God.

In this matter of the antiquity of the Jewish settlement in the land, I sought assistance in order to explain two chapters. I wanted to accept the two chapters as history. But mainly, it was to prove the matter of the choosing of God by the people. This is the greatness of the Jewish people; this is the historical truth; and this is the great act which made the Israelites stand apart. This gave them spiritual strength which other nations did not have. This spiritual strength accompanies it to this day.

CHAPTER ELEVEN

The Antiquity of the Hebrews

At the tenth gathering of Bible scholars, Professor Kaufman's lecture, "The Hebrews in the Book of Genesis and in Biblical Literature," was delivered. In it he differs with my hypothesis regarding Israel's antiquity in its land. I must hasten to point out that in arriving at this hypothesis, I relied on neither Israeli nor foreign Bible scholars, but on the Bible itself, and only on the Bible.

When I come to debate with Professor Kaufman the central question of our early history—a question which affects our understanding of the Bible—I do so with great respect. And I say this not only out of courtesy to someone greater than I in scholarship, but with sincerity and without flattery. Every time I study Professor Kaufman's books, whether it is the monumental *A History of the Israelite Faith,* or his commentaries on the Book of Joshua or the Book of Judges, I am filled with respect for his marvelous erudition, for the sharpness of his intellect, for the profundity of his understanding and, more than anything, for the independence and originality of his thinking. It is not easy for me to differ with him over this or that detail when, in general, I accept his views, and always drink in his words.

First, I will simply define my approach toward history and toward an understanding of the Bible. I am not certain that history, in general, and early history, in particular—for which we only have fragmented documents—falls into the category of science, as do astronomy, physics, biology, and the like—for which we also lack absolute knowledge. However, these can be studied through a microscope or telescope, and it is possible to prove the truth of their laws or their falsity through experimental evidence and observation that cannot be refuted. Historical events which have passed cannot be examined by these means, and we must rely upon written documents and archeological findings which, by their very nature, are incomplete or may contradict one another.

Biblical historiography is almost a "first" in the history of mankind, but its writers had a certain philosophy which served as the purpose of their writings; and there are cases where the historiosophy outweighs the historiography. The Creator's supervision was over everything: the good and the bad, the successes of the Jewish people and its failures. At this point, it should be noted that several sections in the Bible were written without any purpose, and are no more than descriptions of things as they were. We must generally, in my view, accept the stories of the Bible as they are, if there are no inner contradictions, legends or miracles in them.

People—two, three, or four thousand years ago, and at all other times, were like human beings today, to which all the laws of nature applied. But there was a difference in the level of culture, the living conditions, the influence of the environment; and there were differences ingrained in the nature of man and his spirit whose quality and source science has not been able to discover to this day. Consequently, people are not like each other in all eras, and every historical event is almost unique. Whereas the time span, place, and conditions in which man functions never recur with all of their complexities and refinements, we must view the personalities, and the events of history in general, and of the Bible in particular, within the framework of their historical uniqueness, though there is no doubt that they, too, were subject to the same laws or systems which guide the destiny of mankind.

Professor Kaufman recognizes that in the story of the conquest of the land there are mysteries and puzzles, and that "the story is marred by a lack of clarity, and that there are elements in the story which contradict each other and do not agree with other things," and that "it is not clear what went on in one period, and what went on in a later period, hence, the [variety of] suppositions."

I admit that my words on the early history of Israel in its land, which I presented to the Bible Society on the Book of Joshua, and as they were published in "Studies in the Book of Joshua," are only an hypothesis whose truth cannot be proven through direct experiment or observation. As an introduction to my remarks, I said, "I do not consider all of the proof that I will bring as irrefutable evidence, and I myself know how easy it is to question them"; that the main problem is that the stories of the Bible pass almost silently over the existence of a Hebrew people in the land before the exodus from Egypt.

More important, in the Book of Joshua and in the Book of Judges there is no mention of the Hebrews, and according to Professor Kaufman "the solid foundation for the building of the beginning of the history of Israel are not the genealogies and the statistics (in the Torah), but the Book of Joshua and the Book of Judges, and the stories of the Torah which these books expand upon." These books, according to Professor Kaufman, "include faithful contemporary testimony about the events surrounding the conquest of the land and, indirectly, also about the exodus from Egypt, from which we may conclude that at approximately the time of the settlement of the Philistines in the land of Canaan, the land was conquered by the Israelites who came from Egypt via the desert and Transjordan." Professor Kaufman does not spell out which stories in the Torah he does not accept, and which he does accept because they are continued in the books of Joshua and Judges.

It is the undeniable right of a Bible scholar of the rank of Professor Kaufman to reject stories which do not seem reasonable to him and to accept stories which do seem reasonable. It can be said with certainty that the entire Bible was not written by one author, but is a collection of writings, assembled from different sources and documents which differ in accordance with the time, purpose and outlook of the author. They include, as Professor Kaufman rightfully noted, deletions, additions, and alterations according to the taste of the collector or editor. In every attempt which has been made in our day, or in any other era after the canonization of the Bible, to "correct" or "interpret" the hidden and puzzling words of the Bible, there was a certain degree of arbitrariness and personal motivation which depended on the taste of the "corrector" or the "interpreter." We meet up with this phenomenon among the writings of the Rabbis as far back as the two editions of the Talmud, and in the Midrashim.

I hope I will be permitted, not as one who is considered a Bible scholar, but as an average reader of the Bible, and as a Jew who sees the Bible as our people's greatest spiritual legacy from its inception to Second Temple days, to spell out those events in the early history of the nation which, in my humble opinion, are not subject to doubt.

Jewish history begins, in the Book of Genesis, with the appearance of Abraham. The 14 chapters in the Book of Genesis dedicated to the life of Abraham give the impression, not of a legendary or mythological personality, but of an historical, down-to-earth, real person. Though it is possible to doubt several details—even important ones—in these stories, in the main they are stamped with the seal of historical truth, and logic would not demand that we look upon all 14 chapters as legendary. Of the three patriarchs, the image of Isaac is the weakest, and the stories about him contain repetitions from the life of Abraham.

I will not get myself involved in the thicket of research concerning the three sons of Noah: Shem, Ham and Japhet—and their descendants, as described in Genesis 10. Professor Kaufman argues in his lecture that "if there was a Hebrew nation then, its appellation (Hebrew, Hebrews) testifies to its having originated from the stock of the peoples of the descendants of Ever." But, "a list of the peoples of the descendants of Ever has already been provided [according to Professor Kaufman] in Genesis, from chapter 10 on." I examined the text from chapter 10 on, and I did not find any list of nations of the descendants of Ever. Verse 21 of this same chapter does say: "Sons were also born to Shem, ancestor of all the descendants of Ever and older brother of Japheth." But after this, there follows only a list of the descendants of Shem (or the nations of Shem?) and not of the nations of the descendants of Ever. Of Ever it only says that he is the son of Shelach, who is the son of Arpachshad, who is the son of Shem (verses 22-24). Afterwards it says (verse 25): "Two sons were born to Ever; the name of the first was Peleg, for in his days the earth was divided; and the name of his brother was Joktan." And later on, in verses 26-30, the children of Joktan and their places of settlement are listed. It also says: "These are the descendants of Shem according to their clans and languages, by their lands, according to their nations." In chapter 11, Abraham's ancestors from Shem to Terah are listed: Shem begot Arpachshad, Arpachshad begot Shelach, Shelach begot Ever, Ever begot Peleg, Peleg begot Reu, Reu begot Serug, Serug begot Nahor, Nahor begot Terah, Terah begot Abram (Abraham).

Professor Kaufman does not rely on the genealogy given in the Torah. His view can be agreed with or disagreed with, but in these two chapters there is no list of the nations of Ever; only of the nations of Shem (or the sons of Shem and their descendants). First Chronicles, chapter 1, recounts this same genealogy of Abraham, though more briefly: Shem, Arpachshad, Shelach, Ever, Peleg, Reu, Serug, Nahor, Terah, Abram who is Abraham (verses 24-26), and even there no mention is made of the list of the nations of Ever, but rather a recounting of the words of Genesis 10 with slight changes (the author of Chronicles deleted the words "and the descendants of Aram" before the names "Uz, Hul, Gether and Meshech"). I have only one point to make regarding chapter 10: We read there that the descendants of Ham are "Cush, Mitzraim, Put and Canaan." But Canaan does not belong to the family of Ham because the language of Canaan was Hebrew, as we know from the writings of Ras-Shamra (Ugaritic). And in Isaiah 19:18 it says: "When the day comes there shall be five cities in Egypt speaking the language of Canaan and swearing allegiance to the Lord of Hosts." It is clear that "the language of Canaan" meant the Hebrew language.

There are three sections in the Book of Genesis which, in my view, belong to early Jewish history: the first section, from chapter 12 through chapter 25—about the life of Abraham; the second section, from chapter 27 through chapter 35—about the life of Jacob; and the third section, from chapter 37 through chapter 50—about the life of Joseph. There is no compelling reason to cast doubt upon the historicity of these three personalities. To these must be added the chapters in the Book of Exodus on the life and work of Moses.

It is difficult to say with certainty to which generation in the history of the Israelites Jacob and his sons belong. But one thing is clear: Before Jacob this nation was not called by the name "Israel," but by the name "Hebrew." We also find the name Hebrew after Jacob, from the days of Moses (practically speaking from the days of Abraham and Joseph) until the days of Jeremiah, and particularly in the days of Saul, who lived at the end of the era of the judges. It is not to be assumed that the Hebrews were born only in the days of Saul; and if they did exist in the days of Saul, there isn't the slightest doubt that they also existed in the days of the judges and in the days of Joshua, just as they lived in the days of Moses and the days of Joseph (before he went down or was sold to Egypt).

If the name Hebrew or Hebrews is not found in the books of Joshua and Judges, this does not prove that they did not exist then. We should, rather, conclude that we do not know the reason why they were not mentioned in these two books, just as it is not clear why the mighty exploits of one of the greatest kings of Judah (King Uziah or Azariah) were not mentioned in the Book of Kings.

These included territorial conquests (the Philistine cities in the west and the Amorites and Arabs in the east); the liberation and development of Eilat; the fortification of Jerusalem; the irrigation of the lands of the desert; organizing and equipping an army; the invention or development of new weapons; and his great reputation throughout the area. The Book of Kings only tells of his being a leper to the day of his death. In all, the author of Second Kings (chapter 15) dedicated only seven verses to this king (Uziah). Had the author of Second Chronicles not preserved an ancient document and inserted it into his book (chapter 26), we would not know of the conquests and mighty exploits of this great king who is unparalleled by all the kings of Judah. Isaiah, son of Amoz, himself the greatest prophet of his time, wrote "the rest of the events of Uziahu's reign from first to last"; something not done for any other king of Judah, neither before him nor after him. This lends veracity to the known dictum: The fact that we did not see something is no proof [that it didn't happen].

Professor Kaufman erroneously attributes to me—or concludes mistakenly from my hypothesis—that in my view "a monotheistic people existed in the world even before the existence of the Israelites, and the Jewish people are one and the same people, who, in lence of this people has been preserved in the biblical tradition. The biblical tradition knows of no monotheistic people other than Israel, and no such people really existed in the world." This far Professor Kaufman.

According to my way of thinking, the Hebrew people, the Israelites, and the Jewish people are one and the same people, who, in different periods, were called by different names: first Hebrew, later both Hebrew and Israel, and, finally, when the kingdom of Israel was destroyed, they were called Jews. But it is true, as Professor Kaufman notes in his lecture, I do believe (or surmise) that "a Hebrew nation lived in the land of Canaan from antiquity as an indigenous people; they lived there in the days of the patriarchs, and perhaps even before the patriarchal period, if indeed we know when the patriarchal period began." Not all of them went down to Egypt. Only one family went: Joseph's family, which included his father, his brothers, his brothers' children, and various grandchildren; in all some 70 people (there is no logical reason or historical basis to refute what is written in this regard in Genesis 26:27-28, or to deny its validity.

The matter which requires clarification, and which is at the root of the objection of Professor Kaufman, is the existence of the

Hebrews and the importance of Shechem in the early history of our people.

Professor Kaufman refuses to admit the existence of Hebrews —as our people was called at its inception, at least from the days of Abraham until Saul's day (and in my view also in a later period) —and he asks: "Are the Hebrews mentioned at all in the Bible in the sense implied in the hypothesis?" That is: Are Hebrews mentioned as members of a nation (or nations) which were not Israelites, but which were closely related, racially or culturally, to Israel?

I should point out at once that I do not contend that there were Hebrew *nations;* just *one* Hebrew nation. The Hebrews were not closely related racially and culturally to Israel, but the name Israel was adopted later on, and stems from the descendants of the privileged family which went down to Egypt and returned from there. These descendants did not number 603,550 males who were over 20 years of age and fit for military service; but rather several million, if we add in the wives, children and old people who did not fit the category of "being fit for military service," and also the Levites who were not counted among those fit for military service, and "the mixed multitude." Even Professor Kaufman does not accept this enormous total.

In my view, the number of those who left Egypt was much more modest—enlarged only because of the natural increase reflected in the two or three generations of the same Israelites who lived in Egypt. This is proven by the number of Egyptian kings from the days of Joseph until Moses, and from the number of the children of Levi, Reuben and Joseph who were born to the Israelites in Egypt. But this does not have any bearing on the debate about the Hebrews. It demands, rather, clarification on its own account, on some other occasion. I will only say that we should not deny genealogical evidence if it fits in with the facts, and if there is no logical reason to conclude that it was included in the narrative for deceptive purposes or to prove the miraculous events.

Both the number of the kings of Egypt in the stories of Joseph and Moses in Egypt, and the enumeration of the grandchildren of the Israelites (the descendants of Jacob) complement each other. I have no right to claim that the proof which is brought in this regard from the Bible—from Genesis, Exodus, Numbers and Chronicles—is beyond question. I know that Professor Kaufman denies all genealogies and does not rely on them, and I have no way of proving to him or to myself that he is mistaken in this regard, because it is very possible that none of the genealogies of early history can be relied upon, even if the data in different parts of the Bible, regarding the different personalities—Jews and non-Jews—complement each other remarkably.

According to the stories of the Torah, there were three kings in Egypt from the days of Joseph until the time of Moses and the exodus from Egypt. Joseph interpreted the dream of Pharaoh I (Genesis 41:25-36) and, as a result, this same Pharaoh appointed him to be in charge of his household and as ruler over all of his people (41:40). Pharaoh II was "a new Egyptian king who did not know Joseph" (Exodus 1:8). After this Pharaoh died (2:23), a third Pharaoh arose in the days of Moses, and during his reign the Israelites left Egypt (12:31). Obviously, it may be argued that in this span several other Pharaohs who weren't mentioned in the Bible arose and died. And there is no convincing evidence against this claim, just as there is no convincing proof in its favor. But several lists in this same Book of Exodus, which have no connection with Pharaoh, fit in well with the theory that there were two generations of Pharaohs who ruled after Joseph attained his lofty position in Egypt through Pharaoh "the dreamer."

Judah, his son Peretz, and his grandson Hetzron were among those who went down to Egypt (Genesis 46:12). Caleb (or Cluvai), son of Hetzron was among those who left Egypt (I Chronicles 2:9, 18). This Caleb (not to be confused with Caleb, son of Jefuneh) was apparently Hetzron's youngest son, because he had a brother, Ram, whose grandson, Nachshon, son of Aminadav, was among those who left Egypt. According to the Rabbis, he was the first who leaped into the sea. But we must not ignore the fact that the genealogy of Caleb, son of Hetzron, in Chronicles is confused and full of contradictions. Phalu, son of Reuben, was among those who went down to Egypt (Genesis 46:9), and there he begot Eliav, and Eliav begot Dathan and Abiram who were among those who left Egypt (Numbers 16:1). Gershon, Kohath and Merari, sons of Levi, were among those who went down to Egypt (Genesis 46:11). Amram, son of Kohath, and Moses, son of Amram, were born in Egypt (Exodus 6:18; Exodus 14:20; Numbers 26:58). Yitzhar, son of Kohath, was born in Egypt (Exodus 6:18) as was Korach, son of Yitzhar (6:21), and Korach was among those who left Egypt. Gershon, son of Levi was among those who went down to Egypt (as stated above), and his sons Livni and Shimei were born in Egypt (Numbers 3:18; I Chronicles 6:2). Shimei begot four sons in Egypt: Yachat, Zina, Yeush and Beriah (I Chronicles 23:10). Merari, son of Levi, begot two children in Egypt: Machli and

Mushi (6:19). Machli had two sons: Eleazar and Kish (23:21). And Mushi had three sons: Machli, Eder and Yeramot (23:23).

It can be argued that this genealogy cannot be depended upon; and there may be sound reason for this argument. But the similarity between the two Pharaohs who were born after the Pharaoh who lived in Joseph's day and continued until the exodus from Egypt, and the two generations of Amram, son of Kohath and Moses, son of Amram, who were born in Egypt, cannot be viewed as a reconciliation based on legend. Moses occupies a central position in the Torah (from Exodus to Deuteronomy) and in the history of Israel. It is difficult to imagine that incorrect information was given in the Torah about his origin. But I must admit that if Professor Kaufman doubts the accuracy of this genealogy, there is no way to prove, with any degree of certainty, that he is in error.

It appears clear that the Jews did not live in Egypt for 430 years, as is recorded in Exodus 13. All of the early commentators (the Septuagint, the Rabbis of the Midrash, Rabbi David Kimchi) take issue with the alleged fact, mentioned twice in the Torah, that our people lived in Egypt for 400 years. The first time, it is mentioned in Genesis 15:13: ". . . and they shall be enslaved and oppressed for four hundred years." (Concerning this Nachmanides says simply: "There are many instances of distortion in the sources.") The second time, it is mentioned in Exodus 12:40: "The length of time that the Israelites lived in Egypt was four hundred and thirty years." The Septuagint corrected this verse to read: "The length of time that the Israelites lived in Egypt *and in Canaan* was four hundred and thirty years." Our rabbis (in Megillah 9a) confirmed this correction of the Septuagint, though their actual version was slightly different from that of the Septuagint. They wrote, "in Egypt and in other lands," instead of, "in Egypt and in Canaan."

But the two main problems wherein I differ with Professor Kaufman concern the existence of Hebrews as the earliest members of our people, which at a later date was called the Jewish people, and in the Middle Ages was called the people of Israel; and secondly, the importance of Shechem.

The first person called by the name Hebrew was Abram (Abraham), in Genesis 14:13. Abraham was not Ever's son, nor his grandson, nor his great-grandson; and there is no point in attributing this name to Ever, son of Shelach, son of Arpachshad who, according to the genealogies of Genesis 10 and First Chronicles, was seven generations removed from Abraham (Though he was only ten generations removed from Shem, he was not called a Semite.)

But Abraham isn't the only Hebrew in the Bible. Potiphar's wife called Joseph a "Hebrew man" and a "Hebrew slave" (Genesis 39:14, 17) and Joseph said to his comrades in the Egyptian prison: "I was kidnapped from the land of the Hebrews" (40:15). The chief butler in speaking to Pharaoh about Joseph said: "A Hebrew youth was there with us" (41:12), and the Torah tells that after Jacob's family "came down to Egypt," the Egyptians "could not dine with the Hebrews" (43:32). In the Book of Exodus, Pharaoh says to the Hebrew midwives: "When you deliver the Hebrew women, look at the birthstool, and if it is a boy, kill him . . ." (1:16). The midwives said ". . . the Hebrew women are not like the Egyptian women" (1:19). When Pharaoh's daughter saw the baby Moses in the basket among the reeds she said: "This must be a Hebrew child" (2:6). It is also written of Moses that after he grew up, "he went out to his kinsfolk and witnessed their toil; and he saw an Egyptian beating a Hebrew, one of his kinsmen" (2:11). And again when he went out on the second day he saw "two Hebrews fighting" (2:13). And when Moses was sent to Pharaoh by God he was told to say: "The Lord God of the Hebrews has manifested himself to us." And Moses and Aaron said to Pharaoh: "The God of the Hebrews has manifested himself to us" (5:3). Again Moses was commanded to say to Pharaoh: "The Lord God of the Hebrews sent me to you . . ." (7:16). And again: "Thus says the Lord God of the Hebrews: 'Let my people go out to worship me' " (9:1). And further, in the same book, without having any connection with Pharaoh, it says: "When you acquire a Hebrew slave, he shall serve six years" (21:2); and this command is repeated in Deuteronomy (15:12): "If a Hebrew, man or woman is sold to you, he shall serve you six years. . . ."

In his lecture, Professor Kaufman asks: "Were Hebrews mentioned as members of a nation who were not Israelites?" And he calls those people Israelites, who at a later period were called Jews (from Jeremiah's day on, and in fact even from the days of Hezekiah). My hypothesis includes no Hebrews who are not Israelites in Professor Kaufman's sense; and the Hebrews about whom I am talking are not poetic figures, but historical facts mentioned in the books of Genesis, Exodus and others. The name Hebrew is not "the name of all of the house of Jacob," as Professor Kaufman says, because Abraham certainly did not belong to the house of Jacob, who lived much later. Indeed, according to my hypothesis, Hebrews lived in the land of Canaan; and Joseph calls Canaan, where the Hebrews lived, "the land of the Hebrews."

Professor Kaufman argues that "Hebrews was the name given to the Israelites by the Egyptians," but the Egyptians did not write the chapters of the Torah in which Hebrews are mentioned. These chapters—and the matter at hand is not affected by the date they were written—were without a shadow of a doubt written by Jews, and they used the name Hebrew not only in connection with the story of Egypt, but also in other instances, such as the case where Moses saw an Egyptian striking his brother, a Hebrew (his brother here means not his father's son, of course, but his countryman); or when he saw "two Hebrews fighting." A Jew wrote this verse, not an Egyptian, and it was not necessarily written in Egypt. The name, too, was well known to Egyptians—and as is known, the Egyptians ruled in Canaan for a long while—proof that they knew of a Hebrew nation in this land, and not only of Joseph, his father, and his brothers.

There is no need at all to identify the Hebrews with the Habiru or Apiru in the Tel Amarna writings and in other documents who, according to some scholars, were laborers or slaves. The author of the Book of Exodus would not have said "the Lord God of the Hebrews" had he not been referring to a Hebrew nation free in its own land, but a group of slaves. The God of the Hebrews was not the God of slaves, but the God of the Hebrew people; the same people to whom Abraham belonged; and to whom the Hebrew, struck by the Egyptian, belonged; and to whom the two Hebrews who were fighting belonged—i.e., Moses' people.

The Hebrew slaves in the books of Exodus and Deuteronomy do not belong to the slave class, but to the Hebrew people. We know from the Book of Jeremiah that King Zedekiah made a covenant with all the people in Jerusalem; that "all who had Hebrew slaves, male or female, were to set them free; they were not to keep their fellow Jews in servitude" (Jeremiah 34:9). The people did so, but afterwards they regressed, repossessed them, and enslaved them. Jeremiah was embittered, and recalled the days of the exodus from Egypt when it was said: "Within seven years each of you shall set free any fellow Hebrew. . . . But you, too, have profaned my name. You have all taken back the slaves, male and female. . . . Therefore, these are the words of the Lord . . . and I will proclaim a deliverance for you . . . to a sword, to pestilence, and to famine, and I will make you repugnant to all the kingdoms of the earth" (34:14-17). Here, there is a complete identity of terms between Hebrew and Jew, between Hebrew and Israelite, despite what is written about the Habiru or the Apiru in the writings of Tel Amarna. A male and female Hebrew servant are the brethren of their masters—members of the same people—the same as Abraham the Hebrew, or the Hebrews fighting in the presence of Moses. The Book of Samuel, which cannot be considered less reliable than the books of Joshua or Judges, offers eternal proof of this.

When the Israelites carried the "ark of the covenant of the Lord" from Shilo to the army camp in Aphek, and sounded a great blast, the Philistines were puzzled and asked: "What is the great shouting in the camp of the Hebrews?" (I Samuel 4:6). This is certainly not a reference to a slave class, but to the Israelites who were known among the nations by the name Hebrews. Again, it should be noted that a Jew wrote this chapter and not a Philistine. The author goes on to tell that the Philistines said among themselves: "Have courage, Philistines, and act like men, or you will become slaves to the Hebrews" (I Samuel 4:9). It is obvious from chapters 13 and 14 in First Samuel that the Hebrews, or a part of them, were subjugated by the Philistines. In chapter 13 it says: "Saul sounded the trumpet throughout the land saying: 'Let the Hebrews hear!' " It is not Philistines, but Saul saying these things. Further it is written: "Some of the Hebrews crossed the Jordan in the direction of Gad and Gilead, but Saul remained at Gilgal" (13:7). Apparently, the Philistines fled out of fear. In the next chapter (14), we discover that a portion of the Israelites, called Hebrews, came with the Philistines to fight the Israelites, and only after Jonathan succeeded in raising bedlam in the Philistine camp, by making the daring crossing between Bozez and Seneh, did the Hebrews, who had joined ranks with the Philistines, come over to the side of Saul and Jonathan (14:21). From this, two things are clear: That the Hebrews and the Israelites belonged to one people, and that there was a difference between them. The Hebrews had been living in their own land all the time; the Israelites had returned from Egypt. We find the name Hebrew for the last time in the Book of Jonah, when the foreign sailors asked Jonah: "What is your occupation? Where do you come from? Of what people are you?" (Jonah 1:8). And Jonah answered them: "I am a Hebrew, and I worship the Lord God of heaven" (1:9). It is clear that Jonah was monotheistic, and the Hebrew people to which he belonged was identical with the Israelites.

Our people has been called by different names in different periods. In the early period, it was called by the name Hebrew—Hebrews. And Abraham belonged to this people (whether it originated with him as many believe, or whether he joined it, as I believe). One family went down to Egypt—Joseph's family, with his father, his brothers and their children—and they were called

Israelites. They lived in Egypt for two or three generations; and, in the days of Moses, left Egypt. This was the elite family of the Hebrew people that was able to absorb the high culture of Egypt of those days. The great man who arose among it in Egypt, Moses, son of Amram, refined, purified and deepened his faith and his awareness at the revelation on Mt. Sinai. Only a small group, descendants of one family for a period of two or three generations, could maintain its Hebrew language in a foreign land. It is inconceivable that a nation which grew up in Egypt for hundreds of years, even if we accept Rashi's figure of 210 years, and reached tens of thousands—even less than 600,000—would be capable of preserving its language, and would find food in the Sinai desert over a span of 40 years. It was already said of those exiled to Babylonia [sic], who had been absent from their country for only 50 to 70 years: "Half their children spoke the language of Ashdod and could not speak the language of the Jews" (Nehemiah 13:24).

When the Israelites returned to their land under the leadership of Joshua, here and there they had to fight hostile neighbors from among the peoples of Canaan. There is no doubt that they were aided by their Hebrew countrymen, though for some unknown reason the matter was not mentioned in the Book of Joshua or in the Book of Judges. In general, what these two books contain can be relied upon, but no conclusion can be drawn from what they do not contain, for there is no other single book in the Bible whose purpose it was to give the complete history of the people in a certain period. Even a distinguished and objective historian such as Thucydides did not write down everything that he knew about Athens, the city of his birth. Had the book on the Peloponnesian War not survived, we would not know anything about the literary and artistic greatness of Athens, though, in Thucydides' book, words of praise were showered on Athens for being the school of Hellas through the mouth of Pericles (apparently based on a real speech which Thucydides heard from the Athenian leader).

The fact that the Hebrews are mentioned in the same breath as the Israelites in the Book of Samuel proves, beyond the shadow of a doubt, that there were also Hebrews in the days of Joshua and the judges, just as there were in the days of Abraham and Joseph (before he went down to Egypt). The silence of these two books about the existence of Hebrews is no proof of their nonexistence.

There is no doubt that the descendants of the family that went down to Egypt were also called Israelites, and that they were an influential, and perhaps a decisive spiritual force by virtue of the influence that Moses and Joshua held over all of the Hebrew tribes which lived in Canaan from the days of Abraham the Hebrew. In the books of Joshua and Judges we see clearly that the Hebrew inhabitants of Israel still lived tribal lives, and that at different times these or other tribes used to fight with their Canaanite neighbors as well as with other ancient peoples: Moab (in the days of Ehud), Midian, Amalek and others (in the days of Gideon), Ammon (in the days of Jephthah). The name Hebrew is not mentioned in these wars, perhaps because Ehud, Deborah, Gideon and Jephthah were descendants of those who had left Egypt, and were called Israelites. But the Book of Samuel testifies to the fact that in Samuel's day—and therefore, also, in the days before Samuel—there were Hebrews; and it is possible that there was a large cultural gap between the smaller number of Israelites who were spiritually minded, and the more numerous Hebrews who were closer in spirit to their Canaanite neighbors, until all became one people in the days of the monarchy. But the name Hebrew survived until the days of Jeremiah, though by that time a new name, Jews, was in use, which took in both the name Hebrews and the name Israel. Even the language which our people spoke then was called Jewish (II Kings 18:26; Isaiah 36:11, 13; II Chronicles 32:18; Nehemiah 13:24). The name Jews is already mentioned in the days of Ahaz, son of Jotham, king of Judah (II Kings 16:6), but this name became popular only in the days of Jeremiah, after the destruction of the kingdom of Israel, and is commonly found in the Book of Jeremiah (32:12; 38:19; 40:11, 12; 41:3, 44:1); in the Book of Nehemiah (1:2; 2:16; 3:33, 34; 4:6; 5:1, 8, 17; 6:6; 13:23); and is very common in the Book of Esther. It is found in its Aramaic form in the books of Ezra and Daniel: *Yehuda-yay* (Ezra 4:12; 5:1, 5; 6:7, 8, 14). Just as the Israelites and the Jews were not two different peoples, so the Hebrews and the Israelites were not two different peoples. Rather, the name Hebrew was older, while the name Israelite applied to those who went down to, and later left, Egypt. As a result of the qualitative importance of this group, from which came Moses and Joshua, the name Israel spread to the entire nation, until the name Jews came to take its place.

Professor Kaufman establishes one thing which strengthens my hypothesis. He refers to Genesis 43:32, where it says that "the Egyptians could not eat together with the Hebrews because it is repulsive to them." There is no doubt that this Egyptian law of abomination was created, not with reference to the descendants of Jacob with whom the Egyptians were not at all acquainted, but with reference to a large group of Hebrews, who, together with their customs, were known to the Egyptians. Nevertheless, the biblical narrator sees the law as directed towards the descendants of Jacob.

Two conclusions, which strengthen my hypothesis, emerge from these words of Professor Kaufman: 1) that in the eyes of the Egyptians, the descendants of Jacob were Hebrews; and so they appear to me, and 2) that a larger group of Hebrews existed then, who, together with their customs, were known to the Egyptians. That is, there were Hebrews in the land of Canaan (excluding Jacob's children who went down to Egypt), even before Jacob's children went down to Egypt; and they were all circumcised and they believed in the one God that Abraham and Malkitzedek, king of Shalem, believed in. The latter was also a priest to Almighty God, implying that it was not he alone who believed in this God, but also members of his tribe.

And now to the question of Shechem, where, according to Joshua 24, there was a "sanctuary of the Lord," and where Joshua made a covenant with his people: "He drew up a statute and an ordinance for them in Shechem. And Joshua wrote these things in the Torah of God" (Joshua 24:25-26). According to Professor Kaufman: "There is no support for the hypothesis that Shechem was a city of Hebrews who believed in one God." It is hard to reconcile this statement with everything written about Shechem in the Bible and in the Prophets. Even someone who doubts the historicity of all its stories cannot deny that the things written about Shechem were not written by Samaritans or foreigners, but by Jews. And, if the Torah and the Prophets said what they said about Shechem, it is possible to conclude that for different considerations, either because of the importance of Jerusalem after its conquest by David, or because of the dispute with the Samaritans, the authors or editors played down the importance of Shechem. But it is inconceivable that the authors of the Bible attributed favorable events and an importance to Shechem that it did not merit.

These are the main episodes associated with Shechem: When Abraham came from Harran, according to the narrative in Genesis, his first stop was in Shechem, where God revealed Himself to him and said: "I will give this land to your offspring." Professor Kaufman, who stresses so strongly the ancient faith of the Hebrew people (Abraham was certainly not an Israelite), must surely see of primary importance the fact that the land was promised to it as an inheritance, not because the people was indigenous to the land. It simply had come to take over a land already inhabited by other people—Canaanites. Shechem was not the northern border of the Promised Land, but its heartland. Why does the author or the editor of the Book of Genesis relate that God appeared to Abraham *in* Shechem, and that *here* the land was promised to his offspring? In Shechem Abraham built an altar to the Lord who appeared to him. This was the first altar built by Abraham.

Abraham, who came to the land with great flocks and herds, wandered southward, to areas not so heavily populated. From Genesis 13 we learn of Abraham's vast possessions—in sheep, cattle, and tents—and that Lot, the son of his brother, was also rich, to the point where "the land could not support their staying together" (13:6), and that Abraham settled in Aylonei Mamre. We learn that Abraham was not alone; he was able to assemble 318 followers in a short period in order to conduct a war. From the next chapter we learn that in his new homeland there was a priest of Almighty God who shared Abraham's belief—Malkitzedek, king of Shalem. It is obvious that Malkitzedek was not a priest to himself alone, but undoubtedly headed a congregation, or a sect. Even though this is not written explicitly in the narrative, it is clearly implied. One should not wonder that more is not written about Malkitzedek, for the hero of 14 chapters (12-25) in Genesis is Abraham. The others are only mentioned to the extent that the stories about Abraham require their inclusion. From the stories in these chapters it is clear that not only was Abraham circumcised as a "sign of the covenant" with God, but that so were all the children born in his family, all of the male members of his household, and without doubt the 318 "charges" as well; and that they were all associated with the "covenant" for which circumcision served as a sign.

In the story concerning the purchase of Ephron's field at the Machpelah, the Hittites in Hebron say to Abraham: "You are the prince of God in our midst" (Genesis 23:6). Professor Kaufman elucidates: "Abraham is the prince of God not among a Hebrew nation, but among the Hittites in Hebron." Professor Kaufman certainly does not contend that the Hittites were members of the same faith as Abraham, and that the God of Abraham was the god of the Hittites. The words spoken to Abraham were expressions of courtesy (and not especially sincere, because in the end Abraham had to weigh out 400 shekels of silver at the market price, to pay for the field that seemingly the Hittites had been ready to give him as a present). But their words prove that it was known in the land that Abraham was a prince of God, and not a prince to himself, just as Malkitzedek was not a priest to himself, and that he was the head of a large following. As to the intermarriage of Abraham's children and grandchildren (assuming that Isaac was his son and Jacob his grandson—inasmuch as Professor Kaufman does not trust genealogies in the Bible), it is clear that it was their custom to marry with their privileged relatives (because without a doubt they belonged to the aristocratic class and not to common people of lower rank).

Professor Kaufman poses the question: Why didn't Isaac go to Shechem? According to chapter 18, Isaac was fond of hunting; and he was also fond of Esau, the hunter; and nothing is said of any independent initiative on the part of Isaac who, as was already noted, is the most colorless and hazy personality in all the stories of the patriarchs. But it is interesting that it is also said about Isaac that he wished for Jacob to marry into his own family, even though according to the story, Isaac, and not his son was the believer in Almighty God. Family kinship was, apparently, a more important factor in those days than religious affinity.

Again we hear of Shechem when Jacob returns from Paddan Aram (Mesopotamia) with his wives and his children. He came to Succot and built himself a house there, and later came to Shechem where he erected an altar which he called "El Elohei Yisrael"—the Lord God of Israel (Genesis 33:20). This was after the angel had changed his name from Jacob to Israel (32:29).

A complete chapter (34) is later dedicated to Shechem and to Dinah's "mishap." The people in Shechem were Hivites, and the son of the prince of Shechem fell in love with Dinah and did what he did. According to the narrative, two sons of Jacob—Simeon and Levi—"killed every male." It is hard to believe that this story is precise. How could two men kill all the males in the city, even if it occurred on the third day after their circumcision "when they were in pain." From what we know about the custom of avenging the blood and of exacting revenge in instances of lewd behavior practiced by the people of the area, we can deduce that they killed several of the relatives of Shechem, son of Hamor, and not "every male." Professor Kaufman himself, in his commentary on the Book of Judges, deals with the words of Gaal, son of Eved to the people of Shechem: "Who is Abimelech and who are the Shechemites, that we should be his subjects? . . . Have they not been the subjects of the men of Hamor, father of Shechem?" (Judges 9:28). And he [Professor Kaufman] says: "It is possible that there was still a small remnant of Hivites in Shechem, who are called 'men of Hamor, father of Shechem.' " This "possibility" makes sense only if every male in Hivite Shechem was not killed in the days of Jacob.

At least eight generations passed from the days of Jacob to the time of Abimelech, son of Gideon. If my hypothesis is correct (that not all the males of Shechem were killed, but only a few of the relatives of Shechem, son of Hamor), there is no doubt that in seven or eight generations their numbers increased, and they were not merely "a small remnant of Hivites." In my view, the Hivites in the days of Jacob joined the Israelites through the covenant of circumcision, and according to this hypothesis—and I admit that this is no more than a hypothesis—several items concerning Shechem can be understood which are later referred to in the Torah and the Early Prophets. Each item, of itself, can be belittled or denied, but when everything recorded about Shechem and its surrounding areas is taken into account, there is no way of dismissing the facts or playing down their special importance.

Before his death, Israel (Jacob) said to Joseph: "And now, I give you one portion more than to your brothers, which I wrested from the Amorites with my sword and bow" (Genesis 48:22). This verse is troublesome because of the word "one" which comes after the word *shechem.* The Septuagint doesn't use the word "one." It translates it as *shechem*—the city of Shechem. Rashi also interprets the phrase *shechem echad* to be the city of Shechem (i.e., it will be one portion more than to your brothers), though the translation of Onkelos reads: "And I give you one portion more than to your brothers."

In the Book of Deuteronomy it says: "When the Lord your God brings you into the land which you are about to invade and occupy, you shall pronounce the blessing at Mt. Gerizim and the curse at Mt. Eval" (11:29). These are two mountains to the north and south of Shechem. And again, in chapter 27, it says: "Thereupon, Moses charged the people, saying, 'After you have crossed the Jordan, the following shall stand on Mt. Gerizim when the blessing for the people is spoken: Simeon, Levi, Judah, Issachar, Joseph and Benjamin. And for the curse, the following shall stand on Mt. Eval: Reuben, Gad, Asher, Zebulun, Dan and Naphtali'" (27:11-13). Why, of all the mountains in the land of Israel, were these two mountains north and south of Shechem chosen? (The name Shechem isn't explicitly mentioned here.) These hills were not particularly close to the place where the Israelites crossed the Jordan in the days of Joshua, and there are mountains much closer to Jericho and to Ai where the Israelites fought immediately after crossing the Jordan.

After the first two battles, after Joshua devastated Jericho and burned Ai, he went northward and built "an altar to the Lord God of Israel on Mt. Eval, following the commandments given to the Israelites by Moses, the servant of the Lord. . . . There, in the presence of the Israelites, he engraved on blocks of stone a copy of the Torah of Moses" (Joshua 8:30-32). In his commentary on Joshua, Professor Kaufman already dealt with the fact that the description in Joshua does not coincide in several details with what is written in Deuteronomy. But the two questions remain: 1) Why were the two mountains north and south of Shechem chosen? and 2) How did Joshua reach Shechem without any resistance from the local population?

There is a dispute between the Jews and the Samaritans over Mt. Gerizim. This dispute has no bearing on my explanations regarding the antiquity of Israel, because the Samaritan dispute began only after the return to Zion from the Babylonian exile, whereas the importance of Shechem is proven according to the Bible—proven both according to the traditional version of the books of the Torah, and according to the books of the Prophets which the Samaritans do not accept.

There is a dispute among Bible scholars over the date of the writing and publication of the Book of Deuteronomy or, as it is called, *Mishne Torah.* This dispute also has no bearing on my explanations, because, according to those who believe that Deuteronomy belongs to the period of Hezekiah and Isaiah, it is even more mystifying why this honor was bestowed upon Shechem when the center of Israel in the days of David and Solomon, and later in the days of the kings of Judah, was Jerusalem—where Solomon built his Temple.

According to Professor Kaufman, "the books of Joshua and Judges include reliable evidence—contemporary to the events—of the conquest of the land," and they are "the solid base for the building of the beginning of the history of Israel." However, the question is asked: Why did Joshua go to Mt. Eval and to Mt. Gerizim, build an altar there, and write the Torah of God? All this, without doubt, took a great deal of time—and none of the Canaanite or Amorite inhabitants of the land interfered with them. Yet, how does one explain that not once is it mentioned that Shechem was conquered by Joshua? Professor Kaufman establishes that Shechem wasn't mentioned at all in the story about Mt. Gerizim and Mt. Eval, but Shechem did exist at that time as is proven from the Book of Joshua itself (17:7; 20:7; 21:21—all from chapter 24). According to the words of Professor Kaufman: "When those who had left Egypt went up to the land, Shechem was still in ruins and impoverished. There was no real war over Shechem. The tribes went to Shechem without any apprehension. Shechem became an important city once again only after the Israelites settled in it. According to Joshua 24, this occurred in the lifetime of Joshua."

In an introduction to the Book of Joshua, Professor Kaufman expands upon this question, and says: "At first glance, the absence of any information about Shechem is truly puzzling, because Shechem was a principal city in this area. Here, during the Tel Amarna period, ruled Lavaya and his sons (maybe he should be called Lavie?), who played an important role in the disputes of the kings of Canaan at this very time. Shechem is mentioned in the stories of the patriarchs.

"In the days of Abimelech an attempt was made to establish a monarchy there (Judges 9). How is it possible that this city should not be mentioned in the story of the conquest of the land?"

Professor Kaufman answers that Shechem was in ruins and was desolate in the days of the conquest. And he adds: "In the commandment about the ceremony on Mt. Gerizim in Deuteronomy 11:29-30, in Deuteronomy 27, and also in Joshua 8, Shechem is not mentioned at all."

These two arguments are not well taken. There is no basis whatever to conclude that Shechem was in ruins and unpopulated in the days of Joshua. There simply was no need to mention it when speaking of Mt. Gerizim and Mt. Eval, just as it is possible to speak of Mt. Moriah without mentioning Jerusalem, for everyone knows that Mt. Eval is north of Shechem, and Mt. Gerizim south of it.

In Joshua 24 we read that all the tribes of Israel gathered in Shechem where Joshua made a covenant with them, which was secondary only to the revelation at Mt. Sinai. Shechem is mentioned earlier in the description of the territory of Manasseh (Joshua 17:7), and it is designated as one of the three cities of refuge by Joshua (20:7). And a city of refuge, by its very nature, cannot be in ruins. Kadesh in the Galilee, Shechem in the hills of Ephraim, and Hebron in the Judean hills (the three cities of refuge west of the Jordan) were populated cities.

The great importance of Shechem in the days of Joshua stands out in the last chapter of the Book of Joshua—chapter 24. According to Professor Kaufman, this chapter is a later addition, but this is the claim not proven by any compelling evidence, and resembles, somewhat, the claim of Bible scholars from Wellhausen's school, which Professor Kaufman, justly, and with deep understanding, refuted.

One of the most important events—if not the most important event—in the history of Israel in its land is told in this chapter: that of Israel's choosing of its God, which is unlike the accepted version in the rest of the books of the Bible: that God chose Israel as his people.

After Joshua's pithy speech on the early history of his people and a call to worship the Lord wholeheartedly, the people say: "God forbid that we should forsake the Lord to worship other gods." Joshua warns them again: "You cannot worship the Lord. He is a holy god, a jealous god, and he will not forgive your rebellion and your sins." And the people say: "No! We will worship the Lord." And then Joshua says a very significant thing: "You are witnesses against yourselves that you have chosen the Lord and will worship him." And they said: "We are witnesses" (24:22). This is one of the most important and enlightening sections in the history of the Israelite faith, for here the truth about the choosing of God by the Israelites is established—and this reveals the spiritual greatness of our people in those days. And this, incidentally, is one of the most important discoveries in Professor Kaufman's great book: that the belief in one God came early and grew from within the nation, and did not come to it from without, as several Gentile scholars attempt to prove through their distorted commentaries on the Bible and through remnants of the literature of the peoples of the region—Egypt, Babylonia and Aram.

According to Professor Kaufman, "the last two chapters of the Book of Joshua are, to a certain extent, parallel. Both of them tell of assemblies of the people at Joshua's invitation; in both, Joshua reviews the past; and in both, he imposes certain obligations on the people and warns them concerning the future." But Professor Kaufman rejects the view that chapter 24 is the original end of the Book of Joshua, and he believes that chapter 23 was written in an identical style, as a supplement to it. In his view, chapter 24 is an "apocryphal" chapter which has no connection with the body of the book, and which does not serve as its conclusion. This chapter is not a conclusion; Joshua isn't old, isn't about to die, and is not leaving the nation. The assembly takes place in Shechem, and Shechem is not mentioned earlier at all. In chapters 1-23 no mention is made of sanctuaries, but in chapter 24, there is a sanctuary in Shechem. In Joshua 1-23 idolatry is not mentioned, but in chapter 24 Joshua demands the removal of foreign gods. The "hornet" (24:12) is not mentioned previously.

Chapter 23 is linked by its language, by its background, and by its ideas to chapters 1-22, and it is the actual end of the Book of Joshua. This chapter is the last testament of Joshua to the nation, as "conqueror of the land," etc. Chapter 23 is tied organically to the Book of Joshua. Therefore, 23:1-16 and 24:29-33 should be viewed as the original ending of the book; while 24:1-28 is the appended chapter.

In my humble opinion, this distinction, and the gradation of the two chapters is invalid. There is no basis for the removal of the six final verses of chapter 24, to join them to chapter 23, and to consider the heart of chapter 24 as a later addition. In my opinion these two chapters tell of two assemblies—different in audience and different in purpose. It doesn't say in chapter 23 that Joshua assembled all of the tribes, but only the elders of Israel. In chapter 24, however, Joshua assembled "all the tribes of Israel"—their leaders—and the assembly was held in Shechem. (In chapter 23 it doesn't say to which place Joshua summoned the elders and leaders.) In my view, this is not pure chance. The first speech was delivered to those Israelites who had left Egypt, had accompanied Joshua in the desert, and entered the land with him. There was no need to tell them all of the history of the patriarchs, about what happened in Egypt, and what happened in the desert. They were members of Joshua's generation, and had marched together with him through the desert and returned together with him to the land. Now, he was parting from them, for he had reached old age.

But chapter 24 talks about the assembly of the tribes of Israel and its leaders; that is, the native population which had not been in Egypt, and had remained in its land all the while. For them, Joshua describes the early history, the exodus from Egypt, and the story of the wars. The matter of the "hornet" is puzzling; but it is mentioned in the Torah. Professor Kaufman says: "There are those who interpret its meaning as 'panic' or 'terror' and this is comparable to: 'I will send forth my terror before you' " (Exodus 23:27). It is very possible that verses 12 and 13 are a later addition. Professor Kaufman also feels that there are "words left dangling" here.

It is doubtful if the people's reply in verses 17-18 is authentic, because it is hard to believe that the entire people, or its representatives, said all of these things. In the following verses, the nation's reply is brief: "No! We will worship the Lord" (verse 21), "we are witnesses"; and then comes the key verse: "Joshua said to the nation: 'You are witnesses unto yourselves that you have chosen the Lord and will worship him.' And they answered: 'We are witnesses' " (verse 22).

There is no question at all as to why Joshua said to the representatives of the tribes: "Remove the foreign gods in your midst . . ." (verse 23). There were no foreign gods in the midst of those who had left Egypt, but, among those who lived their entire lives in the land, there were certainly many who also worshipped other gods. Because, if this is not so, then the Book of Judges, which Professor Kaufman also considers "the solid base of the origin of the history of Israel," is not intelligible. It is inconceivable that a people which was born in Egypt in its entirety (from one family of the children of Jacob or the children of Israel which went down to Egypt), preserved its Hebrew language all this while (according to the Torah, 400 years; according to the commentators, 210 years; according to my hypothesis, just two or three generations), and remained united [in the words of Professor Kaufman] "under one prophetic leader—as a nation in which tremendous religious enthusiasm prevailed, and which conquered the land in a war with all its inhabitants, where they didn't find one friendly settlement; a people which did not worship any other gods from the day of its birth until the death of Joshua and his contemporary elders who lived on after Joshua—it is inconceivable that they should suddenly split into tribes and begin to worship idols: "And they did evil in the eyes of the Lord and worshipped the Baalim. And they left the Lord, God of their fathers, who took them out of Egypt, and they pursued other gods from among the gods of the nations surrounding them" (Judges 2:11-12). And again: "And the Israelites continued to do evil in the eyes of God" (4:1). And once again: "And the Israelites did evil in the eyes of the Lord" (6:1). This is only possible if there were two separate groups within our people: those who left Egypt "who were unified under one prophetic leader, and among whom tremendous religious enthusiasm prevailed"; and the permanent inhabitants of "the land of the Hebrews" who believed in one God, but were influenced by the Canaanites and other neighbors from among the nations of old: Moab, Ammon, Midian, etc. There were also "foreign gods" among this latter group in the days of Joshua, and Joshua assembled them for the special purpose of asking them to remove the foreign gods. They answered: "We will worship the Lord our God and will heed his voice" (24:24). At that time Joshua made a covenant with the people and wrote the provisions in the Torah of God; he drew up a statute and an ordinance for the people and erected a large stone under the oak tree near the sanctuary of the Lord. It is very probable that this dialogue between Joshua and the tribes of the nation living in the land (because those who had left Egypt were one unified national unit) took place during the last years of Joshua, who had waged several wars and had been accepted by the entire nation as its leader, just as Samuel was accepted after him. There is no need to remove the last six verses of chapter 24 and to attach them to chapter 23.

Chapter 24 can't be denied in its entirety because it testifies to the existence of the sanctuary of the Lord at Shechem. The spiritual importance of Shechem in the early history of our people is confirmed by stories about the lives of Abraham and Jacob, by the commandments of Moses, and by Joshua's journey to Mt. Eval and Mt. Gerizim after his first victory in Ai. Shechem was not uninhabited. Its inhabitants were the grandchildren of the Hivites who had joined the people of God in the days of Jacob—not all of whom were killed by Simeon and Levi. And perhaps it is not mere coincidence that the Hivites, in particular (Joshua 9:7), who lived in Gibeon, Kefirah, Beerot, and Kiryat Jearim (9:17), cleverly made a covenant with Joshua and his princes that they would not fight each other.

It is clear from Judges 9 that Shechem was not desolate, nor was it Canaanite. Jotham, son of Gideon stood at the top of Mt. Gezirim and in his speech to the residents of Shechem, proclaims, "my father fought for you and threw himself into the forefront of the battle and delivered you from the Midianites" (9:17), though there was no reason for Gideon to give his life to save a Canaanite city. Even Professor Kaufman admits that Shechem, in the days of Gideon and Abimelech, was "Israelite" and according to him there was also a remnant of Hivites there. From the words of the Book of Judges, it is clear that Abimelech did not reign over Shechem, but over the whole nation, as it is written: "And Abimelech ruled over Israel for three years" (9:22). But Abimelech was crowned in Shechem (9:6), and this again proves the importance of this city in those days. Even after the conquest of Jerusalem in the days of David, and the building of the Temple in Jerusalem by Solomon, Shechem remained an important city. And when Solomon died, Rehoboam journeyed to Shechem "for all Israel had gone to Shechem to crown him" (I Kings 12:1).

The later editors of the Bible—if there were such editors—had no reason to glorify Shechem and embellish it with legends about Abraham, Jacob, and Joshua, and to say that there, and only there, was there a sanctuary to the Lord before the building of the Temple in Jerusalem by Solomon. These stories prove that in the period before the monarchy in Israel, and particularly in the ancient period, Shechem was the spiritual center of the Hebrews and, therefore, the patriarchs (Abraham and Jacob) went to it; and therefore those who left Egypt were ordered to assemble in the vicinity of the two hills in Shechem—Mt. Eval and Mt. Gerizim. So Joshua went there after his first victory and made a covenant with the Children of Israel—with those who had returned from Egypt and with those who had always lived in the land.

Chapter 24 in Joshua, with the possible exception of several verses which were added later, is one of the principal and most important documents—if not the most important—in the history of the spiritual life of our people in the early period. This chapter bears the stamp of historical truth, and isn't adorned with miracles and supernatural feats. This is a lofty dialogue between the nation's leader—its political and spiritual leader—and the nation's most prominent people from every stratum of society.

If later authors or editors did make changes in this chapter, it could only be with the intention to detract from the image of this great revelation, and not to enhance it. The regard in which Shechem and Joshua were held in later periods should also not be viewed as an exaggeration aimed at lavishing praise and approbation. It is also inconceivable that at a later date someone invented the idea that there existed in Shechem a sanctuary of the Lord, and that the revelation to the patriarchs of the nation had to take place in this city. The narrative in chapter 24 reflects the spirit and content of the entire chapter: "And Israel worshipped the Lord during the lifetime of Joshua and the elders," because Joshua's influence was great on all levels of national society—those who came out of Egypt and those called "Hebrews" in the Book of Samuel.

CHAPTER TWELVE

On the Book of Deuteronomy

The Book of Deuteronomy is the fifth and last book of the Torah. In the Bible it is called *Mishne Torah* (Deut. 17:18), and in the Septuagint, *Deuteronomion,* because the greater part of the book is no more than a review of the stories and laws written in the books of Exodus, Leviticus and Numbers. Occasionally, it is a literal repetition; sometimes, with minor editorial changes, and, occasionally, with significant changes. But this book has an independent image, with a decided moral and prophetic purpose, which comes much closer to the Literary Prophets: Hosea, Amos and Isaiah, son of Amoz, than do the earlier books of the Bible, in a few of which—especially several paragraphs in the Book of Genesis—can be recognized traces of the influence of Mesopotamian literature and its legends.

The school of Wellhausen argues that the Jewish faith, until the days of the Literary Prophets, was not a belief in one God (known as monotheism), but monolatry, the worship of one God, a national God, without the denial of the existence of other gods—the gods of neighboring nations. The Jewish God, according to Wellhausen's school, was not the only god in the world, but the only god to Israel alone. Thus, this school post-dates the existence of the Torah of Moses, which is based on a belief in one God—like whom there is none other—to a later period; to the period of the Literary Prophets, who appeared (in the days of Uziahu, king of Judah, and Jeroboam II, king of Israel) in the eighth century B.C.

Lecture at the 13th Bible Conference, April 1, 1965.

The late Professor Ezekiel Kaufman in his great book, *A History of the Israelite Faith* (which unfortunately was not completed), shook Wellhausen's views to their very roots. But he, too, recognizes that although the five books of the Torah derive from an ancient source—from the days of the patriarchs and Moses—their established version, and what we have today, was put together in the course of generations, based on ancient scrolls which were passed down from generation to generation. Even some of the Rabbis of the Talmud believed that the Torah was given portion by portion; as Rabbi Jochanan in the name of Rabbi Benaya said (Gittin 60): "There is proof for this from the Torah itself. In Deuteronomy 3:14 it is recorded in the name of Moses: 'Jair, son of Manasseh, received the entire Argov region (that is Bashan) as far as the boundary of the Geshurites and Maacathites and named it after himself—Havot Jair [the villages of Jair] so known to this day.'" The conquest of Og, king of Bashan, took place at the end of Moses' life, and so the words "to this day" were, without a doubt, spoken at a much later period. There are similar verses in other books of the Torah. What Professor Kaufman says makes sense: that a distinction must be made between biblical literature which is ancient, and which, as Rabbi Jochanan says, was handed down in small portions, and the books of the Torah, which were put together in the course of time, beginning with the days of Literary Prophets. There is no doubt that the four books, from Genesis through Numbers, came earlier than the Book of Deuteronomy, both with regard to their narrative and their legal content.

The Book of Deuteronomy, as we have it today, also did not appear all at once. Rather, it should be viewed as the first consolidated book found in the Temple by Hilkiyahu, in the days of King Josiah (II Kings 22:8) in the seventh century B.C. The discovery of this book and its presentation to the king brought about the basic reform which was carried out in the days of Josiah: the removal of all traces of idolatry, the removal of the scattered altars, and the concentration of the worship of the true God in one place—at the Temple in Jerusalem as is recorded in chapter 23 of Second Kings. Then, too, "the king ordered all the people to keep the passover of the Lord their God, as this Book of Covenant prescribed. No such Passover had been kept—either when the judges were ruling Israel or during the times of the kings of Israel and Judah. But in the eighteenth year of Josiah's reign, Passover was observed for the Lord in Jerusalem" (II Kings 23:21-23). "Further, Josiah got rid of all who practiced necromancy, all who kept household gods and idols, and all the loathesome objects seen in the land of Judah and in Jerusalem, so that he might fulfill the requirements of the law as prescribed in the book which the priest Hilkiyahu had discovered in the house of the Lord" (23:24).

There are strong words in the Book of Deuteronomy against necromancy: "Let no one be found among you . . . who is an augur, a soothsayer, a diviner, a sorcerer, one who casts spells, or one who consults ghosts or familiar spirits, or one who inquires of the dead. For anyone who does such things is abhorrent to the Lord" (Deuteronomy 18:10-12). But there are also words no less vehement against ghosts and spirits in the Book of Leviticus (19:31; 10:16). But neither in the Book of Leviticus nor in the rest of the Torah, with the exception of the Book of Deuteronomy, is there a prohibition against altars, or a request to concentrate worship in one place. The removal of the altars outside of the Temple already began with King Hezekiah (who ruled 720-690 B.C.), and there is no doubt that the doctrine of a central place of worship was also known in his days, from one of the Deuteronomy scrolls.

It is difficult to conceive that the Book of Deuteronomy was written in its entirety in the days of Josiah, the great-grandson of Hezekiah, because a new book, without a tradition rooted in the people, would not have made a revolutionary impression as did the discovery of the Torah in the Temple, as Professor Kaufman rightly argues. And several scrolls of the Book of Deuteronomy were already known of in the days of Hezekiah, and this king functioned in accordance with them. Hezekiah's attempt to burn the altars did not succeed, because his son Manasseh, whose reign lasted for 55 years, did not follow in his father's footsteps. "He rebuilt the altars which his father Hezekiah had destroyed, he erected altars to Baal and made a sacred pole, as Ahab, king of Israel had done. . . . He built altars for all the hosts of heaven" (II Kings 21:3-5).

Manasseh's son Amon, in turn, followed in his path until his grandson Josiah became king. "And he did what was right in the eyes of the Lord and followed all the paths of his father David." In the eighteenth year of his reign, the Torah was found. Then, the great change took place, and the altars were removed, destroyed and smashed, not to return. The book of the Torah which was discovered in the days of Josiah continued to function among the people as the Torah of God. Thus, with the return to Zion in the days of Ezra and Nehemiah, when the building of the Temple was renewed, altars were no longer built in the land, and the worship of God was concentrated in Jerusalem.

Until the appearance of the "Book of the Torah" in the days of Josiah, judges, prophets, priests and kings ruled the nation. From the days of Josiah, until the return of Zion in the days of Ezra and Nehemiah, the Book took over and ruled.

As has been said, Professor Kaufman distinguishes between biblical *literature* and the *books* of the Bible. Biblical literature existed from early times. The oldest of materials was preserved in scrolls from which the Book of Genesis was formed in the course of time, and afterward the books of Exodus, Leviticus and Numbers. In his view, the consolidation began with the second group of scrolls, which included the material gathered and formulated in the Book of Deuteronomy, which is the first book of the Torah that was discovered in the days of Josiah—even though the origin of this book is also much earlier (earlier than the other four books, which were put together in their present form—after the Book of Deuteronomy). This is a plausible hypothesis, though it should not be accepted with complete certainty. Just as in the days of Josiah they celebrated Passover for the first time on the occasion of the first discovery of the Torah, so in the days of Ezra and Nehemiah they celebrated the holiday of Succot for the first time after "the heads of families of the whole people, with the priests and Levites, assembled before Ezra the scribe, to study the Torah. And they found recorded in the Torah that the Lord had commanded through Moses that the Israelites should live in booths during the feasts of the seventh month, and that they should proclaim it throughout all their cities, and in Jerusalem: 'Go out into the hills and fetch branches of olive and wild olive, myrtle and palm and other leafy boughs to make booths as prescribed.' So the people went out and fetched them and made for themselves . . . a thing that the Israelites had not done from the days of Joshua, son of Nun, to that day" (Nehemiah 8:13-17).

It is interesting that even though the holiday of Succot is mentioned three times in the Book of Deuteronomy (16:13, 16; 31:10), living in the booth is not mentioned at all, and no leaves of fruit trees were specified. And because of this, apparently, we do not hear about living in the booth in the days of Josiah, but rather about the holiday of Passover. Only in the Book of Leviticus (23:40) does it say concerning the holiday of Succot: "On the first day you shall take the product of Hadar trees, branches of palm trees, boughs of leafy trees, and willows of the brook, and you shall rejoice before the Lord your God seven days. . . . You shall live in booths seven days; all citizens of Israel shall live in booths" (23:40, 42)). This contradicts the view of Professor Yavin that the "Sefer

Torah" already existed before Hezekiah. It is clear that what they did in the days of Nehemiah, they did according to the Book of Leviticus, though no olive, wild olive, or willows of the brook are mentioned there. However, palm trees, leafy trees and Hadar trees (apparently referring to the myrtle) are mentioned in the Book of Nehemiah. In any case, it is clear from what is written in the Book of Nehemiah that neither in the days of Josiah, nor in the days of Hezekiah, was the holiday of Succot celebrated, nor did they live in booths or use the trees mentioned in the Book of Leviticus. It appears, however, that this book, or this place in the Book of Leviticus, was not known then. And it is possible that mention of the holiday of Succot was not yet made in the "Book of the Torah" which was discovered in the days of Josiah (i.e. the Book of Deuteronomy).

I do not want to decide at this point the date of the appearance of the books of the Torah, and whether they were formed from scrolls or existed as complete books. Those who accept the orthodox tradition have no need of any proof. But everyone agrees that the Book of Deuteronomy has existed in its present form for more than 2,500 years, has been with us all these years, and without doubt has made a profound influence on the life of our people and on its spirit. In my brief remarks, I will concentrate on the special attributes of this book.

As has been said, the Book of Deuteronomy is no more than a review of the Torah; that is, it reviews the stories and events from the exodus from Egypt, the receiving of the Torah and the wanderings in the desert, to the conquest of the land of the Amorites—Sihon, king of Heshbon and Og, king of Bashan—on the other side of the Jordan. It repeats many of the commandments, statutes and laws, but it stands out because of its strong emphasis on the unity of the Creator and his love; prevention of injustice and love of justice and peace, aid to the poor, to the stranger, to the orphan, to the widow, and the existence of the people of Israel as a chosen people.

This book contains the most adored verse in the faith of Israel: "Hear O Israel, the Lord is our God, the Lord is One" (Deuteronomy 6:4). And after it: "Thou shalt love the Lord God, with all your heart, with all your soul, and with all your might" (6:5). In none of the other books of the Torah is the obligation to love God stressed to the degree that we find it in the Book of Deuteronomy. This verse also recurs in chapter 10: "And now, O Israel, what does the Lord your God demand of you? Only this: to revere the Lord your God, to walk only in his paths, to love him, and to serve the Lord God with all your heart and soul" (10:12). And again it says: "If, then, you obey the commandments which I enjoined upon you this day, loving the Lord your God . . ." (11:13). And again in verse 1 of the same chapter: "Love the Lord your God." Apparently, Baruch Spinoza learned the love of God from these verses which he placed at the center of his ethical system.

In no place in the Torah is the negation of the personification of God stronger than in verses 15-19 of Deuteronomy 4, a condemnation of every picture, statue, image of man, animal, bird, fish, sun, moon, star and heavenly body—everything which at that time served neighboring countries as likenesses of God. The point of the uniqueness of God recurs elsewhere with stark brevity: "It has been clearly demonstrated to you that the Lord alone is God; there is none beside him" (4:35).

The essence of the commandments in the Torah—the "Ten Words" [Hebrew: *Aseret Hadevarim*] in the language of the Torah, or the "Ten Commandments" as we customarily call them—which were given on Mt. Sinai, described in the Book of Exodus, recurs in the Book of Deuteronomy (5:6-18). Most of the commandments recur in the Book of Deuteronomy word for word, or with minor changes, which do not change the gist of the commandment. But, in one commandment the text is fundamentally different in Deuteronomy from what it is in Exodus. That commandment deals with the Sabbath which the Talmud says "outweighs all the other commandments" (Jerusalem Talmud, Berachot 1). In Exodus it says "Remember the Sabbath day to keep it holy. Six days you shall labor and do all your work, but the seventh day is a Sabbath of the Lord your God. You shall not do any work—you, your son or daughter, your male or female slave, or your cattle, or the stranger who is within your settlements. For in six days the Lord made heaven and earth and sea, and all that is in them, and he rested on the seventh day; therefore the Lord blessed the Sabbath day and hallowed it" (20:8-11). But in Deuteronomy, the cosmological rationale that the earth was created in six days and on the seventh day God rested disappears completely. Rather, it says: "Observe the Sabbath day and keep it holy, as the Lord your God has commanded you. Six days you shall labor and do all your work, but the seventh day is a Sabbath of the Lord your God: you shall not do any work—you, your son or your daughter, your male or female slave, your ox or your ass, or any of your cattle, or the stranger in your settlements." And then comes a completely different rationale: ". . . so that your male and female slave may rest as you do. Remember that you were a slave in the land of Egypt and the Lord your God freed you from there with a mighty hand and an outstretched arm; therefore the Lord your God has commanded you to observe the Sabbath day" (Deuteronomy 5:12-15). The rationale to rest offered here is social—humane, and is tied to the memory of the enslavement of the Israelites in Egypt, not with the creation of heaven and earth.

It is desirable to point out that in addition to the chapter on the Ten Commandments, the Sabbath is also presented in this light in one other place (Exodus 23:12): "Six days you shall do your work, but on the seventh day you shall cease from labor, in order that your ox and your ass may rest, and that your bondsman and the stranger may be refreshed." In Deuteronomy it says: "So that your male and female slave may rest as you do." Concern for the male and female servants recurs several times in the Book of Deuteronomy: "And you shall rejoice before the Lord your God with your sons and daughters and with your male and female slaves, along with the Levite of your settlement" (12:12). And again: "You shall rejoice before the Lord your God with your son and daughter, your male and female slave, the Levites in your communities, and the stranger, the fatherless, and the widow in your midst" (16:11). And the same explanation for the holiday of Succot: "You shall rejoice in your festival, with your son and daughter, your male and female slave, the Levite, the stranger, the fatherless, and the widow in your communities" (16:14). In each instance comes the addition: "Bear in mind that you were slaves in Egypt."

The Book of Deuteronomy equates the law pertaining to the female slave with that pertaining to the male slave, while the law in Exodus discriminates against the girl sold into slavery, and she does not go free in the seventh year as does the male: "If you purchase a male Hebrew slave, he shall work for six years and on the seventh go free. And if someone sells his daughter into slavery, she shall not go free as shall the male slaves." But in the Book of Deuteronomy, it says: "If a fellow-Hebrew, man or woman, is sold to you, he shall serve you six years, and in the seventh year you shall set him free" (15:12)—without distinction between male and female servants.

According to the Book of Exodus, the law of the fallow year (*shemitah*), obligates us, on the seventh year, to abandon the field and the vineyard and the olive grove, to the poor and to the wild beasts (23:11). In the Book of Deuteronomy the fallow year is given a much more humanistic interpretation: "Every seventh year you shall practice remission of debts. This shall be the nature of the remission: Every creditor shall remit the due that he claims from his neighbor; he shall not oppress his neighbor or kinsman, for the remission proclaimed is of the Lord" (15:1-2). It is clear that such a *shemitah* had a greater social implication. According to the Book of Numbers (18:18) every firstborn ox, sheep, or goat belongs to the priest; according to Deuteronomy (15:20) it is to be eaten by its owner.

The influence of a prophecy that demands justice is much more pronounced in the Book of Deuteronomy than in any other book of the Torah. Only in Leviticus 19:15—one of the loftiest chapters in the Bible—does it say: "You shall not render an unfair decision . . . judge your neighbor fairly." And again: "You shall have an honest balance, honest weights, an honest *ephah,* and an honest *hin*" (19:36). In contrast, the plea for justice recurs several times in the Book of Deuteronomy in various forms: "Decide justly between any man and a fellow Israelite or stranger" (1:16); "Or what great nation has laws and rules as perfect as this teaching that I set before you this day?" (4:8); "It will therefore be to our merit before the Lord our God to observe faithfully this whole instruction" (6:25). "You shall appoint magistrates and officials for your tribes, in all the settlements . . . and they shall govern the people with due justice. You shall not judge unfairly; you shall show no partiality. . . . Justice, justice shall you pursue" (16:18-20); "You shall not have in your pouch alternate weights—larger and smaller. You shall not have in your house alternate measures—a larger and a smaller. You must have completely honest weights and completely honest measures. . . . For everyone who does those things, everyone who deals dishonestly, is abhorrent to the Lord your God" (25:13-16). "When there is a dispute between men and they go to court, a decision is rendered declaring the one in the right and the other in the wrong . . ." (25:1). Just as the Book of Deuteronomy orders justice, so does it order the prevention of exploitation: "You shall not abuse a needy and a destitute laborer, whether a fellow countryman or a stranger in one of the communities of your land. You must pay him his wages on the same day, before the sun sets, for he is needy and urgently depends on it . . ." (24:14-15).

In the Book of Deuteronomy it says for the first time: "You shall not turn over to his master a slave who seeks refuge with you from his master. He shall live with you in any place he may choose among the settlements in your midst, wherever he pleases; you must not ill-treat him" (23:16-17). This was said in Israel some 3,000 years ago, yet some 100 years ago there was a civil war in the United States over slavery in the southern states.

The Book of Deuteronomy was the first to declare the principle that the members of a family are not responsible for the misdeeds of their relatives: "Parents shall not be put to death for children, nor children be put to death for parents: a person shall be put to death only for his own crime" (24:16). It is puzzling that just two of the prophets who were in Babylonia during the exile brought this idea up again. Jeremiah says in chapter 31 (29-30): "In those days it shall no longer be said: 'The fathers have eaten sour grapes and the children's teeth are set on edge.' For a man shall die for his own wrongdoing; the man who eats sour grapes shall have his own teeth set on edge." Ezekiel dedicated an entire chapter to this theme. He even finds merit in the wicked person who has repented from his wickedness: "It may be that a wicked man gives up his sinful ways and keeps all my laws, doing what is just and right. That man shall live; he shall not die. None of the offenses he has committed shall be remembered against him; he shall live because of his righteous deeds. Have I any desire, says the Lord God, for the death of a wicked man? Would I not rather that he mend his ways and live?" (18:21-23).

Let us remember that in our own lifetime the custom of the redemption of the blood existed among the Arabs, and 56 years ago (in Passover 1909) two of my friends were killed when two guests who arrived at Segerah were attacked on the road by an Arab gang from Kfar Kanna. One of the guests defended himself and wounded one of the Arabs who attacked him, and the Arab later died from his wounds. As a result, on the seventh day of that Passover, two of our people were killed—the watchman, Israel Korngold, and the young farmer, Shimon Melamed. Thus, this simple idea, accepted today by all cultured peoples, that only the criminal is accountable for his actions and not his relatives, was an exceptional and revolutionary idea when it was expressed over 2,500 years ago in our land. It should not surprise us that this was one of the central ideas of the Book of Deuteronomy: the Israelites being a holy and chosen people.

In Exodus it is written that God commanded Moses to tell the Israelites: "Now then, if you will obey me faithfully and keep my covenant, you shall be my treasured possession among all the peoples. . . . But you shall be to me a kingdom of priests and a holy nation" (19:5-6). This is stated in the Book of Deuteronomy more decisively and forcefully: "For you are a people consecrated to the Lord your God. Of all the peoples on earth, the Lord your

God chose you to be his treasured people. It is not because you are the most numerous of peoples that the Lord set his heart on you and chose you—indeed you are the smallest of peoples; but rather because the Lord loved you and kept the oath he made to your fathers. . . . Know, therefore, that only the Lord your God is God, the steadfast God who keeps his gracious covenant to the thousandth generation of those who love him and keep his commandments" (7:6-9). This is repeated in chapter 14: "You are children of the Lord your God. . . . For you are a people consecrated to the Lord your God. The Lord your God chose you from among all other peoples on earth to be his treasured people" (14:1-2). This is reiterated at the end of Moses' speech in chapter 26: "And the Lord has affirmed this day that you are, as He promised you, His treasured people that will observe all His commandments; and that He will acclaim you in glory, above all the nations that He has made; and that you shall be, as He promised, a holy people to the Lord your God" (26:18-19).

The theme of the selection of Israel recurs several times in Isaiah: "The Lord will show compassion for Jacob and will once again make Israel His choice" (14:1). "But you, Israel My servant; you, Israel whom I have chosen . . ." (41:5). "Hear Me now, Jacob My servant, hear Me, My chosen Israel" (44:1). "Have no fear, Jacob My servant, Jeshurun whom I have chosen . . ." (44:2). The choosing of Israel by God also recurs in other books of the Bible (Amos 2:2; Psalms 35:4; Haggai 2:23; Nehemiah 9:7), and to this day every Jew recites the words, "You have chosen us from all the nations," in his prayers. Not only Baruch Spinoza had difficulty with the idea of the selection of Israel; the Rabbis in the Talmud did as well. Is it really possible that God would differentiate between nations, and choose one nation as His own? And so the Agaddah [the Legends] tells us that when the place where the Torah would be given was revealed, it was not revealed to Israel alone, but to all the nations. First, he went to the descendants of Esau and said to them: Do you accept the Torah? They said to Him: We cannot accept the Torah. Then He went to the Ammonites, the Moabites, and the Ishmaelites—there was not one nation on whose door He did not knock to ask if they wanted to accept the Torah. All refused. Only then did he approach Israel.

They said: "We will do and we will listen."

In the last chapter of the Book of Joshua, chapter 24, we find a completely different version of the selection—different from all other biblical sources and accepted tradition—which fits in much better with the legend in the Talmud. In this chapter it says that

God did not choose Israel, but that Israel chose God. Joshua turned to the nation which had assembled in the city of Shechem —in the city in which God appeared to Abraham after He came to the land, and promised him: "I will give this land to your offspring" (Genesis 12:7). And he says to them: "Hold the Lord in awe, and worship him in loyalty and truth. Banish the gods whom your fathers worshipped on the other side of the river and in Egypt, and worship the Lord. But if it does not please you to worship the Lord, choose here and now whom you will worship. . . . The people answered: 'God forbid that we should forsake the Lord to worship other gods. . . .' And Joshua answered the nation: 'You cannot worship the Lord, He is a holy God. . . .' The people said to Joshua: 'No! We will worship the Lord.' And Joshua said to them: 'You yourselves are witnesses that you have chosen the Lord and will worship him.' And they said: 'We are witnesses. . . .' So Joshua made a covenant that day with the people. He drew up a statute and an ordinance for them in Shechem and wrote its terms in the Book of the Torah of God" (Joshua 24:14-26).

There is no doubt that this is a true and faithful historical document, and that there is no contradiction between it and the verses in the Torah and the Prophets which refer to the selection of Israel; since it is because of Israel's choosing the one and only God, that Israel became a chosen people, a treasured people.

There is one more thing in the Book of Deuteronomy unlike anything found in the other books of Torah—the prophecy of the ingathering of exiles: "Then the Lord your God will restore your fortunes and take you back in love. He will bring you together again from all the peoples where the Lord your God has scattered you. Even if your outcasts are at the ends of the earth, from there will the Lord assemble you, from there will he fetch you. And the Lord your God will bring you to the land which your fathers occupied, and you shall occupy it; and he will make you more prospersous and more numerous than your fathers" (Deuteronomy 30: 3-5).

Intelligent and practical people ridicule the apparent chauvinistic destiny of the Children of Israel; to be a chosen people. It is not difficult to find among the greatest of our prophets those who claim that the people of Israel is "a sinful nation, a people laden with iniquity, a race of evildoers; wanton, destructive children." These were the words of Isaiah (1:4). And Jeremiah says: "My people are fools, they know nothing of Me; silly children with no understanding, they are clever only in wrongdoing, and of doing right they know nothing" (4:22). And Hosea cries out: "Hear the word of the Lord, O Israel; for the Lord has a charge to bring against the people of the land. There is no truth, no mercy and no knowledge of God in the land. Oaths are imposed and broken; they kill and rob. There is nothing but adultery. They break all bounds; one murder follows another" (4:1-2).

And Amos cries out: "For three transgressions of Judah, for four I will grant no reprieve, because they have spurned the Torah of God and not observed his decrees and have been led astray by the false gods which their fathers followed. . . . For three transgressions of Israel, for four I will grant them no reprieve, because they sell the innocent for silver and the destitute for a pair of shoes. They grind the heads of the poor into the earth and thrust the humble out of their way" (2:4-7). And Micah wails: "Shame on those who lie in bed planning evil and wicked deeds, and rise at daybreak and do them, knowing that they have the power. They covet land and take it by force; if they want a house, they seize it; they rob a man of his home, and steal every man's inheritance" (2:1-2).

These bitter and harsh words, spoken by the prophets about the Israelites, and which the nation preserved for hundreds and thousands of years, prove the moral greatness of this people. Yet, Isaiah the Second (who lived some 200 years after the first of the literary prophets) said of this "sinful people laden with iniquity": "I, the Lord, have called you with righteous purpose and have taken you by the hand; I have formed you, and appointed you to be a covenant to all peoples, a beacon for the peoples . . ." (42:6). Anyone who is familiar with Jewish history must certainly admit that these are not empty words; that this history is one of the most marvelous in the annals of nations, if not unique.

Wise and practical people ridicule those who continue to believe in the promise of Moses that we are a chosen people, and in Isaiah's vision that we are to be a beacon for the nations. Certainly, one cannot ignore the many dark shadows which cast themselves on our lives here and there—levity, cynicism, hypocrisy, fraud, maliciousness, deceit. But there is not enough in all of these to becloud the great light which bursts forth from the Jewish revival in Israel; from the joyful manifestations almost unduplicated in other lands: new social groupings within the working population which realizes the yearnings of the greatest ancient and contemporary social thinkers; the pioneering character of our unique army; the cultural, economic, and social uplift of hundreds of thousands of immigrants who were imprisoned in lands of exile, oppressed by poverty and ignorance; the appearance of the first buds in the reclamation of the desert; the efficient and blessed aid which tiny, young Israel is extending to new nations on the awakening continents.

Since the founding of the first agricultural school, Mikve Yisrael, in 1870, and the first Hebrew village, Petach Tikvah, in 1878, a pioneering and cultural propensity has been revealed in those who have returned to Zion. Since that time this ability has served us to develop a Hebrew agriculture—the most advanced on the Asian continent, with the exception of Japan—though we had been cut off from tilling the soil for hundreds of years. This ability helped us to institute Hebrew labor in all branches of agriculture, industry, transportation, seamanship, aviation and mining. Through this ability we have revived our Hebrew language which for hundreds of years had been thought of as a dead language; we cultivated a Hebrew literature and advanced scientific and research institutions with world-wide reputations; and we established thriving villages and cities in the desert. And all this seemed to "practical people" 50 or 60 years ago, an empty dream, an idle fantasy. By being a spiritual center for world Jewry, we are becoming, more and more, a covenant-nation, a spiritual fortress to diaspora Jewry. And as such, we are indeed becoming a beacon for developing nations.

The prophetic vision of Israel has not been disappointing. And if we will continue to follow its light, we will succeed. Our nation will be a chosen people, if it will always succeed in establishing an exemplary government which will serve as an example to the masses.

CHAPTER THIRTEEN

Saul and David

In the days of Saul and David, a new era began in the life of the Jewish people—a period of national solidarity, independence and political strength. Until the days of Saul, the Israelites lived in their land as separate tribes, recognizing that they shared a common origin and a common belief in one God.

In the Book of Judges, the verse: "In those days there was no king in Israel; everyone did what was proper in his own eyes," is repeated several times. Nevertheless, even in the days of the judges, common projects were carried out by several tribes, whether to defend themselves from attack by non-Canaanite nations such as Moab, Ammon, Midian and Philistia, or for the purpose of ruling over the rest of the Canaanite people, as in the days of the prophetess Deborah. But only in the days of Samuel did the recognition of the need for full and continuous unification gain strength among the Israelites, and it is this which brought about the request to appoint a king over them. Samuel accepted this request with great reluctance. As it is written: "The request for a king to govern them displeased Samuel" (I Samuel 8:6), because until then he was the judge in Israel (I Samuel 7:17).

As is known, in the Book of Deuteronomy it said: "If after you have entered the land that the Lord your God has given you, and occupied it, and settled in it, you decide, 'I will set a king over me, as do all the nations about me,' you shall be free to set a king over yourself; one chosen by the Lord your God . . ." (17:14-15). Anyone who clings to tradition and believes that these words, as the entire Book of Deuteronomy, were written by Moses, will have difficulty understanding Samuel's position, which runs counter to things explicitly written in the Torah (of Moses). The only limitation set down in the Book of Deuteronomy is no more than: "Be sure to set a king over yourself, one chosen from your own people; you must not set a foreigner over you, one who is not your kinsman" (17:15). We do not know what evil Samuel saw in the desire of the people that he give them a king, nor why he tried to frighten them with the "code of the king" who would govern them: "He will take your sons and make them serve his chariots and with his cavalry; and will make them run before his chariot. . . . He will take your daughters for perfumers, cooks, and confectioners, and will seize the best of your corn fields, vineyards, and olive groves, and give them to his lackeys. . . . He will take a tenth of your flocks, and you yourselves will become his slaves" (I Samuel 8:11-17). Such "rule" never came about in Israel, as we know from the story of Ahab, king of Israel, and his neighbor Navot who had a vineyard close to the king's house. The king wanted to acquire it for full payment. Navot refused to sell it to him and King Ahab didn't dare take the vineyard by force or to coerce his neighbor to sell it to him (I Kings 21:1-3).

As is known, in the eighteenth year of the reign of King Josiah, king of Judah, a scroll of the Torah was found in the Temple, and the supposition is that this was the Book of Deuteronomy. But it is clear that this book was not written in the days of Josiah, because the monarchy was already in existence for close to 400 years, and they would not have written: "Set a king over yourselves." The commandments which accompanied this chapter in the Book of Deuteronomy pertaining to the king: "He shall not keep many horses. . . . And he shall not have many wives, lest his heart go astray; nor shall he amass silver and gold to excess" (Deuteronomy 17:16-17), clearly refer to Solomon's kingdom, because Solomon loved many non-Jewish women. "He had 700 wives who were princesses, and 300 concubines, and they turned his heart from the truth" (I Kings 11:3). He even brought many horses from Egypt (10:28), and accumulated a great deal of gold. "The weight of gold which Solomon received yearly was 666 talents . . ." (10:14). In any case, Samuel's opposition to a king in Israel was not justified from any point of view, and Saul, the first king whom Samuel himself had anointed, was to a large extent a casualty of this opposition. The nation was not frightened by the threats of the "code of the king" which Samuel tried to impose on them, and persisted in its demand and said: "No, we will have a king over us; then we will be like other nations, with a king to govern us, to lead us out to war and fight our battles" (I Samuel 8:19-20), and Samuel was forced to accede to the will of the people. Of Saul it says: "There was a man from the district of Benjamin, whose name was Kish . . . who was a man of valour. And he had a son by the name of Saul, a young man in his prime; there was no better man among the Israelites than he. He was a head taller than any of his fellows" (I Samuel 9:1-2).

There are two different versions of Saul's being chosen as king, in the Book of Samuel. The first time was a chance occurrence. Saul went to look for the asses which his father had lost, and in the course of his search, which lasted for three days, he met Samuel the seer, and "Samuel took a flask of oil and poured it over Saul's head, and he kissed him, and said: 'The Lord anoints you prince over his inheritance' " (I Samuel 10:1). Immediately thereafter, Samuel summoned the people to Mizpah and said to the entire nation: " 'Look at the man whom the Lord has chosen; there is no one like him in this whole nation.' And they all acclaimed him shouting: 'Long live the king' " (10:24).

Immediately after this, we find a second story about the coronation of Saul: Nahash the Ammonite threatened Yavesh Gilad with war, and the elders of Yavesh sent messengers to the hill where Saul lived (*Givat Shaul*) and told him of the Ammonite threat. Those of the nation who heard this began to cry, and Saul, coming from a morning in the field, asked why the nation was weeping, and they told him what the people of Yavesh had said. When he heard this, the spirit of God came upon Saul and he recruited the nation, went to war with the Ammonites and defeated them. And then, "Samuel said to the people: 'Let us now go to Gilgal and renew the kingdom there.' So they all went to Gilgal, and invested Saul there in the presence of the Lord at Gilgal" (I Samuel 11:14-15).

There are also two different versions in the Book of Samuel regarding the circumstances of Samuel's opposition to Saul. The first version is that Samuel said to Saul that he should wait seven days for him before going to war with the Philistines, and while Saul waited Samuel did not come. Those of the nation who had gathered for this meeting left him, and then Saul said: " 'Bring me the burnt-offering' . . . and just as he had finished offering up the burnt-offering, Samuel came." Immediately, Samuel asked in anger: "What have you done?" And Saul answered: "I saw the people were drifting away from me, and you had not come at the time promised, and the Philistines were assembling at Michmash; and I thought:

The Philistines will now move against me at Gilgal, and I have not placated the Lord; so I felt compelled to make the burnt-offering." And Samuel answered him angrily: "You have behaved foolishly. You have not kept the command laid on you by the Lord your God. If you had, he would have established your dynasty over Israel for all time. But now, your line will not endure; the Lord will seek a man of his own heart, and will appoint him prince over his people, because you have not kept the Lord's command" (13:9-13).

But later it is written that Samuel ordered Saul to defeat Amalek "and destroy all that they have, and do not spare them. Put them all to death, men and women, infant and suckling, ox and sheep, camel and ass" (15:3). And Saul conducted the war with Amalek and destroyed the entire nation. But, "Saul and the nation spared Agag and the best of the sheep and the cattle, the young of the second birth and the lambs and everything worth keeping they were not willing to destroy. . . ." And then Samuel said to Saul: ". . . you have rejected the word of the Lord and, therefore, the Lord has rejected you as king over Israel. . . And Samuel never saw Saul again to the day of his death" (15:9-35). And Samuel went to the house of Jesse in Bethlehem and anointed his young son, David, to be king over Israel (16:13).

It was Saul's unique lot to be the first king in the history of our people, and he was worthy of it. But this privilege, in a period of transition, proved a burden to him. The prophet Samuel could not make his peace with the new government which the nation imposed on him against his will. And though he himself crowned Saul, and announced to the people "that there is no one like him in the entire nation," he had never liked the idea of a monarchy in Israel, let alone this king. It is very possible that the moral decadence of his two sons who "were attracted by enticements, took bribes and perverted justice" (8:3), intensified his bitterness, as can be heard in his confession before the nation right after he crowned Saul (12:1-3). It isn't clear if he intended to vindicate his sons in the eyes of the nation through these words, or merely to give public sanction to his own purity. But bitterness and disappointment can be seen in his words.

Samuel was a representative of the old order that saw God alone as king over Israel, and himself as God's emissary; and he looked with disfavor at the nation's wish to change the order. He saw this wish as a threat to the kingdom of God and, without doubt, a threat to his own authority. But he was commanded to listen to the voice of the people and to anoint a king over them. A suitable person was found: Saul, son of Kish, from the tribe of Benjamin—"a young man in his prime; there was no better man among the Israelites than he. He was a head taller than any of his fellows" (9:2). And along with this, he was a modest person "hiding among the baggage" (10:22); a big-hearted person who harbored no resentment against those who scorned him and said: 'How can this fellow deliver us?' And they despised him, and brought him no gifts, and he was silent" (10:27). And even after his first victory over the Ammonites when he saved Yavesh Gilad, and when the nation demanded the death of those who hated him, Saul said: "No one shall be put to death on a day when the Lord has won such a victory in Israel" (11:13). Saul didn't credit himself with the victory, but said that God brought forward the deliverance.

But in addition to his modesty, and his hiding among the "baggage," Saul was a brave man and a fierce warrior. No sooner did he hear of the danger that lay ahead for Yavesh Gilad from the Ammonites, than the spirit of God enveloped him, and he aroused the entire nation to prepare for war. And he was victorious.

Saul also had a brave son by the name of Jonathan who stood up bravely to the Philistines who had camped at Michmash. Together with his soldiers, he attacked the Philistine camp and created panic within it. The Hebrews who had come with the Philistines as their subjects and aides "joined the Israelites under Saul and Jonathan" (14:22).

The author of First Samuel summarizes Saul's deeds and victories in two verses: "When Saul had made his throne secure in Israel, he fought against his enemies on every side: the Moabites, the Ammonites, the Edomites, the kings of Zobah and the Philistines. . . . And he displayed valor, and defeated the Amalekites, and delivered Israel from the hands of those who had raided them" (14:47-48). But this strength and ability were not sufficient to enable him to remain as the head of the nation during the decisive period of transition, when it was transformed from a tribal order to a national entity; from an order of temporary judges who became heads of a tribe, or a group of tribes, through battle, such as Gideon and Jephthah had done—to an institutionalized, hereditary monarchy. And Samuel, who was without doubt among the greatest of the judges, if not the greatest leader after the death of Moses and Joshua, could not make peace with the new monarchical order and saw to it that each of his decrees be carried out by Saul precisely and with respect. As a result, the friction between these two personalities—Samuel and Saul—grew, until finally Samuel estranged himself from Saul. This estrangement left its mark on Saul, and an evil spirit overcame him. Samuel understood that the nation would not return to the old order, and so he sought another suitable candidate for the throne—and the suitable candidate was David, son of Jesse.

It is interesting to note what the sages of the Talmud said of the greatness of Saul. Rabbi Judah said in the name of Rabbi Samuel: Why did the reign of the house of Saul not continue? Because it had more than one blemish. As Rabbi Jochanan said in the name of Rabbi Shimon, son of Jehotzadak: We should only appoint one as a chief over a congregation behind whom dangles a coil of reptiles, so that if he becomes arrogant, they say to him: "Look backward" (Yoma 22b). Rabbi Judah said in the name of Rav: Why was Saul punished? Because he disregarded his personal honor. As it is written: There were scoundrels who said, "How can this fellow deliver us?" They despised him and brought him no gifts. And he was silent (I Samuel 10:27).

As his father's shepherd, near Bethlehem, in the region of Judea, David, son of Jesse, excelled from his youth because of his lofty traits. He was known in his area as "one who can play; as a brave man and a good fighter who is wise in speech and handsome" (16:18). In the course of watching his father's sheep in the desert, he fought with a lion or a bear which had snatched a lamb from the flock, and he beat it and killed it (17:34-35). There is no doubt that such a man would envision a great destiny for himself at a time when Israel was unstable. Apparently, he found his way to Samuel, and Samuel encouraged him in his secret yearnings.

Perhaps it is not coincidental that when an evil spirit overcame Saul, his advisors suggested to him that he seek a man who knew how to play the harp. When Saul accepted this advice, one of the members of his court told him to invite David, son of Jesse, from Bethlehem. In this way, David became close with the royal family, and he pleased Saul; and his daughter, Michal, fell in love with him. He also won over the heart of Saul's son, Jonathan (which is one of the most glorious episodes in the Bible, though not the most glorious), who was of great help to him as he progressed toward his destiny of becoming the prince of Israel—an independent king (not dependent, as was Saul, upon the prophet Samuel).

There is no doubt that the time that David spent in Saul's house was sufficient for him to study Saul's unstable nature. This experience convinced him that he was the person best suited to open a new chapter in the life of Israel—the period of the monarchy which unified the entire nation and saved it from all of its neighbors. His stature grew, little by little, among the masses, and his superiority over Saul was recognized. This recognition was openly expressed in the verse: "Saul killed thousands, but David ten thousands." This came after the fight between David and Goliath. The Philistines assembled to do battle with Israel and camped between Socho and Azekah at Ephes Damim. Saul and the Israelites camped in the Valley of Elah. Then "a champion came out of the Philistine camps, a man named Goliath. . . .* He had a copper helmet on his head, and he was clad with a coat of mail, and the weight of the mail was 5,000 shekels of copper. On his legs were copper greaves, and a copper javelin between his shoulders. The shaft of his spear was like a weaver's beam, and the head of his spear weighed 600 shekels of iron" (I Samuel 17:1-7). This armed giant spread fear over Israel. When David the shepherd heard of this, he abandoned his sheep and hastened to the battle, and because he was blessed with a keen sense of strategy, he immediately grasped that Goliath's heavy armor was the root of his weakness, and that rather than battling him face to face, he would be able to defeat him from a distance, for in this way Goliath would not be able to lay a hand on him. So he declined the heavy uniform which they wished to give him, and went out to meet the Philistine giant with pebbles from the brook and with a slingshot that would shoot from a distance.

As a shepherd, David was used to shooting stones over distances past sheep which had strayed from the flock, and when he went to meet the Philistine giant, he shot a stone from a distance which hit him in his forehead, and the giant fell to the ground dead. Then David went up to his enemy, drew his sword from its sheath, and cut off his head. Abner, Saul's chief officer, brought David before Saul with the head of the giant in his hand. Saul was astounded by the sight of David's valor. He did not recognize him, perhaps seeing him for the first time. He asked: Whose son are you, lad? And David replied humbly: The son of your servant, Jesse of Bethlehem. Saul would not let him return to his father's house, and appointed him an officer over a thousand men. But when he heard the women singing: "Saul killed his thousands, but David his ten thousands," he began to fear him. David's second

* This name is doubtful, because in II Samuel 21:19 it says: "In another war with the Philistines in Gob, Elchanan son of Jaarei Orgim of Bethlehem killed Goliath of Gath, whose spear had a shaft like a weaver's beam." This was after David ruled over all of Israel. And this is also told in I Chronicles 20:5: "In another war with the Philistines, Elchanan son of Jair killed Lachmi, brother of Goliath of Gath, whose spear had a shaft like a weaver's beam."

success in the battle with 200 Philistines intensified Saul's suspicion and gave impetus to a plot to kill David.

Jonathan, son of Saul, who recognized David's military prowess, became the bodyguard and deliverer of the person hated by his father, though he was not unaware that David could very well inherit his father's crown in his place. It is difficult to find another example of this magnanimous spirit, shown by Jonathan, in the annals of monarchies in world history. Michal, Saul's younger daughter, also loved him—and married him.

Initially, Jonathan tried to persuade his father not to sin by killing David for no valid reason. At first, it appeared as if he had influenced him, and Saul swore to Jonathan: "As the Lord lives, he shall not be put to death" (I Samuel 19:6). Jonathan returned David to Saul: "And he was in attendance before him as before." But after another battle with the Philistines in which David was victorious, "an evil spirit from the Lord came upon Saul as he was sitting in his house with his spear in his hand; and David was playing the harp. Saul tried to pin David to the wall with the spear, but he side-stepped, and the king drove the spear into the wall. That night David fled" (19:9-10). David fled to his house where he lived with his wife Michal. Saul sent men to Michal's house to kill David, but Michal, his wife, smuggled him away in the dark of the night. At that time, the decision was made by Saul to have David killed wherever he might be. However, Jonathan stood between his father and his beloved David, and revealed to David the schemes of Saul to kill him, and gave him encouragement. In the language of the Bible: "He gave him courage in God's name." While David was hiding from Saul, in the wilderness of Ziph in a forest, Jonathan came and said to him: "Do not be afraid, the hand of Saul my father will not find you; the hand of Saul my father will not touch you. You will become king of Israel and I shall hold rank after you; and my father knows it" (I Samuel 23:17).

David was turned into a fugitive, an outlaw. Certain of the destiny which had directed his life, David knew how to exploit this situation. He surrounded himself with a nucleus of warriors, daring and desperate men, and made an effort to win his first allies.

In the south, where he hid from Saul, there gathered around him "men in any kind of distress, or in debt, or discontented" (22:2); and from among them he built up a regiment of 400 men who would be loyal to him and who would follow him everywhere. David tried to get close to the king of Moab—perhaps out of a family relationship, because David's father was the grandson of Ruth the Moabite. In particular, David revealed his far-sighted, political wisdom in the course of the many opportunities given him by Saul, when the king of Israel tried to capture David and kill him while hiding in the Judean desert, in the cave of Ein Gedi, in the wilderness of Ziph, and in other places. Saul would go out in search of David accompanied by quite a large force, as befitted a king. David had a small band of guerrilla fighters and he was completely familiar with every hiding place in the Judean desert—with its caves and natural fortifications. It was easy for him to hide from Saul and wait in ambush for any movement of his, as well as to catch him when he was alone (as in the cave in Ein Gedi). Someone not as great as, and less far-sighted than, David, would have used this opportunity to kill Saul.

David, who knew how to restrain himself in political and military situations (in personal and family matters, David was subject to uncontrollable moods, more so than Saul), understood that harming God's messiah (and the king of Israel in those days was thought of as the anointed of God) would only arouse the nation against him. Hence, in those instances where Saul fell into his hands, David exhibited patience, and did not listen to his closest advisors and friends, such as Avishai, son of Tzeruiah—one of his most select officers—who also had close family ties to David. He did not harm Saul though he did all he could to prove to him that if he only wished to, he could put an end to his life. Saul, who was basically an emotional person, was moved and said: "A blessing on you, David my son! You will do great things and be victorious" (I Samuel 26:25). But David understood that these words were the result of Saul's momentary excitement and could not be depended upon, because in a similar instance Saul had said to him: "You are more righteous than I, for you have treated me well while I have treated you badly. . . . I know now for certain that you will become king, and that the kingdom of Israel will be established under you" (24:17-20).

David decided to cross over with his regiment—which in the meantime had grown to 600 men—to the land of the Philistines, to Achish, king of Gath, as if to serve him. To make sure that the Philistine rulers would not be aroused against him, he asked the king to put land at his disposal in one of the country towns, and Achish gave him Ziklag (27:6). Here, begins David's military career which was destined first to elevate him to be king of Judah and, later, king over all of Israel.

David began with organized raids against the Geshurites, the Gizrites, and the Amalekites (27:8) who used to oppress the

Hebrew tribes at the southern border. Achish saw a loyal vassal in David because he thought (according to David's official reports) that he had raided the Israelite settlements in the south, and thus "had made his people Israel abhor him, and would remain my subject all his life" (27:12). Then came the big Philistine attack against Aphekah, where it seemed as though David and his men had joined with Achish the Philistine. But under pressure from the Philistine rulers who didn't trust David, Achish was forced to have David "return to the land of the Philistines, and David returned to Ziklag."

The Philistines fought with Israel in the Gilboa region and inflicted many casualties among the Israelites; among them, Saul's three sons: Jonathan, Avinadav and Malkishua. When Saul saw that his situation was desperate, he requested his retainer to stab him, lest the uncircumcised come and mistreat him. But his retainer did not dare do this, and Saul fell on his own sword and died; and his retainer did likewise.

When this became known to David at Ziklag, he understood that his time had come. Even before this, David had won the hearts of the people of Judah by his raids against the Hebrew [sic.] inhabitants of the south and the Negev. He had even sent the spoils to the elders of Judah in Bethel, to Ramot Hanegev, to the cities of the Jerachmielites and the Kenites, to Hebron and elsewhere (I Samuel 30:26-31). When David heard in Ziklag that the king of Israel, as well as his beloved Jonathan, were dead he composed the great lament over Saul and Jonathan:

> Delightful and dearly loved were they in life;
> In death, they were not parted.
> They were swifter than eagles, stronger than lions . . .
> I grieve for you, Jonathan my brother,
> Dear and delightful were you to me,
> Your love for me was wonderful,
> Surpassing the love of women.
> (II Samuel 1:23-27)

This lament, if it was uttered by David (and there is no reason to doubt it), strengthens the supposition that many of the verses of Psalms, attributed to David, are really the product of the pen and spirit of this great king. This great king was not only a brilliant military man and statesman, but also an exalted poet with a warm and sensitive heart. In contrast to Saul, not once did his emotions prevail over his political sense and his obligation to the nation.

David understood that it would not be easy for him to stand

at the head of all of Israel, and he did not rush to attain this—not only when Saul was alive, but even after his death. Nevertheless his every move was directed toward the ultimate destiny which he knew was imposed upon him—to be king over Israel.

With the death of Saul, David saw that henceforth he would have to direct his energy towards becoming king of Israel. Samuel was no longer alive, and no one of such spirit arose to take his place. The institution of the monarchy had already gained a foothold among the people. David was well respected by the masses of the population, but there were also many who hated him, and were jealous of him. Thus, it was with great wisdom that, initially, David limited himself at Hebron to the kingdom of Judah. The wars that he waged before becoming king (in the days of Saul and in his service); the war to save the city of Keilah from the Philistines (I Samuel 23:5)—Saul tried to trap him, but David fled immediately because he knew that the people of Keilah would hand him over to Saul; and his wars with Amalek and the rest of the tribes of the Negev which had oppressed their Hebrew neighbors—all these, without doubt, made a great impression throughout Israel. David's noble behavior toward Saul also certainly became known throughout the land. But Saul had also been a brave king and his wars with Moab, Ammon, Edom, the kings of Zobah, the Philistines and Amalek—though the author or authors of the Book of Samuel didn't give many particulars about them—without doubt had built up great respect for Saul in Israel. Even after his failure and death at Mt. Gilboa many still bore allegiance to his family. David didn't rush to conquer the kingdom by force, and in the first years was content with the kingdom of Judah which was given to him by the people of Judah. Though we read of feuds between David's chief officers, Joab, son of Tzeruiah and his brothers, and Abner, Saul's commander-in-chief, there is no indication that this came about through the initiative, or with the knowledge of David (II Samuel 2:12-23).

But the friction between the "House of Saul" and the "House of David" didn't end. It was David's good fortune that Saul left no successor worthy of the position, and Abner, his commander-in-chief, who had coronated Ish-Boshet, son of Saul, became alienated from Saul, and, in the course of time, surrounded himself with supporters of David in Israel. As Second Samuel tells it: "Abner now spoke to the elders of Israel and said: 'For some time you have wanted David to be your king; now is the time to act, for the Lord said to David: By the hand of my servant David, I will deliver my people Israel from the Philistines and from all their enemies'" (3:8-17). Abner actually came to David with 20 men from Israel—without a doubt important members of the tribes of Israel. Again, when Joab became jealous of Abner and secretly killed him, David decreed a fast, wrote a eulogy, and refused to eat until sunset. And this action made an impression to which the narrative testifies: "Everyone throughout Israel knew on that day that the king had had no hand in the murder of Abner, son of Ner" (3:27). Then the Israelites came to Hebron to crown David king over Israel (5:3).

David attained the throne, neither through craftiness nor through connections, but rather thanks to his military ability, his political wisdom, and his inner stability at difficult and crucial times. Because of these traits he won the heart of the nation, and because of it he prevailed over Saul. David's weaknesses—and the Bible makes no effort to conceal them—were limited to family matters. In these, Saul was superior to David, and the Rabbis rightly said that in this area Saul had no fault. Saul was kind-hearted and of noble spirit; but he couldn't control his temper. Fate charged him with a difficult task; the transition from a tribal anarchy to national government at a time when Samuel, the most respected spiritual personality in the nation was still alive, and his influence over the people was still substantial. (He opposed national government strongly, and eyed every step that Saul took sternly.) Saul, too, was a great and brave military man, but he lacked the inner stability and the deep political wisdom of David, though from a human point of view he was not inferior to David, and possibly was his superior.

The author of the Bible saw David's life and deeds through a theological conduit which was the legacy of all other authors of the Bible. But the lives of Saul and David, as they are told in the Bible, are more naturally understood if we look thoroughly at the particular circumstances of the times in which they lived. Both are tragic figures. One is tragic as the first king at a time of difficult transition, not wanted by the spiritual leader of the nation, the prophet Samuel. The other succeeded in his reign, thanks to his great political and military prowess, but was tragic in his family life, because he was terribly emotional and was unable to control his impulses. This is well known from the incident of Bathsheba and Uriah the Hittite.

Our Rabbis said: "Anyone who says that David sinned, errs." From this point of view, I am among those who have erred. David himself said: "I sinned before the Lord," but this does not diminish David's greatness as a king.

CHAPTER FOURTEEN

The Image of King Cyrus

Mr. Chairman, Bible devotees, ladies and gentlemen:

Before I get to the essence of my discussion, first I wish to welcome you in the name of the government of Israel. It seems to me that I will not be detracting from my remarks, if I say that the force which has kept us alive since the Proclamation of Cyrus (for some 2,500 years), and which brought us here, was not that we had been persecuted (there were persecutions, and I do not deny their part in the return to Zion, both then and today), but the Book of Books—which for the ninth time we have gathered to study together. It seems to me that only in the land of its birth, through the regeneration of our independence, can we penetrate that very special atmosphere and environment in which the Bible appeared and which the Bible helped create.

But let us not pretend—even as the third generation to return to Zion—that we will conclude this work. As in science, where the more it discovers the secrets of nature, the more it reveals to us the riddles of nature, so, the more we delve into the Bible and begin to understand it, all the more are the new problems that confront us. I am sure that this generation which has only now returned to the task of tilling the soil of the homeland and to investigate its spiritual greatness—which is the Bible—and to understand it, will also leave for the coming generations problems to be studied in the Bible. This study has no end. This gathering

---

Delivered at the Ninth National Bible Conference, April, 1951 (Nissan, 5711).

will be a success if it brings us a little closer to an understanding of the eternal book from which we draw the secret of our existence.

And now to the matter assigned to me for this session.

The Bible, as it has come down to us, ends with these two very significant verses: "Now in the first year of Cyrus, king of Persia, so that the word of the Lord spoken through Jeremiah might be fulfilled, the Lord stirred up the spirit of Cyrus, king of Persia; and he issued a proclamation throughout his kingdom, both by word of mouth and in writing, to this effect: 'This is the word of Cyrus, king of Persia: The Lord God of heaven has given me all the kingdoms of the earth, and he has given me the task of building a house for him in Jerusalem, in Judah. To every man of his people now among you I say, the Lord his God be with him, and let him go up'" (II Chronicles 36:22-23).

This was a unique privilege to be merited by a non-Jewish ruler; to complete the Book of Books, and to complete it with a word which even today has fateful significance for all of the Jewish people, for both those who live in Israel, and those who live in the diaspora. The word is, *vayaal* (let him go up). There was no other non-Jewish ruler who merited praise from the greatest prophets of Israel as did Cyrus from the prophet Isaiah, whom Bible critics call by the name of Isaiah the Second: "I say to Cyrus: 'You shall be My shepherd and carry out My purpose, so that Jerusalem may be rebuilt and the foundations of the temple may be laid.' Thus says the Lord to Cyrus His anointed, Cyrus whose right hand I have strengthened to subdue nations before him and loosen the loins of kings; before whom gates shall be opened and no doors be shut. I shall go before you and level the uneven hills; I will break down doors of brass and hack through bars of iron. I will give you treasures from dark vaults, and hidden treasures of secret places" (Isaiah 44:28; 45:1-3).

Without a doubt, Cyrus deserved this praise, not merely because of his proclamation and the permission which he gave the Babylonian exiles to return to their land and to rebuild the Temple in Jerusalem. Cyrus was also one of the greatest figures, from a general historical point of view. He was one of the greatest military men in the history of nations, one of the greatest politicians of all time and, in addition, a merciful and big-hearted man at a time when there were few exceptional individuals among the great conquerors.

Cyrus' rise from governor of a small principality by the name of Anshan in Elam, to the founder of the largest empire to arise in the world until that time, is by itself one of the most marvelous events in the history of nations. But this phenomenon takes on additional importance because of four very important facts: 1) This great empire of Cyrus was established within a very short period of time: in the 11 years which passed from the conquest of Achmetah, capital of Media, in the year 550 B.C., to the conquest of Babylonia in 539. 2) The Persian empire endured for 200 years under the rule of the Cyrus dynasty, while the empire of Alexander the Great, which was, as is known, the inheritor of the Persian empire, survived only during his lifetime, and fell apart immediately after he died. 3) Cyrus exhibited a compassionate spirit toward his enemies and a unique tolerance toward all religions; 4) He played a decisive role in the first return to Zion.

We have information about Cyrus the Great from ancient Babylonian writings, in the books of the Bible (Isaiah, Daniel, Ezra, Chronicles), and a great deal more in Greek literature. The great dramatist Aeschylus, who was born four or five years (525) after the death of Cyrus (529), wrote these words of praise in the play, *The Persians,* in which he described the Persian war with Greece: "Cyrus, blessed with good fortune, promised peace to all his friends. He took in the peoples of Lydia and Phrygia, and conquered all of the land of the Greeks through his might. God loved him for he was full of understanding."

Many Greek authors wrote about his life, including Heron, Dionysius, Herodotus, and others. Xenephon, who was born 100 years after the death of Cyrus, wrote an entire book dedicated to the life of Cyrus. It was called, *Kuro Phediae,* meaning, the education of Cyrus, but the author did not limit himself to the story of Cyrus' education. He covered all aspects of his life. The truth of the matter is that this isn't history, but a historical novel, though without a doubt there is factual material here and there.

We have contradictory information about Cyrus' childhood and teenage years. It is replete with legends and falsehoods taken from Greek literature (which apparently took them from lost Persian sources). There are those who say that he was the son of a robber, and some say that he was the son of a Persian shepherd from Pasargadae. Horodotus himself heard four different versions of the early years of Cyrus' life. It is conceivable that Cyrus stemmed from a family of governors of a small Persian principality by the name of Anshan, part of the kingdom of Elam. As far back as the sixth century, we find hints in Ezekiel of a Persian army in Tyre. In chapter 27:10 he says: "Men of Persia, Lydia and Put served as warriors in your army. They hung shield and helmet around you, and it was they who gave you glory."

In 38:5, Ezekiel foresaw that Persia would be included in the army of Gog, king of Magog: "Persia, Cush [in the place of Lydia, there it is Cush], and Put with them, all of them with shield and helmet." Both Jeremiah and Ezekiel prophesied about the destruction of Elam. Jeremiah said (49:35) in the year 597: "Thus says the Lord of hosts: 'I will break the bow of Elam, the chief weapon of their might.'" And Ezekiel (32:24) says (in the year 588): "There is Elam, with all her hordes buried around her, all of them slain, fallen by the sword; they have gone down without strength to the nether world, men who struck terror in the land of the living, but now share the disgrace of those that descend to the abyss."

We have knowledge of three kings of Anshan who lived before Cyrus: "Tysfais (Sheshphesh), Cyrus (this Cyrus was the grandfather of our Cyrus the Great), and Cambyses. Cyrus II, (our Cyrus) the son of Cambyses—Cyrus the Great—was king of Anshan in 559 or 558, and died 30 years later (in 529) in a war with one of the tribes in East Persia on the Indian border, after building a gigantic empire which stretched from the remote areas of India, from the western side to the eastern Mediterranean.

Xenophon who lived in the fourth century B.C. (he was born at the end of the fifth century), more than 100 years after the death of Cyrus the Great, tells that while he was still alive, stories and legends about Cyrus abounded among all the nations of the East. And Antistenus who lived in the middle of the fourth century, composed a dialogue entitled: "Cyrus, or the Kingdom."

Cyrus' first conquest was the kingdom of Media, ruled by Ishtovega (in Greek Astyages), who, according to several sources, was Cyrus' grandfather. He gave his daughter, Mandana, to Cambyses for a wife, and she was Cyrus' mother. Astyages, the last king of Media, was not particularly acceptable to his army.

According to one legend, Astyages ordered his chief officer, Harpagos, to kill the child Cyrus, but he didn't carry out the king's command. When, ten years later, it became known to the king that Cyrus was alive, and was living with a certain shepherd, he invited Harpagos to a feast at his palace and fed him the flesh of his son. This chief officer, who betrayed the king, was of great help to Cyrus in his wars against Astyages, Media and Persia—all of which were mixed racially, and merged into one kingdom under Cyrus. This was the first step in the establishment of the great empire.

When Cyrus took his enemy Astyages captive, he treated him kindly, as was his way; and he did him no harm. It is interesting that at least five times Media and Persia are mentioned in the Bible as one kingdom, and there is no doubt that these tribes were close to each other. In Isaiah 21:2, Elam is mentioned together with Media; and Darius, a descendant of Cyrus the Great, is called Madaah or Ha-Madi (i.e., of Media) in Aramaic (Daniel 6:1; 11:1).

Four years after conquering Media, Cyrus fought with Croesus, king of Lydia. The oracle of Delphi, that Croesus visited before his war with Cyrus, is famous. The priest of Delphi said: "If he crosses the river Helos, which divides him from the countries east of him, he will destroy a great power"; and Croesus was certain that the allusion was to the destruction of Cyrus' great power. Croesus had reason for his belief because he had powerful allies: Egypt, Babylon and Sparta. But when Cyrus lost no time in attacking Croesus' army, his allies didn't come to his aid and, in 546, Cyrus conquered Sardis, capital of Lydia, and gained control over all the Greeks in Asia Minor. And then came Babylonia's turn which, like Media, also had a king who wasn't particularly loved. And especially hated by the Babylonia priesthood was Nabonidus, the last king of Babylonia.

In *Tishrei* [September] of 540 Cyrus' army entered Babylonia, and on the third of *Heshvan* [month after *Tishrei*], King Cyrus entered the Babylonian capital city. The priests, who didn't like the Babylonian king because of his religious aberrations, apparently opened the gates to Cyrus.

A great Jewish prophet who arose at the time of the decline of Babylonia's glory—and whose prophecy became part of the Book of Isaiah—prophesied in the "Prophecy Concerning Babylon" (Isaiah 13:17-19): "I will stir up against them the Medes who care nothing for silver, and are not tempted by gold . . . and Babylon, fairest of kingdoms, proud beauty of the Chaldees, shall be like Sodom and Gomorrah." This prophet linked the fall of Babylonia with the revival of the Jewish people and the return to Zion: "The Lord will show compassion for Jacob and will once again make Israel his choice. He will settle them on their own soil, and strangers will come to join them and attach themselves to Jacob. Many nations shall escort Israel to her place in the land of the Lord . . ." (14:1-2).

In his great book, *A History of the Israelite Faith* (Book 6, pp. 175-181), Professor Kaufman explains the intention of this prophecy another way. In his view, instead of calling it the "Prophecy

Concerning Babylon," it should be called the "Prophecy Concerning Assyria." He sees the verses: "The Lord will show compassion for Jacob and will once again make Israel his choice. He will settle them on their own soil . . ."—as later additions, not really belonging to this chapter. The word "Chaldees" in the verse: ". . . and Babylon, fairest of kingdoms, proud beauty of the Chaldees," found its way into this prophecy by mistake. In his view, the king of Assyria is called the king of Babylonia here, for the kings of Persia prided themselves with the title "king of Babylon." And as for the words: "I will stir up the Medes against them," in Professor Kaufman's view, this does not refer to the Medes who were associated with Persia in the Bible and in history, but a distant nation from the north, from the same barbaric nations whose coming the prophets foresaw "from the outer extremes of the land," as is described in Jeremiah 51:27-28, where Media appears together with the kingdoms of Ararat, Mini and Ashkenaz.

Despite all my admiration for Professor Kaufman, it is difficult for me to accept these explanations by the author of *A History of the Israelite Faith.* Media is not mentioned together with Ararat, Mini and Ashkenaz in Jeremiah 51. These three kingdoms are mentioned in verse 27, while the kings of Media are spoken of in verse 28, and it is clear there, without a doubt, that the reference is to Media, the twin of Persia. In my humble opinion there is no basis for the view that the Media described in chapter 13 of Isaiah is an abbreviation of Media, Ararat, Mini and Ashkenaz. Professor Kaufman's deletion of the word "Chaldees" seems to me completely arbitrary. If you delete the word Chaldees, something is missing, and the structure of the entire verse is altered. Changing "Prophecy Concerning Babylon" to "Prophecy Concerning Assyria" is also arbitrary. The kings of Persia called themselves kings of Babylonia after Cyrus captured Babylonia, and Babylonia remained in Cyrus' dynasty for the entire 200 years that the Persian empire existed. It is hard to doubt that the last verses of Isaiah 13, and the first two verses of Isaiah 14, prophesy about the conquest of Babylonia by the kings of Media and Persia and the redemption of Israel which was to come soon. There is no logical connection between these verses; between what preceded them in chapter 13, and what came after, in chapter 14. Apparently, at that point, a prophecy from another source was inserted, as we find in many other places in the Bible.

In chapter 45 of Isaiah, the prophet calls Cyrus the "Messiah of God." The word "messiah" cannot be understood here in its later eschatological sense of "redeemer of Israel and the world."

Rather, it must be understood in its biblical and historical sense: "anointed for the throne."

In the Cyrus Cylinder (inscription) discovered in Babylonia in 1879, or in shorter inscriptions discovered in Babylonia in 1850, there is no mention whatsoever of Jews in Cyrus' life. His relationship to the Jews is also not mentioned in the Greek literature on Cyrus. We only know of Cyrus' connection with the exiles of Babylonia and the return to Zion, from biblical sources. In addition to the prophecies in the Book of Isaiah, historical narratives are found in Ezra, Nehemiah and Second Chronicles. In Ezra it says: "Now in the first year of Cyrus, king of Persia ["first" here refers to his reign in Babylonia—539 or 538 B.C.] so that the word of the Lord spoken through Jeremiah might be fulfilled, the Lord stirred up the heart of Cyrus, king of Persia; and he issued a proclamation throughout his kingdom, both by word of mouth and in writing, to this effect: 'This is the word of Cyrus, king of Persia: The Lord God of heaven has given me all the kingdoms of the earth, and He himself has charged me to build him a house in Jerusalem which is in Judah. To every man of his people, now among you, I say, God be with him, and let him go up to Jerusalem in Judah and rebuild the house of the Lord God of Israel, the God who is in Jerusalem' " (1:1-4).

In Ezra 1, almost the same things, word for word, are said about Cyrus' proclamation as are found at the end of Second Chronicles, except that the words "the Lord God of Israel, the God who is in Jerusalem," are added. Cyrus' proclamation, in which he mentions the Lord God of Israel, should not be interpreted as implying that he recognized the God of Israel according to the Jewish concept: God of the world, the one and only God. But this does not imply that he did not use the term "God of Israel," only because he didn't believe in one God as the Jews did. It is known that Cyrus was tolerant in religious matters, and acknowledged the gods of all the lands which he conquered. He acknowledged the gods of Babylonia, and after his son Cambyses conquered Egypt, he acknowledged the gods of Egypt. In Babylonia he also spoke in the name of Merodach.

But what is mentioned in Ezra 1 and in Chronicles is apparently not Cyrus' proclamation in his own words. We know this from chapter 6 of Ezra, from the reply which King Darius sent to the question which Tattenai, governor beyond the river, and Shetar-Bozenai and their friends asked, in which they requested clarification of the authority under which the Jews were building the Temple. The Jews claimed, in the presence of Tattenai and his friends, that they received permission to do so in the days of Cyrus, king of Persia. But the governor wanted to look into the matter and turned to Darius. The decree was issued in Echbatana, the capital of Media or, as is written in Ezra: "But it was in Ahmetha in the royal residence in the province of Media, that a scroll was found, on which was written the following memorandum" (I would suggest that in place of the word "decree" we use the word "memorandum"). And in verses 3-5 (chapter 6), the text of the decree, in its original Aramaic form, is given. According to this decree which was found in Ganzach, in Ahmetha (or Echbatana, as the Greeks call it), King Darius ordered Tattenai, governor beyond the river, and Shetar-Bozenai to permit the Jews to continue building the Temple and to give them all the necessary assistance. The building of the Temple then continued in the days of Haggai and Zechariah, the last of the prophets of Israel, and the Temple was completed on the third day of the month of Adar, in the sixth year of the reign of Darius. This was in 516, in the days of Zerubabel, son of Shealtiel. Then, too, all of the Jews did not return from Babylonia. The call of the prophet Isaiah II: "Come out of Babylon, hasten away from the Chaldeans; proclaim it with loud songs of triumph, crying the news to the ends of the earth; tell them, 'The Lord has ransomed his servant Jacob,'" was not heeded by all of the Jews. According to Ezra, only 47,000 Jews returned, and the Babylonian exiles stayed there until 10 years ago—until 1951—when three times the number returned. We are fortunate that we have lived to see the day when almost all of the descendants of the Babylonian exiles of 2,500 years ago have returned.

The historian Josephus, son of Mattathias, called Flavius, tries to explain in his book, *Antiquities of the Jews* (Book XI), Cyrus' relationship with the Jews through the fact that the Jews ascribed to Cyrus a prophecy which Isaiah had prophesied 210 years earlier. It is doubtful that there is any basis for this explanation. All contemporary scholars agree that the prophetic chapters in Isaiah on Cyrus were spoken by another prophet who lived in Cyrus' day and is known as Isaiah II. There is reason to believe that the Jews of Babylonia helped Cyrus in his wars, just as most Jews were sympathetic to England in World War I. Without a doubt, it was politically important to Cyrus that he have loyal allies in the western part of his kingdom—the Eastern Mediterranean. But Cyrus' decree cannot be explained by these motivations alone. This decree fits in with Cyrus' general policy reflecting the manner in which he dealt with other nations he conquered.

The great conqueror who arose in Persia over 2,500 years ago did not behave as did the kings of Assyria and Babylonia, who exiled conquered nations and imported other nations to replace them. He also did not yearn, as did Alexander the Great and his descendants, to smother the conquered nations with his country's culture, nor did he make any attempt, as did the descendants of Mohammed, to impose his language and religion upon the defeated nations. Cyrus dealt forthrightly with the vanquished. He respected the religion and ritual of every nation and acknowledged its gods.

When he said in his decree: "To every man of his people now among you, I say, God be with him, and let him go up to Jerusalem in Judah, and rebuild the house of the Lord God of Israel, the God who is in Jerusalem," he did not deceive, was not hypocritical, and also did not acknowledge the God of Israel in the way the Jews did; as is written in Isaiah 45:5-6: "I am the Lord, there is no other; there is no God beside me . . . there is none but I. I am the Lord, there is no other." Rather, he believed, as was customary among other nations, that every people had its god, and that "the Lord God of Israel is the god in Jerusalem."

Cyrus granted every nation spiritual and ritual autonomy, and retained only his political and military rule. This was the policy of the kings of Persia for 200 years, until the conquest of Alexander the Great. And during the span of these 200 years, the Jews enjoyed religious autonomy. During this period, Judaism was consolidated and strengthened, and was able to endure for the entire period of the Second Temple. The Jews only attained political independence in the days of the Seleucids (in the period of the Second Temple)—the Greek rule in Syria—after the Hasmonean revolt against the Hellenists.

In closing, I must note that it is not clear if this year marks 2,500 years since Cyrus' decree, or whether it is next year. But it is quite certain that the event took place in the month of Nisan (April). It is possible that this month marks the 2,500th year of the decree. There is no doubt that Cyrus' greatness as a mighty and enlightened ruler, and as the first to permit the return to Zion, should be remembered by us and by all civilized people. I am pleased to see two delegates here from modern Persia, now known as Iran. Here, two ancient peoples meet again in the international arena as friendly nations, working together for the common good, and for world peace. On behalf of the government, I extend to them and to their people our best wishes.

CHAPTER FIFTEEN

The Return to Zion

Three central events concerning the return to Zion are known in our history. The most important, which according to tradition is the point of origin of Jewish history, and which has been celebrated for 3,300 years all over the world in every place where a quorum of Jews, or even one Jew is to be found, is the return to Zion after the exodus from Egypt. The second event is the return to Zion from Babylonia 2,500 years ago, which opened a new chapter in the history of Judaism. And the third event—the return to Zion in our day, which brought with it the revival of a sovereign Israel as well as the ingathering of exiles; both unparalleled since we became a nation.

In the Bible, we have two different versions of the exodus from Egypt. According to the Book of Exodus, all of the Israelites left Egypt at the same time, and after 40 years reached the promised land. According to First Chronicles (7:20-22), the descendants of Ephraim left Egypt separately before the rest of the Israelites, and were killed by "people from Gath who were born in the land." The great Babylonian Amora, known as Rav, offered the following interpretation (Sanhedrin 92b) of the "dry bones" which Ezekiel, the prophet, brought to life (Ezekiel 37). These were the bones of the descendants of Ephraim who miscalculated—that is, they erred in counting the "four hundred years" which Abraham was told about during the Covenant of Circumcision: "Know well that your offspring will be strangers in a foreign land, and they shall be enslaved and oppressed four hundred years" (Genesis 15:13). According to the commentators, they should not have included in the count the date of the decree, "they shall be enslaved and oppressed four hundred years," but started with the birth of Isaac. Instead, they counted the years from the time these words were spoken to Abraham. We read in the book *Seder Olam:* When Abraham was spoken to at the time of the Covenant, he was 70, and by the time Isaac was born, he was 100 years old; it is written (Genesis 21:5): "Abraham was 100 when Isaac, his son, was born to him." Accordingly, the descendants of Ephraim left Egypt 30 years before the appointed time; that is, before the Israelites left under the leadership of Moses.

Indeed, there have been many scholars who have held that the entrance into the promised land didn't take place at one time, but in waves. But my purpose here is to clarify the exodus from Babylonia, and not the exodus from Egypt. This was of a different nature than the exodus from Egypt—in its numbers, in its motivation, and in the political circumstances which surrounded it.

According to the accepted tradition, the Jewish people was born in Egypt, for only Jacob and his family went down to Egypt, as it is written in the Book of Genesis: "All the persons belonging to Jacob who came to Egypt—his own issue, aside from the wives of Jacob's sons—all these persons numbered 66. And Joseph's sons who were born in Egypt were two in number. Thus, the total of Jacob's household who came to Egypt was 70 persons" (46:26-27). But, there is reason to believe, as I have explained elsewhere, that most of the Hebrew people, or a large part of them, remained in their land all the while and did not go down to Egypt at all. According to the Book of Numbers: "All the Israelites, age 20 years and over, enrolled by ancestral households, all those in Israel who were able to bear arms—all who were enrolled, came to 603,550. The Levites, however, were not recorded among them by ancestral tribe" (1:45-47). Elsewhere, in the Book of Numbers (26:51) it says: "This is the enrollment of the Israelites: 601,730." Here, too, the members of the tribe of Levi were not included: "They were not part of the regular enrollment of the Israelites, since no land was assigned to them among the Children of Israel" (26:62). These two figures imply that the number of Israelites who left Egypt approached 3,000,000 people. Moreover, according to the Rabbis, the Israelites lived in Egypt not 400 years, as Abraham was told in the Covenant of Circumcision, and not 430 years, as it says in the Book of Exodus (12:40), but *only* 210 years. And in this short span of time they reached such a vast number, far too many considering the population rate of those days! It is obvious that this figure is legendary and exaggerated.

In the two immigrations from Babylonia, only about 52,000 people immigrated. In the first immigration led by Zerubabel, son of Shealtiel in 538 B.C., immediately after Cyrus' decree, "forty-two thousand, three hundred and sixty" people immigrated, and, together with their male and female servants and singers, the number amounted to 49,894. The second immigration, led by Ezra approximately 80 years after Cyrus' decree, numbered only 3,000 people. The two immigrations from Babylonia amounted to 10% of the number (482,000) who immigrated to Israel in the 30 years from the Balfour Declaration until the establishment of the state, and less than 50% of the number of immigrants in the first 15 years of the state. In our day, from Babylonia alone (today Iraq) 7,994 people arrived during the Mandate period, and 123,265 people in the period 1950-1951. This immigration from Babylonia was larger than any that came in such a short period from any country in Europe, Asia, or Africa in our lifetime. Only the immigration from Poland in the 30 years of the Mandate was greater, and numbered 170,127 people.

The second difference between the exodus from Babylonia and the exodus from Egypt lies in the fact that according to accepted tradition (and a very doubtful tradition, in my view), before the exodus from Egypt there was not any Jewish settlement in the Promised Land. The formation of the renewed State of Israel can be dated from the establishment of the first cooperatives (*moshavot*) in 1870-1878, at a time when only a tiny urban population—close to 24,000 people—lived in the country. But, when the immigrants came from Babylonia in the days of Zerubabel, and later in the days of Ezra and Nehemiah, they found a large Jewish settlement in the country, because Nebuchadnezzar, king of Babylonia "carried the people of Jerusalem into exile, the officers and the fighting men, 10,000 in number, together with all the craftsmen and smiths" (II Kings 24:14). But the "poorest segment of the population" remained, and they were the majority of the population in Judah. Even Nebuzaradan, who came eleven years after Nebuchadnezzar, and burned the Temple and all the houses of Jerusalem, razed the walls of the city and exiled many of the people to Babylonia—kept the poorest people of the country as vine-dressers and husbandmen (II Kings 25:12). This means that the people who had been engaged in agriculture was not exiled, as is reported in Jeremiah 39:10: "At that time Nebuzaradan, captain of the guard in Judah, left behind the weakest class of people, those who owned nothing at all, and made them vine-dressers and husbandmen." Thus, those who returned to Zion from Babylonia did not return to a land uninhabited by Jews.

However, the return to Zion in the days of Zerubabel differed from the exodus from Egypt and the ingathering of exiles in our day, in the international circumstances and geopolitical framework in which it was carried out.

The history of the Jewish people from its beginning to this day is unique, and, it appears to me, is without parallel in all of human history. But the historical laws which apply to all nations also apply to us, and one of these laws is that international events and geopolitical circumstances influence and, sometimes, decide the fate of a nation—the fate of our nation is much like the fate of other nations—and that only the will of the people, its inner strength, and its determination, and its spirit can make it master of its own fate. The State of Israel, today, is surrounded on all of its land-borders by Arabic-speaking moslems, who are quarreling and competing with each other, and who are, to no small extent, undermining one another. But they are united by one declared aspiration: To destroy Israel and to throw our people into the sea.

In the days of the First Temple conditions on our borders were much better. The different nations: Edom, Moab, Ammon and Philistia in the southern sector, and the Canaanite nations, Sidon and Tyre in the north—were also small nations. But they were not united, and not all were constantly hostile to Israel. In those days, the kingdom of Israel, especially after the division following the death of Solomon—the only king in Israel to rule with a cosmopolitan outlook—was under the pressure and influence of two great and mighty powers who were competing with each other in the Mediterranean: Egypt from the south, and Assyria, followed by Babylonia, from the north. The cold and often the hot war between these two powers, for whom the land of Israel served as a crossroads, was occasionally responsible for strengthening and awakening Israel, and occasionally the cause of its enslavement and ruin.

Hoshea, son of Elah, the last king of the kingdom of Israel in the north, first turned into a vassal, subservient to Shalmaneser, king of Assyria, and after he tried to contact Soh, king of Egypt, the king of Assyria captured Samaria "and deported the people of Israel to Assyria and settled them in Halah, and on the Habor, the river of Gozan, and in the cities of Media" (II Kings 17:6). This was in 722 or 721 B.C. Seventy years after the destruction of the kingdom of Israel, in the days of King Hezekiah, Sennacherib, king of Assyria, "attacked and captured all of the fortified cities of

Judah" (II Kings 18:13)—among them the two big cities in the south, Lachish and Dvir.

But the kingdom of Judah lasted until 587—that is, another 135 years after the destruction of Israel—because in the interim, the kingdom of Assyria began to falter, until it was completely conquered by the revived kingdom of Babylonia. This weakening of Assyria made possible the expansion of the kingdom of Judah into the territory of the kingdom of Israel by young King Josiah who ruled from 640 to 609 and who strengthened the fabric of the State materially and spiritually; for one of the books of the Torah was found in the Lord's house during his reign, and the covenant between the people and the God of Israel was renewed. In Second Chronicles (34:5-6) we read that Josiah not only cleansed Judah and Jerusalem, but also smashed altars in the cities in Manasseh and Ephraim, from Simeon to Naphtali. It is clear from this that his kingdom also extended to Samaria and the Galilee. The prophet Zephaniah, who lived during the days of Josiah, prophesies about the destruction of Assyria and the devastation of Nineveh, and utters these words of consolation to his people: "Zion, cry out for joy; raise the shout of triumph, Israel; be glad, rejoice with all your heart, daughter of Jerusalem. The Lord freed you of your adversaries, he has swept away your foes; the Lord is among you as King, O Israel; never again shall you fear disaster" (Zephaniah 3:14-15).

Indeed, in the days of Josiah, in 623, Babylonia was relieved of the yoke of Assyria, and the king of Babylonia, Nabopolasar, fortified his position and prepared to attack and destroy Assyria. In 612, Nineveh fell, and the king of Assyria and his army fled to the northern part of Aram Naharaim (Mesopotamia). But after three or four years (608-609), Assyria was subdued by the Babylonians who were aided by the armies of Media in the War of Harran.

The disintegration of the kingdom of Assyria only helped to strengthen the kingdom of Judah temporarily. A strong Babylonia also became a severe threat to Israel, and in the days of Jehoiakim, son of Josiah, "Nebuchadnezzar, king of Babylonia, came up and Jehoiakim became his vassal; but three years later he broke with him and revolted" (II Kings 24:1). Jehoiakim tried to rely on Egypt, but in the interim Egypt had weakened and "the king of Egypt did not leave his own land again, because the king of Babylonia had taken from the king of Egypt all of his possessions, from the 'river of Egypt' to the Euphrates" (24:7).

In the days of King Jehoiachin, son of Jehoiakim, Nebuchadnezzar besieged Jerusalem once again, and deported Jehoiachin to Babylonia, and together with him were deported "all the men of might, seven thousand in number, and a thousand craftsmen and smiths, all able-bodied men and skilled warriors. The king of Babylonia brought them as captives to Babylonia" (24:16).

This was the first Judean exile, in the years 598-597. It was 123 or 124 years after the destruction of the kingdom of Israel. Judah became subject to Babylonia, but was not yet destroyed, because in place of Jehoiachin, Nebuchadnezzar had crowned Mattaniah, his uncle, son of Josiah, who had changed his name to Zedekiah (II Kings 24:17).

The new king, too, was inclined to rely on Egypt, contrary to the thinking of Jeremiah, the prophet, and in the year 588 B.C. he rebelled against Babylonia (II Kings 24:20). The king of Babylonia returned to place Jerusalem under siege. The neighboring pro-Egyptian kings in whom Zedekiah placed his faith didn't come to his aid, and Judah remained alone in her war against a mighty and war-hardened enemy. The walls of Jerusalem held fast for about a year and a half, but famine engulfed the city and the people were no longer able to fight. An erroneous international assessment was at the root of the downfall of the kingdom of Judah, and brought on a great catastrophe.

On the ninth day of the month of Tammuz, 587, the city was breached. The children of King Zedekiah were slaughtered before his eyes, and afterwards the Babylonians gouged out his own eyes. This king of Judah was bound in chains and carried off to Babylonia (II Kings 25:7). And, "on the seventh day of the fifth month"—the seventh day of Ab—Nebuzaradan came to Jerusalem and burned the Temple of the Lord and the palace of the king.

According to the Book of Jeremiah, the event took place, not on the seventh of Ab, but on the tenth of Ab. As it is written: "In the fifth month, on the tenth day of the month, in the nineteenth year of Nebuchadnezzar, king of Babylonia, Nebuzaradan, captain of the kings' guard came . . . and set fire to the house of the Lord and the royal palace. . . . The Chaldean forces with the captain of the guard pulled down the walls around Jerusalem" (Jeremiah 52:12-14). This was the second and final exile at the hands of the king of Babylonia in 586—some 135 or 136 years after the exile of Israel. With the banishment of Zedekiah, the House of David came to an end, but the end had not yet come to all the independent settlements in Judah. It is true that the monarchy no longer existed, but the king of Babylonia appointed a Jewish representative over "those people who remained in Judah" (II Kings 25:22)—Gedaliah, son of Ahikam, son of Shaphan; one of the noblest figures of the Bible; one whose compassion and humanity remind us of Jonathan, son of Saul, David's friend.

But, Gedaliah, like the prophet Jeremiah, favored Babylonia, and his entire family was outspokenly pro-Babylonian, unlike the supporters of the monarchy who were pro-Egyptian. Thus, the zealots of the royal house plotted against Gedaliah and killed him seven months after his appointment (II Kings 25:25). The remainder of the population was then overcome by fear, for they feared the vengeance of the king of Babylonia, despite Jeremiah's appeal to the people to stay in the country, and despite his promise to them in the name of God: "If you will stay in this land. . . . Do not be afraid of the king of Babylon whom you now fear. Do not be afraid of him, says the Lord; for I am with you, to save you and deliver you from his power. I will show you compassion, and he, too, will have compassion on you; he will let you stay on your own soil" (Jeremiah 42:10-12). And although he warned them not to leave for Egypt, the leader of the pro-Egyptian group did not listen to him and even dared say to Jeremiah: "You are lying; the Lord our God has not sent you to forbid us to go and make our homes in Egypt. Baruch, son of Neriah has incited you against us in order to hand us over to the Chaldeans, so that they may kill us and deport us to Babylonia" (43:2-3). And it also says there: "Johanan, son of Kareah, and the captains of the armed bands, collected the remnant of Judah, all who had returned from the countries among whom they had been scattered, to make their home in Judah—men, women and children, including the king's daughters, all the people whom Nebuzaradan, captain of the guard, had left with Gedaliah. . . . Those all went to Egypt, and came to Tahpanhes, disobeying the Lord" (43:5-7).

A Jewish exile already existed in Egypt in the days of King Zedekiah, as we learn from the Book of Jeremiah (24:8). There were also Jews who fled to Moab, Ammon and Edom (Jeremiah 40:11-12), and there were also Jewish settlements in the distant sea islands (Isaiah 60:9; 66:19-20). But the most important exile was in Babylonia, consisting of all of the officers and warriors, as well as all of the craftsmen and smiths who were banished in the days of King Jehoiachin (II Kings 24:14).

Only the poorest of the nation remained in the country; and there is reason to believe that this constituted a majority of the people in Judah.

Again there were events of an international nature which the prophets of Israel saw as manifestations of God and which led to the second return to Zion some 50 years after the exile of Zedekiah.

Just as the First World War, in our lifetime, helped bring about the Balfour Declaration, so did the wars of Persia and Media against Babylonia lead to Cyrus' declaration with which the Bible, as we now have it, ends. These are the last verses of Second Chronicles: "Now, in the first year of Cyrus, king of Persia, so the word of the Lord spoken through Jeremiah might be fulfilled, the Lord aroused the spirit of Cyrus, king of Persia; and he issued a proclamation throughout his kingdom, both by word of mouth and in writing, to this effect: 'This is the word of Cyrus, king of Persia: The Lord, the God of heaven, has given me all the kingdoms of the earth, and He himself has charged me to build him a house in Jerusalem, in Judah. To every man of his people now among you I say, the Lord his God be with him, and let him go up' " (II Chronicles 32:22-23).

Though the Book of Chronicles is the last book of our Bible, there are books which were written after it, including Ezra and Nehemiah, which are really no more than a continuation of Chronicles. With minor changes, the Book of Ezra begins with the words with which Second Chronicles ends.

Cyrus, king of Persia, is one of the greatest historical figures in the annals of mankind. He built the largest empire in existence to his day, and he excelled not only as a great conqueror, but as a distinguished statesman and a brilliant leader who knew how to respect his defeated opponents, who acknowledged and respected the leaders and religions of all nations, who granted every nation full spiritual and religious autonomy and ritual freedom, and who also excelled in the planning and organization of transportation between near and distant lands.

There are many statements to be found on Cyrus (who was rightly noted in history as "The Great" in order to distinguish him from Cyrus I, who preceded him, and the younger Cyrus who came after him) in the books of the Bible (Isaiah, Chronicles, Ezra, Nehemiah and Daniel), even more so in Greek literature. There are also testimonies in ancient Babylonian writings: the cylinder inscription found in 1879; a long inscription of several columns; and a shorter inscription found in 1850. An inscription has also been found in three languages—Persian, Babylonian and Elamite—about which it is not yet clear whether it pertains to Cyrus the Great, or Cyrus the Younger.

Cyrus' first conquest was the seizure of the kingdom of Media. Later, he fought with Croesus, the rich king of Lydia in Asia Minor. In 546, Cyrus conquered Sardis, capital of Lydia, and also ruled over the Greeks in Asia Minor. Then came Babylonia's turn.

The rise in Cyrus' fortune sparked hopes of redemption in the hearts of the Jewish exiles in Babylonia. The prophet of compassion, Isaiah II, enthusiastically declared: "I make My servant's prophecy come true, and give effect to My messengers' designs. I say of Jerusalem, 'She shall be inhabited,' and of the cities of Judah, 'They shall be rebuilt; all their ruins I will restore.' I say to the deep waters, 'Be dried up; I will make your streams run dry.' I say to Cyrus, 'You shall be my shepherd to carry out all my purpose, so that Jerusalem may be rebuilt and the foundations of the Temple may be laid' " (Isaiah 44:26-28).

He said things about Cyrus which no prophet of Israel ever before uttered about a foreign king: "Thus says the Lord to Cyrus, His anointed; Cyrus, whom He has taken by the hand in order to subdue nations before him and to undo the might of kings; before whom gates shall be opened and no doors be shut. I will go before you and level the swelling hills; I will break down gates of brass and hack through iron bars. . . . For the sake of Jacob my servant and Israel, my chosen, I have called you by name and given you your title, though you have not known Me" (Isaiah 45:1-4).

As has been said, after the conquest of Asia Minor, Cyrus attacked Babylonia. At that time, Nabonidus who spent most of his time away from the capital of Babylonia, was on the throne, and he dedicated most of his time to the renovation of the ancient temples of Sin, god of the moon, which aroused the ire of the priests of Marduk, Babylonia's god at that time. The enmity of the priests for their king who was being lured by a foreign god made it easier for Cyrus to conquer Babylonia, which voluntarily opened its gates to the Persian conqueror. In Tishrei, 539, Cyrus' army entered Babylonia, and on the third day of the month of Heshvan the king entered the capital city of Babylonia.

The great prophet who arose at the time of Babylonia's decline, and whose prophecy has been incorporated in the Book of Isaiah, prophesied in his "Prophecy Concerning Babylon" (Isaiah 13:17-19): "I will stir up against them the Medes, who care nothing for silver and are not tempted by gold. . . . And Babylon, fairest of kingdoms, proud beauty of the Chaldeans shall be like Sodom and Gomorrah when God overthrew them." This prophet associated the fall of Babylonia with the revival of the Jewish people and the return to Zion, and he added: "The Lord will show compassion for Jacob, and will once again make Israel His choice. He will settle them on their own soil, and strangers will come to join them and attach themselves to the house of Jacob. Many nations shall escort Israel to her place, and she shall employ them as male and female slaves on the land of the Lord; she shall take her captors captive and rule over her taskmasters" (14:1-2).

In non-Jewish sources—in ancient Babylonian, Greek and Roman writings on Cyrus—there is no mention at all of Cyrus' declaration to the Jews. Concerning this, we have only the references in Second Isaiah, Second Chronicles, Ezra and Nehemiah. But there is no basis for the doubting of Christian scholars, especially the Germans. Cyrus' declaration in Chronicles and the Book of Ezra—both the short and festive form in Hebrew, and the longer and more prosaic form in Aramaic (Ezra 6), fits in with Cyrus' governmental policy in its entirety as implemented in Media, Asia Minor and Babylonia.

We find that Cyrus speaks with the same reverence and the same language in his proclamation concerning the God of Israel as in his speech about Marduk, god of Babylonia. This, too, should be mentioned with special emphasis: Cyrus did *not* grant the Jews political independence or autonomy—only spiritual, religious and ritual independence. Permission was granted to go up to Jerusalem to rebuild the Temple of God. He also allowed those who remained to make donations to the house of God in Jerusalem, but the government of the country remained in the hands of the Persians and their governors.

However, opponents to the return to Zion arose, just as happened several years after the issuance of the Balfour Declaration, in our day. "Then the people of the land caused the people of Judah to lose heart and made them afraid to continue building; and in order to defeat their purpose, they bribed officials at court to act against them. This continued throughout the reign of Cyrus, and into the reign of Darius, king of Persia" (Ezra 4:4-5). And during the reign of Ahasueros—Bishlam, Mithredath, Tabeel and the rest of their companions wrote an indictment against the inhabitants of Judah and Jerusalem and sent it to Artaxerxes; and in it they informed the king (in Aramaic) that the Jews who had left his land arrived in Jerusalem and are building the evil and rebellious city. They warned the king that if the Jews are permitted to rebuild this city he will lose all the taxes, and the king's treasury will be hurt. At the king's command, building was halted, and it started again only in the second year of Darius' reign. King Darius issued an order to search the archives where the treasures brought from Babylonia were kept. During the search a memorandum was found in which was written (in Aramaic): "In the first years of King Cyrus, the king issued a declaration concerning the house of

God in Jerusalem: Let the house be rebuilt as a place where sacrifices are offered. Its height shall be sixty cubits, and its breadth sixty cubits, with three courses of massive stones and one course of fresh timber. The cost is to be defrayed from the royal treasury. Also, the gold and silver vessels of the house of God, which Nebuchadnezzar took out of the Temple in Jerusalem and brought to Babylonia, shall be restored; they shall be taken back to the Temple in Jerusalem, and restored each to its place in the house of God" (Ezra 6:3-5).

The Babylonian exiles were cut off from their land for only 50 or 60 years: the exile of Jehoiachin took place in 598-597 B.C., and the exile of Zedekiah in 587-586. Cyrus' decree was issued in 538—60 years after Jehoiachin's exile and 49 years after Zedekiah's exile. In this short period, two generations were born in Babylonia, or at the most three. There were two immigrations: the first immigration led by Zerubabel, son of Shealtiel immediately after Cyrus' decree in 538; and the second immigration in the days of Ezra in the 7th year of the reign of King Artaxerxes who ruled in the years 465-424. Ezra's immigration was in the year 458; that is, 80 years after Cyrus' decree. This relatively short period provided enough time for those exiled to Babylonia to assimilate. And Nehemiah, who immigrated to the land 13 years after Ezra, found that the earlier immigrants had wed women from Ashdod, Ammon and Moab, and that "half their children spoke the language of Ashdod, and could not speak the language of the Jews" (Nehemiah 13: 25-26).

The immigrants who came after the Balfour Declaration in our day, after hundreds of years of living and wandering in exile, spoke 70 tongues, and very few "spoke the language of the Jews" before they came to the land.

The immigrants from Iraq, in our day, returned to the land after almost 2,500 years since the Babylonian exile, and after a period of only a few years in the land, the entire younger generation was speaking Hebrew. But the outstanding difference is that after the return from Zion in the days of Cyrus and Zerubabel, 373 years passed before the Jewish settlement in the land became independent in a political sense. This happened after the conquest and purification of Jerusalem in 165 by Judah the Maccabee. In our day, the immigrants attained independence 30 years after the Balfour Declaration. The similarity between the two "returns"—that of 2,500 years ago, and that of our generation—lies in the fact that both encountered enemies in the land who tried, by force and provocation, to interfere with the building of the homeland.

"Then the people of the land thwarted the people of Judah and made them afraid to continue building, and in order to frustrate their purpose they bribed court officials to act against them. This continued throughout the reign of Cyrus and into the reign of Darius, king of Persia" (Ezra 4:4-5). So it was in our generation, in the days of Chancellor and Passfield, and later on in the days of Chamberlain and MacDonald. The Darius of our day, who issued the "righteous" document, was Henderson, the British Foreign Minister of the Labor Party who rescinded the White Paper in a letter known as MacDonald's Letter, which was really Henderson's Letter, which once again permitted immigration. By 1935, the wave of immigration grew from several thousand to 61,000 per year.

The first returnees to Zion lived under the rule of Persia for 200 years as a religious sect, without political independence; until the Persian empire was conquered by Alexander the Great.

Alexander followed in the footsteps of Cyrus the Great, giving freedom to all peoples, and not oppressing them; and he also dealt mercifully with the Jews. But he did not last long, living only eleven years after establishing his great empire. After his death, his kingdom was split apart; and his heirs divided it. The Land of Israel was first made a part of Egypt, and later a part of Syria. Then the Hellenistic rulers began to oppress the Jews religiously. Even spiritual autonomy was taken from the Jews. But even more, there was religious pressure to assimilate them into the Hellenistic world. The decrees of Antiochus Epiphanes aimed at annihilation, and lasted until the Maccabees revolted in 167 B.C.; and on the 25th of the month of Kislev, 165, Judah the Maccabee conquered Jerusalem and liberated it.

It was not the Balfour Declaration—and I hasten to add, not the General Assembly decision of November 29, 1947 either—which gave us the State of Israel.

One should not deny the part that Cyrus' proclamation played, nor that of the Balfour Declaration. And one should certainly not downgrade the part played by the U.N. General Assembly. But the U.N. decision did not bring about the establishment of the state, nor did it guarantee its existence; for we know that eight hours after our Declaration of Independence, on May 14, 1948, the Arab armies invaded the young state. The Arabs rebelled against the decision of the General Assembly which was supported by more than two-thirds of the members of the U.N., and included in this majority was America, on the one hand, and Russia on the other. This was the first time, after World War II, that both shared a common view. But when the Arab armies invaded Israel, not one outside person raised a finger to defend us, and no one asked the invaders to withdraw to the previous lines. Had it not been for the Israeli army which knew how to fight and how to drive out the invaders, not a trace of the U.N. decision would have remained, and the Jewish settlement in Israel would have been erased from the face of the earth. Because of this we can say it was not the U.N. decision, but the strength and might of the Israeli army which gave us the State of Israel.

From this a lesson can be learned. Cyrus' decree was also a great act. After strangers came and argued against the building of the Temple, the Jews relied upon Cyrus' declaration. Darius, king of Persia, issued an order to look for it, and it was found. Then, the building of the Temple was completed, and, for a period of 200 years, the Persians did not interfere with the freedom of the Israelite religion. But the Jews only obtained independence through the war which the army of Judah the Maccabee and his brothers waged. In our generation, too, independence was only obtained thanks to the power and might of the Israeli army.

CHAPTER SIXTEEN

The Bible and the Jewish People

The history of the Jewish people is one of the most amazing, if not *the* most amazing, in the history of nations. It is a threefold wonder:

1) The existence of our people for hundreds of years while it was dispersed throughout the world and was surrounded by the enmity of the peoples in whose midst it lived. There is no other example in world history of a people cut off from its land, scattered and separated, and wandering from land to land, that preserved its existence, uniqueness and unity for close to 2,000 years without being forced off the stage of world history.

2) The national revival and renewal of its independence under conditions unparalleled in the annals of any other nation.

From the time when the Hebrew state was revived in the ancient homeland of the Jewish people a little over 16 years ago, more than 40 nations in Africa and Asia freed themselves of their enslavement and attained freedom and independence. But all these nations had spent all of their years in their own land, and were enslaved for scores and even hundreds of years by European empires: Britain, France, Russia, Belgium, Holland, etc. Israel was revived only after a prolonged process of returning to Zion—the return of a scattered and separated people which was cut off from its homeland for more than 1,800 years.

Delivered at Nahalal, July 20, 1964.

At the end of World War I, the Jewish settlement of Israel numbered only 65,000 people. On the eve of the establishment of the state, in the middle of May, 1948, it numbered 650,000. And, today, it numbers over 2,000,000. No other nation has arisen under such conditions—not in our age, and not in any other. There is no other example in human history of a nation renewing its independence in its homeland after being exiled and wandering for 1,813 years (if we take our count from Bar Kochba's defeat in 135 A.D.). The people of Israel is the only Mediterranean people to preserve its faith from antiquity, and to speak the language that its forefathers spoke three and four thousand years ago. Egypt, Babylonia, Syria, and Canaan do not even know their early names, and not one of their rulers knows how to converse in the language of his forefathers. They received their religion from foreigners—willingly, or under duress. Only the faith and language of Israel lives, once again, in its ancient land.

3) Its influence on world history—despite its being a small nation deprived of its independence: Only the Greeks of the classical period had such an extraordinary influence on the shaping of world history as did the Jewish people. And this influence was not only apparent in those years when the Christian and Islamic religions were spreading among the nations of the world, but also in the last few hundred years, from the days of Spinoza to Marx, Freud, Einstein and the rest of the great Jewish scientists; and in the short period of the renewal of Israel's independence during which time the young, small state became a significant factor among "developing" nations on three continents: Africa, Asia, and Latin America.

The secret of this threefold wonder lies in the immortal creation of our people in antiquity—the Bible, which has accompanied our people in all of its metamorphoses and wanderings for some 2,500 years.

In the books of the Bible, for the first time in human historiography, we are given the story of the birth, growth and struggles of a nation. The writing of Hebrew history predated the works of Herodotus and Thucydides and other books of history written by Greeks and Romans in days of old.

The Bible bequeathed to the Jewish people an awareness of its origin, its great past, its political, military, cultural and spiritual struggles with its neighbors, its moral and religious uniqueness, as well as its historical destiny for the future.

From the Bible the Jewish people drew its faith in the return to Zion after its independence was destroyed and its land devastated twice: by the Babylonians 2,500 years ago; and by the Romans 1,900 years ago. Every Jewish child studied the Book of Deuteronomy, where it says: "Then the Lord your God will restore your fortunes and take you back in love. He will bring you together again from all the peoples where the Lord your God has scattered you. Even if your outcasts are at the ends of the world, from there the Lord your God will gather you, from there He will fetch you. And the Lord your God will bring you to the land which your fathers occupied, and you shall occupy it; and He will make you more prosperous and more numerous than your fathers" (Deuteronomy 30:3-5).

Every Jewish child studied and read about the ingathering of exiles in the Book of Isaiah: "Have no fear; for I am with you; I will bring your children from the east and gather you all from the west. I will say to the north, 'Give them up,' and to the south, 'Do not hold them back. Bring my sons from afar, bring them from the ends of the earth'" (Isaiah 43:5-6). The same thoughts are found in the prophecies of Jeremiah: "I will restore your fortunes and gather you again from all the nations and all the places to which I have banished you, says the Lord, and bring you back from the place from which I have carried you into exile" (Jeremiah 29:14).

From the Bible, our people also learned the process of redeeming and rebuilding the land. Amos, the shepherd-prophet who said of himself that he is neither a prophet nor the son of a prophet, but a herdsman and a dresser of sycamore trees, prophesied the following about the Return: "I will restore the fortunes of my people Israel; they shall rebuild deserted cities and live in them, they shall plant vineyards and drink their wine, make gardens and eat their fruit. Once more I will plant them on their own soil, and they shall never again be uprooted from the soil I have given them. It is the word of the Lord your God" (Amos 9:14-15).

Just as the words of the Prophet of Destruction cried out: "I saw, and behold the farmland was wilderness, and the towns all razed to the ground, before the Lord in his anger. These are the words of the Lord: 'The whole land shall be desolate'" (Jeremiah 4:26-27), so did the Prophet of Compassion cry out: "Ancient ruins shall be rebuilt and sites long desolate, restored; they shall repair the ruined cities and restore what has long lain desolate" (Isaiah 61:4). Even an arid and desolate land will bloom again, because water will spring up in the desert: "Let the wilderness and the thirsty land be glad, and the desert shall rejoice and flower as the lily . . . for water springs up in the wilderness, and brooks in the desert. And the parched land shall be a pool, and the thirsty ground springs of water" (Isaiah 35:1-7).

Throughout the hundreds of years of wandering, scattered Jewry was accompanied by the Book of Books, and by its promise of redemption and return to Zion; a promise of making desolation bloom and of an ingathering of exiles. The nation didn't lose heart and its spirits didn't drop. For hundreds of years every Jew prayed daily: "Blow the mighty shofar to herald our freedom, and raise a banner to gather in our exiles; and gather us speedily into our land from the four corners of the earth . . . and return mercifully to Jerusalem your city . . . and rebuild it speedily in our day for eternity." And three generations ago this silent prayer turned into a program of pioneering settlement: In 1870 the Mikve Yisrael Agricultural School was founded; in 1878 the first Hebrew village by the name of Petach Tikvah was founded, and after it Hebrew villages by the score and by the hundreds were set up. In 1948 the establishment of a Hebrew state and the independence of Israel were declared, because our people were sure that their prayer would be answered if they would return to the land which their forefathers bequeathed to them, and if they would reconstruct its ruins. And in our day this marvel was achieved. We are still at the beginning of the revival: making the desert bloom and gathering in the exiles. The road ahead of us is still long and difficult, but we know that our hopes and faith and efforts have not turned to disappointment.

It is not only a knowledge of its past and its hope for its future that the Jewish people has drawn from the Book of Books. The Bible has bequeathed to our nation—and through us, to all of humanity—not only a belief in one God who created all, but also lofty human values: the values of human brotherhood, the values of justice and mercy, truth and compassion, equality of nations and peace—all of which are the kernel of the thoughts of the prophets and the morality of Judaism.

In a three-word [Hebrew] phrase our Torah has expressed the loftiest moral truth: "Love thy neighbor as thyself," about which the greatest of the Mishnaic scholars said: "This is the greatest precept in the Torah." It is interesting that this supreme human command is found in the same book of the five books of the Torah which Bible critics speak of with contempt, as if it is no more than a Book of Priests dealing with religious ritual: the Book of Leviticus. Lest this command be interpreted as being intended only for Jews, the Bible reminds us in the same chapter: "When a stranger resides with you in your land, you shall not wrong him. The stranger who resides with you shall be to you as one of your citizens; you shall love him as yourself, for you were strangers in the land of Egypt: I am the Lord your God" (Leviticus 19:33-34). The entire chapter is one of the most sublime in the Bible, and it demands concern for the poor and the stranger ("You shall not pick your vineyard bare, or gather the fallen fruit of your vineyard; you shall leave them for the poor and the stranger"—19:10). It demands just conduct ("You shall not steal; you shall not deal deceitfully or falsely with one another. . . . You shall not defraud your neighbor. You shall not commit robbery. The wages of a laborer shall not remain with you until morning. . . . You shall not render an unfair decision: do not favor the poor or show deference to the rich; judge your neighbor fairly. Do not deal basely with your fellows. Do not profit by the blood of your neighbor. . . . You shall not hate your kinsman in your heart. Reprove your neighbor, but incur no guilt because of him. You shall not take vengeance nor bear a grudge against your kinsfolk. . . . You shall not falsify measures of length, weight, or capacity. You shall have an honest balance, honest weights, an honest *ephah,* and an honest *hin.* I am the Lord your God who freed you from the land of Egypt").

One of the first Literary Prophets, Hosea, son of Beeri, established the covenant between the God of Israel and his people on four principles: "I will betroth you to myself in righteousness, and in justice, in loving-kindness, and in compassion" (Hosea 2:21); and when he grew bitter over the tottering foundations of morality in Israel, he cried out with all his might: "Hear the word of the Lord, O Israel; for the Lord has a charge to bring against the people of the land: There is no truth nor mercy nor knowledge of God in the land. Swearing, and lying, and killing, and stealing, and committing adultery! They break all bounds, and blood touches blood. Therefore is the land in mourning, and everyone that dwells within it languishes" (4:1-3).

Almost all of the prophets deal with righteousness and justice. We already find in the Book of Genesis: "Abraham is to become a great and populous nation, and all the nations of the earth are to bless themselves through him. For I have singled him out, that he may instruct his children and his posterity to keep the way of the Lord by doing what is just and right . . ." (18:18-19). Whether we accept the traditional view, that these words were written by Moses before the period of all the literary prophets, or the view of Bible scholars, that these are later utterances, the Jewish people, throughout the generations, for at least 2,500 years, has read these words in the belief that they were written by Moses and given by God. And when before his death Moses blesses the tribe of Gad, he concludes his blessing and praise of this tribe with the words: "It executed the Lord's judgments and his decisions for Israel" (Deuteronomy 33:21).

When the author of Second Samuel summarized the reign of King David, he wrote: "David ruled over the whole of Israel and maintained law and justice among all his people" (II Samuel 8:15). The same is true of the author of First Chronicles (18:14). And when the queen of Sheba came to King Solomon, she naturally praised his wisdom, but saw his function as that of practicing justice and righteousness: "He has made you king to do justice and righteousness" (I Kings 10:9). The prophet Isaiah stated that: "Justice shall redeem Zion and righteousness her repentant people" (Isaiah 1:27), and reiterated the principles of justice and righteousness several times in his prophecies (9:5-6; 16:5; 28:7; 33:5). The same applies to Second Isaiah (56:1; 58:2). Jeremiah stresses this strongly when he states that a wise person should not boast of his own wisdom, a brave man of his strength, or a rich man of his wealth; "rather, if any man should boast, let him boast of this: that he understands and knows Me, because I am the Lord who exercises mercy, justice, and righteousness on earth. It is in these things that I delight. This is the word of the Lord" (Jeremiah 9:22-23). He repeats this several times in his addresses and prophecies (4:2; 21:3; 22:15; 23:5; 33:15). The same holds true for the prophet Ezekiel and the Minor Prophets.

The composer of Psalms asks: "O Lord, who may dwell in thy tabernacle? Who may dwell on thy holy mountain?" And he answers: "The man of blameless life, who does what is right and speaks the truth from his heart" (15:1-2). He praises and glorifies the God of Israel: "Thou hast established equity, thou hast executed justice and righteousness in Jacob" (99:4). Several times the Psalmist repeats the words: "Lover of righteousness and justice," "Acts of justice and righteousness," "To observe your laws of righteousness." And the same applies to the Book of Proverbs.

But the prophets of Israel did not limit themselves to preaching about justice and righteousness between individuals. They also held aloft the ideals of equality among nations and peace in the world—something unheard of in any of the literature of ancient, cultured peoples: Greece, Egypt and Babylonia in the Mediterranean region; India and China in the Far East. (The peoples of Europe, and the rest of the nations of Asia and Africa above the Sahara, were not recipients of the benefits of human culture in those days, and the existence of America and Australia was not yet known in the three older continents.)

Amos, a herdsman and a dresser of sycamore trees, who angrily prophesied against the transgressions of all the nations surrounding Israel, also said about his own nation: "Are you Israelites not like the Ethiopians to me, says the Lord? Did I not bring Israel up from Egypt, the Philistines from Caphtor, and Aram from Kir?" (Amos 9:7). All nations are equal before the Lord God of Israel. Isaiah and Micah saw a vision that in the end of days peace would reign between nations, and "nation shall not lift up sword against nation, neither shall they learn war anymore" (Isaiah 2:4; Micah 4:3). This is the vision of peace which the prophets of Israel foresaw—a vision which all of the large nations of our day, who wholeheartedly reject war, have not yet attained. They are wasting a large part of their wealth, and their manpower, which runs into the tens of thousands and millions, in "learning warfare." These two prophets of Israel foresaw an age of peace in which not only would "nation not lift up sword against nation," but during which time they would not learn war anymore.

A prophecy such as this is not to be found in the great literatures of antiquity—not in China, not in India, and also not in Greece. The greatest Greek philosopher, Plato, who lived some 300 years after Isaiah, preached in favor of the cessation of the wars between the Greek tribes, because in his youth he had been a witness to the war of destruction which the Dorians of Sparta and the Ionians of Athens conducted against each other. But he didn't oppose the war of the Greeks against the barbarians, as the Greeks then called all non-Greeks.

The prophets of Israel preached peace among all nations and they believed that this peace would come in "the end of days," even without being aware of the great danger of the atomic bomb which is capable of destroying all humanity. Through their deep insight into the lives of people, and because of the deep sense of justice which beat within them, they believed that a day would come—though not in the near future (for which reason they used the phrase "in the end of days")—when nations will destroy their weapons, will not wage war against each other, and will no longer even learn the art of war. They will not possess weapons, because this is the only real and faithful guarantee for a reign of lasting peace, and for the reduction of mutual fear.

The Bible not only bequeathed to the Jewish people and the nations of the world the lofty, human and international values that will cause justice, mercy, truth and peace to reign in the world, but also established a great destiny for the people of Israel—to be a beacon for other nations. "I the Lord have called you with righteous purpose, and taken you by the hand, and created you to be a covenant among the nations and a beacon to all people," says the prophet in the name of God. He also explains the purpose of all this: "To open up blind eyes, to bring captives out of prison, out of the dungeons where they lie in darkness" (Isaiah 42:6-7). Elsewhere, he repeats this and expands upon the goal: "I will make you a light to the nations, that my salvation may reach to the ends of the earth" (49:6).

Realistic and shrewd people belittle this envisioned destiny. "We aren't a light to ourselves, so how can we be a light to other nations?"—so they argue. This overlooks the great light which shines forth from the enterprise of the Jewish revival in Israel. Of course, there is no lack of dark spots in our life: emptiness, cynicism, hypocrisy, transgressions, fraud, thievery, prostitution, cruelty, maliciousness and deceit. All this is also found in other countries to a greater or lesser extent, in one form or another. But there are positive manifestations and deeds in Israel the like of which are not found elsewhere in the world. New social relationships within the working population correspond to the dreams of the greatest social philosophers of the past and present. The pioneering character of our army is unique. The effect of the efficient and beneficent aid which young and small Israel is extending to new nations in Africa and to old nations which are developing in Asia and Latin America, is in no way inferior to that of the mighty powers —the biggest and richest in the world. Our pioneering capacity has come to the surface—an ability which perhaps every person possesses, but for some reason isn't aware of, or doesn't want to put to use. This capacity has developed here in the last three generations, since the first Hebrew village was established in 1878. Since that time, the capacity has served us to build up a Hebrew agriculture which is the best on the Asian continent (with the exception of Japan), though for hundreds of years we were cut off from the earth; to apply Hebrew labor to all branches of agriculture, industry, communications on land, in the sea, and in the air; to revive a language which for 2,000 years was thought to be a dead language, and which became a spoken language in Israel; to create a thriving Hebrew literature; and to develop and cultivate advanced scientific and research institutes with world-wide reputations. All these appeared as empty dreams, as pure fancy, as something impossible, to "practical people" 50 or 60 years ago.

The pioneering capacity which was revealed—or more correctly, awakened—and which has been increased in the last three generations, was linked to the vision of the prophets: a vision of national and universal revival, so that a people scattered and wandering for hundreds of years, from country to country, is now rebuilding its new land. In the first 15 years of the existence of the State of Israel, the Jewish population in the land has trebled. The mass migration which has reached Israel from all the countries of the world has come mainly from the countries of Asia and Africa—from backward and depressed countries, both in a material and cultural sense. And within the confines of this small land, which doesn't consist of more than 20,000 square kilometers, one great problem has been placed before us, which is now perhaps the most serious and essential challenge before humanity: the challenge of closing the gap between the developed countries, who are rich materially and spiritually, and the poor, backward countries, who are deprived educationally. This is not to say that Israel, for itself, has already solved this problem, but there is no doubt that she is working towards its solution successfully and resourcefully. And there is no doubt that in the not too distant future she will reach the point where immigrants from Europe, America and the Ukraine on the one hand, and Asia and Africa on the other will reach an equal social and educational level, and the differences between the various communities will be a mere remnant of the past.

This capability, which we have discovered in our land, served us well as we began to give assistance to both backward and developing nations in Asia, Africa and Latin America. In those countries, Israel is regarded with respect and admiration, and our destiny, to be "a beacon for the nations," is neither rhetoric nor fanciful thought. Although our Arab neighbors have as yet not made peace with our existence, and their leaders are declaring their desire to destroy us, Israel's position in the international arena is becoming stronger, thanks to the beacon which shines forth because of the feat of our revival, which is reflected both in our accomplishments in the developing countries, and in the creativity within our own land; for we are creating new social structures free of competition, exploitation and discrimination, characterized by mutual assistance, truthful cooperation, love of humanity and human brotherhood.

The Book of Books has been our most faithful and instructive guide, and has implanted in our hearts universal redemption. If we continue to walk in its light, both the nation and its leaders will be successful.

CHAPTER SEVENTEEN

The Monarchy and the Prophethood

Ladies and Gentlemen:

In the first days of the nation, the monarchy and the prophethood were concentrated in the hands of one man whose title was neither king nor prophet, though in fact he was both of these at once. Such a person was Moses. He was a leader, a legislator, a teacher, a guide, the head of a nation, and an emissary of God all rolled into one. The title given to Moses in most of the books of the Bible is "servant of God" or "servant of the Lord," and perhaps this is the noblest title; a meaningful title. Not once is he called king, ruler, or prince, and only rarely is he called by the title "prophet." The Torah ends with these words: "Never again did there arise in Israel a prophet like Moses—whom the Lord knew face to face, for the various signs and portents that the Lord sent him to display in the land of Egypt, against Pharaoh and all his courtiers, and his whole country; and for all the great might and awesome power that Moses displayed before all Israel" (Deuteronomy 34:10-12). But not often is he called by the title "prophet."

Joshua, son of Nun, continued the work of Moses, but he is called by the title "servant of Moses," and not once is he addressed as a prophet, though he was promised in the name of the Lord "as I was with Moses, so will I be with you; I will not fail

---

Lecture before the Bible Study Group at the Sde Boker Teachers Seminary, October 8, 1968 (16th of *Tishrei,* 5729).

you or forsake you. . . . Do not be fearful or dismayed, for the Lord your God is with you wherever you go" (Joshua 1:5-9). According to Jewish tradition and Jewish faith, there is no one else like Moses. The doubt over the historical existence of Moses, which to some extent also ensnared Ahad Haam, has in my opinion, no basis in fact. I have already addressed myself to that point elsewhere.

Joshua was the disciple (both in the Torah and the Book of Joshua he is called "his servant") and successor of Moses—chiefly as a statesman, commander, and leader. Though we find several times in the Book of Joshua that God spoke to Joshua, these very stories show up the spiritual distance between Moses and Joshua. In the Book of Deuteronomy it says of Joshua that "he was filled with the spirit of wisdom, because Moses had laid his hands upon him; and the Israelites needed him, doing as the Lord had commanded Moses" (34:9). But the title "prophet" or "man of God" is not ascribed to him once; not in the Book of Joshua, nor in any other book of the Bible, although before he crossed the Jordan it is told that God said to Joshua: "Today I will begin to exalt you in the eyes of all Israel, and they shall know that I will be with you as I was with Moses" (Joshua 3:7). After he crossed the Jordan it says: "That day the Lord exalted Joshua in the eyes of all Israel, and the people revered him, as they had revered Moses all his life" (Joshua 4:14).

There are many different meanings to the term prophet in the Bible. In a dream, Abimelech, king of Gerar, is told that Abraham is a prophet: "Therefore, restore the man's wife—since he is a prophet he will intercede for you" (Genesis 20:7). But this title is not given to Abraham, Isaac, or Jacob even once in the books of the Bible. In the eyes of the people of Canaan, Abraham was "a prince of God" (Genesis 23:6). In the Book of Numbers it tells of 70 of the nation's elders whom Moses gathered and "stationed around the tent. Then the Lord came down in a cloud and spoke to him. He [God] drew upon the spirit that was on him, and placed it upon the 70 elders. And when the spirit rested upon them, they prophesied, but did not continue. Two men, one named Eldad and the other Medad, had remained in camp; yet the spirit rested upon them—they were among those recorded, but they had not gone out to the tent—and they prophesied in the camp. A youth ran out and told Moses, saying, 'Eldad and Medad are acting the prophet in the camp!' And Joshua, son of Nun, Moses' attendant from his youth, spoke up and said 'My master Moses, restrain them!' But Moses said to him, 'Are you wrought up on my account? Would that all the Lord's people were prophets; that the Lord put his spirit upon them'" (Numbers 11:24-29).

In the Torah, a spokesman—someone who is capable of speaking about, and explaining, things—is called a prophet. God said to Moses: "See, I place you in the role of a god to Pharaoh, with your brother Aaron as your prophet. You shall repeat all that I command you, and your brother Aaron shall speak to Pharaoh" (Exodus 7:1-2). He did not mean to say that Moses would be God, so to speak, and that Aaron, his brother, would be his prophet, but that Moses would speak in the name of God, and Aaron would explain what he asid. Once, Miriam, Moses' sister, is called a prophetess as she comes out dancing and singing accompanied by timbrels, together with all the other women, after the parting of the Red Sea (Exodus 15:20). This honorable title was apparently given to her at that time since she was Moses' sister.

But there were two real prophetesses: Deborah, the wife of Lappidot, of whom it is said: "She judged Israel at that time," that is, she was also a judge, and the Israelites came up to her for judgment (Judges 4:4-5). When Barak, son of Abinoam, who commanded an army of 10,000 people from the tribes of Naphtali and Zebulun, was ordered by Deborah, the prophetess, to go out and war against Sisera, commander-in-chief of Jabin, he said to her: "If you go with me, I will go; but if you will not go, neither will I" (4:8). So spoke a military man to a prophetess. So great was the esteem in which Deborah the prophetess-judge was held.

One other famous prophetess is mentioned in the Bible: Huldah the prophetess. When Hilkiah, the high priest, found the Torah in the Temple in the days of King Josiah, and sent it to the king with Shaphan the scribe, and the king read the scroll that had been discovered, the king commanded Hilkiah the priest, Achikam, son of Shaphan, and others from among his men to go and seek guidance from the Lord, "for myself, for the people, and for all of Judah, about what was written in this book that has been discovered, for great is the wrath of the Lord that has been kindled against us, because our forefathers did not obey the commands in this book and do all that is laid upon us [by this book]. So Hilkiah the priest, Achikam, Achbor, Shaphan and Asaiah went to Huldah the prophetess, wife of Shallum, son of Tikvah, son of Harhas, keeper of the wardrobe, and consulted her at her home in the second quarter of Jerusalem" (II Kings 22:13-14). She ordered the king to do what was written in the scroll, and the king then wrought a total revolution in Judah, in accordance with the words of the book of the Torah which had been found, as the prophetess had ordered him (II Kings 22; II Chronicles 34). This was the greatest religious revolution which was carried on in the days of the First Temple. At that time they also observed a Passover in honor of the Lord, "for no Passover such as this had been observed from the days of the judges that judged Israel and through all the days of the kings of Israel and the kings of Judah" (II Kings 23:22).

Something of a combination of prophet and king in one man also took place at the end of the period of the judges in the days of Samuel. Samuel's youth is known to every student of the Bible. He was educated according to the will of his mother and father in the house of Eli the priest, who himself was a righteous priest, but whose sons were corrupt. Samuel's name was well publicized among the people: "All of Israel, from Dan to Beersheba, knew that Samuel was confirmed as a prophet of the Lord" (I Samuel 3:20). In the encounter with the Philistines which erupted at that time, the Philistines prevailed. Many Israelites fell in the war, among them Eli's two sons, Chafni and Pinchas. When Eli heard of this, he died, for he was already 98 years old—and Samuel became the judge over Israel. "And Samuel judged Israel throughout his lifetime" (I Samuel 7:15). He was both a judge and a prophet—the last person to combine these two roles.

"When Samuel grew old, he appointed his sons to be judges in Israel . . . judges in Beersheba. His sons did not follow in their father's footsteps, but were intent on their own profit, taking bribes and perverting the course of justice" (I Samuel 8:1-2). This fact, which became known to the people, led to a basic change in the course of the nation. It brought to an end the rule of the judges, which was basically anarchic rule, as the concluding verses of the Book of Judges tells us: "In those days there was no king in Israel; each person did what was right in his own eyes" (Judges 21:25). And Samuel was the last judge in Israel. "All of the elders of Israel met, and came to Samuel at Ramah and said to him: 'You are now old, and your sons have not followed in your footsteps; appoint us a king to govern us like other nations.' And the matter displeased Samuel" (I Samuel 8:4-6).

On the surface, this sounds a bit strange. Why did this displease Samuel? Doesn't it say in the Book of Deuteronomy: "If, after you entered the land that the Lord your God has given you, and occupied it, and settled in it, you decide, 'I will set a king over me, as do all the nations about me,' you shall be free to set a king over yourself, one chosen by the Lord your God. Be sure to set as king over yourself one of your own people" (Deuteronomy 17:14-15). If this is so, why did Samuel oppose the wishes of the people? It is possible that the Book of Deuteronomy was not known to Samuel, or that he didn't take the words of the Torah into consideration, because he knew that the appointment of a king would remove from his hands control over the people. He tried to cast fear in the people by describing "the manner of a king." He said: "This will be the manner of the king who will rule over you. He will take your sons . . . and will make them run before his chariot. . . . He will take your daughters for perfumers, cooks, and bakers, and will seize the best of your cornfields, vineyards, and olive-yards, and give them to his lackey's . . . and you yourselves will become his slaves" (I Samuel 8:11-17). But such a "manner of a king" had not existed in Israel.

From First Kings 21:1-15, we know that one of the great kings of Israel, Ahab, son of Omri, coveted the vineyard of Navot the Jezreelite which was adjacent to the king's palace. "And Ahab spoke to Navot: 'Give me your vineyard so that I may have it as a garden, because it is close to my house, and in its place I will give you a better garden. If you prefer, I will give you its value in silver.' And Navot said to Ahab: 'The Lord forbid that I should let you have land which has always been in my family' " (I Kings 21:2-3). And Ahab didn't lay a hand on Navot. But, Jezebel his wicked wife, stirred up several of his officers and scoundrels to plan a wicked plot against Navot because he cursed God and a king. Two false witnesses testified to this effect, and on this basis Navot was sentenced to death. Only then did Jezebel say to her husband: "Get up and take possession of the vineyard which Navot refused to sell you, for he is no longer alive." And Ahab went down to the vineyard of Navot to take possession of it, and immediately Elijah the Tishbite came to him and said: "Have you killed and also taken possession? . . . Where dogs licked the blood of Navot, there dogs shall lick your blood" (21:15-19). So said the prophet to the king, to one of the greatest kings of Israel! It is thus clear that there is no "manner of kings" in Israel as Samuel portrayed to the elders of Israel—that is, that he would take the sons and daughters, the houses, vineyards and olive trees and give them to his slaves.

But, despite the dark prophecy which Samuel described, the nation refused to listen to him and said: "No! We will have a king over us." And at this point Samuel was forced to yield to their wishes and crowned Saul, son of Kish.

In First Samuel there are two stories on the coronation of Saul, but these stories aren't particularly significant and there is no great contradiction between them. What *does* emerge from these stories is that Saul is a modest man, a brave warrior who was head and shoulders above the rest of the nation—not only in height but in character. Upon merely hearing about the danger expected for Yavesh Gilead from Nachash the Ammonite, he immediately gathered together the entire army of Israel and went to the aid of Yavesh Gilead.

There were scoundrels among the nation who despised Saul and said: "How will this man help us?" And when the people heard these words, they were very angry and said: "Turn these men over to us and we will put them to death." But Saul said: "No man shall be put to death on a day when the Lord has wrought salvation in Israel" (I Samuel 11:13). Here we see the moral greatness of Saul.

In the story of the meeting between Samuel and Saul, when the latter went to look for the asses of his father, it is told that in those days a prophet was known as a seer, and anyone frequenting a seer had to give him a present or payment. When Saul claimed that he had nothing to give "the man of God," his servant said to him: "I have here a quarter-shekel of silver to give to the man of God so that he might tell us what we should do" (I Samuel 9:8). When they came to Samuel, he crowned Saul king over Israel.

After Saul's victory over Ammon at Yavesh Gilead, Samuel said to the people: "Let us go to Gilgal and there renew our allegiance to the kingdom." Because he had already coronated him, and because Saul had won a great victory, Samuel wanted to renew the allegiance to the kingdom. "So all of the nation went to Gilgal and invested Saul there before God; and Saul and all of the Israelites celebrated with great joy" (11:15).

At that point, Samuel sensed that his role as a judge in Israel had come to an end. So when he learned that his sons were not worthy of his position and that the people knew that they were perverting justice and taking bribery, Samuel had to test the nation's faith in his justice as well as his honesty, and he said to the people: "I have listened to your request and installed a king to rule over you. And the king is now your leader . . . but I have been your leader ever since I was a child. Here I am. Lay your complaints against me in the presence of the Lord and his anointed one [so they called Saul]: Whose ox have I taken, and whose ass have I taken? Whom have I wronged, and whom have I oppressed? From whom have I taken a bribe to turn a blind eye? Tell me, and I will make restitution." And they answered: "You have not wronged us, you have not oppressed us, you have not taken anything from any man." And he said to them: "This day the Lord is witness among you, his anointed king is witness, that you have found nothing in my hands." And the people said: "We are witnesses" (I Samuel 12:1-5).

From all that transpired in the relationship between Samuel and Saul after this episode, it is clear that Samuel saw the establishment of a king as a severe blow to himself, and that he showed animosity toward Saul. This is quite obvious from what he said to the nation after his speech: "You will see and you will know how wicked it was in the Lord's eyes for you to ask for a king." And at the conclusion of his remarks: "But if you persist in wickedness, you shall be swept away, you and your king" (I Samuel 12:17, 25), and his opposition to Saul wasn't long in coming.

After Samuel poured oil on Saul's head and said: "The Lord has anointed you prince over his inheritance" (10:1), Samuel ordered Saul to go down to Gilgal ahead of him, and added: "I will come to you to offer burnt-offerings and to sacrifice peace-offerings. Wait seven days till I joint you; then I will tell you what to do" (10:8). After Jonathan, son of Saul, defeated the Philistines at Geva, "and the Philistines gathered to fight with Israel" it says of Saul: "He waited seven days for his meeting with Samuel, but Samuel did not come to Gilgal; so the people began to drift away from him. Then Saul said: 'Bring me the burnt-offerings and the peace-offerings,' and he offered up the burnt-offering. As he had finished offering the burnt-offering Samuel came, and Saul went out to greet him and bless him. And Samuel said: 'What have you done?' and Saul answered: 'I saw that the people were drifting away from me and you yourself had not come at the appointed time, and the Philistines were assembling at Michmash; and I thought: "The Philistines will now move against me at Gilgal,, and I have not placated the Lord," so I felt compelled to make the burnt-offering alone.' Samuel said to Saul: 'You have behaved foolishly. You have not kept the command laid on you by the Lord your god. . . . Now your line will not endure; the Lord will seek a man after his own heart, and will appoint him prince over his people, because you have not kept the Lord's command' " (I Samuel 13:5-14). It is clear from this that Samuel had already met with David and told him that he would be king of Israel in place of Saul, though we are only told of this in chapter 16, verses 1-12.

In the meantime, Saul and his son Jonathan defeated the Philistines. That is what the Bible says about him: "When Saul had made his throne secure in Israel, he fought against his enemies on every side, the Moabites, the Ammonites, the Edomites, the kings of Zobah, and the Philistines. . . . He displayed his strength by defeating the Amalekites and freeing Israel from its spoilers" (I Kings 14:47-48). "There was bitter warfare with the Philistines throughout Saul's lifetime; any strong man and any brave man that he found, he took into his service" (14:52). Obviously, all of these wars were not fought in one day, though we are not told for how long Samuel was not seen before he came to Saul, and said to him: "This is the word of the Lord of Hosts: 'I have remembered what the Amalekites did to Israel; how they attacked them on their way up from Egypt. Go, now, and smite the Amalekites and destroy everything that they have, and do not spare anyone. Slay men and women, infants and sucklings, oxen and sheep, camels and asses' " (15:2-3). If I am not mistaken, no similar order was given all the years that Israel was in its land. I studied carefully what is written in Exodus 17:8-16 regarding Amalek, and it is difficult to square this with the words of Ezekiel in chapter 18—one of the most marvelous chapters in the Prophets—and the words of Jeremiah (31:28-29): "They shall no longer say: 'The fathers have eaten sour grapes and the teeth of their children will be set on edge, but . . . the person who eats the sour grapes, his teeth will be set on edge."

The bitterness of Samuel who was a judge in Israel all of his life—until he became old and the people asked him to appoint a king over them—is understandable. He found a good king for his people, a modest and withdrawn but brave man—a man neither vengeful nor vindictive. But, when Samuel was late in coming, and Saul could no longer wait for him, Samuel became angry and said to him: "Your line will not endure." And after Saul didn't carry out Samuel's precise order, and did not slay "oxen and sheep, camels and asses," Samuel said to him: "You have rejected the word of the Lord, and therefore the Lord has rejected you as king over Israel" (I Samuel 15:26). "And Samuel saw no more of Saul as long as he was alive" (15:35). It is only natural that after such a speech Saul's mood changed and "he became another person" —one of the most tragic of the kings of Israel. David's lament over Saul was certainly spoken with sincerity and true feeling, and it portrays Saul's true character.

Prophets arose also in the days of the kings of Judah and Israel, both in Judah and in Israel, but until the days of Uziah, king of Judah, and Jeroboam, son of Joash, king of Israel, some 200 years before the destruction of the First Temple and some 40 years before the destruction of Samaria, most of them were false prophets, as in the days of Ahab, son of Omri. The few true prophets in those days were also, in the main, court prophets, such as the prophet Nathan who dared chastise King David for what he had done to Uriah the Hittite. He had caused Uriah the Hittite to be killed after he (King David) had slept with his wife, whom he later married. King David confessed: "I have sinned against the Lord" (II Samuel 12:1-12). And there was the prophet Achiyah of Shilo who prophesied that after the death of Solomon, Jeroboam, son of Nevat, would be given the reign over the 10 tribes and only one tribe would remain in the hands of the House of David. But these prophets were not well-known to the people, though there were such "men of God" among them as Elijah the prophet (in the days of Ahab) who didn't think twice about chastising the king for what he had done to Navot and for his persistence in doing evil in the eyes of the Lord (I Kings 21:20-26). These words [of Elijah] made a deep impression on Ahab. As it is written: "When Ahab heard this, he rent his clothes, put on sackcloth and fasted; he lay down in his sackcloth and muttered to himself. Then the word of the Lord came to Elijah the Tishbite: 'Have you seen how Ahab has humbled himself before me? Because he has thus humbled himself, I will not bring disaster upon his house in his own lifetime, but in his son's' " (21:27-29).

In the days of Ahab there was one more prophet—not so well-known—Michayahu, son of Yimlah. He dared bring bad tidings to the king, while all of the king's other prophets—the false prophets —only brought good tidings. The messenger who was sent to bring Michayahu, son of Yimlah, asked of him that he speak only favorably about the king, as did the rest of the prophets—i.e. the false prophets. But, Michayahu said: "As the Lord lives, I will only say what the Lord tells me to say" (I Kings 22:14). And when Michayahu came and said to the king derisively: "Go up and prosper, and the Lord will deliver it into the hands of the king," Ahab sensed that he was speaking with derision and said to him: "How often must I adjure you to tell me nothing but the truth in the name of the Lord" (22:15-16). Then, Michayahu said to him: "I saw all Israel scattered on the mountains, like sheep without a shepherd [i.e. 'You are not Israel's shepherd']. The Lord said: 'They have no master; let them go home in peace' " (22:17). Then Ahab, King of Israel, said to Jehoshaphat, king of Judah: "Did I not tell you that he never prophesies good for me, nothing but evil?" (22:18). Zedekiah, son of Kenaanah, one of the false prophets, slapped Michayahu on the cheek, and they put Michayahu in prison and fed him scant bread and scant water. Then Michayahu said to the king: "If you do return in safety, the Lord has not spoken through me" (22:28). That is: 'It will be a sign that my prophecy was not a true prophecy.' And, indeed, in this war with the army of Aram, Ahab was killed (22:36). What Michayahu said in the Lord's name was indeed the truth.

Perhaps, false prophets have not ceased to function even to this day. It is not difficult work. But true and just prophecy was unique in Israel, and to no small degree left its mark on a good portion of mankind. In the main, it was the work of the Literary Prophets who began to preach in the days of Uziahu, king of Judah, and Jeroboam, son of Joash, king of Israel—two great kings who lived almost 200 years before the destruction of the First Temple (i.e., more than 2,700 years ago). Even before the Literary Prophets, there were true prophets such as Elijah the prophet, and Elisha, his disciple, as well as Michayahu, son of Yimlah who, like Elijah, prophesied in the days of Ahab, son of Omri, king of Israel. But we do not know if they, too, tried to persuade and guide the entire nation as the Literary Prophets did, or if they only met with the king, his officers and courtiers with whom he had contact. In any case, their words have almost completely disappeared.

The Literary Prophets from the days of Amos of Tekoah to Jeremiah of Anatot, functioned during two important periods in the history of Israel—in the days when the kingdoms of Assyria and Babylonia (which in the end destroyed Israel and later Judah) became strong. These prophets not only preached against the moral and social decadence, and about the people's tendency toward foreign gods, but they were also seasoned philosophers on political and national matters. They were not only familiar with what went on among the people, but also with what was happening among neighboring nations. There were some among them whose understanding of political and international affairs was superior to that of the king, his officers, and his advisers. There were prophets whom the kings and officers consulted with and to whose advice they listened, as was the case of King Hezekiah who consulted with the prophet Isaiah and listened to him. They were far-sighted prophets whom the king admired deeply, but who were rejected by his corrupt or shortsighted officers. Such was the case with Zedekiah, the last king of Judah, in his relationship with the prophet Jeremiah—one of the greatest Literary Prophets, if not the greatest.

Most of the prophets opposed the sacrificial cult. The prophet Hosea, son of Beeri, said in the name of God: "For I desire mercy and not sacrifices; the knowledge of God rather than burnt offerings" (Hosea 6:6). Micah the Morashtite said: "Wherewith shall I come before the Lord, and bow myself before God on high? Shall I come before him with burnt-offerings, with calves a year old? Will the Lord be pleased with thousands of rams, with tens of thousands of rivers of oil?" (Micah 6:6-7). Isaiah also said: "Your countless sacrifices, what are they to me? says the Lord. I am sated with the burnt-offerings of rams, and the fat of fed beasts; and I delight not in the blood of bullocks, or of lambs, or of he-goats. . . . Bring no more oblations. It is an offering of abomination unto me" (Isaiah 1:11-13). The prophet Jeremiah was a complete non-believer in the Lord's command concerning the offering of sacrifices. I should note that our great teacher, whom we have been blessed with in our lifetime, the late Ezekiel Kaufman, differs with me on this point, but what I am reading is written in the Bible. And these are the words of Jeremiah: "These are the words of the Lord of hosts, God of Israel: 'Add burnt-offerings to your sacrifices, and eat the flesh.' But when I brought your forefathers out of Egypt, I gave them no commands about burnt-offerings and sacrifices. What I did command them was this: 'If you obey me, I will be your God and you shall be my people. You must conform to all my commands, if you would prosper'" (Jeremiah 7:21-23).

The prophets demanded belief in one God, God of heaven and earth, and preached truth and justice, mercy and righteousness, assistance for the needy, the orphan, and the widow. Most of their rebukes were directed against evil and oppression, wickedness and deceit, bribery and enticement. Isaiah—not the Isaiah with whom we are familiar, but a prophet who isn't known to us by his own name and is called "Isaiah II," and whose message begins with chapter 40—preached to his people: "Is it a fast like this that I require, a day of mortification such as this? Is it to bow down his head as a bullrush, and to spread sackcloth and ashes under him? Will you call this a fast and an acceptable day to the Lord? Is not this the fast that I have chosen: To loosen the fetters of wickedness, to undo the bands of the yoke, to let the oppressed go free, and to break every yoke? Is it not to deal your bread to the hungry, and to bring the poor that are cast out to your house? When you see a naked person, that you should cover him, and not shirk from your obligations to your kinfolk? Then shall your light break forth like the dawn, and soon you will grow healthy as a wound newly healed; your own righteousness shall be your vanguard, and the glory of the Lord your rear-guard" (Isaiah 58:5-8). This was the main theme which the Literary Prophets dealt with in those years, from the days of Hezekiah until the last king, Zedekiah.

As already said, the true prophets, from Amos to Jeremiah, prophesied in the days of the kingdoms of Assyria and Babylonia. From the beginning of reign of Manasseh, son of Hezekiah, until the middle of the reign of King Josiah—almost 50 years (677-628)—Judah was subject to Assyria where Assurbanipal (669-622-1) ruled. This king gained control over Egypt in 661 B.C. But, at the end of his days, the kingdom of Assyria began to crumble, and in the days of King Psammetichus I, founder of the 26th Egyptian dynasty (663-625), Egypt grew in strength. Initially, Psammetichus was subject to Assurbanipal, king of Assyria. When this king aged, Psammetichus slowly became free of this Assyrian enslavement. At that time, the kingdom of Babylonia also began to gain strength and to expand at the expense of Assyria. At the end of the life of Psammetichus, the Egyptian (he ruled for 54 years), Nineveh, capital of Assyria was conquered by the army of Media, Babylonia's ally. Pharaoh Necho, who assumed the throne of his father, Psammetichus, in 609 B.C., saw the increasing weakness of Assyria, and again made an attempt to subdue the Canaanite kingdom. King Josiah went to war with Pharaoh Necho, perhaps because he heard what Ravshakeh had said in the days of King Hezekiah: "Behold, you depend on Egypt—on a broken reed. If a man leans upon it, it will run into his hand and pierce it. Such a man is Pharaoh, king of Egypt to all who rely on him" (Isaiah 36:6). Or, perhaps, it is because he believed in what Isaiah the prophet had himself said in the days of Hezekiah: "Vain and worthless is the help of Egypt; therefore I have called her, 'arrogance that sits still'" (30:7). It is difficult to understand exactly what is meant by *rahav* or *shavet,* but apparently King Josiah relied on his prophecy which warned that Egypt could not be relied upon, and went to battle against Pharaoh Necho. But he was critically wounded at Megiddo and he died, and his followers took him to Jerusalem for burial, and crowned his son, Jehoachaz. But he too was not loyal to Pharaoh, and after three months Pharaoh Necho arrested him and brought him to Egypt, and invested his brother Eliakim or Jehoiakim in his stead, who ruled for 11 years. In the interim, the kingdom of Babylonia had gained a tremendous amount of strength, and Nebuchadnezzar, king of Babylonia, defeated Pharaoh Necho, and "the king of Egypt did not leave his own land again, because the king of Babylonia had divested him of all his possessions, from the brook of Egypt to the river Euphrates" (II Kings 24:7). The last king to rule Judah was Zedekiah, Eliakim's brother, and the third son of Josiah. In the days of Nebuchadnezzar II, the greatest of the kings of Babylonia, Jerusalem was sacked because King Zedekiah, son of Josiah, was not wise enough to listen to the advice of Jeremiah—perhaps the greatest statesman, and without doubt the bravest and most tragic of all the Literary Prophets. King Zedekiah admired Jeremiah very much and believed in him. But, he was afraid of his officers and of the people who hated Jeremiah, and had, several times, wanted to kill him.

The greatest poet of the last years of the Haskalah period, Y. L. Gordon, in his epic poem, "Zedekiah in Prison," attempted to describe the two historical personalities: Jeremiah the prophet and Zedekiah the king—both tragic, unhappy characters filled with sorrow and hurt, but different from each other in their inner faith and in the steadfastness of their spirit. Y. L. Gordon's portrayal is far from historic truth and is more like an argument between a maskil [modern educated person] of Gordon's generation, and a zealous rabbi, lacking all practical understanding.

In Y. L. Gordon's poem, King Zedekiah asks:

> Blind and lonely, imprisoned by iron and poverty,
> Is there another one in the land as unfortunate as I?
> . . . .
> Locked up in a cage like an animal, like an antelope in a net;
> Why did this miserable lot befall me,
> To rule over Israel in such days of anguish?
> And why has destruction reached us now?

Up to this point, the question is natural and understandable; the facts are almost compelling to anyone who knows what happened to this king, as is told in Second Kings: "Zedekiah's sons were slain before his eyes; and then his eyes were gouged out, and he was bound in fetters and carried off to Babylonia. . . . And he burnt the house of the Lord and the king's house and all the houses of Jerusalem, and smashed the walls all around Jerusalem" (25:7-10).

Therefore, King Zedekiah's sorrow is natural and understandable. But the answer which the poet puts in Zedekiah's mouth to these bitter questions is puzzling, distorted and groundless. What is the answer which Y. L. Gordon puts in the mouth of the unfortunate king?

> What evil have I done, wherein have I transgressed?
> Because I did not bow down to Jeremiah,
> Before the soft-hearted man, the man with a conciliatory soul,
> Who advised us the path of shame, subjugation, and docility?

Was Jeremiah really like this? The poet tries to portray Jeremiah's image:

And what does this priest from Anatot ask?
Not to carry a burden on the Sabbath?
Was there time, then, for holidays and Sabbaths?
The enemy surrounded the land, and laid waste the cities.
Their batteries reached the gates of the royal city

. . . .

And day after day he stands at the gate of the people.
He stands and calls in the ears of those who come there,
Not to carry a burden on the Sabbath.

But is this the only thing which Jeremiah asked for? Jeremiah did say: "Do not carry a burden on the Sabbath . . . sanctify the Sabbath day, as I commanded your forefathers" (Jeremiah 17: 21-22). The Romans later ridiculed the Jews on this account, and called them "a nation of idlers" because they didn't work for one entire day every week. But the importance of the Sabbath was bequeathed by the prophets of Israel to almost all of the nations of the world, even to our day. It is impossible that Gordon would not have known that the Maccabees—who were without doubt orthodox Jews—fought their enemies on the Sabbath. There is, thus, no reason to believe that the Jews were defeated by the Babylonian army because of the Sabbath; or that King Zedekiah thought so in his day. Jeremiah opposed warring against King Nebuchadnezzar on week-days as well, because he knew the balance of powers and was certain that the Jews would be routed. But Gordon was not satisfied with this complaint, and he put words in the mouth of the king of Judah which he didn't say and could not have said:

This too, a new covenant did he create for Judah:
All the people of the land, from young to old
Should study the words of the Torah and its testimony.
The entire people—from farmer to prince—
All should become scribes and sons of prophets.
The workers of the field will forsake their ploughing
And the men of war, their banners and weapons.

. . . .

And then axe and mallet will cease from the land,
All earthen vessels will be burned in their place.
And they shall beat ploughshares into writing implements,
and pruning hooks into musical instruments,
Axe and thresher into lyre and harp.

. . . .

On that day you will search Judah with candles,
And you will not find a farmer, a living man of achievements.
Artisans will be despised and lowly;
. . . .
Can such a people exist under the heavens?
If it can exist, will it survive one day or two?
Who will plow his furrows, who will produce bread for him?
And on a day of siege, who will fight for him?

Y. L. Gordon, who was well acquainted with the Bible, and knew what the prophets did and did not say, without doubt knew that all of the ideas which he attributed to Jeremiah, and put in the mouth of Zedekiah, had no basis.

Jeremiah said to the people of Judah and Jerusalem in God's name: "Plow yourselves furrows, and do not sow among thorns" Jeremiah 4:3). Jeremiah even sent a letter to the exiles whom Nebuchadnezzar had banished from Jerusalem to Babylonia, and told them: "So said the Lord of hosts, the God of Israel: '. . . build yourselves houses and live in them, plant yourselves gardens and eat of their fruit' " (29:4). And when Jeremiah prophesies about the return to Zion, he says: "So said the Lord of hosts, God of Israel: 'Once more shall these words be heard in the land of Judah and in her cities, when I return them from captivity: 'The Lord bless thee, O habitation of righteousness, O mountain of holiness.' And Judah and all her cities shall dwell there together, and they who wander with their flocks' " (31:23-24). Jeremiah, like all the Literary Prophets, asked that they swear "in truth, in justice, and in righteousness" (4:2). "Do not oppress the alien, the orphan or the widow, and do not shed innocent blood . . . and do not run after other gods to your own ruin" (7:6). And he uttered these marvelous verses: "These are the words of the Lord: 'Let not the wise man glory in his wisdom nor the valiant in his valour; let not the rich man glory in his riches. But if any man would boast, let him boast of this, that he understands and knows Me; that I am the Lord who exercises mercy, justice, and righteousness in the land. Because it is in these that I delight.' These are the words of the Lord" (9:22-23). But he did not say that there was no need for farmers.

Jeremiah also dared "to reason" with God, though he knew how to do this with all the required humility. "You would be just, O Lord, if I were to contend with You, yet I will reason with You. Why do the wicked prosper and traitors live at ease" (12:1). But this difficult and bitter question, which remains unanswered in the writings of the prophets, did not diminish his faith in the Lord. During his lifetime (and perhaps after his death), the same prophet whom we call Isaiah III, said: "I am the Lord . . . I make light and create darkness, I make peace and create evil. I, the Lord do all of this" (Isaiah 45:6-7). The prophet says that the Lord also creates evil, but doesn't explain why and how. It is possible that this was said in the days of the ascendancy of Persian Zoroastrianism, which provides for two gods—a god of righteousness and a god of evil—and the prophet negates this.

Though Jeremiah did not receive an answer to his bitter question, and though others asked this question and were not answered, the faith of the prophet was not shaken or weakened, and he did not cease to preach against immorality, oppression, fraud and iniquity. Even though his enemies multiplied—either because he rebuked them for their evil deeds or, even more so, because he prophesied disaster for Judah (and he did this from the thirteenth year of the reign of Josiah, son of Amon to the fourth year of Jehoiakim, son of Josiah—that is, for a period of 23 years and more), and the priests and the officers and the people became his arch enemies and wanted to kill him—the prophet was not deterred. Indeed, Jeremiah was an unfortunate man, and in the bitterness of his soul said: "Cursed be the day I was born! Be it forever cursed, the day on which my mother bore me! Cursed be the man who brought word to my father, 'A child is born to you, a son' " (Jeremiah 20:14-15). No one of his generation was as hated as Jeremiah, and many beat him and tried to kill him. When he once wanted to go to the land of Benjamin, "and when he was at the gate of Benjamin, an officer of the guard was there whose name was Yiriyah, son of Shelemyah, son of Hananiah, and he arrested the prophet saying: 'You are siding with the Chaldeans.' And Jeremiah said: 'It is a lie! I am not siding with the Chaldeans.' And Yiriyah seized Jeremiah and brought him before the officers. The officers were indignant with Jeremiah, flogged him, and imprisoned him in the house of Jonathan the scribe which they had converted into a prison . . . and Jeremiah stayed there for a long while" (37:13-16), until King Zedekiah removed him and put him in the court of the guard.

Jeremiah continued undauntedly to express his gloomy prophecy, and when the officers Shephatiah, son of Mattan, Gedalyahu, son of Pashhur, Yuchal, son of Shelemyahu, and Pashhur, son of Malkiyah heard the words of Jeremiah: "These are the words of the Lord: 'This city will fall into the hands of the king of Babylonia's army.' Then the officers said to the king, 'The man must be put to death. By talking in this way he is discouraging the soldiers, and the rest of the people left in the city. . . .' King Zedekiah said: 'He is in your hands. The king is powerless against you.' So they took Jeremiah and threw him into the pit . . . in the court of the guard, lowering Jeremiah down with ropes. There was no water in the pit, only mire; and Jeremiah sank in the mire. Now Eved-melech, a Cushite and an officer in the king's court, heard that Jeremiah had been cast into the pit. . . . He said to the king: 'Your majesty, these people have shown great wickedness in their treatment of the prophet Jeremiah. They threw him into the pit and he is likely to die there because of the famine. . . .' Thereupon the king instructed Eved-melech as follows: 'Take 30 men and lift Jeremiah the prophet from the pit before he dies.' Eved-melech took the men . . . and they hoisted Jeremiah up from the pit with ropes, and Jeremiah lived in the court of the guard until the day that Jerusalem fell" (Jeremiah 38). Before this, the prophet had said to the people: "I will make this house like Shilo and this city a curse to all nations on earth. . . And priests, prophets and all of the people seized him and said: 'You shall surely die. Why did you prophesy in the Lord's name saying: "This house shall be like Shilo and this city shall be razed" (26:6, 8-9). The officers of Judah heard these words, and the priests and the prophets said to them: "Condemn this man to death for he has prophesied against this city as you have heard with your own ears" (26:11). They didn't ask whether or not this was correct, only why he had said this. But Jeremiah was neither taken aback nor deterred. "And Jeremiah said to all the officers and to all of the people: 'The Lord sent me to prophesy again this house and against this city everything which you have heard. So now mend your ways and actions and listen to the voice of the Lord your God, and the Lord will relent of the evil he had threatened you with. But I, I am in your hands. Do with me what is just and proper in your eyes' " (26:12-14). There were both officers and fair-minded people among the masses who said to the priests and prophets: "This man should not be condemned to die, for it is in the name of the Lord our God that he spoke to us" (26:16). And several of the country's elders brought historical proof and said: "Micah the Morashtite prophesied in the days of Hezekiah, king of Judah. And he said to the entire people of Judah: 'This is the word of the Lord of hosts: "Zion shall be plowed under as a field, and Jerusalem shall become heaps, and the Temple Mount as the high places of a hill." ' Did Hezekiah, king of Judah and all of Judah put him to death? Did he not fear the Lord, and seek to placate the Lord?

And the Lord relented and revoked the evil which he had spoken upon them. Thus we might invite great evil against our own souls. Nevertheless, the hand of Achikam, son of Shaphan, was with Jeremiah and saw to it that he was not given over to the people to be put to death" (26:18-24).

This Achikam was already active in the days of Josiah after the scroll of the Torah was found in the Temple, and he, together with some of the other officers from among those loyal to King Josiah, was sent to consult Huldah the prophetess and she calmed the emissaries, and the king who sent them to her (II Kings 22: 12-20). Achikam's family believed in the Literary Prophets, and when Jeremiah opposed with all his might the revolt against Nebuchadnezzar, king of Babylonia, this family supported him, and, as a result, Achikam's son Gedalyahu, became one of those loyal to the king of Babylonia. When Nebuchadnezzar defeated Zedekiah and did what he did to the sons of Zedekiah and to Zedekiah himself, the king of Babylonia put Gedalyahu, son of Achikam in charge of that part of the nation which remained. But Ishmael, son of Netanyah, of the royal line, together with his cohorts, killed Gedalyahu, and fled to Egypt (II Kings 25:22-26).

This was not the end of Jeremiah's troubles. The officer Jochanan, son of Kereach, and his friends, who had opposed the assassination carried out by Ishmael, son of Netanyah of the royal line, approached Jeremiah that he might pray on their behalf and tell them what to do, and they promised to heed his advice. Ten days later, Jeremiah called Jochanan, son of Kereach and his friends, and told them, in the name of the Lord, that they should remain in the country, should not fear the king of Babylonia, and should not go to Egypt. But Jochanan, son of Kereach and his friends did not listen to Jeremiah, even though they had agreed to do so; and they did not want to stay in Judea, occupied by Babylonia. They took all those remaining, including Jeremiah and his aide and secretary, Baruch, son of Neriah, and went down to Egypt.

Even in Egypt, Jeremiah continued to beseech the Jews living there to return to the land of Judah, but the Jews didn't listen to him; and we do not know Jeremiah's final fate.

Most of Jeremiah's words are rebukes against injustice and thievery, lying and iniquity, oppression and deceit; and, as a result, he prophesied catastrophe and destruction. The fact is that a corrupt people cannot stand up against a large nation. But he also preached words of comfort, and tidings of redemption, and said: "Behold the days come, says the Lord, when I will make a righteous shoot spring from David's line, and he shall reign as king and prosper, and shall execute justice and righteousness in the land. In his days Judah shall be saved, and Israel shall dwell safely; and this is his name whereby he shall be called: 'The Lord is our righteousness' " (Jeremiah 23:5-6). He also prophesied: "I will gather the remnant of my flock from all the countries where I have driven them, and will bring them back to their folds; and they shall be fruitful and multiply" (23:3). "Therefore, fear not, Jacob my servant, says the Lord; and do not be dismayed, O Israel; for I will save you from afar, and your seed from the land of their captivity; and Jacob shall again be quiet and at ease, and no one shall make him afraid" (30:10). "For the days are coming, says the Lord, when I will return the captivity of my people Israel and Judah, and I will return them to the land which I gave to their forefathers, and they shall possess it" (30:3).

Jeremiah was also the first prophet who declared a new principle regarding punishment: the principle of individual responsibility. "In those days it shall no longer be said: 'The fathers have eaten sour grapes and the children's teeth are set on edge.' A man shall die for his own wrongdoing. Any man who eats sour grapes shall have his own teeth set on edge" (31:29-30). Here too I must differ with Professor Kaufman, who denigrates this statement.

After Jeremiah, the prophet Ezekiel, who lived in exile, expanded and deepened this principle. He also opposed the saying: "The fathers have eaten sour grapes and the children's teeth are set on edge." He went even further and dedicated an entire chapter to it—chapter 18—in his book. I will note only the principal verses: "It may be that a righteous man turns his back from his righteous ways, and commits every kind of abomination that the wicked practice. . . . None of his former righteousness shall be remembered. He has broken his faith, he has sinned, and he shall die. . . . And if a wicked man turns from his wicked ways and does what is just and right, he will save his life. If he recognizes his offenses and turns his back on them, then he shall live; he shall not die" (Ezekiel 18:24, 27:28).

The lot of the first king, Saul, during the era of the prophets was not a good one. Nor was the lot of the last prophet, Jeremiah, in the era of the monarchy. Because King Saul—the modest, forgiving king who was a brave warrior and a withdrawn person—did not wait more than the appointed time which Samuel had set, the angry prophet said to him: "You have behaved foolishly. You have not kept the command laid on you by the Lord your God. . . .

Now, your line will not endure; the Lord will seek a man of his own heart, and will appoint him a prince over his people, because you have not kept the Lord's command" (I Samuel 13:13-14). Samuel had already secretly anointed another man, David, son of Jesse, to be king over Israel.

The fate of the prophet Jeremiah in the days of the last king —Zedekiah, son of Josiah—was much worse than that; and not because of the hatred of the king. On the contrary, Zedekiah, the last of the kings of Judah, had faith in the prophet Jeremiah, and respected him. Everything that happened was because of his officers and his priests who did not want to listen to the bitter words, the merciless reproach, and the demand for surrender to the king of Babylonia which came out of Jeremiah's mouth. There were other prophets before Jeremiah who were not deterred from speaking the bitter truth to the king; and the king listened without becoming angry. Nathan the prophet, who opposed King David's actions with Bathsheba and Uriah the Hittite, her husband, told him the parable of the poor man's lamb; and David became angry and said: "A man who has done such a deed shall die." At which point the prophet said to him: "You are the man! You took the wife of Uriah the Hittite and killed him." David did not become angry, but said: "I have sinned" (II Samuel 12).

Elijah the prophet did not hesitate to rebuke King Ahab severely for killing Navot, and said to him: "Have you murdered and also inherited?" Ahab was neither offended nor did he become angry. Rather, he rent his clothes, covered his body with a sack, and fasted; and, as a result, God pardoned him (I Kings 21:1-9).

And there was another prophet in the days of Ahab, Michayahu, son of Yimlah, who was asked by the king's courier to prophesy tidings for Ahab who was planning to go to war, together with Jehoshafat, king of Judah, against the king of Aram. But Michayahu did not want to tell a lie, and repeated only the words that God had put in his mouth. One of Ahab's false prophets slapped him on his cheek for this, and Michayahu was even put in prison. But he refused to retract his harsh prophecy.

In general, the relationship with the prophet of God was one of trust, as was the relationship of King Hezekiah with the prophet Isaiah. No one prevented the prophet Hosea from divulging to the people the harsh and bitter prophecy that "there is no truth, no mercy, nor any knowledge of God in the land"; but only "swearing, and lying, and killing, and stealing, and committing adultery! They break all bounds, and blood touches blood. For this reason does the land mourn, and everyone who dwells therein does languish. . . . And Israel and Ephraim will stumble in their iniquity, and Judah also shall stumble with them" (Hosea 5:1-3; 5:5). Only about Amos, who prophesied evil for Israel, did Amatziah, the priest of Bethel, report to Jeroboam, king of Israel; and in the name of the king he was asked to flee to the land of Judah and to prophesy there ("Prophesy no longer in Bethel for it is the king's sanctuary, and it is a royal house"). And Amos answered: "I am neither a prophet nor the son of a prophet, but a herdsman and a dresser of sycamore trees. And the Lord took me from the flock and said to me: "Go prophesy unto my people Israel." He did not listen to the priest, but continued to deliver harsh prophecies (Amos 7:12-16).

As far as is known, the other prophets were not prevented from prophesying, though they all severely reproved their people.

Micah the Morashtite said bravely and with conviction: "But I am filled with power by the spirit of the Lord, and of justice and of might, to declare to Jacob his transgression, and to Israel his sin" (Micah 3:8).

In my view, there is no doubt that the greatest prophet who arose during the monarchy period, before the destruction of Jerusalem, and also the most unfortunate, despised, and courageous was Jeremiah, as I have already noted above. He was not frightened by prison, by flogging and even by the threat of death itself. To the very end, he chose to tell his people the bitter truth. He did, indeed, curse the day he was born, but continued, courageously, to utter bitter words of reproof to the people and the king, though the king's officers beat him, put him in prison, requested that he be put to death, and finally threw him into a pit without water—containing only mire, so that he might sink in it. During his lifetime, one of the prophets, Uriah, son of Shmayahu, who prophesied evil for Judah, was killed. King Jehoiakim, son of Josiah, asked that he be put to death, and Uriah fled to Egypt. But the king sent special emissaries there to bring him back to Jerusalem; had him killed, and threw "his corpse into the grave of the common people" (Jeremiah 26:20-24). Despite this, the danger did not deter Jeremiah, and he continued to pronounce his severe prophecies throughout his life. King Zedekiah, Josiah's third son, stood behind Jeremiah, and saved him from his enemies, although he himself was a weak person, afraid of public opinion and afraid of his officers: both were against Jeremiah. Jeremiah requested that the army of Judah surrender to the king of Babylonia; and such words certainly would not have been pleasing to their ears. But, Jeremiah was thoroughly familiar with the situation and the balance of power, and it was clear to him that if the Judeans were to continue in rebellion, Jerusalem would be destroyed. As a result, he didn't hesitate to advise the king: "Bring your necks under the yoke of the king of Babylonia, and serve him and his people, and live" (Jeremiah 27:12). He knew well that one cannot remain strong indefinitely, and was certain that not much time would elapse—not more than 70 years—before Babylonia would totter and fall. He, therefore, promised in the name of the Lord: "I will restore your captivity and gather you from all the nations, and from all the places to which I have driven you, says the Lord, and I will bring you back to the place from which I have banished you" (29:14). Jeremiah loved his people, and also believed in its future—and his faith was vindicated in our time.

I will conclude my remarks on a personal note. In my youth I studied the Bible and read the poems of Y. L. Gordon. And when I read the beautiful and sad poem, "Zedekiah in Prison," I was unequivocally on Gordon's side, and against Jeremiah. Only after I immigrated to Israel—62 years ago—and read the Bible here, did I know and understand that justice was on the side of the "Prophets of Rebuke." I saw what was in store for us here for the first time when I worked in Sajrah, and two of my friends: Israel Korngold, watchman of the settlement, and a young farmer by the name of Shimon Melamed, were needlessly killed by Arabs (Passover, 1909), merely to satisfy the custom of "redeeming the blood," a practice accepted among the Arabs. Only then did I understand what was in store for us, and what was required of us in this land.

I learned two things from the reality of life in the land, and from the Bible which I have read in an altogether different light since I came to the land: 1) that words alone, even the most beautiful words, if not accompanied by appropriate deeds, have no significance at all. As a result, I was compelled to say at some international gathering that I am no longer a "Zionist." And 2) that Moses was correct. We are the smallest of nations and, thus, we must be a special people. Only our superior quality has sustained us. We succeeded in the Six Day War because we succeeded in building up a special army. And we need not fear evil if we also succeed in establishing a special government. The Jewish people has the needed traits to be a special people, but to achieve this, more than any other nation in the world, we need a special government. For we are a small nation, and the world does not understand that we are different from all other nations—both in days of old and today—and need a special government. Without such a government, which will arouse respect and trust from Jews as well as from the best nations in the world, we will not long endure. This, in my view, is the moral lesson of the Bible and of Jewish history, from ancient days to our own.